FLASH FLOODS IN TEXAS

RIVER BOOKS
Sponsored by
 the River Systems Institute
at Texas State University
Andrew Sansom,
General Editor

FLASH FLOODS
IN TEXAS

~~~~~~~~

JONATHAN BURNETT

A&M nature guides

TEXAS A&M UNIVERSITY PRESS
COLLEGE STATION

LIBRARY OF CONGRESS
CATALOGING-IN-PUBLICATION DATA

Library of Congress Cataloging-in-Publication
Data

Burnett, Jonathan, 1962–
  Flash floods in Texas/Jonathan Burnett. —1st ed.
    p. cm.—(River books) (ATM nature guides)
  Includes bibliographical references and index.
  ISBN-13: 978-1-58544-590-5 (cloth : alk. paper)
  ISBN-10: 1-58544-590-8 (cloth : alk. paper)
  1. Floods—Texas—History. I. Title.
  GB1399.4.T4B87 2007
  551.48'909764—dc22

                              2007022335

On the cover: Austin Dam Break, 1900 (Austin History Center, Austin Public Library,
  Photo ID: PICA 12238); I-45/I-10 interchange
  in Houston, 2001 (Copyright 2001 Houston
  Chronicle Publishing Company, reprinted
  with permission, all rights reserved)

To my father, J. P.,
and my mother, Vida,
and to my sons,
Isaac and Jesse

CONTENTS

~~~~~~~~

SERIES EDITOR'S FOREWORD, *by Andrew Sansom*   ix

ACKNOWLEDGMENTS   xi

INTRODUCTION   xiii

APRIL 1900 — Austin Dam Break   1

DECEMBER 1913 — Nolan Creek and Brazos River Floods   10

APRIL 1915 — Floods on Shoal and Waller Creeks   22

SEPTEMBER 1921 — Downtown San Antonio Flood   28

SEPTEMBER 1921 — Thrall Record Rainfall and Little River Flood   37

JULY 1932 — Guadalupe River Basin Flood   50

SEPTEMBER 1932 — Devil's River and Rio Grande River Floods   58

MAY 1935 — D'Hanis Flash Flood   66

JUNE 1935 — Llano and Nueces Rivers Floods   72

DECEMBER 1935 — Downtown Houston Flood   86

SEPTEMBER 1936 — Concho River Flood   94

JULY 1938 — Brady Creek and San Saba River Floods   111

MAY 1949 — Downtown Fort Worth Flood   129

SEPTEMBER 1952 — Pedernales River Flood   136

JUNE 1954 — Pecos River's Eighty-Six-Foot Wall of Water   151

MAY 1957 — Lampasas Mother's Day Flood   162

JUNE 1965 — Sanderson Flash Flood   173

MAY 1966 — Dallas Flash Flood   186

MAY 1970 — San Marcos River Flood   192

MAY 1972 — New Braunfels Flood   199

MAY 1978 — Canyon, Texas, and Palo Duro Canyon Flood   205

AUGUST 1978 — Hill Country Flood   216

AUGUST 1978 — Albany, Texas, Flood   232

MAY 1981 — Memorial Day Flood in Austin   246

AUGUST 1998 — Del Rio Flood   261

OCTOBER 1998 — Hill Country Flash Floods   273

JUNE 2001 — Tropical Storm Allison Flood in Houston   284

JULY 2002 — Guadalupe River Flooding   291

APPENDIX — Overview of Significant Texas Floods   299

NOTES   309

INDEX   325

SERIES EDITOR'S FOREWORD

~~~~~~~~

YOU KNOW WHAT they say about the weather in Texas: "If you don't like it, wait around for a day or so because it is going to change."

People who monitor the weather around the country know that Texas experiences the most extreme weather conditions and most rapid weather changes of any state. In this volume of our series *River Books,* Jonathan Burnett portrays some of the most powerful of these in a narrative that is both dramatic and well researched. *Flash Floods in Texas* is as informative a page-turner as you are going to find, as Burnett takes readers through devastating floods spanning a century and the entire breadth of the State.

With descriptions of alligators being washed out of Aquarena Springs in San Marcos, of homes tumbling over the dam on the Colorado in Austin, or of bodies being transferred by cable across Nolan Creek in Belton after the bridges have washed out, Burnett keeps our attention and helps us understand how serious these events can be and the permanence of their impact.

The book is an engaging read and, I am proud to say, the work of an alumnus of Texas State University, where water issues are a core value. Burnett clearly articulates how our natural climatologic and hydrologic conditions set the stage for these extreme events, but he also provides equally compelling evidence that the actions of humans—including decades of overgraz-

ing and urban development—contribute substantially to the problem. Ultimately, the book should cause us to look carefully at policies that allow and even encourage the rebuilding of homes and other structures in flood-prone areas and at inadequate planning and management in watersheds that exacerbates runoff and flooding when it occurs.

The author, and the *River Books* series, is fortunate to have a generous patron as knowledgeable of the subject as Terry Hershey, whose support made this book possible. Hershey, who pioneered sound management of the bayous in Houston, has been actively involved in flooding and floodplain management issues for many years. We are not only grateful to her for believing in this project but also are graced to have her distinguished name attached to it.

And so, as we move into a period of uncertainty about our climate, the only thing certain about the weather in Texas, as always, is that it is going to change. The best research available today suggests that as the climate changes on a global scale, which it seems destined to do, the extremes of Texas, both flooding and drought, will get worse. We need to recognize the dangers ahead but also watch for opportunities to adjust and make improvements. In a thoughtful and yet gripping way, *Flash Floods in Texas* sets the stage for us to do both.

—ANDREW SANSOM

ACKNOWLEDGMENTS

~~~~~~~~~

A book of this type cannot be written and published without help from many sources. There are more than twenty sources for photographs alone and dozens of sources from newspapers and libraries throughout Texas. Initially, I was driven by the research of Texas weather and an interest in nature. As the project progressed, some of my favorite discoveries were the generous and helpful people of Texas, who were found at libraries, museums, newspapers, historical celebrations, and parks. I am grateful to everyone who shared resources to help me research, write, and publish this book.

I thank the editors and staff affiliated with Texas A&M University Press whose vision and dedicated efforts allowed this book to be published, especially Jennifer Ann Hobson, Diana Vance, Shannon Davies, and Carol Hoke. I am also grateful to Andrew Sansom and Terry Hershey for their support in this field of research, specifically the River Books series at Texas A&M University Press.

While researching these flash flood events, I met and worked with several experts in the study of Texas floods. I am grateful to Roy Sedwick, Raymond Slade, Lynn Lovell, William Asquith, and the late John Patton for their work in the field and for their support of my interest in flash floods and hydrology. I also thank the late Gunnar Brune for a meaningful and insightful interview about what he learned from writing *Springs of Texas*. Dan Yates and Melinda Luna at the Lower Colorado River Authority also have supported me and exchanged their knowledge related to flood studies. I thank them for their support over the years, too.

I thank George Bomar for his research and for his classic book *Texas Weather*. I was reading that book on a camping trip in 1990 to Garner State Park and the Davis Mountains State Park that included a stop in Sanderson. The mix of learning about Texas weather and visiting Sanderson made a connection that later inspired me to write this book on flash floods.

I am also very appreciative of the professors and graduate students in the hydrology field of the geography department at Texas State University, especially Richard Earl and Joanna Curran, who is now teaching at the University of Virginia.

The list of people from libraries, museums, historical commissions, and other entities that helped me is long. I specifically want to acknowledge the following individuals and parties for their help: the late Wayne Spiller, Anne Cook, Texas Department of Transportation, Ben Grillot, Austin History Center at the Austin Public Library, Kim Adelle Kroll, Lena Armstrong Public Library, Bill Stein, Nesbitt Memorial Library, Billy Moore, Melinda Curley, Lower Colorado River Authority Archives, Patrick Lemelle, University of Texas at San Antonio's Institute of Texan Cultures, Karen Ellis, Taylor Public Library, Linda Dietert, Sopheinburg Museum and Archives, Hondo Anvil Herald, Frederica Wyatt, Kimble County Historical Museum, Virginia Davis, El Progreso Library, Houston Metropolitan Research Center, Shannon Strum, West

xii   Texas Collection at Porter Henderson Library at Angelo State University, Bert Striegler, Heart of Texas Historical Museum, Ann Shuffler, E. M. Richards Library, Karen Faught, San Saba News & Star, Donna S. Kruse, Fort Worth Public Library, Cathy Spitzenberger, University of Texas at Arlington Library, Special Collections, John Anderson, Texas State Library Archives, Gladden Corbin, Kay Briggs, Amy McDaniel, Keystone Square Museum, Dorothy Marquart, Terrell County Historical Commission, David Woo, Dallas Morning News, Rowe Ray, San Marcos Record, Brad Tooley, Canyon News, Donnie Lucas, Albany News, Joe San Miguel, Del Rio News-Herald, Jo Guiterrez, Houston Chronicle. Thanks to the many other libraries, parks and museums I visited throughout the state while researching this book.

A few of my friends who are writers provided constant and unwavering encouragement to me and this project. I thank Scott Blackwood, Jerry Young, and Clara Serrano for their support. I also thank my friends Frank Markle, Tom McNair, and Michael and Julie Allen. I thank my family for their patience and understanding while I spent many hours on this project. Thanks go to Maggie, Isaac, and Jesse.

I want to acknowledge several other people who taught me the perseverance needed to span the fourteen years it took to write this book. I thank my mother, Vida, whose dedication to teaching music in small towns throughout Texas showed me the rewards of sharing her talents with others on a daily basis. I thank Bob McNair and his family, who taught me that the next bale of hay needs to hauled the right way, even if you are exhausted and you have already banged your head on the rafters of the barn a dozen times. I also thank Donna Anglin for teaching me the discipline of everyday hard work and focus in academic pursuits.

One final thank you goes to my father, James Park (J.P.) Burnett. He was a sixth-generation Texan with a great and lively knowledge of Texas and natural history. His interests encouraged me to learn about Texas. His gentle and caring way with people demonstrated how to listen to and learn from others. Without these experiences, I never would have been able to research and write this book.

INTRODUCTION

~~~~~~~~

TEXANS ENJOY BEING number one in many fields. Unfortunately, one area in which Texas is consistently foremost in the United States is the number of deaths attributed to flooding. From 1995 to 2004, Texas topped this list in seven of these ten years.

One reason that Texas is typically near the head of this list is that the location and landscape of the Lone Star State make it prone to flash floods. Deluges at Del Rio in August 1998, in the Hill Country in October 1998, in Houston in 2001, and in the summer of 2007 in Marble Falls (where 12–18 inches fell in less than four hours) solidified Texas' reputation as having some of the most flash flood–prone land in the world.

No part of Texas is immune to flash floods. The state lies in the path of sources of copious moisture from the Gulf of Mexico and the Pacific Ocean. Hurricanes and tropical storms frequently visit the state and release enormous amounts of water as they dissipate over land. Slow-moving cold fronts and the Texas dry line interact with the jet stream to build supercells that can drop torrential amounts of rain in a very short time. Compounding their threat, these supercells have a tendency to strike at night, when the flash flood danger is hidden in darkness.

The Balcones Escarpment and Edwards Plateau in Central and West Texas are ideal flash flood locations. Their soils are rocky, and the gradient of the land provides rapid runoff. The rise in altitude along the escarpments creates orographic lift to trigger storms, especially from easterly waves moving in from the Gulf of Mexico.

From 1930s to the 1970s William Hoyt and Walter Langbein studied floods extensively. In 1955 they published *Floods,* in which they commented: "It is a striking fact that many of the greatest flood discharges occurred in East-Central Texas. . . . [Tropical storms] may not achieve their maximum rates or amounts of precipitation along the coastline, being more likely to do so while crossing the high barrier known as the Balcones Fault, some 100 to 200 miles inland. . . . There is a startling contrast between the usually near-dry state of the river channels and the parched soil with desert types of vegetation predominating, on the one hand, and the torrential flows that break all records for intensity, on the other."[1]

In a 2004 report, two U.S. Geological Service (USGS) hydrologists noted, "Within the conterminous United States, the greatest concentration of exceptional unit discharges is at the Balcones Escarpment of central Texas, where maximum U.S. rainfall amounts apparently coincide with appropriate basin physiography to produce many of the largest measured U.S. floods."[2]

This book provides historical accounts of major flash floods in Texas. Some of these raged through major cities such as San Antonio in 1921, Forth Worth in 1949, Austin in 1981, Dallas in 1966 and 1995, and Houston in 2001. Others tore through arid West Texas canyons, like the Pecos River Canyon in 1954 and Sanderson Canyon in 1965. One flash flood in 1900 occurred as a result of human error during the construction of the Austin Dam almost a decade earlier.

Flash floods have changed the landscape throughout the state. The town of

Ben Ficklin served as Tom Green's county seat until it was wiped out by a flash flood in August 1882. The seat of government then moved to San Angelo, another city ravaged by flash floods until large reservoirs were built upstream on the North, South, and Middle Concho rivers.

For years, San Antonio debated ways to control the San Antonio River, which flows through its downtown. The growing city was alerted to the danger after it was hit by two floods between October and December of 1913. Eight years later, a disastrous flood in September 1921 inundated the city. Pontoon boats floated along the downtown streets, and seals rode the flood wave out of the zoo to freedom downstream. San Antonio responded this time by building flood-protection structures such as the Olmos Dam along the Olmos Creek and the San Antonio River. The city's flood-protection projects prevented severe damage along the San Antonio River in the October 1998 floods.

Texas flash floods have produced events that tax the imagination. In 1954 the Pecos River flood produced an eighty-six-foot wall of water that destroyed the existing highway bridge over the river. Just upstream of that structure stood the famous Pecos River High Bridge for the railroad. When the highway bridge was rebuilt, the state of Texas built a massive overpass that spanned the top of the canyon, just like the railroad bridge.

In several events covered in this book, flood-prevention measures were not finished in time to prevent flash floods from occurring. The 1957 Lampasas flood came down from the hills west of town during the same month when the Soil Conservation Service was surveying locations for flood and conservation dams. Similarly, the ferocious 1972 flood in New Braunfels roared down basins where dams had been planned for more than a decade but not built due to disputes over their exact location.

As this book explains, flash floods often strike the same location. Nolan Creek in Belton created great losses in 1913 and rose well into the Yettie Polk Park and parking lots for nearby apartments as recently as December 1997. Shoal Creek tore through the west side of Austin in 1915, 1981, 1991, and 2001.

This book also provides a brief synopsis of the weather conditions prior to the flash floods and recounts rainfall totals and the resultant discharges of most of the events. In addition, the material focuses on the human element of these events.

Large-scale development of Texas has surged in the past one hundred years. Floodplains have been developed without knowledge of the historical flood data—and even in spite of this crucial information. This development has placed the residents of Texas in the path of the some of the most extreme flash floods in not only the United States but also the world. In many such inundations, the deadly surges arrive in the middle of the night. Victims of these events often remember the terror of being awakened as water floated their beds away or as debris broke open door and windows.

The tragedies related to flooding in Texas are almost too numerous to catalog. In covering them, this book brings to light many of the catastrophes associated with flash floods. Some of the most noteworthy include the following:

• workers in the powerhouse of the Austin Dam, who were drowned in an ultimate case of being in the wrong place at the wrong time
• the loss of most of the Polk family in downtown Belton during the town's 1913 flash flood
• a boy's tale of survival in the middle of the Guadalupe River in Kerrville and the loss of several would-be rescuers during the July 1932 flash flood

• rescue workers stranded in the middle of the railroad bridge over the Rio Grande River in the September 1932 flood

• hotel guests who survived flood waves in downtown Houston in 1935 and downtown San Angelo in 1936

• Fort Worth residents who paddled to safety in the 1949 flash flood, which struck in the middle of the night

• Ozona residents who attempted to escape the flash flood surging through town and the loss of fishermen along Independence Creek in the massive flash floods of June 1954

• Lampasas residents who battled gushing floodwaters downtown on Mother's Day in 1957

• the staggering and tragic destruction of much of Sanderson in the June 1965 flash flood

• violent floodwaters that tore through New Braunfels in May 1972, forcing residents to their rooftops as their houses floated down the city's streams

• the usually serene Medina River ripping through idyllic Hill Country camps in the early morning hours and carrying away residents and campers in August 1978

• just days after the 1978 Hill Country flash flood, the same storm system unleashing a torrent of floodwater through Albany, sweeping trucks away and burying them in several feet of gravel and sediment

• the loss of longtime residents of central Austin as an unprecedented flash flood smashed through their neighborhood along Shoal Creek in May 1981

• a horrific flash flood that rampaged through Del Rio, down the beautiful and life-giving waters of San Felipe Creek, which invaded houses several blocks away in the middle of the night in August 1998

• the five-hundred-year flood event in downtown Houston, in which elevators became death traps and flood waves rushed through underground tunnels in 2001

• the unthinkable incident of water topping the Canyon Dam spillway and destroying houses and camps along the Guadalupe River above New Braunfels in 2002

Life in Texas has always been intertwined with the weather. Flash floods bring extreme and sudden destruction to the state. The accounts in this book help to define our unfolding understanding of Texans and their physical environment.

FLASH FLOODS IN TEXAS

APRIL 1900

~~~~~~~

Austin Dam Break

SINCE THE EARLIEST days of Austin, the immense power of the Colorado River has motivated citizens and community leaders to take action to protect the city's residents. After decades of talk and inaction, in 1889 the city of Austin held an election to decide on the building of a dam. The proposed dam was the major topic in the mayoral race of that year. The incumbent, Joseph Nalle, opposed the project; the challenger, John McDonald, favored it. McDonald won. Less than a year after he was elected, the people of Austin overwhelmingly approved construction by a vote of 1,354 to 50. Excavation started on November 5, 1890, and on May 2, 1893, workers laid the final brick in the dam, creating Lake McDonald.

During their first few years, the dam and lake garnered great praise for the recreational opportunities and power they created. Mayor McDonald proclaimed, "The City of Austin is the owner and operates the best water power, waterworks, electric light and electric power plant owned by any city in the United States, and we have a right to feel proud of our achievement."[1] Power generated by the dam enhanced life in Austin by halving utility rates and lighting the town's moonlight towers, and Austin thus became known as the "City with the Violet Crown."[2]

By 1897, the glory days of the dam had faded because it failed to consistently supply the power promised when it was funded. The Colorado provided neither a reliable nor a sufficient base flow. While studying the river's characteristics, the dam's first lead engineer, Joseph Frizell, assessed the minimum flow at 1,000 cubic feet per second (cfs). In 1899 the average flow was 1,170 cfs, and the minimum flow was only 180 cfs (eighteen percent of Frizell's predicted minimum). If the low flow in 1899 had been unusual, the dam would perhaps not have been a failure in terms of power generation. To the despair of the dam's supporters and the citizenry, minimum flows for the years 1896, 1897, and 1898 were similar: 180, 200, 210 cfs, respectively.

In May 1897 T. U. Taylor, a professor at the University of Texas, noted that the lake was filling with silt, thus robbing that body of water of its storage capacity. In January 1900 Taylor calculated that the lake had lost forty-eight percent of the reservoir volume to silt. He described the sediment found two miles from the head of the lake as a "fine, impalpable, absolutely gritless deposit."[3] Moreover, in the late 1890s a few Austinites noticed a development that foretold a greater danger than an unreliable power source. The rock support beneath the toe of the dam was vanishing. While fishing in that area, one Austin resident ran his fishing pole along the toe of the dam and did not bump into the bottom, as he expected.[4]

On April 8, 1896, J. P. Frizell sent a letter to the mayor of Austin. In it Frizell warned that he had found a "very friable foundation of rock" 300–400 feet from the east end while he was building the dam. He added, "The rock was poor for the entire easterly half of the river." He was writing to "suggest that you cause soundings to be made along the toe of the dam to ascertain if dangerous abrasion is in progress in that locality." Though Frizell did not provide details, he mentioned that he planned to "execute some supplementary work of protection which would have been easy to do" if his plans had been followed.[5]

Highs and Lows of 1899 Streamflow

In June 1899 the Austin Dam experienced the biggest rise of its lifetime. Heavy rains upstream near San Angelo and along the Pedernales, Llano, and San Saba rivers propelled the Colorado to flood stage, and water flowed 9.8 feet over the dam. This spectacle inspired the following account from the *Austin Daily Statesman:* "The Colorado is wild with energy and is swinging over the crest of the vast granite wall that would check its magnificent dash to unbridled flow, with scornful roar as if to thunder its protests against the efforts of mortal man to restrain one iota, the terrific velocity of its tremendous currents." Spectators were "hastening to look upon the spectacle of an awful flood plunging like an unleashed animal, to liberty . . . to see the flotsam of the great flood—uprooted trees, grim and aged logs, tufts of green grass, shocks of grain, an occasional skiff, now and then a box and all the trophies that angry waters gather to their wild bosoms in their mad sweep to the far away ocean."[6]

The big rise filled the lake and bolstered the city's power supply for several months. By the fall of 1899, however, the low-flow conditions had returned, limiting the supply of water from the lake. When the temporary state capitol building burned on September 30, 1899, a private company's hydrants supplied the water to fight the fire.[7]

April 1900: Weather

In early April of 1900 a strong low-pressure area stationed in the southeastern Rocky Mountains determined the weather

in the central United States, while a high-pressure system over the Mississippi and Missouri valleys blocked its movement. As the high pressure began to shift eastward into Tennessee, the low-pressure area moved southward into West Texas. On April 6 the *Monthly Weather Review* noted a "well-defined cyclonic movement of the atmosphere" over West Texas. The low-pressure system eventually tracked into the Gulf of Mexico, east of the mouth of the Rio Grande.[8] The slow-moving low-pressure system produced rains across most of the state, especially the central and west-central area. The heaviest rains fell over the Guadalupe

Austin Dam in the years before the break (Austin History Center, Austin Public Library; Photo ID: PICA16819).

Austin Dam break and how it progressed.

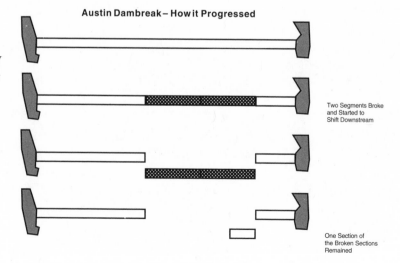

Austin Dambreak – How it Progressed

Two Segments Broke and Started to Shift Downstream

One Section of the Broken Sections Remained

River's upper reaches, the central Colorado basin, and the central Brazos.

The *Monthly Weather Review*'s account tracked the storms in Val Verde, Kinney, and Maverick counties on April 5 and in the Panhandle on April 6. According to the report, "The two rain areas appear to have united over the central part of the State."[9] Irion County near San Angelo was hit by a cloudburst, while rises on the South Concho damaged Christoval and fed a minor flood in San Angelo. An account in the *San Angelo Standard Times* commented, "Every ravine was a river."[10]

Closer to Austin, San Antonio reported 4.27 inches of rainfall from 7 P.M. on April 6 to 7 A.M. on April 7, and Landa Park in New Braunfels reported 6.5 inches in twenty-four hours. The *San Antonio Express* called the tempest, which raged from midnight to 6 AM on April 7, the "heaviest rain and electrical storm to visit the southwest".[11] Lockhart received its "heaviest rain in 20 years."[12] In the Colorado basin during this same period, Llano reported 4.65 inches, Fredericksburg 4.81 inches, and Burnet 4.08 inches of rain. The city of Austin received 5 inches between 1 P.M. on April 6 and 1 A.M. on April 7, and some locations measured 4 inches in a single hour.

April 7, 1900, at the Dam

On the morning of April 7, the floodwaters of the Colorado were rising rapidly (some residents estimated 2–4 feet an hour at the dam). The river challenged the dam with its largest flow ever over the structure, as it surpassed the high-water mark set in June 1899. By 10 A.M. the river was flowing 10 feet over the dam. That morning a crowd of approximately five hundred people gathered along the shore and near the powerhouse to watch the water pour over the barrier. At approximately 11:20 A.M., with no warning, the dam suddenly gave way to the muddy Colorado, breaking at a point about 300 feet from the east end. Witnesses said it appeared that "the wild current had simply pushed its way through the structure." According to an account in the *San Antonio Express*, "sooner than it takes to write these words" two 250-foot sections of the dam were moved 60 feet downstream by the currents, and water poured through the gap "with a roar that could be heard for several miles."[13]

One eyewitness gave this account of the rupture:

I was gazing intently at the great body of water as it swept gracefully over the crest of the dam. . . . It was grand and awe-inspiring, and nothing in my opinion could in any measure compare with it, except the falls of Niagara.

While thus gazing with awe on a sight such as I had never before witnessed, I noticed a sudden commotion of the waters near the center of the dam. For a moment the water where the commotion occurred seemed to recede, but it was only for a moment. It then shot upward in a tremendous spout to a height of perhaps fifty feet, as if in gleeful fury, and I saw that the dam was giving way. The commotion spread toward the east end

One of the pastimes at the Austin Dam (Austin History Center, Austin Public Library; Photo ID: C00066-B).

Watching the flood from south (downstream) of the dam on the day of the break (Austin History Center, Austin Public Library; Photo ID: PICA 12238).

of the dam and there was a trembling of the earth. The mighty waters roared and plunged with an indescribable fury, and the river, which a moment before had presented a scene of graceful grandeur as it curved over the dam, was turned into a seething maelstrom, so awful and so terrible, that nothing save the pen of a Dante or a Byron could do it justice.

I was appalled and entranced. My feelings were such as I had never before and never again hope to experience. Suddenly, above the dismal roar of the surging raging waters, there came a cry "The dam is breaking, the dam is breaking." The sound of the cry was as dismal as that of the maelstrom and people shuddered and their blood seemed chilled, although the sun shone warmly from a cloudless sky. . . . Imagine then if you can a body of water forty feet in height and of great width

Watching the flood from east of the dam on the day of the break (Austin History Center, Austin Public Library; Photo ID: PICA 17933).

and length suddenly released from confinement, and you will have a faint idea of the scene that I witnessed at the great dam across the Colorado River.[14]

Tragically, the location of the dam break directed the ensuing forty-foot wave of water toward the powerhouse, which sat at the same elevation as the base of the stream, some fifty feet below the crest of the dam. Employees working in the lower reaches of the powerhouse were caught in a nearly inescapable death trap. Eight of the workers drowned "like so many rats in a hole."[15] One worker survived by "grabbing a bolt and hauling himself out hand over hand through an opening in the roof of the building before water reached him."[16] The torrent carried eight other men standing below the dam a quarter mile downriver, where they were rescued.

H. M. Chance, a mechanical engineer who was studying the private waterworks downstream, heard shouting: "Looking up the river, a turbulent wave of water, 6 or 8 feet high, was seen coming rapidly downstream." Chance made his way to the dam in about twenty minutes. Once there, he saw one of the broken, displaced sections roll over into the water and disappear. He stated that the undamaged sections of the dam retarded the remaining streamflow and that the silt prevented a still bigger wall of water from pouring through.[17]

One eyewitness described the sound of the dam breaking as "a dull thud, something like a pile-driver makes when driving a pile into the ground." The observer added that he "saw the water spread out and everything seemed to go down at once. Then it appeared as if a tidal wave had suddenly come rushing down the river."[18]

Of the watercraft lost in the flood, the most noteworthy casualty was the steamboat *Ben Hur*. Measuring 181 feet in length and featuring a 130-foot-long saloon and thirty private cabins, the side-wheel steamer was the showpiece of the Lake McDonald fleet. It was docked when the dam broke and was left stranded on a sandbar when the water drained out of the lake. The ship broke into pieces, and months later its engines were sold. Residents picked up the wood from the *Ben Hur* and used some of it to build houses. The steering wheel was salvaged and still functions today on one of the riverboats that glide along Lake Austin.

Downtown Austin

Downstream of the dam, witnesses of the break raced to notify residents of the impending flood wave. In what was called "[a]nother Paul Revere's ride," one man mounted his horse to warn the lower sections of Austin of the imminent swells.[19] The lower reaches received warning about three minutes before the water hit. One group was crossing over the wagon bridge at Congress Avenue and allegedly escaped only a minute before the wave arrived. A young boy named Tom Miller was part of the group that witnessed the rise. Thirty-three years later Miller was elected to the city council

View of the dam shortly after the break (Austin History Center, Austin Public Library; Photo ID: PICA 09067).

5

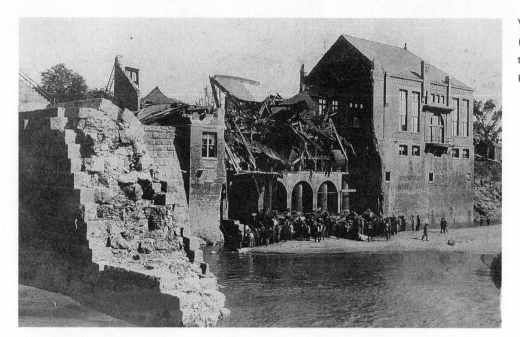

and began serving as mayor of Austin. In 1940 the dam built at the site of the original Austin Dam was completed and named for him.[20]

When they heard the roar of the water, residents evacuated their houses amid "such scenes of excitement [that] were never before witnessed in Austin," according to the *San Antonio Express*.[21] A San Antonio resident recounted what he saw downstream from the dam:

At the time we were crossing the railroad bridge. At the bridge the water was three quarters of a mile in width. . . . Both sides of the bridge were lined with people watching the boiling waters.

We had just gotten across the bridge and were turning into the Y near the dispatcher's station when the cry was raised that the dam had broken. . . . When the warning cry was heard, everybody looked ahead in the direction of the dam. Ahead of us, at a distance of about 300 yards, a wall of water was coming in our direction. The water, I suppose, was 15 feet in height, although it seemed greater. From the time it was first seen by us until the volume of water reached the

railroad bridge, hardly a half minute had elapsed. Almost in an instant the water came within five feet of where our train was standing.

The people residing along the river in small huts came out of them like rats. Their homes were lifted by the torrent as if they were only a match. . . . When the people standing on the bridge saw the water bearing down upon them, hardly before they could utter a cry, it had already reached there. Within ten minutes we saw at least thirty houses passing by in the river. Everything imaginable was in the stream.[22]

As the flood moved through town, it inundated the creeks that flow into the river. Shoal Creek rose twenty feet in two hours. The surge dislodged a steel bridge at Twelfth Street and a stone bridge at Sixth Street.[23] On Barton Creek, the water washed away the elegant, arched, eighty-foot stone bridge above Barton Springs.[24]

Downstream of Austin

On April 7, news of the dam break arrived at the Galveston weather bureau by telegram from Austin around 6:30 P.M. The message read, "Six and half inches of rain last night. Dam broken." Immediately the office sent out a warning that the Colorado River would experience a "sudden and decided rise" in the next few days.[25]

In Bastrop, the river peaked at 43 feet on April 8. At Smithville, the crest reached 40 feet, and at La Grange, the highest point was measured at 47 feet in the evening of April 9. The flood brought a 34-foot rise in Columbus on April 10. At Wharton, the Colorado was "higher than any previous overflow," according to the *Monthly Weather Review*. Floodwaters were 2–4 miles wide in Wharton County and 4–12 miles wide in Matagorda County.[26]

Austin after the Breach

The morning after the dam break, the powerhouse fell into the river after the water that had filled the building the day before forced its outer walls to give way. The *Austin Daily Statesman* described the powerhouse as looking "like a crippled monster . . . lying half in and half out of the water."[27]

Following the dam break and powerhouse collapse, residents of central Texas rushed to the site. Two days later, the *Austin Statesman* reported that "every vehicle that could stand on wheels, save a wheel

Wreck of the *Ben Hur* (Austin History Center, Austin Public Library; Photo ID: PICA 03977).

barrow, was pressed into service and every horse that was capable of placing one foot before the other, was trotted out."[28] The *San Antonio Express* added, "Almost every man, woman and child in Austin and for a distance of many miles around have visited the wrecked dam and power station during the past two days."[29] Only after viewing the wrecked dam did many citizens realize that the structure was not built of solid granite. Instead, its interior was made up of fill and rubble, not granite blocks. Many of the observers believed that this inner layer may have led to the rupture.

The April 11 issue of the *Austin Semi-Weekly Statesman* described the dam break as "without parallel in history of the state."[30] The *Dallas Morning News* added that Austin was now home to the "greatest blunder ever made by a Texas city or town."[31]

As news of the dam break spread throughout the United States, the nation's financial community focused on Austin's loss. The outstanding bonds for the project totaled $1,300,000 (the three largest ones were $400,000 in St. Louis, $300,000 in New York City, and $200,000 in Cleveland), and Austinites hoped the state would dedicate money to buy back the bonds. A rumor circulated throughout the town that Andrew Carnegie had given the city $100,000.[32]

Reasons for the Dam's Failure

Explanations for the collapse of the dam came from many sources. Local citizens blamed the rubble fill, the silt from the lake, and the debris in the floodwaters. Those who had built and studied the dam focused on its foundation. Within days of the breach, the *Engineering News* posted a report on the failure, which stated that "no overturning but a lift up and shove down stream" occurred.[33]

The April 19 edition of the *Engineering*

News included a thorough, five-page account of the dam's history. It featured a letter from Joseph Frizell, the first engineer in charge of the construction project. He wrote, "So far as any sense of responsibility for the late deplorable accident at Austin is concerned, I don't feel called on to say anything, having as I think, sufficiently washed my hands of that responsibility." He included his letter of resignation (dated June 1892) and a copy of the letter he had sent to Mayor Louis Hancock on April 8, 1896, in which he called attention to the friable rock at the base of the dam.[34]

J. T. Fanning, the lead engineer who succeeded Frizell, contributed a brief letter, in which he hypothesized that the break had resulted from an undermining created by a current "which had found its way under the rock of the river bed on which the dam rested."[35] Engineer E. C. Geyelin, who had reviewed plans of the dam in 1892, weighed in by reminding readers that he had suggested the pump house be placed about one hundred feet below the dam, "in which case

had it been done, it is likely the injury would not have been so great as it was."[36]

The following month, USGS geologist Robert T. Hill told *Engineering News* that the "site of the dam . . . [crossed] the river sub-parallel to one of the most conspicuous of the fault lines" and stated that, during excavation, springs had developed. He added that, if the dam had been placed two miles upstream, the "structural condition would have been avoided."[37]

E. W. Groves, who served as "engineer in charge of construction" in 1893, also wrote to *Engineering News* and said that, when excavation was under way, he had noticed a fault that consisted mostly of adobe. He believed the water flowed under the dam and floated sections that had settled. He closed his letter by extending sympathy to the people of Austin and then stating that "the attitude of the president of the board of public works toward Mr. Frizell was not such as should exist, if the best results were to be obtained during construction."[38]

The April 28, 1900, issue of *Scientific*

View of the dam site years after the break (Austin History Center, Austin Public Library; Photo ID: PICA 18022).

Surveying the wreckage of the powerhouse (Austin History Center, Austin Public Library; Photo ID: PICA 03987).

American offered an explanation for the collapse of the dam and the reason it was of interest to the scientific community: "The great size and importance of the dam across the Colorado River at Austin, Texas, and the peculiar features attending its recent failure render this wreck one of the most interesting on record." The article briefly recounted the differences between the engineer in charge during the first part of the project and his successor. It added that springs brought "considerable trouble" during the construction of the dam's foundation. These springs indicated the "unreliable nature of the limestone upon which the dam was built [and] must have shaken the faith of the engineers in the security and permanence of this great structure."[39]

The *Scientific American* summarized its findings as follows:

It will doubtless be found that the impact of the enormous mass of falling water upon the bed of the river below the toe of the dam had washed away the limestone rock, leaving nothing but the frictional resistance between the base of the masonry and the bed of the river to oppose the downstream thrust of the water. It is stated that the section of the dam, as originally designed, provided for four cut-off trenches in underlying bedrock, but it now seems that only two trenches were built. . . . If any washing away of the rock below the toe of the dam actually took place, the resistance offered by the downstream cut-off trench would be destroyed, and there would be nothing but the holding power of the masonry in the upstream trench coupled with the frictional resistance, to prevent the whole structure from sliding bodily down the bed of the river.[40]

In his report of 1910, T. U. Taylor reprinted part of a letter from one of the dam's engineers, N. Werenskiold. The letter read, "There can be no doubt that the failure was not caused by any defective work in the dam itself, but by the entire body being pushed downstream and broken from the lateral pressure on account of too small frictional resistance under the dam." He added, "I think it possible that the foundation might have been good enough for a dam without overfall, but it proved not to be good enough for this bold structure."[41] Years later, borings "demonstrated indisputably the very undesirable condition existing at the site," according to a 1917 report on the troubled structure.[42]

DECEMBER 1913

Nolan Creek and Brazos River Floods

FLASH FLOODS ARE usually associated with springtime storms and summertime hurricanes or tropical systems. In the last fifteen years, however, several large rain events have hit Central Texas in November and December (e.g., the storms of December 20–26, 1991, and November 15, 2001.)

In early December 1913, fourteen years after a record flood in the Brazos River valley, a weather system centered its heavy rainfall on the same region. This time it struck in the central part of the river valley, along major tributaries in the Temple and Belton areas, including Nolan Creek, the Leon River, the Lampasas River, and the Little River.

The flash flooding produced by the storm ripped through Belton, washed away houses, and tore bridges from their foundations along Nolan Creek. One of the greatest tragedies in the December 1913 flood was the loss of the Polk family of Belton. Today, just a block from the courthouse in town and on the banks of Nolan Creek, a park is named for Yettie Polk, the mother of the clan, who lost her life in the floodwaters early in the morning of December 2, 1913.

Precedent Conditions

The weather prior to the tragic flood exhibited one of the most extreme climate shifts in Texas in the last one hundred years. From January through May, Temple's rainfall was almost 7.5 inches below normal. Waco's tally was more than 5 inches delinquent for the same period. From April through August, Austin, San Marcos, and San Antonio all had rainfall deficits of more than 6.5 inches. During the summer months, the drought in Central Texas intensified and spread throughout the state. Precipitation totals for the July–August period dipped to an all-time record low for the entire state in the twenty-six years for which records had been kept.

In September, the local weather pattern finally began to shift. Rainfall in San Antonio, Lampasas, and Temple was more than 3 inches above average. That month's totals for Austin and Waco were 5 and 8 inches above normal, respectively.

October's weather brought flood-producing rains along the Guadalupe and the San Antonio rivers. San Antonio gauged 8.86 inches for that month, while New Braunfels and San Marcos exceeded that figure by tallying more than 12 and 15 inches, respectively, in October.

In November, above-normal rains doused Central Texas. By the end of the month, all of the streams in that region had climbed to the tops of their banks. Streamflow rates on the Brazos, Colorado, and Guadalupe rivers were at their highest levels in ten years. The *Engineering News* commented that the "ground was thoroughly saturated by heavy rains during the last 10 days of November."[1]

Storm Rainfall

At the end of November, a low-pressure system stalled west of Texas, causing warm,

Remnants of Main Street destroyed by the December 1913 flood in Belton (in the collection of the Lena Armstrong Public Library, Belton, Texas).

Rope pulley system for transferring goods across Nolan Creek (in the collection of the Lena Armstrong Public Library, Belton, Texas).

humid air to flow into the Lone Star State ahead of it. For several days (December 1–4), the system triggered continuous rain showers and storms over areas that had been soaked by the October and November rains.

At 7:30 P.M. on December 1, ominous clouds to the west and southwest of Temple unleashed their copious caches of moisture. Observers noted that "the very flood gates of heaven were opened, and the water fell in sheets on the stricken territory."[2] Their accounts stated that the rains were accompanied by light winds and little thunder, although "livid sheets of lightning were as si-

lent as the tomb, seeming more awful from that very fact."[3]

At Lampasas, upstream from Belton on the Lampasas River, 6.05 inches fell. Salado officially received more than 8.5 inches on December 2 and 3. Eight miles northeast of Belton, Temple received approximately 7.5 inches. By noon on December 3, Mart had recorded 10 inches of rain. Telephone operators in Lorena reported 10.5 inches of precipitation in the same period.

Nolan Creek Streamflow

The deluge of early December fell on drenched soils and poured into already full streams. The runoff from the intense rains was extreme and immediate. Early in the morning of December 2, a flood wave along Nolan Creek tore into Belton. The water level surged, invading houses built along the stream. One of these belonged to the William Polk family and was the home in which Yettie Tobler Polk, the mother of the family, had been raised.

Shortly after midnight, two men warned the Polks of the impending floodwaters. Mr. Polk rushed out to get his horse to carry his family to safety. His eldest son followed close behind. When Mr. Polk attempted to return on horseback to rescue his wife and the rest of the children, a rush of water swept both horse and rider downstream into a fence. The swell, which also carried away the jailhouse bridge, picked up the Polk house and smashed it. Mrs. Polk and the remaining children were caught in the raging waters and drowned. Mr. Polk made a "furious effort" to go back out into the floodwater but was held back by bystanders.[4] Onlookers of this tragedy remembered the "screaming of the doomed mother and her children as they floated past in the house. The watchers stood helpless, powerless to render aid."[5] The *Temple Daily Telegram*

reported that Mrs. Polk was "born in the same house in which she was bourne [*sic*] to her death. All her life she had spent in the house. Repeated floods had failed to shake her faith in the strength of her lifetime abode and she lost her life in the darkness of the night still firm in that belief."[6]

Within hours of the awful event, search parties were out looking for the bodies of the Polk family members. Mrs. Polk was found by the family dog, who barked to alert searchers when he spotted her body. The dog would "shake with cold and fear, but not for a minute would he take his eyes from the form of his dead mistress."[7]

Once searchers located Mrs. Polk's body, retrieving it was difficult and dangerous. Several attempts to reach the drift pile holding her were thwarted, including one in which the rescue boat fell apart. When the rescuers finally reached the corpse, with the dog barking excitedly, they loaded it into their boat. However, the return trip met with misfortune when the boat hit a whirlpool and overturned, returning the body to the water. The rescuers struggled to reach shore but lost sight of the corpse. Another rescue party on the east side of the Leon River located it later.[8]

On the night of December 2, another rise came down Nolan Creek. As the water reached levels almost as high as those twenty-four hours earlier, houses along Central Avenue were again flooded. Damage, however, was minimal this time.

Nolan Creek Aftermath

Three bridges linked north and south Belton prior to the flood. All three bridges—on Central Avenue, Main Street, and Penelope Street—were washed away in the deluge. To transport supplies to the isolated section south of the creek, Belton residents devised a cable system that stretched across the gap at Main Street. By December 4 eighty-three

loads of provisions had been sent to south Belton.

By that same day, all but one of the bodies of the doomed Polk family had been found. Mr. Polk expressed his wish that they be buried in the cemetery north of the creek. However, the only way to transport the bodies there was via the cable system. Witnesses of the event remembered that "one of the saddest spectacles the eye of man ever beheld took place in Belton yesterday shortly after noon. Over the improvised cable . . . was sent the body of Florence Polk, 14, who was drowned in the first flood Tuesday morning with her mother, sister and two brothers. . . . As the body started on its journey across the creek the hundreds of men who lined the bank on either side lifted their hats and stood with bared heads. Women and children in the crowd of watchers sobbed openly and it was the most tense moment in the city since the flood first tore its way through the place." Shortly after, the corpse of the four-year-old son was brought over, and later the mother's body was brought in to town from the spot where it had been recovered, 1½ miles below Belton. Businesses closed that afternoon so that the townspeople could pay their respects to the surviving members of the Polk family.[9] Lost were mother Yettie, daughters Yettie and Florence, and sons Marion and James.

Hero dog from Belton (in the collection of the Lena Armstrong Public Library, Belton, Texas)

Flood scene in Belton from 1900 (in the collection of the Lena Armstrong Public Library, Belton, Texas).

Footbridge across Nolan Creek (in the collection of the Lena Armstrong Public Library, Belton, Texas).

The Central Avenue bridge destroyed by the flood in Belton, December 1913 (in the collection of the Lena Armstrong Public Library, Belton, Texas).

Salado Creek and Little River

Salado Creek was flooding in Salado and Sparta, reaching eighteen feet in the latter and flowing three feet deeper than the October flood in Salado. One mile above its junction with the Leon River, Salado Creek joins the Lampasas River. This junction forms the start of the Little River. With its tributaries flooding, the Little River was transformed into what the *Temple Daily Telegram* called "a veritable monster, snorting its way south-ward and laying waste to valuable farms and their products."[10]

The Little River invaded the Burgess community, twelve miles southeast of Temple. Anticipating the floodwaters, one family chained their home to a large tree after drilling holes in the house walls. The floodwaters moved the house off its foundation blocks, but the chains drew tight and kept the home from floating away in the current. The same family managed to coax two of their hogs and a cow into the house to save them from the deluge.[11] At Cameron, the Little River swept away the Santa Fe railroad bridge.

Two motorboats were used to rescue stranded residents, one of whom had been stranded in a tree for forty-eight hours. Another woman, in an attempt to stay awake during the ordeal, rubbed her forehead until "the skin was worn to the flesh."[12]

Brazos River

At 7 A.M. on December 1 the Brazos River at Waco stood at 13 feet. Over the next two

	NOV. 20–30	DEC. 1	DEC. 2	DEC. 3	DEC. 4	DEC. 5	DEC. 1–5 TOTAL
Albany	5.37	0.26	0.25	0.30	0.85	0.13	1.79
Comanche	6.10	0.10	1		1.25	0.35	2.7
Dublin	5.31		0.11	0.81	1.08	0.61	2.61
Lampasas	3.09	0.00	6.05	1.57	1.67	1.03	10.32
Waco	3.52		1.42	2	5.4	1	9.82
Temple	2.63	0.00	1	4.43	2.93	1.4	9.76
Cameron	2.67	0.62	4.09	4.29	0.97	0	9.97
Taylor	2.28	0.05	2.25	5.6	1.83	0.3	10.03
Georgetown	3.24		4	4.51	5.05	0.02	13.58
Hewitt	2.72	trace	2.22	7.86	0.8	0.96	11.84
Salado	2.3		2.67	5.9	1.5	1.15	11.22
Brenham	8.4		0.16	0.42	3.73	0.5	4.81
Somerville	11		0.3	5	7.75	0.5	13.55
Austin	1.86	0.06	1.85	6.34	4.32	1.5	14.07
Marble Falls	1.7		5.6	2	2.5	0.65	10.75
Blanco	3.62	0.04	1.25	0.65	4.12	0.65	6.71
San Marcos	4.51	0.00	2	2.45	10	1.05	15.5
New Braunfels	5.98	0.2	0.37	0.73	4.2	0.94	6.44

days, the river rose almost 27 feet, peaking at 39.7 feet on December 3 at 6 P.M. On December 2 Waco citizens lined the bridges across the Brazos and watched the river rise. At the Washington Street Bridge, a man known as "Galveston Charlie" jumped into the swirling floodwaters after gathering ten dollars from the crowd, who had paid him to swim across the river. After being tossed about for a few hundred feet, he avoided a dangerous current and drifted another two hundred yards below the suspension bridge, where he waded to shore. He then announced that he would repeat the feat later in the afternoon.[13]

Around 9 A.M. on December 3 floodwaters broke through the levee and began to spread into East Waco, where merchants had been warned to prepare for high water. They had spent the previous night moving goods to upper shelves or second-story locations. Wagon operators from American Express and Wells Fargo sold their perishable goods once they discovered they were stranded in Waco. Later the wagons were used to rescue marooned residents. As the

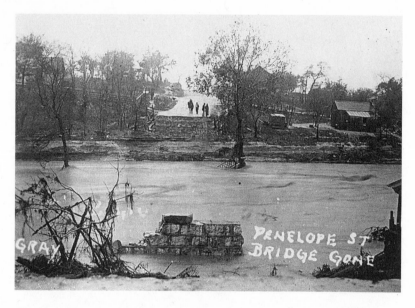

floodwater poured into East Waco, planing mills began building boats for county and city authorities to use for rescue work. Elm Street in East Waco filled with twelve feet of water.

One hero in Waco turned out to be Lazaro Amador, who had been jailed for drunkenness after he attempted to dive into the river at the Washington Street Bridge. When a policeman was trapped while rescuing another

This is all that remained of the Penelope Street bridge after the December 1913 flood in Belton (in the collection of the Lena Armstrong Public Library, Belton, Texas).

Footbridge in use after the flood in Belton (in the collection of the Lena Armstrong Public Library, Belton, Texas).

man, a fellow officer who remembered hearing stories of Amador's swimming prowess released the prisoner and brought him to where the policeman had been stranded. There Amador placed a rope in his mouth and dived into the churning water. He reached the raft where the two were stuck and secured them before heading back to shore. The *Waco Daily Times-Herald* said, "It looked like certain death, but not once did [Amador] falter." Afterward a collection was taken up for Amador, but he refused it, stating, "as he covered his heart with both hands, 'Me no save him for money. Me save him for love.'" Amador continued his work that day and saved several other victims as well.[14]

South Waco also suffered. Water from Waco Creek poured out of its banks, flooding 250 homes and washing through the grounds of the Cotton Palace.

The Brazos Watershed near Waco

Close to Waco, in the South Bosque community, a ten-foot wall of water from the Bosque River and Harris Creek rushed through the town. Houses were swept off their blocks, and the force of the water nearly toppled the passenger depot of the Cotton Belt Railroad. The surge washed away one thousand feet of Cotton Belt track.

The flood from the Brazos also affected the Marlin area, even though the town sits five miles from the river. The big story there involved a passenger train that was trapped by high water that stretched "two miles from land in any direction," according to the *Waco Daily Times-Herald*.[15] The 175 passengers, many of whom lived south of Marlin and were fleeing the floodwaters, filled the train, which was "struck by a mighty rush of water."[16] The high water flowed into the firebox, bringing the engine to a halt. During the harrowing experience, which lasted throughout the night of December 3, water lapped at the lower steps of the passenger cars. The next day passengers floated to safety on light boats and skiffs.[17] The river also flooded Marlin's new pump station, which was built with the previous high-water marks in mind and was thought to be safe.[18]

16   At Valley Junction, the Brazos River was joined by the Little River, and the swirling water there formed an "immense sea" six miles wide.[19] Robert H. Martin, a vice president and general manager of the International and Great Northern Railroad, was working with others to rescue flood victims when his boat overturned and he was swallowed up by the currents.

After this point, the high water on the Brazos surged downstream, and Bryan-area residents knew this would be the big test for their new twenty-seven-mile "great levee." Unfortunately, the embankment failed when water spilled over it around 3 P.M. on December 4 and piled up in the lowlands, forming a lake five miles wide.[20] Rescue parties from Bryan rounded up twenty boats and used them to reach those who were marooned in the lowlands.

Choosing not to leave their farms, many of the owners of the large plantations along the river tried to save their stock. In an attempt to keep the animals from drowning, they tore down barns and sheds to build platforms. As many as 3,000 people were trapped on the upper floors of houses and barns, on rooftops, and in trees. However, even the usually safe rooftops and trees were not sufficient in many instances. Boatmen reported that "Not even the chimneys showed above the water when they made their final trips." One night more than 1,500 people were rescued using only eight motorboats. One of the rescuers stated, "God knows how many there were left in the bottoms. When we left last night, we could hear cries and shouts in the darkness. They are all huddled together in the gins and high places. There were 180 people in one gin house. We caught three hogs drifting down the river and the people killed and skinned them in the gin, but they had no bread to eat with the meat."[21]

After the flood-producing low-pressure system moved to the east, the counterclockwise circulation pushed cold air into Texas. According to the *Engineering News,* there was "great suffering due to exposure and hunger." From December 5 to December 7 temperatures dipped to 45 degrees. On December 8 and 9 they fell to the mid-thirties. To survive, people "subsisted on raw meat from animals fished out of the water."[22] At Hempstead, the water reached 52.8 feet at the U.S. Weather Bureau gage. Water covered an area that was six to eight miles wide.

By December 6 the flood wave was emptying into the Gulf of Mexico at Freeport. An indication of its power was seen in the debris: A large section of a railroad bridge and a wrecked residence were washed down in the middle of the stream early in the morning.[23]

Colorado River

South of the Belton and Temple area, extremely heavy rain fell from Austin southward to San Antonio. From December 1 to December 5 fourteen inches fell in Austin. There, floodwaters from the Pedernales River and other tributaries upstream of the city spurred the river to its highest level since April 1900, when the Austin Dam failed. The river in Marble Falls rose from 9.3 feet on December 1 to 21 feet on December 3. Reports of this stage were interpreted wrongly in Austin, as its residents expected

Colorado River flood at ballpark in Austin (Austin History Center, Austin Public Library; Photo ID: PICA 04009).

a 21-foot wall of water to come rushing down from Marble Falls.

In Austin, the river stood at 10.3 feet at 7 A.M. on December 2. Slightly less than ten hours later, the river was flowing 25 feet deep. The peak stage of the event in Austin occurred at 1 A.M. on December 5, when the river reached 27 feet. This high point came within 1.5 feet of the top of the refurbished Austin Dam. The partially completed structure held well, but the cofferdams were washed away.[24] Water rushed through the gap in the unfinished structure, "making a show almost equal to that of the gorge of Niagara Falls." Driftwood pounded it but did little damage. The flood covered the Deep Eddy swimming hole with 15 feet of water.[25] Near the railroad bridge, the Texas League ballpark on the south side of the river was submerged in several feet of water.

The rains in Austin were extreme enough to cause evangelist Doctor Biederwolf to cancel a speaking engagement for the first

time in seventeen years. According to the *Austin Daily Statesman,* Biederwolf's party was "used to all sorts of storms and weather but this time for the once, all their plans are baffled." [26] Downstream, parts of Bastrop were under 2–3 feet of water when the river crested, although the depth was still 7 feet lower than during the epic flood of 1869.

The Colorado River flood grew as it moved downstream. The flood there matched the record inundation of July 9, 1869 when it reached an estimated discharge of 380,000 cubic feet per second (cfs), exceeding that of the one-hundred-year flood at La Grange by 90,000 cfs. The shock experienced by residents in the La Grange area was well recorded in the *La Grange Journal:*

Customary as it is to refer to an incident in the history of a community, the application of that custom is permissible in this instance when we sit here in our demoralized office and attempt to describe the visit of the floodwaters upon the beautiful little city of La Grange, and the appalling sight when the waters receded. Truly might it be said with impunity, with the exception of the yellow fever siege in 1867, La Grange has not been visited by a calamity heretofore that has left so many sad hearts and creates so much concern as that of the weeks just passed.

When the last issue of the Journal *made its appearance on the afternoon of December 4, the citizens living in the flat were beginning to pack their household effects and removing to the Northern and Eastern end as fast as teams could be procured. . . . The hope was prevalent everywhere that the waters would not be in excess of those of 1900.*[27]

However, the waters climbed well past the mark set in 1900 and extended to the courthouse square, where, on the night of December 4, they reached a depth of four feet. According to the reporter from the *La Grange Journal* who looked out the next morning,

Colorado River flood at bridge in Columbus, December 1913 (courtesy of the Nesbitt Memorial Library, Columbus Texas).

"There was presented a scene that the artist from his standpoint could have raved over. Marooned on the second floor, we appeared like the Biblical Noah and gazed out upon a vast area of water, and the scene was such as to melt even the heart of a tyrant."[28]

The record rise created a harrowing experience at Columbus. On December 4 telephone reports from La Grange indicated that the town would be an island by morning. At the time of the warning, Columbus residents could still escape along the railroad track to the west, which was passable until the water exceeded the level reached during the historic 1869 flood, which was another 12 feet.[29] Two days later, on December 6, the river crested at 44.1 feet—20 feet above flood stage—thereby surpassing the 1869 level by 2.9 feet.

Columbus residents fled the town in boxcars that were brought in via a switch engine from Glidden, three miles away. The second group of people "saw water eating away the dirt from under the tracks." A few minutes later, the track snapped from the strain.[30] Near the Gulf of Mexico, Wharton was surrounded by water, and Bay City guarded its levees with as many as three hundred men. According to unverified reports, the extreme floods on the Colorado and Brazos rivers joined, creating a section of water thirty miles wide in the coastal area.[31]

Guadalupe River

After its 15-inch rain total in October, the town of San Marcos received 15.5 inches between December 1 and December 5. At Luling, the San Marcos River hit 38 feet, several inches higher than the October flood. Plum Creek at Luling reached a level of 30–40 feet,[32] which was 4 feet higher than ever before.[33]

The floodwaters of the San Marcos River fed into the Guadalupe River and pushed it

to record highs from Gonzales to Victoria. The gage at Gonzales read 8.2 feet at 6 P.M. on December 2. The following day the river was at 21 feet, and by the next morning it had reached 25 feet and was still rising at 1.1 feet per hour.

San Marcos reported a ten-inch rain during the daytime hours of December 3. The deluge in San Marcos left "no doubt . . . that new high-water marks would be established." By 7 P.M. the full effects of the downpour were felt at Gonzales, as the river reached 38.1 feet, the flood's peak. The previous high-water mark had been set only two months earlier—at 36.7 feet.[34]

Colorado River flood, railroad bridge outside of Columbus, December 1913 (courtesy of the Nesbitt Memorial Library, Columbus Texas).

Scenes from Colorado River flood at Columbus, December 1913 (courtesy of the Nesbitt Memorial Library, Columbus Texas).

Main Street in Columbus during the Colorado River flood, December 1913 (courtesy of the Nesbitt Memorial Library, Columbus Texas).

Nolan Creek and Little River basins

San Antonio

In San Antonio, the six to nine inches of rain resurrected a topic that the city's residents had discussed just two month before—how to handle the flooding of the San Antonio River and area creeks. Observers of the San Antonio River noted that the "first angry swirl of the Olmos red outpouring had tumbled under the Navarro Street bridge" at 10:45 P.M.[35] In the early morning hours, the river rose again, and by 6 A.M. the river had passed its October flood mark. It raged for the next two hours before falling rapidly.

In the downtown business district, the river overflowed into St. Mary's Street. Most of the businesses had not fully repopulated the lower quarters and basements of their dwellings, which had been damaged by the October flood. Two landmarks, the Gunter Hotel and the Royal Theatre, were also in need of repair. The Alamo Stables were inundated with five to eight feet of water, and the Bowles Ponytorium was inundated. Overall, however, destruction was less than might have been expected, largely due to warnings from police and firemen, which the citizens heeded. The *San Antonio Express* stated that the San Antonio populace "weathered this later visitation of the storm king with far more satisfaction and far less of cost than surprised the metropolis a few weeks ago."[36]

One afflicted area was "Convent Bend," a section of town bounded by St. Mary's, Martin, and Navarro streets and the San Antonio River. When a number of neighborhood residents doubted the predictions of more flooding along the river, the *San Antonio Express* colorfully described the situation this way: "Many of the denizens of the Bend regarded flood forecasts as cries of 'Wolf, wolf!' They refused to believe that devastation was approaching them from beyond Brackenridge Park, that destruction was coming in marathon bounds. Like unto the scoffers in the time of the first and only world flood, some of the whiskered men stroked their chins, shook their heads significantly and observed, 'There's no use getting in the ark; it's only going to be a shower anyway.'" Hours later, several of these skeptics had to be rescued. When the flood receded, many Convent Bend residents came back to homes that had been invaded by three inches of slimy ooze.[37]

Elsewhere in the San Antonio area, Salado Creek reached its highest level in fifty years. It was estimated to be 50 feet deep at

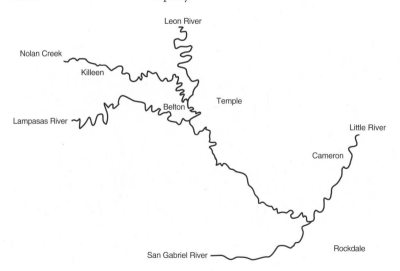

STATION	JANUARY	FEBRUARY	MARCH	APRIL	MAY	JUNE	JULY	AUGUST	SEPTEMBER	OCTOBER	NOVEMBER	DECEMBER
Lampasas	2.09	2.14	0.59	2.05	3.08	2.76	0.29	1.34	6.55	4.4	6.71	11.3
Hewitt	2.1	2.25	0.34	1.7	1.28	2	1.02	1.42	8.4	3.54	5.43	13.37
Waco	1.78	2.47	0.78	3.4	1.2	1.16	0.15	4.07	11.17	3.52	5.32	11.76
Temple	2.09	2.58	1.02	1.8	1.95	1.78	0.5	0.81	6.55	6.72	6.33	11.16
Salado	2.09	2.33	0.84	1.62	1.6	2.56	0.92	0.72	4.49	6.06	5.45	12.12

points, more than 18 feet deeper than during the October overflow. Leon Creek also reached new highs when it rose to 25 feet, which was 15 feet higher than in October.[38]

After the flood, San Antonio residents and officials recalled other deluges and promoted their solutions to alleviate them. One of the most common recommendations was to "dam the Olmos."[39] The *San Antonio Express* stated, "Wherever men congregated, the chief topic was what to do with the river. There were suggestions almost as numerous as the conversations and every one was uttered with a vehemence that left no doubt but that the plan suggested was the only proper one to be pursued in the safeguarding of the lives and property of San Antonians."[40]

River Commissioner George Surkey believed the chief problem was the San Antonio River's inability to transport all of the floodwaters. He proposed the building of an underground spillway from Romana Street to the Mill Bridge, which connected Navarro and Garden streets. The spillway would accommodate any overflow when water rose above a safe level.[41]

The *San Antonio Express* repeatedly urged the city's leaders and citizens to develop a flood-prevention plan. Its editorial of December 5, "Twice the Warning Has Come—Let Us Act," summarizes the paper's ideas:

The San Antonio River must never again be permitted to go on a rampage such as that of yesterday and of two months ago. This is the most important work today facing the city administration and the people of San Antonio. It shadows every other development, for, unless safety from this always possible menace is obtained, progress along the line of building the greater San Antonio will be handicapped by the knowledge that some day another and perhaps far more disastrous flood will make naught the work of the builders.

Procrastination is not only the thief of time, but it is the trapdoor to ruin. After the flood of October, even the old timers said, "This will not occur again for twenty years"—yet within 62 days a greater flood swirls throughout the city. Something must be done and done at once to obviate a reoccurrence. . . .

Some distance beyond Brackenridge Park, at the headwaters of the San Antonio River there are two high bluffs, marking the entrance of the Olmos Valley. Firmly anchored into these bluffs a reinforced concrete wall, at 20 feet in height and of sufficient strength to resist the impact of a great body of water and approximately one thousand feet in length could be built. This wall would be pierced by two openings. . . . These openings would permit the water even though it should come in flood volume, to be diverted in such measure that it would not overflow the present height of the banks of the San Antonio River. In other words, it would take 24 hours for the passage of a volume of water that now requires three hours. . . .

Under no circumstances must water be allowed to remain or lake to form.[42]

Another proposal suggested straightening the river, but the *Express* also had an argument against that project: "San Antonio will never submit to seeing its historic river mutilated, when that mutilation will not serve the purpose intended. The river as a scenic attraction has incalculable value. There is no other city in the United States that has such a winding picturesque stream. We are essentially and for years to come will be a winter tourist resort. The charm of San Antonio lies in the unusual, the old, the historical, all of which it has possession in abundant measure, although today we have little left. The charge has been made that by tearing down one building after another in the making of a greater city, we are killing the goose that lays the golden egg. Let us keep the greatest natural resource assets we possess; let us improve and beautify instead of abandoning it."[43]

Summing Up

The *Engineering News* concluded that the December floods "exceeded all previous records, not only as to depth of water recorded but also as to extent of territory covered."[44] The flooded area covered more than three thousand square miles.

In reviewing the event, the *Texas Coaster* of Richmond, Texas, on December 13 commented, "While the loss will not reach the magnitude of the 1899 flood by hundreds of thousands, it will still be enormous and make untold hardships for many thousand[s of] families. . . . One lesson has been thoroughly taught dwellers in the bottoms. Perhaps two. The first is that they must not ignore the reports of the U.S.W.B. [United States Weather Bureau]; and when the river makes a record rise at a point from three to five days above us to heed the warning and cease to believe and hope that God Almighty will in some way stop the waters on their way to the sea and prevent them from reaching lower points. The other lesson, if it be one, is that in a safe retreat there is less danger than to stand your ground until you are surrounded by water. It is better to prepare for a big flood and move everything out and then no flood come, than to stay and perhaps be deceived."[45]

APRIL 1915

~~~~~~~~~

Floods on Shoal and Waller Creeks

THE APRIL 1915 flash flood that hit Austin, Texas, is an example of a relatively small storm dropping intense rain on vulnerable locations to produce a raging flash flood. Downtown and central Austin are flanked by two creeks: Shoal Creek to the west and Waller Creek to the east. The eastern edge of the University of Texas was built along the latter.

The April 1915 flash flood also pointed out the danger posed by debris in the floodwaters and obstructions along the streams. Wreckage from the flood formed small dams, created whirlpools, and clogged the flow of water under bridges. Victims lost their lives in the currents and traps formed by the debris, especially at the bridges over Waller and Shoal creeks.

Precedent Conditions

Prior to the flash flood, rainfall in Austin in the spring of 1915 was near normal. The most unusual feature of Central Texas weather that spring was snow and sleet. In March, two inches of snow fell in Austin. In April, sleet fell southeast of Austin—in Sealy, Flatonia, Luling, and Hallettsville.[1]

Storm Description

The flash flood was triggered by a trademark storm for localized flash flooding in a Texas—a slow-moving tempest that dropped large amounts of rain in only a few hours. At 7:45 P.M. on April 22 a thunderstorm began dumping heavy precipitation on Aus-

tin, which persisted throughout the night. By 1 A.M. rainfall estimates ranged from eight inches in three hours to ten inches in less than two hours. Reliable records indicated that eight inches fell before midnight.[2] One newspaper account called the storm the "greatest in Austin history."[3] Others labeled it "the severest rain and electrical storm in the history of Austin,"[4] as well as the "heaviest cloudburst in the history of Central Texas."[5]

Austin Creek Runoff

The eight to ten inches that fell over Austin flowed quickly into the two main creeks running through the central part of the city. In 1915 these two streams, Shoal and Waller, responded with rapid and unprecedented rises for many Austinites. One of the few warnings to residents living along their banks came in the form of rats running through houses in search of higher ground.

The runoff brought disaster to Austin. The *Austin American* of April 23, 1915, stated that "Austin this morning arouses from a veritable night of terror, during which the worst flood and storm in the history of the city and probably the state swirled and raged for hours. . . . Houses were washed away, cows, horses, chickens and other fowls went careening down swelled Shoal and Waller Creeks to join the human corpses that had gone swirling before them to the bosom of the Colorado. . . . Austin is a pitiable sight. . . . There is not a section of the

DAILY RAINFALL (IN INCHES) FOR THE APRIL 1915 FLOOD

	APR. 18	APR. 19	APR. 20	APR. 21	APR. 22	APR. 23	APR. 24	APR. 25	APR. 26	TOTAL
Austin	1.13	0.83	0.78			10	0.29	3.05	3	19.08
Taylor	0.18	0.99	0.11		8.29	1.5	2.01	1.95		15.03
Cameron	0.22	0.13	1.54		7.3	0.22	3.51	1.27		14.19
Temple	0.26	0.10	1.55			3.3	0.2	0.59	2.53	8.53
San Marcos	0.76		0.24			1.5	0.49	0.71	0.61	4.31
New Braunfels	3.11	2.3				2.3	0.52	0.57	0.22	9.02
San Antonio	6.78	trace			trace	1.51	0.26	1.84		10.39

city traversed by the treacherous little stream, docile most months of the year, which has not felt the finger of death. . . . Caught like rats in a trap, strong men and fragile women had their lives snuffed out without warning."[6]

Along Waller Creek, the flood debris, consisting of houses, fences, bridges, barns, and outhouses, was likened to that in the aftermath of a cyclone. Near Fifteenth and Trinity streets, the wreckage formed a chute in which several victims were sucked in and drowned.

Along Shoal Creek, the primary damage occurred between Fourth and Twelfth streets, where the floodwaters demolished thirty-one houses. The currents swept away most of the buildings along Wood Street, which backs up to the stream.[7] Outhouses along West Sixth Street were de-

posited along the sidewalk bordering the road. Shoal Creek also washed out the tracks to Austin's trolley system. The *Austin American* described the grim situation: "Houses that were made the pawns of the furious waters as they were in Shoal Creek's rise . . . were hurled, smashed and crashed as though they were eggshells afloat in the sea."[8]

During the deluge, debris blocked the openings under bridges, causing flood water to back up into houses. After the flood, citizens living along Shoal Creek sued the city, contending that it had built the bridges "too low to allow the water to pass under them" and thereby caused the bridges to act as dams.[9] Even along streets not adjacent to creeks, the rapid runoff created dangerous conditions for pedestrians. One young man was swept into a two-foot-deep

Searching for bodies in the debris at Fifteenth Street and Waller Creek (Austin History Center, Austin Public Library; Photo ID: PICA 27260).

Street scene during the September 1915 flood (Austin History Center, Austin Public Library, Photo ID: C08541).

Waller Creek in flood (Austin History Center, Austin Public Library; Photo ID: PICA 14517).

September 1915 flood in Austin (Austin History Center, Austin Public Library, Photo ID: C08530).

Submerged trolley car (Austin History Center, Austin Public Library; Photo ID: C08542).

Man posing next to tree that he and his wife climbed to escape Waller Creek flood (Austin History Center, Austin Public Library; Photo ID: PICA 27255).

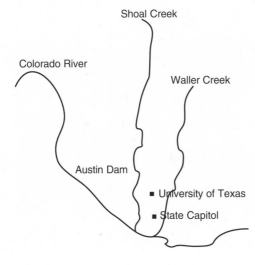

Map of Shoal and Waller creeks

torrent that was heading to a storm sewer, but a passerby reached down and yanked him from the waters. Another man was swept for three blocks until a police officer pulled him to safety.

Austin's police chief noted how the citizens living near Waller Creek had cooperated in helping each other. Police Chief Morris commented, "I want to say, first of all, that if the wealthy people of Austin could have seen what I saw last night and today, they would liberally subscribe for the relief of the people. . . . [The] remarkable unselfishness of the really poor in lending assistance to the unfortunates is one of the most striking features."[10] In the 600 block of Congress Street, J. T. Taylor's restaurant offered free food to the victims. The invitations went out to "Negroes, Mexicans and whites alike, and without price."[11]

With close to one thousand people left homeless and thirty-two dead, the *Austin American* summarized the scene after the event: "Ere dawn had thrown its gentle glow over the scenes of ruin and wreckage of yesterday, the waters of the two miserable little freshets, Shoal and Waller Creeks, had sunk back into their channels, leaving a panorama of waste, desolation, death and destruction

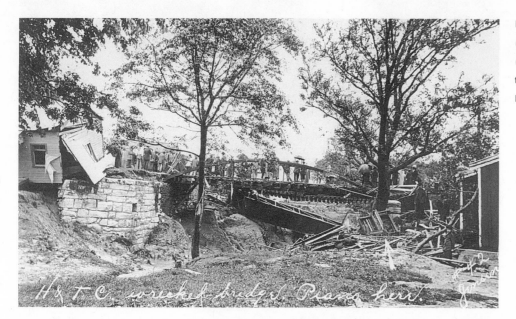

Debris at railroad bridge (piano is in wreckage at tree) (Austin History Center, Austin Public Library; Photo ID: PICA 27264).

Austin Dam in 1915 after repairs (Austin History Center, Austin Public Library, Photo ID: C11079).

Trolley line wreckage (Austin History Center, Austin Public Library; Photo ID: PICA 27239).

Floodwaters at Austin Dam in 1922 (Austin History Center, Austin Public Library; Photo ID: Co8581).

in their wake. . . . By daylight the treacherous little streams resembled rills, which rippled and played as though they had not a few hours earlier stabbed the city in its vitals."[12]

Colorado River

With the torrential rain and wild flooding along Austin's creeks, the recipient of these waters, the Colorado River, rose sharply. One fisherman was tossed from his small boat when the flood came down the Colorado from the creeks in an eight-to-eleven-foot wave.[13]

Outside of Austin

In Oak Hill, to the west of Austin, homes that had stood along Williamson Creek for thirty years were flooded. Other streams in the Austin area, including Wilbarger, Willow, Dry, Brushy, and Little and Big Walnut creeks, were at their highest levels in that same period. In eastern Travis County, the Swedish tabernacle was destroyed. The inundation was described as the "largest that has ever been in this county."[14]

Floodwater at Austin Dam, September 1915 (Austin History Center, Austin Public Library, Photo ID: Co8538).

SEPTEMBER 1921

~~~~~~~~~

Downtown San Antonio Flood

PRIOR TO HIS tenure as superintendent of Central Park in New York City, Frederick Law Olmsted toured Texas and subsequently wrote *Journey through Texas, or, A Saddle-trip on the Southwestern Frontier*. The beauty of the San Antonio River inspired Olmsted to describe the river as "a rich blue and as pure as crystal, flowing rapidly but noiselessly over pebbles and between reedy banks. One could lean for hours over the bridge rail."[1]

The city of San Antonio grew up around this enchanting river. In the 1800s its banks became home to gristmills and breweries, and its water supplied local bathhouses. The river also became part of the city's celebrations. In 1905 the king of San Antonio's Fiesta was escorted on the river for the first time.

However, the river also brought risk to San Antonio residents living along its banks. Located at the edge of the Balcones Escarpment and near the river's headwaters, San Antonio was susceptible to flash floods. In 1819, 1845, 1865, 1869, and 1903 the river overflowed. In early 1913 Mayor pro tem Albert Steves advocated damming Olmos Creek, the primary tributary above downtown San Antonio. Before major planning or discussion advanced, the river flooded severely twice more that year.

In 1920 the city contracted with a nationally known engineering firm to study the problem. In December of that year, the company concluded that flooding could be averted by straightening the river, extending its flood-carrying capacity, and constructing a dam above Brackenridge Park, close to the mouth of Olmos Creek.

To increase its flood-carrying capacity, the river would be deepened, and obstructions, included picturesque cypress trees, would be removed. Once the citizens of San Antonio heard about this plan, they protested mightily. The program was then halted, and the river remained as it was prior to the study. The engineers stated, "We doubt if the citizens realize the ruinous loss which would result today with the present condition of the river channels from such a flood as that of a century ago. When such a flood will recur, no man can say. A very great flood ought to be expected in the near future. . . . This disastrous flood is just as likely to occur next year as at any other time."[2]

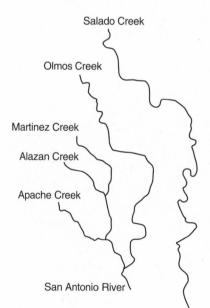

San Antonio River and the creeks that flooded in 1921

Map of downtown San Antonio (based on present day)

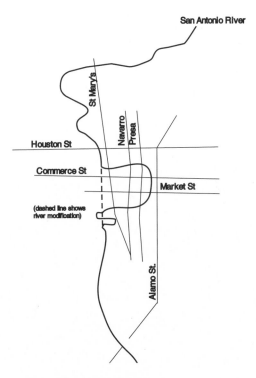

San Antonio River

St Mary's

Navarro Presa

Houston St

Commerce St

Market St

(dashed line shows river modification)

Alamo St.

Debris at Alamo Street bridge (UTSA's Institute of Texan Cultures, San Antonio, Texas, No. 91-291).

54 - Alamo St Concrete Bridge

Precedent Conditions

As river modification was being debated, the weather in San Antonio followed a familiar shift from wet to dry. From March to June 1921 San Antonio recorded 15.29 inches of rain. In July and August the wet pattern reversed, as the city received only 0.93 inches of rain. The rest of the state shared in the droughty August. For that month, precipitation in Texas was the lowest in thirty-four years of record keeping by the U.S. Weather Bureau. Austin and San Marcos received no rain at all in August.

As frequently happens along the Gulf Coast, the hot, dry conditions that baked the land also heated the Gulf of Mexico waters and cooked up a tropical disturbance that moved into South Texas in early September. Evidence of the weather system appeared on September 7, when Laredo recorded 0.20 inches of rain. The following night, the city received 6 inches of rain. The resulting runoff washed away the pontoon bridge over the Rio Grande River. That same day San Antonio received general showers totaling 0.55 inches, prompting the *San Antonio Express* to label the rains as "the most timely showers since 1919."[3]

Storm Rainfall

On September 9 in San Antonio, showers started early in the morning and fell all day. In the evening the precipitation turned into an intense electrical storm that lasted from approximately 6 to 9 P.M. and brought torrential rains to the area. Officially, the San Antonio Weather Bureau received 6.84 inches for the twenty-four-hour period ending at 11 P.M. on September 9, with 1.46 inches falling between 7 and 11 P.M.

Considerably heavier rains hit areas to the north and west of the city. A station 2 miles north of the weather bureau gauged 9.50 inches for the day and more than 3 inches after 7 P.M. A location 3 miles northwest of the city reported more than 10 inches. The heaviest rains, up to 15 inches, fell 5–6 miles northwest of downtown. Along the San Antonio River basin, rainfall totals averaged 12.5 inches, with the northern reaches receiving up to 15 inches. Over its basin, Olmos Creek averaged more than 14 inches of rain for the day.

Olmos Creek and San Antonio River Flood

Upstream of the downtown area—at the Alamo Street Bridge—the San Antonio River rose one to two feet by 6 P.M. on September 9. That meager rise occurred before the intense evening rains fell to the north and west of downtown. Powered by the fourteen-inch rain over the Olmos Basin, Olmos Creek first overflowed its banks around 10 P.M. and then devastated some of San Antonio's most scenic and popular landscapes and parkland. The high water from the Olmos inundated Brackenridge Park, cutting off campers there from the rest of the city. Police initially feared the campers would be lost in the flood, but they fled to safety on a high cliff.

The high water in Brackenridge Park also disrupted animal life at the zoo, where two sea lions floated away from their enclosure. One was captured two miles from home af-ter visiting several porches the following morning. The other was seen seventy-five miles down the river. Jazz trombone great Jack Teagarden allegedly spotted one of the sea lions riding a flood crest.[4]

Near the park, water was four feet deep on River Avenue. Autos stalled while attempting to dash through the rapidly rising currents. Many residents did not heed warnings and had to be carried out by rescuers. One police officer was credited with rescuing twenty to thirty people in the 1400 block of River Avenue.

Alazan Creek and Martínez Creek Floods

The rains transformed Olmos Creek into a torrent of about 30,000 cfs that hit the headwaters of the San Antonio River around 10:30 P.M. At approximately the same time, Alazan and Martínez creeks were blasting through the western portion of San Anto-

Crowd watching men in canoe on the floodwaters of the San Antonio River at St. Mary's and Travis streets (UTSA's Institute of Texan Cultures, San Antonio, Texas, No. L-1278-B).

Debris at Alazan Creek
(UTSA's Institute of Texan
Cultures, San Antonio,
Texas, No. 84-455).

nio, where Alazan Creek swept away three houses on South Laredo Street around 11 P.M. Wading through shoulder-deep water to reach trapped residents, police, fire fighters, and soldiers from Fort Sam Houston and Camp Travis rescued at least five hundred people.

Water rose 8 feet within twenty minutes. Some witnesses reported a flood wave between 10 and 30 feet tall. Small frame houses built near the creeks were carried away, and many of them piled up against the International and Great Northern Railroad trestle. According to an account in the *Austin American,* "By midnight, 40 or 50 houses that a few minutes before vomited

men, women and children in all stages of dress and undress, were being churned into a shapeless mass of debris where they lodged against the railroad bridge."[5] Most of the damage along the Alazan occurred in the vicinity of South Flores Street at Cass Street and South Laredo and West Cevallos, where, at one point, four houses were seen floating down the stream. Before the creek receded around 1 A.M. water covered North Laredo Street for almost one mile.

West End Lake, where floodwaters peaked around midnight, lost a third of its dam. At the peak of the flood, water topped the structure by two feet, while eighteen inches of water covered the dance floor at the park. The massive pile of debris at the International and Great Northern Railroad bridge required days for clean-up crews to sift through. After the first two days, two power tractors and fifty men had barely dented the forty-foot-tall pile.

San Antonio River Flood in Downtown San Antonio

The waters of the rising San Antonio River surged toward the city's downtown business section. At 11:30 while water was

Automobile in water at
South Flores Street (UTSA's
Institute of Texan Cultures,
San Antonio, Texas,
No. 91-292).

DOWNTOWN SAN ANTONIO FLOOD

several feet deep on River Avenue, the water level in the downtown area rose within four feet of the embankment on Pecan Street. The *San Antonio Express* commented, "At that hour, it appeared the flood might equal the 1913 record in the business district, but there was no intimation it would be more severe. Shortly after midnight, however, water began flowing down St. Mary's Street, and in 20 minutes College Street was flooded as far east as Navarro." [6]

Shortly after midnight the river flowed over the embankments protecting St. Mary's Street, and the water then swept down it into Houston and Navarro streets. A four-by-six-block area was inundated. Water also invaded the ground floor of the Gunter Hotel, the Gunter office building, and the Brady building. At 1 A.M. currents reached the *San Antonio Express* building and were flowing at 21,000 cfs down Houston Street. The *San Antonio*

Looking north on St. Mary's Street (UTSA's Institute of Texan Cultures, San Antonio, Texas, No. 91-290).

DAILY RAINFALL (IN INCHES) FOR SOUTH CENTRAL TEXAS DURING THE FLOOD OF SEPTEMBER 1921

	SEPT. 6	SEPT. 7	SEPT. 8	SEPT. 9	SEPT. 10	SEPT. 11	TOTAL
Austin	0.03	0.15	0.05	15	4.03	trace	19.26
Blanco	0	0.18	0.15	1.72	5.8	0	7.85
Brady	0	0.83	1.84	1.75	0.31	0	4.73
Burnet	0.18	0	0.05	3.4	5.3	trace	8.93
Cameron	0	0.3	0.77	0.85	12.45	0	14.37
Del Rio	0	0	0	0	0	0	0
Junction	trace	0	0.15	trace	0	0	0.15
Kerrville	0	0.02	0.01	0.26	2.87	0.04	3.2
Lampasas	0	1.5	0	0.03	1.1	0.7	3.33
Llano	0	0	0	0.14	1.65	0	1.79
New Braunfels	0	0	0.18	9.38	0	0	9.56
San Antonio	0.01	0.55	6.83	trace	0	0	7.39
San Marcos	0	0	2	8	1.5	0	11.5
Taylor	0.9	0.04	0.28	16.11	7.87	0.18	25.38
Temple	0	0.04	0	0.35	9	2.55	11.94
Uvalde	0.03	0.2	0.5	0.53	0	0	1.26

Express lost the use of its printing machinery for the September 11 edition when water flooded the pressroom, causing the power to go out.

The peak of the downtown flood occurred around 1:45 A.M. when water was more than eight feet deep at Houston and St. Mary's streets and five to six feet deep on Crockett Street. Throughout the night, wooden paving planks clanked together and "produce[d] a sound like that of automatic guns," according to observers.[7] Autos were driven to the water's edge to provide light.

Around 4 A.M. at Alamo Street, the concrete bridge housing the river's water-monitoring station collapsed. The station was unable to operate from 1:45 to 5:45 A.M. The USGS estimated that the river reached a peak of 20.14 feet, which, one of its officials noted, was "clearly marked in the gage house" and eyewitnesses estimated to have occurred at 3.[8]

Entrance to Gunter Hotel on Houston Street (UTSA's Institute of Texan Cultures, San Antonio, Texas, No. 80-135).

Accounts of Flooding

The *Austin American* reported that the first eyewitness accounts given in Austin came from three men who were traveling through San Antonio after a visit to Fredericksburg. They arrived in San Antonio around 11:30 P.M. when the downtown flood was beginning. One of the three recalled: "I drove into San Antonio and came up to the Lanier Hotel on St. Mary's Street and noticed the wood block paving bulging up in places. Directly I saw a man step on one of the humps and go down through the paving, and I turned my car around. I drove on into the business district and noticed the water steadily coming up on Houston Street. I parked my car and directly the water had come up a little farther, and kept on rising and rising." His party stayed at the Travelers Hotel, where water was knee high in the lobby. He added, "The whole thing came up so suddenly that I can't understand yet just how it all happened. Practically all of the stores in San Antonio's business district, except those on Alamo Plaza, were flooded. . . . One can find any sort of article of furniture about the streets—sofas, roll-top desks, chairs, tables. . . . Lights went off about 12:30 on Saturday morning, and the only sounds were the crashing of wreckage, the roar of the water and an occasional scream." [9]

On Saturday morning, thousands of

	JAN.	FEB.	MAR.	APR.	MAY	JUNE	JULY	AUG.	SEPT.	OCT.	NOV.	DEC.	TOTAL
Blanco	1.94	0.6	3.17	5.11	2.07	3.4	0.81	1.42	8.08	0.54	0.43	1.1	28.67
Junction	0.41	1.9	3.63	1.65	1.8	3.25	1.3	1.6	1.35	0.3	0.1	0.3	17.59
Kerrville	0.95	0.52	2.69	2.4	2.51	9.91	0.48	0.13	3.5	0.85	0.38	0.83	25.15
New Braunfels	3.11	0.67	5.7	5.6	1.68	5.04	0.23	0.9	10.07	0.98	0.38	1.16	35.52
San Antonio	1.4	0.23	5.91	2.78	2.01	4.59	0.48	0.45	8.27	1.02	1.16	0.23	28.53
San Marcos	2.66	1.45	9.4	8	2.4	7	0.8	0	12.64	0.5	0	0	44.85
Uvalde	0.46	0.78	4.09	0.6	5.22	2.92	1.44	0.4	1.46	1.55	0.38	0.2	19.5

people filled the downtown area to observe the damage. The September 11 issue of the *San Antonio Express* stated, "Practically all of the San Antonio business district is damaged. The commercial life of the Alamo City is paralyzed. All theaters are closed. Banks are closed. In all the vast section of the principal business portion not a store opened for business; not a wheel turned at the usual hour yesterday morning. Not one building escaped. . . . The principle business thoroughfares have been practically floated away, and, with the coming of daylight, the street bore all the signs of having suffered a successful heavy artillery barrage and airplane siege combined." In addition, the *Monthly Weather Review* reported that

fifty-one people lost their lives in the flood, which caused $5 million in damages.[10]

Rescues

Many spectacular and unusual rescues took place during the deluge. In one, a five-year-old boy sat on his twelve-year-old brother's shoulders for five hours while the latter held on to a tree on South Flores Street. In another, a five-year-old boy begged rescuers to "save my donkey," which was standing on a table in his family's house. When a man waded into the shoulder-deep water in the house, he heard the yells of people from the second floor, so he rescued them also.

Additional incidents involved floating

St. Mary's church (UTSA's Institute of Texan Cultures, San Antonio, Texas, No. 80-134).

GUNTER HOTEL
E. HOUSTON ST

Looking east at Houston Street (UTSA's Institute of Texan Cultures, San Antonio, Texas, No. 80-137).

furniture or other objects. A dog that had been sleeping in a baby bed was awakened when the floodwaters lifted the bed. The dog's barking woke the family, who escaped the high water by moving to the upper story of the house. A man used his cork leg as a life-saver to help them float out of the inundated residence and into shallow water. Other survivors were saved by riding on floating mattresses; some actually slept through the flood as their mattresses floated in the water.

With World War I a recent memory, the *San Antonio Express* alluded to battle in reporting on the aftermath. The events reminded witnesses of "scenes of the flight of refugees before advancing armies when the World War . . . [was] at its height in Europe. Only in San Antonio, the flood victims had less warning than the booming of distant cannons." [11]

The San Antonio Abstract Company lost records valued at $70,000. Water spread throughout the first floor of the Wolff Marx store, and the Majestic Theater filled with water up to the second row of boxes on one side of the first balcony. Props from the stage area were washed out into the street. The flood also swept a piano against the door of the city's library.

Commentaries

During the flood in San Antonio, a U.S. Forest Service representative, W. W. Ashe, was visiting in Central Texas to meet with the Texas State Board of Water Engineers. He commented: "Cities of Texas will continue to be devastated by floods, and alluvial lands [will be] flooded and perpetually destroyed until a comprehensive system of flood water control is designed and put into execution. . . . The streams of Texas are erratic and exhibit the same character of flow as those at the southern end of the Appalachian Mountains in the Carolinas, Georgia, and Alabama due to enormously heavy rainfall at irregular intervals and rapid run-off on account of steep slopes. Added to this is the fact that at no period of the year is the surface protected from erosion by freezing, as is the case in the North. For this reason soil erosion is one of the most important factors which must be taken into consideration in the location of storage reservoirs."[12]

In addition to Ashe's comments, editorials in the *San Antonio Express* and *Dallas Morning News* addressed the problem of flood control in Texas cities. The former exercised its right to recount what it had printed nearly eight years earlier. In its editorial of September 11, the *Express* stated that, "After the business district and low-lying residential district along the river and creeks were inundated eight years ago, the *Express* urged that the Olmos be strongly, safely dammed . . . [and] that the city protect itself by construction that would drain off rises in the stream within 48 hours and prevent the swift flooding of a large area neighboring these several water courses. . . . The cause and course of the smashing torrent of Friday night and Saturday morning demand that this remedy be urged again upon the taxpayers and the city government. . . . The community must not allow its river and creeks to run wild any longer. . . . San Antonio now must take heed of its death list and its property destruction—and build for its vital protection." The *Express*

added that the cost of a dam would be less than the flood damage from either the 1913 or the 1921 flood.[13]

The *Dallas Morning News* weighed in with its opinion, too:

Possibly the most distressing feature of San Antonio's disastrous flood experiences is the probability that they were avoidable. It does not seem unreasonable that foresight could have prevented the great loss of life and property which came because of the presence within the heart of the city of a placid little river that has to be petted and coaxed to keep it flowing through the dry months of the year. Doubtless the proof that the occurrence was preventable will come in the decision to take steps at once to prevent the recurrence of the catastrophe. . . . Another week might see such another cloudburst. . . . The lesson is not for the devastated sections alone. Scarcely is there a city of any size in Texas but has within its confines one or more placid water course potentially as murderous as the beautiful San Antonio River.[14]

After listing the levee projects around the Trinity River in the Dallas area designed to mitigate killer floods, the *Dallas Morning News* added, "All these things the engineers—with unimaginative slide rule and chart based upon facts . . . have told the people of Dallas. . . . Nowhere in Texas is there a city set on the banks of a stream which can afford to ignore the lesson." [15]

SEPTEMBER 1921

~~~~~~~

Thrall Record Rainfall and Little River Flood

THE RAINSTORM THAT struck Central Texas on September 9 and 10, 1921, is one of the greatest downpours in the recorded history of the United States. The storm dropped more than 38 inches east of Taylor, Texas, near Thrall. The official rainfall total set a record for the nation, with 19.65 inches recorded in twelve hours. An unofficial total near Thrall recorded 32 inches in the same period.

The cloudburst fell on the fertile soil of the Blackland Prairie, which would typically absorb the runoff better than the rocky outcropping along the Balcones Escarpment, forty miles to the west. However, the rich earth had been baked by weeks of drought and little to no rain. The resulting runoff from one of the greatest storms in recorded history produced astounding increases in local rivers such as the San Gabriel and the Little. To those who were living along the streams, the rain and subsequent rises were unprecedented. Residents there had little chance of escape, especially since the swellings came in the middle of the night. As a result, human suffering caused by this flood was immense—more than 170 people died in the Central Texas floods of September 1921.

Central Texas Rain

Like San Antonio–area residents, Central Texans welcomed the all-day showers of September 8 and the morning showers of September 9 as relief from their summer-long drought. The last measurable rain in Austin had occurred on July 8.

The morning showers of September 9, however, grew into severe thunderstorms. The first sign of serious weather in Central Texas appeared when a tornado touched down in southeastern Travis county near Elroy and Creedmoor. Several people were injured, including one young man who was pitching horseshoes when a seed house wall collapsed, pinning him under its wreckage. The tornado then tracked to the north and northwest, passing over the "deaf and dumb asylum" (as it was known in 1921) in south Austin on Barton Springs Road and the Deep Eddy area of the city. When the tornado passed over South Congress Avenue, citizens watched as huge limbs flew in the air over the institution.

Shortly after the tornado passed, heavy rain began to fall in Austin. By the afternoon of September 9, the rain "was pouring down in a veritable blanket of water."[1] Street gutters overflowed sidewalks, streetcars were forced to cease operation when sand and gravel washed onto the tracks, and wood paving blocks buckled after water flowed underneath them. On Barton Springs Road, near Wende's store, water was eight feet deep at Barton Creek, holding up traffic in front of the establishment. When the rain gauge was read the next morning, Austin had received 18.23 inches in twenty-four hours—a record for the city.

New Braunfels and San Marcos were doused with 9.56 and 11.50 inches, respectively. To the north of Austin, heavy rains fell at Round Rock, Georgetown, Salado, Belton, and Temple.

38

In Georgetown, the official gage tallied more than 15 inches during the storm. At Berry Creek, reports of more than 17 inches were given. In *Land of Good Water,* Clara Stearns Scarbrough's book on the history of Williamson County, the author noted that "observers of the storm described the fierce lightning, the garish green hue of the sky, and the water which fell—not in drops—but in great sheets hour after hour."[2]

Belton received more than 14 inches of rain, and Temple measured 11.90 inches. Farther down the Little River Basin, Cameron, Rockdale, and Milam counties were also hit by the downpours. In Cameron, rainfall exceeded 13 inches on September 8 and 9. Rockdale received a similar deluge, prompting the *Rockdale Reporter* to record this observation on the night of September 8: "Shortly after dark that night the floodgates of the heavens seemed to have loosened, and old residents say that such a rain never before fell in Rockdale. . . . The rainfall was variously estimated at from 12 to 18 inches."[3]

The heavy showers hit west of Austin as well. Marble Falls recorded a substantial, yet welcome, rain on September 8, but on September 9 that feeling of appreciation changed. The *Marble Falls Messenger* noted, "Last Friday and Saturday will be long remembered by the people of Marble Falls and Central Texas. Friday will be remembered because it marked the beginning of the end of a three months drouth. . . . The government gauge at nightfall registered 6.55 inches. Saturday will be remembered because it marks the date of the biggest rain that ever fell in this part of the state in a single day. In less than four hours, according to government measurement, eleven inches of water fell. Some are inclined to think it was much more. . . . We doubt if there is a citizen living in this section who ever witnessed a harder rain or so much destruction in so short a time."[4]

Williamson County Rains

The 12–18-inch rains approached or exceeded record precipitation but were dwarfed by the deluge that hit the Taylor and Thrall areas of Williamson County. The heaviest rainfall occurred a few miles north of Thrall. As more data came in, weather observers increased their initial estimate of 20 inches—first to 24 and then to 30 inches. The final tally from a location two miles north of Thrall was 32 inches in 12 hours, which was the highest "unofficial point-rainfall total" in the United States for that period of time.[5] (Other sources list similarly extreme totals. The *Texas Almanac* reported a 36.4-inch total for an 18-hour period.[6] *One Hundred Years of Texas Weather, 1880–1979* lists a 38.2-inch total for 24 hours but states that this figure was eclipsed by a 38.7-inch rain in Yankeetown, Florida.[7])

J. P. McAuliffe, Taylor's weather observer, reported on the rains in the September 1921 edition of the *Monthly Weather Review.* Water barrels belonging to "trustworthy farmers" were sought out as one recording instrument after the mammoth rainfall. McAuliffe's use of the barrels led him to conclude that "It is stated by these gentlemen that barrels on farms at different places measured 36 inches high by 18 inches in diameter were filled to overflowing on the morning of the 10th. It is certain that not more than 2 inches of water were in the barrels prior to the excessive rain. . . . Allowing for all errors, it seems assured that some 30 inches of rain fell at many places in about 15 hours."[8]

In Taylor, at the official rain gage nearest to Thrall, McAuliffe recorded 23.11 inches in 24 hours, a total that was described as the greatest official 24-hour rainfall on record for the United States at the time. McAuliffe added that the "most remarkable feature of this storm was its duration, covering a period of 35 hours, with an excessive rate over a period of more than 10 hours."[9]

Most of the rain came in two bursts. During the first, 10.5 inches fell in Taylor in a three-hour stretch starting at 6:45 P.M. on September 9. During that deluge, the automatic register ceased working because the tipping bucket was flooded. A second torrent hit around 3 A.M. on September 10 and continued as a steady downpour until 7:30 that morning. At 7 A.M. on September 10, the precipitation total had reached 21.50 inches, with 19.49 inches falling between 6:45 P.M. on September 8 and 7 A.M. on September 10.

Storm Explanation

The September 9–10 deluges over San Antonio and Central Texas were related to what is now known as a disastrous scenario for the Lone Star State—a dying hurricane that is moving slowing over the Balcones Escarpment, Edwards Plateau, or any region with enough orographic lift to concentrate the extremely efficient rain from the diminishing tropical system. In this case, the hurricane hit well south of Texas—near Tampico, Mexico. But the steering currents did not push the storm farther westward into the mountains near Monterrey, Mexico. Instead, the remnants of the hurricane created a northerly and northwesterly arc that passed over the Laredo and Eagle Pass area to San Antonio and Thrall.

Bernard Bunnemeyer of the U.S. Weather Bureau office in Houston stated that the cause of the extreme Texas rains in September 1921 was the "breaking up in Texas of the disturbance that moved westward toward the Mexican coast south of Tampico on September 7, 1921." He added that, "although the distribution of the pressure was such that the storm could not be charted, the shifting winds, the progressive, northeastward extension of the rainfall area, and the profound agitation of the atmosphere, as evidenced by violent squalls and thunderstorms over the stricken sections, can hardly be ascribed to any other cause."[10]

George Lott's 1953 study of the storm added that, "Although all traces of a surface circulation disappeared when the storm reached the Mexican Plateau, pressure falls could be followed through this region and on into south and central Texas." Lott mentioned the effect of the Balcones Escarpment:"[T]he storm['s] isohyetal patterns had an orientation roughly paralleling the ground contours." He concurred that the storm also had twin low-pressure centers that coincided with the two peaks in rainfall observed at Taylor.[11] The storm's rainfall pattern exhibited a sudden drop-off in rain totals to the north and northeast. Curiously, Waco and Somerville received less than one inch of rain from September 7 to September 11.

Runoff and Streamflow: Brushy Creek Basin

Two of Brushy Creek's tributaries, Bull Branch and Mustang Creek, flow through Taylor. The flooding on these two small streams extensively damaged Taylor, washing out bridges and houses and wrecking railroad lines.

Flood in Taylor

At 9 P.M., during the final hour of the first ten-inch deluge, the flooding in Taylor breached the dams at the town's water supply on North Main Street. The fast-flowing currents undermined part of the Texas Power and Light Company's substation, and Taylor lost power shortly afterward. The *Taylor Daily Press* of September 10 commented, "Not until then [the loss of power] did realization come of impending danger. With the city in total darkness, all telephones out of commission, the occasional glare from the headlights of passing motor cars were the only lights to be seen. After this the flood-tide reached its zenith."[12] Throughout Taylor, water in the streets was flowing at depths of from one to four feet.

After installing a temporary generator, the *Taylor Daily Press* started its presses, thus becoming, in its own words, "the first and only newspaper to herald to the world an account of the storm's ravages at Taylor."[13] The paper declared, "Decidedly the most destructive rainstorm in the annals of the history of Taylor and Williamson County cast its pall of sadness over the city Saturday morning."[14]

On Bull Branch, the floodwaters swept away an iron bridge and a house that had stood nearby for forty years. West of downtown, Mustang Creek washed out ninety feet at the south end and eighty feet at the north end of the railroad bridge. Bunnemeyer stated that Mustang Creek damaged many homes on its way to joining Brushy Creek, where it created "a current 10 miles wide."[15] Outside of Taylor to the east and southeast, the smaller communities of Thrall and Thorndale, as well as areas to their north, experienced even heavier rains than in Taylor.

Thrall Flood

The thirty-eight-inch rainfall near Thrall ravaged the countryside. Roads were impassable even on horseback, and the runoff into fields cut gullies six feet wide and several feet deep. A long-time resident of the Thrall area, F. A. Nolte, recorded his remembrances fifty years later in a *Waco Times-Herald* article: "It just came up and started misting, then it got

Taylor flood damage (courtesy of the Taylor Public Library).

heavier and heavier. . . . The wind didn't blow much at our place. It thundered and lightninged [*sic*] a right smart, but I have seen a lot more thunder and lightning in a cloud than there was in that one. It rained all the rest of the day and all night long. You couldn't see anywhere, it rained so hard."[16]

Mrs. Nolte stated that family members could not see the barn from the house, even though it was only a short distance away. Nolte's uncle was staying with them at the time, and Nolte said, "Uncle Harmon would walk back and forth on the porch and look at that rain, and he'd say, 'My God! When is it going to quit!'"[17] When the rain

South Main in Taylor, looking north (courtesy of the Taylor Public Library).

Flood damage in Taylor (courtesy of the Taylor Public Library).

finally let up, Nolte could see a "little branch a half mile from his house and it looked like a river." Water "covered the fields in all directions."[18]

Near Thorndale, the storm dropped 20–25 inches of rain, inundating "every ravine, creek and river in a larger volume than at any time since the 1900 storm."[19] A member of a pioneer family in that area stated that "never before in the history of Thorndale did the water accumulate so fast in Brushy Creek and San Gabriel River."[20]

Brushy Creek

The floodwaters along Brushy Creek awoke many people who were still slumbering in their beds, forcing them to scramble up nearby trees for safety. Several residents climbed into the lofts of their homes and then had to cut holes in the roof to escape the rising water. One survivor was asleep in bed as the flood developed. While turning over, his hand dipped into the water beside his bed. Upon waking, he noticed that the room was filled with floodwater. To escape the currents that eventually reached a depth of ten feet, he hung on to the rafters of his house.

In another home that sat approximately

a mile away from Brushy Creek, floodwaters reached a depth of twelve feet, forcing a farmworker to escape the deluge by climbing a tree in the forks of Brushy Creek. Six days after the floodwaters subsided, he refused to climb down and acted as if the flood were still roiling through the creek bottom.

San Gabriel River

After the shock of the flooding in San Antonio had diminished, the *San Antonio Express* described the effect of the overflow on the San Gabriel River: "The picturesque San Gabriel, river of romance, known for many years to students of Southwestern University and to Georgetown as a beautiful and shady stream for canoeing parties, has become the grimmest among Southwest Texas watercourses in the now historic floods of September 10 and 11."[21] The newspaper added that the destruction along the San Gabriel and Little rivers was "probably three times as great as that of the streams which swept through the business and residential section of San Antonio last Saturday morning."[22]

Like the unfortunate residents along Brushy Creek, many victims were sleeping and knew nothing of the threat until water actually invaded their houses. Others knew of the high water but did not leave because floodwaters had never before reached them. Those who did flee the lowlands had no time to herd livestock or save their household goods.

Headwaters of the San Gabriel River

The two forks of the San Gabriel meet in Georgetown to form the San Gabriel River. Each fork received heavy rain, causing damage upstream of the town. Communities on the headwaters of the river lost livestock and crops and suffered bridge damage but avoided the devastation that struck downstream.

Georgetown

Where the two forks of the San Gabriel join, the flood peaked around 10:30 A.M. on September 10. The bridge over the north fork was torn away, but that over the south fork survived. Campers at San Gabriel Park, just below the confluence of the two forks, had to flee. The park's caretakers themselves took off during the night of September 9 while wearing only their bathing suits. The currents took out the Katy Railroad's iron bridge between Georgetown and Granger, marooning the Texas Special train and its 129 passengers in Georgetown.

Jonah

Jonah, eight miles downstream from Georgetown and built on the river, felt the full effect of the inundation. Every home was invaded by the floodwaters. The *Taylor Daily Press* reported that more than thirty buildings were destroyed and that water was three feet deep in the Jonah post office. The Jonah Christian Church was carried one hundred yards across Mileham Branch before coming to rest at a pigsty, "without even a window breaking."[23] Two other oddities, both related to a pig and a church, also emerged during the flood at Jonah. After the deluge, a man found a three-hundred-pound hog in a bed in his house, and another man used a rope to guide a floating bale of his cotton into the Methodist Church.

The more than 250-foot-long bridge across the river, known as "one of the largest structures of its kind across this river," was demolished by the violent currents. It was "left a twisted, broken mess. The large pier from the middle of the stream is laying [sic]

on its side, the steel beams laid 75 feet from the piers in a pile of twisted metal."[24]

Circleville

At Circleville, approximately seven miles farther down the San Gabriel, the turbulent river took out the large iron bridge there and wrecked the school. Clara Stearns Scarbrough recalled her family's and Centerville's predicament: "Water stood five feet inside the Stearns home nearby, although the home was several feet above ground on stilts to prevent just such an occurrence. Floodwaters had risen rapidly after sundown and by nine o'clock Friday evening the Stearns family was barely able to drive away before being cut off between the river and Pecan Branch to the north, which streams soon joined to form a continuous swirling body of water. . . . For days, water spread almost as far as the eye could see, afar, far out of the river banks. . . . The rail-road crossing at Circleville was washed away and the tracks grotesquely twisted and wrenched as if they were delicate toys."[25]

A Taylor resident who visited Circleville on September 10 reported that at 3 P.M. the river was a mile wide. He noted that boys climbed to the tops of trees to gain a vantage point and reported that the only buildings left on the north side of the river were the Stearns gin and a two-story tenant house. Witnesses of the flood at

The bridge at Jonah before the flood of September 1921 (courtesy of the Taylor Public Library).

Centerville counted eighteen houses floating down the river.

Laneport and Youngstown Communities

One of the most tragic scenes occurred at Laneport, near the present-day dam for Granger Lake, where twenty-three bodies were found. One account stated that the swift river water "picked up homes like so much paper and splintered them against trees." One of the bodies was hanging in a tree; another was buried headfirst in mud.[26]

In another account, one person was awakened by the sound of raindrops. He then woke up the others in the house, all of whom waded through waist-deep water to reach a graveyard, where they took refuge.[27] Around Youngstown, one man commented after the flood that the "air is filled with the odor of the dead."[28]

San Gabriel

As the runoff from the downpour hit the village of San Gabriel, the river water changed from a clear, peaceful riffle to a powerful torrent that peaked at 35 feet in less than three hours. Nearby, Alligator Creek rose to its high mark of 25 feet in even less time.

Fed by rains varying from 5 to 15 inches in its upper reaches and possibly in excess of 35 inches in its lower reaches, the floodwa-

ters of the San Gabriel River came down in several rises. A four-foot wall of water barreled downriver in the middle of the night "with a roar that could be heard for more than a mile."[29] The first rise was followed by a continual increase, estimated at two feet per minute. Subsequent rises "put water to a height never before known,"[30] peaking at "seven feet higher than ever before."[31] A long-time resident commented that the floods of 1854 and 1868 were the only swells to come even close to this one.

The *Thorndale Champion* noted, "The flood came so quickly and unexpectedly that families living below the high water mark were only aroused from sleep by the waters reaching their beds. Others had everything movable washed from their yards, waking after the waters had subsided five or six feet."[32] When one family was roused by their barking dog, they were astonished to discover that they were "surrounded by water and their clothes floating around the house."[33]

The "San Gabriel Gossip" column in the September 22 edition of the *Cameron Herald* reported the following: "Our flood of Friday night and Saturday, the most terrific ever known here, though now a thing of the past will long live in the memory of those who were in the reach of its waters that brought death, destruction, and ruin to man, beast, and all bottom crops. . . . Our iron clad bridges that seemed strong enough and high

Central Avenue in Belton during the flood of September 1921 (in the collection of the Lena Armstrong Public Library, Belton, Texas).

enough to withstand the waters of ages were swept away like bubbles in the air."[34]

An elm tree had served for the past sixty years to document increases along the river as residents cut notches in its trunk to mark high-water levels. Judging from the nicks, this particular deluge was 7.5 feet higher than any previous one.

Little River

With the San Gabriel and one of its major tributaries, Brushy Creek, both in record flood, the next target was the stream it flowed into: the Little River. The upper reaches of the Leon and Lampasas rivers missed the downpour. Their lowest sections received flooding rains and floods from Nolan and Salado creeks.

Belton

Victimized by the deluge of December 1913, Belton received another dose of major flash flooding when more than fourteen inches of rain fell on the night of September 9, 1921, driving Nolan Creek to tear through Belton once again. Floodwaters at the Leon River and Nolan Creek confluence rose to within one inch of the 1913 level. The worst destruction occurred at the Park Lawn Inn,

but other buildings near the park, such as the Confederate camp houses and the confectionery house, were also damaged. After stating that the devastation was not as bad as it had been in 1913, the *Temple Daily Telegram* highlighted the positive aspects of the deluge several days later: "The creek is now cleaner than it has been in years and, when the dam is closed again, the lake will be larger and considerably deeper."[35]

Salado Creek

Floodwater also poured into the Little River from Salado Creek, which rose to record heights in Salado. W. S. Rose Jr. estimated that 25–30 inches of rain fell in the town. The resulting currents ripped the Salado Bridge from its foundation and carried the remnants half a mile downstream. In addition, one-hundred-year-old trees were "torn bare and not even any drift was left along [the] barren banks of the now greatly widened stream." In Rose's words, "It is hard for the people to imagine the Salado River doing as much damage as it did Saturday. It must have rained from 25 to 30 inches there, and I watched the river rise to its maximum stage of 30 feet within hardly 20 minutes."[36]

Three miles below Salado, a superintendent at Jones Mill reported two peaks—one

Wreckage in Taylor (courtesy of the Taylor Public Library).

at 7 A.M. on September 9, which was followed by a plateau, and a second crest that pushed water 8.4 feet higher than the first. The peak stage occurred between 9 and 10 A.M., leaving water marks inside buildings that were used to determine the stream's discharge amounts.

Summers Mill

Salado Creek decimated the quaint creekside setting of Summers Mill. The building itself, built in 1852, was the biggest loss. A report in the *Taylor Daily Press* stated, "Practically nothing is left of the little community village except a few residences on the hill."[37] The operator of the mill at the time described the destruction: "It was plainly seen that there remained a dam by a millsite, but no mill by a damn sight." His mill store and house were also wrecked by the currents, and he later moved his family to Belton.[38]

Little River at Little River Academy

Southeast of Belton, the record flood peaks on Nolan and Salado creeks poured into the Little River Basin and produced the highest stage ever on the Little River at the town of Little River. The Little River reached its new all-time high at 3 P.M. on September 10. The *Taylor Daily Telegram* stated that "Bales of cotton, large drifts of corn . . . cattle, horses [dotted] its surface as it swept over an area of 5–6 miles in width in low-lying sections."[39]

At Burgess, downstream from the community of Little River, the river left its banks at 3:30 A.M. on September 10. The swell continued until 2 P.M., when it was two feet higher than the 1913 flood and five miles wide. The flood caused the greatest destruction in Burgess in sixty years. A hero from the 1913 flood, John Bigham, again used his water skills to rescue stranded residents.

Closer to Cameron, the water reached to within a foot of the top of the Holtzclaw Bridge. The Little River's record flood then joined with the San Gabriel River's record overflow. Waters in the lowlands near these three streams reached a depth of fifteen feet, flooding plantations and rich farmland throughout the valley.

Cameron

The more than eleven inches of rain in Cameron combined with the Little River's already high levels. At Cameron, the Little River rose 45 feet in a twelve-hour period on September 10. The December 1913 flood mark was no match for the 1921 surge, which eclipsed the former by 4.5 feet, hitting a 49.5-foot stage on September 10 at 2:30 P.M., with a peak discharge estimated at 647,000 cfs. This discharge for an area of 7,010 square miles was the "highest rate of discharge that has ever been recorded for so large an area," according to C. E. Ellsworth in the USGS report on the flood.[40] Since approximately 2,000 square miles of the Little River Basin received less than one inch of rain, this record was even more astounding. The floodwaters continued to flow at a depth of 30 feet for more than three days.

The spectacular flood motivated Central Texas communities to unite and undertake dramatic rescue actions. In the Maysfield section, motorboats from Waco were used to reach farmers who remained stuck in trees for two days after trying to save their livestock.

At Cameron, the unprecedented rise inundated the Santa Fe Railroad bridge at noon on September 10. The railroad company sent its personnel, including a division engineer and master mechanic, to inspect the bridge and four thousand feet of track that were under four feet of water. As the engineer and mechanic examined the bridge, their small rowboat capsized, hurl-

46 ing them into the churning water. A notebook they were carrying somehow ended up on the railroad bridge itself.

In the ensuing search for these two prominent railroad employees, powerboats from Temple and Galveston cruised through the muddy Little River. When night fell, tar flames lit up the darkness as the hunt continued. The large-scale effort to find the men also involved an aerial search by future Belton mayor Roy Sanderford, who had racked up twenty-two months of flying experience while serving in the air force. At the time of the 1921 flood, Sanderford was employed as tax collector for Bell County in Belton. A day before he was asked to help find the missing men, he had refused to fly Fort Worth newspaper reporters to San Antonio, maintaining that "he was too badly out of practice." After Sanderford learned about the mission in Cameron, however, he accepted the challenge. The *Cameron Herald* recounted Sanderford's response: "Bell County's steady, routine tax collector closed his huge desk, reached into a closet and took down his flying helmet and goggles, and slipped easily and naturally from the prosaic role of a county official to that of a daring air pilot. . . . Only when he strapped into his pilot's seat the ex-war flyer remarked . . . 'This old ship has not been in service for a long time, and neither have I. I never flew one like her, and I don't know whether I understand her or not, and I think this field is too muddy to ever get her off—but here's hoping. Contact.'"[41] Sanderford's efforts proved fruitless, however. He made several passes over the muddy, swirling stream but spotted no one.

The bodies of the Santa Fe Railroad men were found at 7 A.M. on September 13, only three-quarters of a mile away from the trestle where their boat had capsized, indicating that the bodies had probably become snared by debris and then floated away.

In another high-profile search, Rockdale and Cameron residents attempted to

find the bodies of prominent farmers Bailey Turner and H. C. Sullivan. The flood swept away Turner's house, barns, sheds, and stock, leaving only his car, which was lodged in a drift. Gunshots and cries for help from the Turner place were heard shortly before daylight on September 10. Rockdale Mayor H. C. Meyer asked the town's citizens to turn out and join in the hunt for Sullivan and Turner. On September 13 approximately three hundred men scoured the river bottom. Much of the territory had to be covered by swimming through murky water because of the deep sloughs, thick mud, and large drifts.

The searchers found Turner's body on September 15. The remains were in a slough that was still full of running water. Turner was entirely buried in the mud and was found by searchers who were attracted to the spot by a swarm of green flies. The man who found Sullivan's body declined the reward, saying that he "deemed [the task] their duty."[42]

The search parties found other bodies in the tops of trees and another buried in a bank with only a foot sticking out of the mud. The *Rockdale Centennial* noted that "Searchers reported that the stench in the bottoms was becoming almost intolerable from the countless carcasses of animals. One man was heard to say that the only live things he had seen in the bottoms were one cricket and a butterfly. All living creatures had either fled the country or been drowned."[43]

The leader of the search party for Turner and Sullivan was flood survivor Ed Green. At 2 A.M. on September 10 he discovered two to three feet of water in his own house. His situation worsened as "the rise came so rapidly that there was no chance to get out, and it was only an hour or two until they were forced to climb to the roof of the house." The crest of the flood reached his home at 3:30 A.M., and the house began to float away. Fortunately, a large white oak "extended a convenient branch over the shack," enabling the family to climb into the tree. The house floated away as Green lifted the last of its occupants to the tree.[44]

At daylight on September 10 the water began to recede. During the day, the survivors swam to a nearby building and settled on the rooftop. Later that day, another rise undermined the foundation of the structure, so Green swam back to the tree to check on one of the survivors, an elderly woman. He "swam back and forth . . . a number of times, trying to make her more comfortable and cheer her up, but he observed that she was getting much weaker, and he bound her to the tree with a blanket. Night came on, and some time during the night the grandmother became delirious, untied herself from the tree, and, exclaiming 'I am gone,' allowed herself to drop into the dark waters."[45]

A girl and two boys survived the ordeal. Green especially praised the girl, who, he related, "showed unusual grit and vitality. She kept her brothers awake throughout the long hours of the night, frequently slapping and pinching them into wakefulness when to fall asleep meant death." Throughout their thirty-six-hour ordeal, they had only a five-pound can of sugar and muddy river water to eat and drink.[46]

The end of the Green's trial came on the morning of September 11, when, at 9 A.M., two men reached his farm in a small boat. Able to carry only two passengers, the rescuers took the girl and one of her brothers. While Green waited for the men to return, the relief from "the nervous strain and sleepless hours was so great that both he and the boy lay down on the roof of the shack, which was two or three inches deep in slimy mud, and went sound asleep, sleeping until [the rescuers] came back."[47]

Rockdale

In Rockdale, rain fell intermittently on September 9, but "shortly after dark that night the floodgates of the heavens seemed to have loosened, and old residents say that such a rain never before fell in Rockdale." Water ran through the streets as if they were creeks. Ham Branch reached unprecedented heights, and water advanced into houses that had historically remained dry. The rainfall in town was estimated to range from twelve to eighteen inches.[48]

Mayor H. C. Meyer was very proud of the citizenry's rescue-and-recovery efforts. He proclaimed, "Rockdale people have done many good things since I have been mayor, but never before have I been more pleased than on this occasion. . . . And when I say 'Rockdale people' I mean to include all these brave country boys and men who have joined in the rescue work."[49]

An example of the townspeople's generosity concerns a Rockdale baker, Joe Stein. The commissary department

Washout at Taylor (courtesy of the Taylor Public Library).

notified Stein that a couple of baskets of bread would be necessary to feed the flood victims and that he could charge them to the Chamber of Commerce. Stein replied, "'Charge nothing. I don't sell bread for such purposes as that. You can have all you want free.' "[50]

Damage

Crops such as cotton and corn, which had been awaiting harvest along the river bottom were ruined, and the accompanying damage was "incalculable."[51] Farmhouses, barns, and everything in them, including tools, feed, and vehicles, were washed away or destroyed. Rescue parties estimated that "fully 90% of the cattle, horses, mules and hogs that were in the bottoms were drowned. All those valley farmers lost practically every head of stock they had, the loss including work stock and milch cows. There were literally thousands of dead rabbits, possums and birds, as well as fish."[52] In addition, the floodwaters destroyed miles of the railroad track that ran through the Little River bottom. Sections of track that had never been submerged were inundated with six to eight feet of water.

Brazos River Flood

The Little River flows into the Brazos at Valley Junction, approximately twenty miles downstream of Cameron. On September 10 the enormous flow of 647,000 cfs from the Little River began to invade the Brazos Valley. In September 1921 the condition of the Brazos River was similar to that of the Leon upriver of Belton—dry. In Waco, the discharge for August was only twelve percent of its normal flow.

The flood waves from the Little River began pouring into the Brazos on the morning of September 10. At 7:00 A.M. the gage at Valley Junction near Hearne read 3.5 feet. At

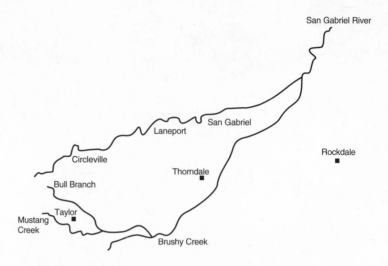

4:40 P.M. the gage hit 25 feet, and the water was rising fast, completely filling the river at 6:30 P.M. At this point, the river observers advised residents to evacuate.

The river at Valley Junction peaked at 58.2 feet, less than a foot below the record set on December 1913. The gage at Valley Junction was not read from September 11 through September 13. Farther downstream, the Jones Branch gauging station near College Station noted a peak of 53 feet sometime between 1 and 3 A.M. on September 12. The river was reported to be three to five miles wide, breaking and eroding levees for a distance of 3,000 feet. At Washington, the river peaked slightly above 50 feet on September 14 and was from one to three miles wide.

Like its upper reaches, the lower reaches of the Brazos were not in flood, thus preventing the massive Little River deluge from setting new records there. At Hempstead, a maximum stage of 40.2 feet was reached at 7 A.M. on September 16, which was below flood stage. Farther downstream at Rosenberg, the peak also did not attain flood stage. As the *Monthly Weather Review* stated, "The flood was remarkable from the fact that it was caused by tremendous rains over a single tributary, the Little River . . . and that the large volume of water spread out at an exceedingly rapid rate as it rushed downstream."[53]

Lower San Gabriel River Basin

Central Texas Floods: Guadalupe Deluge

Rainfall at the headwaters of the Guadalupe was light. The first signs of heavy rain in the Guadalupe basin was a 7.85-inch rain in Blanco. Farther downstream in the Guadalupe basin, New Braunfels received 9.56 inches and San Marcos 11.50 inches.

At Comfort, the river peaked at 12 feet, not a dramatic rise. At New Braunfels, the increase was more extreme, as it rose from a 3-foot stage at noon on September 9 to a 28.5-foot stage at 2 A.M. the next morning. At 4 P.M. on September 10, the water had fallen back to 12.6 feet and was down to its normal 3-foot stage around noon on September 14.

At Gonzales, the river surpassed its flood stage of 22 feet by rising almost 22 feet in a twenty-four-hour span from 7 A.M. on September 10 to 7 A.M. on September 11. It crested at 31.4 feet, running a quarter mile wide. At Victoria, the river reached 4.5 feet above flood stage on September 16.

A troop of Boy Scouts from Austin who were camping on the Guadalupe River outside of New Braunfels were in the Guadalupe's flood path. Following a slight rise in the river, the scouts received reports that the river was falling. Later, however, they noticed that the river began to swell, eventually at the rate of one foot per hour, and the troop moved to a patch of higher ground near Hueco Springs. After the flood wave hit, the New Braunfels fire chief, along with forty to fifty men, worked to rescue the scouts. Several of the men swam the river, tying ropes to treetops. A pulley system was attached, and the boys were removed one by one. The rescue efforts lasted until 4 A.M. on September 10, when the rising water was only a few feet away from overtaking the high ground that the scouts had occupied.

Colorado River Flood

A small area of the Colorado River basin above Austin was hit with very intense rains, driving the Colorado to near flood stage in Austin and downstream. In Marble Falls, the *Marble Falls Messenger* recounted the damage there: "In less time than it takes to tell the story, the earth assumed the appearance of a great lake just as far as the eye could see in any direction you might look. Dry branches and creeks were soon roaring torrents, meting out destruction to property of every kind and character."[54]

One area landowner found huge bones that appeared to be those of a mastodon "in a ravine 30 feet below the surface of the earth" four miles down the river. They consisted of a jawbone weighing 108 pounds and a leg bone weighing 39 pounds.

Other locations in Burnet County were hit by heavy rains as well. Fairland in Burnet County received almost nine inches. At Travis Peak, as a report in the *Marble Falls Messenger* noted, "the people here are almost washed away. Cow Creek got up bigger than it has been in fifty years."[55]

The Colorado at Marble Falls did not rise, reaching a stage of only 3.2 feet. However, downstream, the river rose 18 feet in Austin between 7 A.M. on September 9 and midnight on September 10, with most of the increase taking place in the afternoon. The Pedernales River near Spicewood reached its highest stage ever, according to area residents. According to the USGS Water Supply Paper, its peak discharge "probably exceeded that of the Colorado River at Austin, where the crest was reduced and the flood period prolonged by the retarding effect of Lake Austin and the much wider channel of the Colorado."[56] Swells on the Pedernales at its mouth (near Spicewood) reached 35 feet.

JULY 1932

~~~~~~~

Guadalupe River Basin Flood

IN THE SUMMER of 1932 Franklin Roosevelt selected Uvalde's John Garner as his running mate, and in early July Garner's nomination was the lead story in newspapers across the Lone Star State. But in Garner's hometown of Uvalde, that announcement shared billing with one of the few items that could bump it off the top of the page—a record-breaking flood in the Uvalde area and the Hill Country.

The July 1932 flash floods hit along the Uvalde-area rivers—the Frio and the Nueces—and also to the north and east along the headwaters of the Guadalupe River, upstream from Kerrville. The flash flood wave along the Guadalupe set the high-water mark for the newly established summer camps, which had been built above the 1932 flood line. Subsequent inundations along the forks of the upper Guadalupe over the last seventy years or so have resulted in little damage to these camps.

Precedent Conditions

In the first two months of 1932, rainfall in Texas was well above normal. January was the second-wettest January statewide since 1891, and rivers in Northeast Texas flowed above flood stage for much of February. From March through June, Hill Country rainfall was slightly above average, although May was below average. The most extreme rain shortages in May were in Austin (a 3.35-inch deficit) and Boerne (a 2.35-inch deficit).

Storm Rainfall

Prior to the July storms, showers popped up in the San Angelo area. From June 26 to June 28 San Angelo gauged more than 1.5 inches, and Garden City tallied more than 5 inches. During the last week of June, Kerrville recorded 0.75 inches of rain.

From June 30 through July 2, the light showers developed into torrential downpours. Several locations received 15–20 inches within two days. Some of the higher three-day totals included 10.65 inches at Hondo, 8.74 inches at Montell, 7.92 inches at Kerrville, 15.22 inches at La Pryor, 19.25 inches at Sabinal, and 20.28 inches at Uvalde.

The *Uvalde Leader* called the precipitation in that region the "heaviest rainfall in history."[1] The Kincaid Ranch, southwest of Uvalde, recorded 29 inches. Uvalde itself gauged 11 inches in sixteen hours. While the 20-inch tallies in the Nueces, Frio, and Sabinal valleys were very high, unofficial totals near Kerrville were much higher. At the state fish hatchery on Johnson Creek above Ingram, an astounding 35.56 inches fell in a thirty-six-hour period. Hatchery superintendent E. C. Brady noted that a slow rain fell during the night of June 30 and the morning of July 1. Heavy rains began during the afternoon of July 1 and continued through the morning of July 2, with a lull around sundown on July 1. At Hunt, an observer recorded 26 inches. Upstream on the North Fork, 14.75 and 16 inches were measured at locations nine and sixteen miles upstream, respectively. Almost matching the extreme

1932: View of the flooding of Guadalupe River taken from the foyer of the Blue Bonnet Hotel (The San Antonio Light Collection, UTSA's Institute of Texan Cultures, No. L-1369-K).

total at the fish hatchery was a 33.5-inch tally at Station C of the Humble Pipe Line.

Guadalupe River Flood

In the 1930s, the north and south forks of the Guadalupe River were home to some of the state's most popular summer camps. After 14–20 inches of rain fell over a two-day period on the forks of the Guadalupe, these sites, which were filled with campers during the peak of the camping season, were in the path of the surging rivers. Cabins were washed away at Camp Mystic, Camp Rio Vista, and Camp Stewart. Water invaded the dining halls at Camp Waldemar, Camp Mystic, and Camp Stewart, and the owner of Camp Stewart sought refuge from the floods in a large oak tree. The water both rose and fell rapidly, enabling the cleanup of the mess hall at one of the camps on the same day that water invaded it.

A day after the deluge above Kerrville, an airplane from San Antonio flew over the river and camp region. Campers were excited to see the plane—some waved and cheered at it, and one camper even attempted to communicate via semaphore. The pilot's and passenger's account of the damage was that "some buildings . . . [were] flattened as though they had been stepped on by a giant foot."[2] At Camp Waldemar, the campers spelled out a message with strips of white cloth: "All is well—do not land." Other messages were signaled to the planes that "All are safe."[3] Much to the camps' credit, no campers were lost in the overflow. Authorities and camp owners acknowledged that losses would have been greater if the rise had occurred at night.

Hunt

With a flood wave fueled by 15–20 inch rains coming down each fork of the

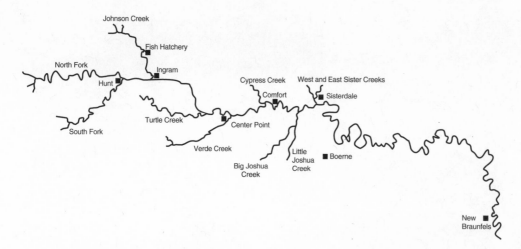

Guadalupe River, the little community of Hunt, where the two forks meet, was the site of a 36.6-foot flood stage. The *Austin American* commented that Hunt was "virtually destroyed by the flood. . . . [The town] was swept off the map so far as all the buildings along the river were concerned."[4] The post office, filling station, and general store were washed away. The only building left standing was the school. Twenty houses were lost, and more than three hundred people were left homeless. As one account summed up the situation in Hunt, "Nothing is left there."[5]

Ingram

The next major tributary along the Guadalupe, Johnson Creek, flows into the river at Ingram. Eight miles upstream from Ingram, at the state fish hatchery on Johnson Creek, the deluge dropped thirty-five inches in thirty-six hours. As the water poured down at the hatchery, an estimated half million fish were swept into the floodwaters of Johnson Creek. The hills above the hatchery "sent down a sheet of water which soon filled drain ditches and then began to boil into the ponds, from the upper side and out the lower, completely cleaning them of the fish or mixing fish from one pond to another." Fourteen catfish that were stuck on the fence were returned to the ponds.[6] At

Ingram itself, the waters covered the town with three feet of water, and people "took to the hills" to escape the floodwaters.[7]

Kerrville

In Kerrville, the floodwaters reached a depth of thirty-nine feet. A rancher originally from the San Angelo area said the flood reminded him of the Ben Ficklin flood of 1882. Kerrville itself was not heavily damaged, although telephone lines were down and roads were impassable. To communicate with the outside world, amateur radio operator Gene Butt sent more than one hundred messages to the outside world about the flood situation in Kerrville. One local authority summed up the deluge there: "Kerrville is all right. It has had a mighty hard lick, but it is taking a toe-hold on the comeback road."[8]

The most dramatic story of the July 1932 flood revolved around a seventeen-year-old boy who became stranded in a cypress tree. He was herding sheep or chasing rabbits, depending on the source of the story, and was treed by a sudden wall of water at 4:30 P.M. Initially he found refuge in a small pecan tree two hundred feet above the dam, but, after the water overwhelmed the small tree and carried the boy downstream, he grasped a low branch on a cypress tree while being washed downriver and eventually managed to crawl to safety.

Several onlookers tried valiantly to reach the boy. One crew attempted to rescue him with a metal boat but was thwarted by the swift water. Two men tried to swim out to him but were swept away and drowned. A proposed rescue plan using a blimp from San Antonio was scuttled when authorities realized the blimp was in Houston. Throughout the boy's ordeal, a crowd of 200–1,000 people on the bank shouted encouragement. To help the boy stay awake, the fire department directed strong lights at him. On the other side of the river his mother called to him, but her cries were overcome by the roaring water.

After twenty-one hours, the boy was finally rescued when the water dropped enough for a man to reach him with food and medicine. After resting and feeding the boy for three hours, the two were assisted out of the water.

Legion

Considerable damage occurred at Legion, a community just below Kerrville on the Guadalupe. There, water from the river and Quinlan Creek reached into the cemetery.

Center Point

At Center Point, water tore away a new bridge as the river reached a forty-two-foot stage, and sections of the metal bridge were carried more than one hundred yards downstream. A traveler who had detoured via Bandera stated that the damage at Center Point was "indescribable."[9] Many large cypresses were uprooted and lined the river from Kerrville to Comfort.

Comfort

The peak flood stage at Comfort reached 38.4 feet. The average daily streamflow in-

creased from 48 cfs on June 30 to 27,100 cfs on July 1 and 37,500 cfs on July 2. Until 7 A.M. on July 4, the river at Comfort was impassable. Vehicles were backed up for miles, waiting to be pulled across the river by four heavy trucks linked by chains. The town's new bridge, made of concrete instead of steel, was lost, "chopped apart as though by a great ax." A makeshift pontoon bridge also failed, and pieces of it ended up in a field. One section "was seen lodged in the tops of trees near the river's edge."[10]

One of the losses in the Comfort and Center Point area was the drowning of a couple of young adults, when the auto they were riding in was washed downriver. Two of their fellow passengers clung to a tree for twelve hours before being rescued.

Just as bridges at Center Point and Comfort were lost in the flood wave, so was that between New Braunfels and Blanco near Spring Branch. A stage line driver reported that he had crossed the structure just moments before it was washed away.

New Braunfels

On July 3 the river hit a thirty-five-foot stage, which was higher than the 1913 flood stage. The overflow took out pecan and cypress trees that had survived fifty years of floods. Backwater flowed into the Comal River and backed up into Comal Creek as well. Camps Warnecke and Giesecke were coated with two inches of mud. Below New Braunfels, water washed out one side of the dam at Lake Dunlap.

Uvalde Area

Receiving more than 20 inches of precipitation, the Uvalde area experienced what the *Uvalde Leader News* called one of the "worst floods in the history of this entire section."[11] The rains near Uvalde started on the night of June 31 and totaled 7.5 inches. Creeks were on a rampage but caused only minor damage. The rainfall continued throughout July 1, with heavy torrents falling on the night of July 1 and in the morning and afternoon of July 2.

Around 9 A.M. on July 2, the Leona River washed away the railing on the wooden bridge at Nopal Street. By noon, the currents had spread to within one block of the courthouse. Streets in the town were inundated, and houses and buildings filled with one to three feet of water. Cook's Slough, an ordinarily dry waterway, "carried more water than has ever been known." The river was nearly two miles wide where the slough crossed Highway 4. At Highway 90 on the western edge of town, the slough was more than half a mile wide.[12]

West of Uvalde, Turkey Creek's floodwaters caused thousands of dollars of damage at the asphalt mines. Although one ranch house along the creek had remained untouched by floods for forty years, water from this deluge reached a depth of thirty inches in the home. Flood victims climbed on top of furniture to escape the waters and then waded seven miles to get food.

By the night of July 2, the Leona was back in its banks, and Cook's Slough was only a foot above the highway, allowing traffic to Carrizo Springs to resume. Twenty miles south of Uvalde, in lower country, the water was several feet deep. One driver abandoned his car three miles north of Batesville and waded through one to four feet of water to reach the town. Residents in the Batesville area estimated that the Leona rose to a depth of forty feet. As the water spread out over the flat country, it formed a lake almost five miles wide and fifteen miles long.

At Batesville, the Baptist minister and his wife were stranded in a tree for eighteen hours. Near Uvalde, two men who were searching for a relative became marooned in a tree for more than eight hours after their boat was damaged by a tree in the turbulent Leona. A crew searched for them throughout the night, and the two men showed up in town on July 3.

Two Batesville women were working in their apiary, which was some distance from their ranch house. As water from Live Oak Creek and the Leona River came up, they tried to reach their house but got lost in the pasture. After wandering for a while, they returned to the apiary house, where they found a compass. With that in hand, they found their house, which had three-foot-deep currents flowing through it. The women rode out the flood by spending two nights in the attic.

Downstream, the Nueces River rose to its highest levels since 1913, reaching twenty-five feet near Crystal City and thirty feet near Carrizo Springs.

Frio River Flood

Near Concan, Rio Frio, and Leakey, 15 to 20 inches fell, and one location near Rio Frio recorded 24 inches. With 20-inch totals over its headwaters region, the Frio was another river on a big rise.

Guadalupe River flooding in New Braunfels, July 1932 (Copyright 1996, Sophienburg Archives, New Braunfels, Texas).

Guadalupe River, New Braunfels, July 1932 (Copyright 1996, Sophienburg Archives, New Braunfels, Texas).

Concan

The Concan and Leakey area reported high water on July 1, as the Frio River rose from an average daily streamflow of 62 cfs on June 30 to 41,200 cfs on July 1. Above Concan, Frio State Park was reported to be under water, and all of its buildings were washed away. Four rises were reported at Concan, and a camper there noted the river had climbed to thirty-six feet on the gage. At Concan, the water stranded residents and campers alike, forcing them to "live on roasting ears and goat meat" until the water dropped and travel could be resumed.[13]

The high water affected several Concan landmarks. An oak that had been "admired by hundreds of tourists for many years" and had an estimated spread of one hundred feet was washed away by the flood.[14] A big cypress tree was carried away at the Shut Inn.

Knippa

Near Knippa, an eighteen-year-old man tried to cross the Frio but was swept away in midstream. He managed to grab a tree, then shed his clothes, and set out again but was sucked under once more. One of his traveling partners searched for him but was also carried away by the treacherous currents and drowned. The would-be rescuer was planning to get married on July 3, and the victim he had tried to save was to have been a member of the wedding party.

Dilley and Derby

Near Derby and south of Pearsall, a thirty-foot flood wave covered the highway bridge with fifteen feet of water. Approaches to the railroad bridge were washed out, and the highway lost more than a mile of roadway. As the water backed up, it formed a lagoon estimated to be two miles wide. As military planes flew overhead and dropped notes to marooned families, requesting them to "keep up their courage as help was coming as rapidly as possible," one family sought refuge on a mound, and another family was rescued by men in boats.[15]

Tilden

On July 4 the river began rising and moving toward Tilden. Residents fled and spent the night of July 5 in the Catholic church on high ground a mile away from town. The telephone operator at Calliham reported that four-foot-deep water was running through the streets of Tilden. Among the last to leave was the owner of the town's only telephone, who stayed at the office of his hotel until the water reached a depth of three feet. As the water rose in town, he relayed information to Calliham about the flood and eventually reported that the waters had reached the roof of his hotel. In La-Salle County, outside of Tilden, the flood frequency of the July 1932 rise was noted when forty-year-old ranch homes were washed away.

Guadalupe River overflow, New Braunfels, July 1932 (Copyright 1996, Sophienburg Archives, New Braunfels, Texas).

July 3, 32. Flood.

Miscellaneous Hill Country Sites

Heavy rains fell between Uvalde and Kerrville, too, producing high runoffs in the streams of that region. Sabinal recorded more than nineteen inches from June 30 to July 2. Near Sabinal, the Blanco River rose twenty feet. In Sabinal, when twelve motorists were stranded due to the high water, residents opened their homes to accommodate the travelers.

At D'Hanis, which sits at the confluence of Seco and Parkers creeks, the heavy rains transformed the two normally dry streams into foaming rivers. On July 1 the high water came down the Seco, washing over the western part of town. More than two thousand acres surrounding D'Hanis were covered with several feet of water. Stores in the downtown area had as much as four feet of water flowing through them. D'Hanis residents fled their houses for higher ground or second stories. Seco Creek was more than two miles wide.

With more than a foot of raining falling in Tarpley, Hondo Creek surged to 35 feet in Hondo, where the streets were full up to the curbs. Surprisingly, minimal property damage resulted. Along the Medina River, more than 14 inches of rain produced a flood that caused Medina Lake to rise 11 feet by 1 P.M. on July 2. At that time, it was rising at a rate of 9 inches per hour. Overall, the lake rose 22.5 feet during the flood.

DAILY PRECIPITATION (IN INCHES), JUNE 24–JULY 6, 1932

	JUNE 24	JUNE 25	JUNE 26	JUNE 27	JUNE 28	JUNE 29	JUNE 24–29	JUNE 30	JULY 1
Uvalde	0.00	0.00	0.00	0.00	0.00	0.00	0.00	0.08	6.67
Sabinal	0.00	0.00	0.00	0.00	0.00	0.00	0.00	1.72	8.28
La Pryor							0.00	5.21	9.83
Hondo	0.04	0.00	0.00	0.00	0.00	0.00	0.04	1.00	2.40
Montell							0.00	0.17	2.94
Kerrville		0.69	0.01	0.01	0.04	0.00	0.75	0.00	1.63
Morris Ranch							0.00		4.5
Junction	0.00	0.00	0.00	0.00	0.00	0.00	0.00	0.30	2.53
San Antonio			trace				0.00	0.46	4.07
Carrizo Springs							0.00		1.55
Boerne	0.00	0.04	0.05	0.00	0.00	0.00	0.09	0.13	0.84
Rocksprings	0.00	0.00	0.00	0.00	0.00	0.00	0.00	0.00	0.04

AVERAGE DAILY DISCHARGE, JUNE 24–JULY 9, 1932

	JUNE 24	JUNE 25	JUNE 26	JUNE 27	JUNE 28	JUNE 29	JUNE 30	JULY 1	JULY 2
Guadalupe at Comfort	48	92	62	59	52	50	48	27,100	37,500
Guadalupe at Spring Branch	67	69	82	100	80	75	67	67	28,500
Comal at New Braunfels	308	311	308	311	308	308	315	315	315
Pedernales at Spicewood	16	18	8.40	7.20	7.20	6.10	6.50	324	8,810
North Llano at Junction	5.90	7.60	6.50	5.40	3	2.10	3.40	7.60	151
Llano at Junction	49	49	49	46	46	46	46	68	11,700
Llano at Castell	31	44	63	64	72	50	40	64	19,400
San Saba at Menard	20	20	20	20	20	20	19	18	27
San Saba at San Saba	136	265	117	111	108	103	99	200	14,400
Frio at Concan	60	60	58	56	54	54	62	52,000	15,300
Nueces at Laguna	41	39	37	37	35	35	37	2,530	15,600
Nueces near Uvalde	6.20	6.20	6.20	6.20	6.20	6.20	7.80	14,100	59,600

Discharge in cubic feet/second

Central Texas Flooding

Farther north of the southern Hill Country, heavy rains pushed Brady Creek and the San Saba River to flood stages. Near Brady, one of the heaviest rains on record lasted throughout the afternoon of July 1. Around 7 P.M. it began falling in sheets and continued without abatement through the night. By 2 A.M., 5.3 inches had caused the Commercial National Bank gage to overflow. The rain filled wash pots and eight-inch-deep lard buckets.

Just upstream of downtown Brady, runoff from the heavy rains washed out the west end of the racetrack and inundated Richards Park. Brady Creek flooded several blocks east of the bridge. Area residents feared that, if the Eden and Melvin areas had received heavy rains, too, Brady might experience a rise on Brady Creek similar to that of 1930.

Coleman

Coleman was hit with the heaviest rain there since 1908. Talpa reported ten inches, and Coleman nine inches. Jim Ned Creek, which flows approximately twelve miles north of Coleman, and Hords Creek, which skirts the north and northeast boundary of Coleman, were higher than they had been since 1900. Many bridges along Hords Creek to the Abilene and Baird highways were washed away. Talpa was partially inundated, with currents reaching into the telephone office.

Brownwood

Jim Ned and Hords creeks both flowed into Pecan Bayou above Brownwood. The new lake on the bayou, Lake Brownwood, was almost finished when the heavy rains arrived. The runoff filled the lake with 150,000 acre-feet of muddy, rushing water. The reservoir filled in a six-hour period (5–11 P.M. on July 3). At 9:45 P.M. water started flowing through the spillway. By the time the lake stopped rising, water to a depth of 1.8 feet was overflowing the spillway.

Around Brownwood, conversation was all about the dam. On July 5 the "Around the Supper Table" column in the *Brownwood Bulletin* remarked:

Brownwood people Monday forgot about the Democratic Convention, let the Declaration of Independence speak for itself, ignored George Washington and even sacrificed golf games in order to visit and talk about Lake Brownwood. Heretofore, it has been merely a dam, but yesterday, it became a lake and what a lake!

JULY 2	JULY 3	JULY 4	JULY 5	JULY 6	TOTAL
13.53	0.00	0.00	0.28	0.53	21.09
9.25	0.00	0.00	0.00	0.11	19.36
0.18					15.22
7.25	0.00	0.00	0.00	0.09	10.78
5.63					8.74
4.60	1.69	0.00	0.00	0.00	8.67
2.29					6.79
2.67	0.00	0.00	0.00	0.10	5.60
0.38					4.91
3.07					4.62
2.05	0.00	0.00	0.03	1.00	4.14
3.06	0.00	0.00	0.00	0.00	3.10

JULY 3	JULY 4	JULY 5	JULY 6	JULY 7	JULY 8	JULY 9
546	546	546	546	546	546	546
62,800	6,800	2,270	1,560	1,400	1,140	945
330	330	330	330	330	330	330
1610	355	179	246	267	108	75
1,500	176	74	48	34	30	28
7,020	1,120	530	379	292	248	218
19,400	19,400	1,700	928	692	532	439
8530	1240	123	68	55	44	49
8,740	7,040	3,790	958	508	482	399
3,900	2,040	1,460	1,240	1,190	930	800
1,860	356	273	233	222	192	186
10,400	3,200	1,500	834	600	520	445

People who have predicted that the reservoir would never be filled were astonished when they learned that the lake had been filled to capacity, and then some, in 24 hours, and incidentally, it may be observed that a number of perennial critics of the project would be terribly disappointed if the dam doesn't break . . .

Enough water for the domestic needs of Brownwood for the next 10 years, if it could be retained but all must be released to allow the dam to be finished.[16]

On July 6, three days after the reservoir was filled, the release of water had lowered the dam four feet from its peak. The only damage to the new structure was some washing of the "soft earth at the north side of the outlet structure."[17]

An editorial in the *Brownwood Bulletin* the following day added this observation:

Brownwood people have had a marvelously forceful illustration of what is meant by flood prevention, and hereafter when they think of the water project they will think not only of the preservation of a domestic supply and of the possibilities of irrigation in the Bayou Valley, but of the value of the project as a protector against devastation by flood waters.

It is impossible to estimate how much damage might have been done to property and life if the big dam had not been available to check the flow of the flood waters down the Bayou Valley. In all likelihood, there would have been as great destruction as there has been in the valley of the Guadalupe . . . .

. . . Causes everyone in the community to look with more favor than ever before upon the whole water project. . . . And including the fact that the dam has withstood the tremendous test of unprecedented flood while it is still unfinished . . . should put an end to the recurring rumors as to the dam's stability.[18]

Summing Up

After the floods had been reported, the *San Antonio Express* added its opinion about flood protection and prevention measures: "Altogether, the cost of this latest flood season to the region probably will run into millions of dollars. And every such visitation reminds the people and their government that money spent for systematic, effective flood-control would be a sound investment and, in the long run, economical."[19]

Prior to the rains of the summer of 1932, the Bandera County History Book Committee recounted what was uttered at a prayer meeting in Bandera, when an attender prayed for a good east wind. When asked why he had not prayed for rain instead, the man replied, "If the wind gets in the east, all h—l can't keep it from rainin'."[20]

SEPTEMBER 1932

~~~~~~~~~~

Devil's River and Rio Grande River Floods

THE FLASH FLOODS of September 1932 were part of a large-scale rain and flood event throughout the Rio Grande River Basin that lasted for almost two months (from late August into October). That year, the September flash floods in the United States moved primarily down the Devil's River, the Pecos River, and smaller streams in the area of Eagle Pass, Del Rio, and the western Edwards Plateau. Additionally, heavy rains hit throughout the Rio Grande River Basin into Mexico. The resulting floods on the Rio Grande produced a dramatic moment when several railroad workers became stranded on the International Bridge.

Rainfall

Late in August, showers spread northward from the southern end of the Rio Grande Basin. The first extreme rains showed up in Mexico at Múzquiz, Coahuila, on August 26 and in Texas at Fort Davis on August 27 and 29. Substation 14, the only formal rainfall site in the Devil's River Basin monitored by the weather bureau at that time, received 7.66 inches on August 31 and 6.08 inches on September 1. Rocksprings officially reported 11.19 inches, but other nearby totals reached 16 inches. Robert Lee in the Colorado River Basin recorded 17 inches.

In thirty-six hours, ending at 2 P.M. on September 1, Sonora received 11.07 inches of rain. Other high totals occurred at Barksdale (14 inches), Fort Clark (8 inches),

Piedras Negras (7.64 inches), and Monclava, Coahuila (6.20 inches), on September 3.[1]

Devil's River

The Devil's River gage data near Del Rio on September 1 was steady at 15 feet throughout most of the morning. Shortly after 12 P.M. the river rose to 18 feet, and in the next five hours it surged to a 30-foot rise. At 5:30 P.M. the river peaked at 48.4 feet. The 33-foot surge not only destroyed the gage but also dislodged and shattered the concrete building that housed it.

Leading up to the flood, the average daily streamflow in the Devil's River at Juno was holding steady at 73–76 cfs. The first full day of the flood records, September 1, registered an average daily flow of 94,200 cfs.

On September 2 the Southern Pacific bridge over the Devil's River went out at 3 A.M. Initially it was reported that the Central Power and Light plant was destroyed, supposedly leaving only remnants of the machinery, but, as it turned out, only the roof and upper rock walls were damaged. Seven people were stranded on the roof of the Central Power and Light plant overnight on September 1. The son of one of the trapped men used a rowboat to reach the plant and rescue the men.

The highway crossing lost half of its concrete causeway, and three spans of the railroad bridge were washed out. The water also cut a new channel east of the causeway.

Along the river from Lake Walk to a point a half mile below the highway, a pecan

grove was completely washed away. Trees estimated to be more than ninety years old were lost. The Sutton County history book of 1979 reports that the "violent run off reduced the Devil's River Valley, at that time one of the most beautiful rivers in Texas and one of the most prolific pecan producing areas on the earth, to a plantless pile of rock."[2] Moreover, H. L. Molyneaux, a Del Rio weather observer, called the floods the greatest in the region's history.

The International Boundary Water Commission also published a report on the inundation. According to the account, the Devil's River flood of September 1, 1932, was the greatest in North America for a stream of 1,000–10,000 square miles. Streamflow per square mile was calculated to reach

138.23 cfs from the 4,033 square miles in the basin. The peak flow was 557,500 cfs. The report concluded that the flood was the greatest on the Devil's River in at least one hundred years.

For the month of September 1932, the Devil's River discharged 896,000 acre-feet, which was almost three times the previously recorded high of 301,000 acre-feet in May 1925. The earlier peak annual discharge was 616,000 acre-feet, making the monthly discharge in September 1932 almost fifty percent greater than the highest yearly discharge on record.[3]

Pecos River

The Pecos River reached a depth of 38.25 feet at 3 P.M. on September 1. The previous

Bridge over Rio Grande between Del Rio and Villa Acuna (the middle span was washed away) (The San Antonio Light Collection, UTSA's Institute of Texan Cultures, No. L-1389-A).

View of Rio Grande with men stranded on bridge, September 1932 (courtesy of the Texas Department of Transportation).

high was 35.75 feet on April 6, 1900. According to the high-water marks, the peak flow was estimated at 101,800 cfs.

Rio Grande River

The Rio Grande River fortunately avoided the July 1932 floods. By August, the river at Rio Grande City was at its lowest point in the previous twenty-four months. The low flow changed dramatically, however, after the rains of late August and the flash-flood-producing rains along the Devil's and Pecos rivers in early September.

At 5:30 P.M. on September 1, the Rio Grande was more than a mile wide at Del Rio. At 8:30 P.M., three hours after the Devil's River peaked, the Rio Grande attained its highest point at 34.5 feet and 604,600 cfs. The highest previous flood at Del Rio occurred on June 18 and 19, 1922, when it reached 32.8 feet.

Smaller streams raged with record floods, too. The Las Moras, Pinto, Sycamore, and Seco creeks all dumped floodwaters into the Rio Grande. The overflow at Pinto Creek was the seventh largest flood in North America for comparably sized watersheds (200–300 square miles). Pinto Creek peaked at 21.08 feet and 54,650 cfs on August 31. The drainage area was 229 square miles, and streamflow was calculated to be 238.6 cfs per square mile.

Eagle Pass

The rise invaded Eagle Pass at noon on September 2, when the peak was measured at 49 feet, 4 feet above the 1922 flood level. The streamflow was 568,630 cfs.

Water flowed eighteen inches deep in the main streets of Eagle Pass and under-mined the foundations of several buildings, causing them to collapse. With twelve city blocks of residences under water, one

thousand people were rendered homeless. Across the Rio Grande, seventy-five percent of Piedras Niegras was covered with water.

Laredo

Laredo residents were warned to expect a swell greater than that of the 1922 flood, when Laredo was hit with a forty-nine-foot crest. With a rise of that proportion on the way, citizens took precautions to preserve the bridges over the Rio Grande. To help stabilize the railroad bridge, empty railroad cars were moved onto the bridge.

The first wave of the floodwaters rushed into Laredo at 10:30 A.M. on September 3. With the crest still on the way, newspapers reported that the water was two feet below the floor of the International Bridge. The peak of the flood arrived at 5 P.M. that day, when the river crested at 52.2 feet and 402,590 cfs, and the Rio Grande remained at that level for two hours. During the peak of the deluge, only the lampposts on the bridge were showing above the water. By 10:30 P.M. the river was slowly receding (at a rate of 1.5 inches per hour). As the flood wave diminished, the *Laredo Times* noted, "The Rio Grande has set a flood record here which probably will never be broken."[4]

The events in Laredo yielded the most intriguing rescue story in the September 1932 flood. The "yellow flood waters" brought trees, houses, dead animals, and miscellaneous debris with them.[5] As the wreckage hit bridges, it formed piles that increased the pressure on those structures. When this happened at Laredo, authorities considered dynamiting the International Bridge to release the rubble. As an alternative to detonating explosives, railroad workers attempted to dislodge the debris. While several men were working near the middle of the bridge, the structure col-

Mexico
RIO GRANDE
zacate Creek
RIO GRANDE
Arroyo Chacon
submerged bridge
FLOOD AT LAREDO, TEX.
Sept. 3-4, 1932
PHOTO BY
AIR CORPS, U.S. ARMY
HIGHWAY No. 2

lapsed, stranding three of them on a drift-wood raft. Two of the three were naked, as the violent waters ripped away their clothes. Adding to their discomfort, rats, armadillos, and snakes gathered on the same pile of driftwood as a refuge from the waters.

In an effort to provide the stranded men with a means to float to shore, an army airplane dropped five inner tubes. From the riverbank, rescuers attempted to shoot a line to the men, first with a bow and arrow and then with a "salute cannon" from the customs house. The first try failed, and the second burned the rope. On the third attempt, the rescuers used a homemade harpoon, but this also failed when the rope became entangled in nearby buildings.[6] Spectators along the shore were kneeling in prayer during the ordeal.

Sixteen hours after the nightmare began,

a 130-pound fireman, Manuel de la Cruz, wrote a "new chapter in border heroism," according to the *San Antonio Light*.[7] To reach the men, de la Cruz slid down the roof of a partially submerged store near the U.S. customs house, clung to a trolley wire, and then tied a rope to the branches of a tree in the parkway. Four other firemen—Higinio Mendoza, Guadalupe Hernandez, Belisario Guera, and Fortunato Mireles—followed him into the waist-deep water and felt their way along the edge of the customs house. At the raft, the stranded men were passed from one fireman to the next. When finally on shore, they were taken to Mercy Hospital, where they were treated for exhaustion.

After he was rescued, one of the stranded men, Vincente Gonzales Flores, said that he still heard roaring waters all through his sleep. The *San Antonio Light* stated, "His ex-

Aerial scene of flooding at Laredo, September 1932 (courtesy of the Texas Department of Transportation).

pression was that of a man who has chatted with death and returned to tell of his conversation"[8] Flores also recounted the threat posed by the snakes: "It seemed the whole world was crawling with them while we were out there." When Flores awoke from a nap on the raft, one of his companions warned him of a rattler two feet away from Flores's face. Flores also mentioned that he was thankful for the inner tubes since he could not swim.[9]

To help the stranded men survive their ordeal, José Rodriguez Trigo assumed the role of leader. Afterward he asked his fellow victims, Julian Lozán and Flores, to forgive him for his rough talk. He had only wanted to keep them together to prevent them from drowning. Trigo said, "Our courage and hopefulness were about to give way to despair as darkness came Saturday, but the big

search light turned on our island from the roof of the Hamilton Hotel made us feel we would be rescued."[10]

Elsewhere in the Laredo area, convicts were released from jail to build a levee in the hope that it would protect the town against the rising currents, which reached nine blocks into Nuevo Laredo. In Laredo, the foundations of buildings up to four blocks away were completely washed out.

Zapata and Roma

Farther downstream, the Rio Grande River at Zapata peaked at 7 P.M. on September 4 with a flow of 261,160 cfs. Flood damage there was light. At Roma, stage height reached 35.4 feet at 11 A.M. on September 5, and the peak flow was 203,420 cfs. According to interviews with old-timers in Roma, the 1932 flood was the greatest since 1860.

South Texas Rio Grande River Valley

The flood struck the Valley on September 5. Water was 26.4 feet deep at Rio Grande City, and Hidalgo reported water 25.6 feet deep on September 7.

In the Valley, the multimillion-dollar floodway starting at Mission was cleared in anticipation of its first real test. By noon on September 7, however, the walls of the floodway were already crumbling. A thirty-foot-wide break in the south floodway wall was located four miles south of Mission. Moreover, a fifteen-foot rupture was reported three miles south of McAllen. Four other gaps were noted in the walls of the south floodway.

West Texas Draws

With heavy rains over West Texas, the normally dry-as-a-bone draws went on a

Devils River Basin

DAILY PRECIPITATION (IN INCHES), AUGUST 24–SEPTEMBER 9, 1932

	AUG. 24	AUG. 25	AUG. 26	AUG. 27	AUG. 28	AUG. 29	AUG. 30	AUG. 31	SEPT. 1	SEPT. 2	SEPT. 3
Alpine							2.06			0.78	0.06
Balmorhea			0.07	0.03	trace	0.05	2.72		trace	1.03	0.05
Carrizo Springs			0.02			0.28	0.04	1.75	3.89	0.03	2.24
Del Rio		0.11	0.20	trace	0.09	trace	1.39	2.15	0.85		0.66
Eagle Pass		trace	0.50	1.13	0.63	0.03	trace	5.13	0.07	0.17	1.05
Eden	0.00	0.00	0.00	0.00	0.20	0.40	0.80	0.00	0.00	0.00	0.10
El Paso				trace	trace	0.10	0.04	trace			
Fort Clark			0.20				8.00				
Fort Davis			0.17	3.90		5.30		0.05		0.12	0.16
Fort Stockton							0.25	0.45	0.30	0.16	
Grandfalls							1.00	0.90		0.40	
Hondo	0.00	0.00	0.00	0.06	0.05	0.00	0.21	1.88	0.83	0.02	0.58
Junction	0.00	0.00	0.00	0.00	0.00	0.00	0.26	2.45	1.75	0.86	0.26
Langtry		0.68	0.12		0.02		0.41		4.11	0.27	0.02
Laredo		trace		trace					1.30	0.93	
Muzquiz	0.01		6.82	trace	0.05	0.05	2.49	0.28		4.25	2.76
Menard	0.00	0.00	0.00	0.00	0.00	0.00	0.00	0.80	0.65	0.95	0.40
Monclava		trace	0.12				trace	0.12		0.79	6.20
Piedras Negras		trace	0.29	1.45	0.12	0.04	trace	7.64	0.16	1.38	
Presidio				trace		0.42	trace				
Rocksprings	0.00	0.00	0.00	0.00	0.00	0.00	0.07	5.06	3.06	3.07	0.00
Sabinal	0.00	0.00	0.05	0.00	0.00	0.00	0.00	2.63	1.90	0.00	0.15
San Antonio		0.15	trace	trace	0.85	0.44	0.01	0.39	0.33	0.46	0.1
San Angelo			trace	0.07	trace	trace		1.23	2.85	0.65	0.71
Sanderson	0.00	0.00	0.00	0.00	0.00	1.83	0.28	0.15	0.41	0.36	0.06
Substation 14	0.04	0.09		0.06			0.07	7.66	6.08	0.78	0.77
Uvalde	0.00	0.00	0.05	0.00	0.00	0.00	0.15	2.60	0.97	0.30	0.55

AVERAGE DAILY DISCHARGE, AUGUST 24–SEPTEMBER 9, 1932

	AUG. 24	AUG. 25	AUG. 26	AUG. 27	AUG. 28	AUG. 29	AUG. 30	AUG. 31
San Saba River at Menard	8.40	10	11	10	9.90	9.50	9.20	9.20
Devil's River at Juno	73	73	73	73	72	72	75	76
North Concho River at Carlsbad	3.40	3.10	3.10	3.10	3.10	2.80	3.40	12
South Concho River at Christoval	11	10	10	11	11	11	12	17
Concho River at Paint Rock	9.40	8.20	7.60	6.30	9.10	5.70	3.60	41

Discharge in cubic feet/second

tear. At Sonora, Lowrey Draw flooded houses. Residents in the lower lands of Sonora spent the nights of August 31 and September 1 in the courthouse and the First National Bank, where they ate leftover beans and chili from a party given on August 31. Homes in back of the Kirkland Hotel were washed from their foundations and carried a distance of 250 feet. In spite of the damage, the rains were welcome in most parts of the county.

A week later, after many sheep, goats, cattle, and horses had drowned in the area streams, the attitude among area residents had changed. The *Devil's River News* noted, "For once ranchmen are willing to admit that enough rain has fallen."[11]

Hill Country Rises

With more big rains in the Divide area, the Llanos, Frio, and Nueces rivers all had

SEPT. 4	SEPT. 5	SEPT. 6	SEPT. 7	SEPT. 8	SEPT. 9	TOTAL
0.46	0.30	0.90	2.10	0.16		6.82
2.63	0.10	0.39	1.83	0.44		9.34
0.87	0.24					9.36
0.72	0.01	0.58	1.04		trace	7.80
	0.02	1.65	0.92	0.01		11.31
1.92	0.98	1.61	0.50	0.00	0.00	6.51
	trace					0.14
2.80		1.60				12.60
0.11		0.38	1.05			11.24
0.35	0.60	0.60	1.32	0.05		4.08
	1.25	0.45				4.00
0.64	0.27	0.00	0.35	0.00	0.00	4.89
0	0.45	1.68	0.35	0.00	0.00	8.06
0.33		1.19	1.52	0.12		8.79
0.05	0.09					2.37
0.30	3.49		0.79	2.00		23.29
0.00	0.00	5.50	0.21	0.04	0.00	8.55
2.76	0.98	0.47	trace	0.32	0.71	11.76
0.28	1.02	0.43				12.81
trace		0.26	1.26	0.25		2.19
0.00	0.00	0.80	0.60	0.00	0.00	12.66
1.35	0.00	0.02	1.65	0.00	0.00	7.75
0.11			0.04			2.88
trace	0.15	0.71	0.35	0.62	trace	7.34
0.00	0.26	0.75	1.98	1.50	0.00	7.58
trace	0.22	0.73	0.59	0.03	0.04	17.12
2.40	0.00	0.00	0.00	0.00	0.00	7.02

SEPT. 1	SEPT. 2	SEPT. 3	SEPT. 4	SEPT. 5	SEPT. 6	SEPT. 7	SEPT. 8	SEPT. 9
30	1,300	668	93	45	8,820	1,200	176	105
94,200	2,920	2,920	2,920	2,920	2,920	2,920	2,920	405
78	26	13	9.20	9.20	961	346	579	398
388	181	25	23	27	47	39	35	33
11,500	3,840	1,170	430	198	541	2,420	3,060	1,540

abrupt but not record increases. The North Llano reported a 30-foot rise, and the South Llano a 20-foot swell. The Frio isolated Leakey and blocked traffic at Derby. On September 1 the Nueces River rose 25 feet near Uvalde.

A USGS employee was measuring water flow in the Nueces River by using a trolley on a cable that spanned the river. When a log hit the cable and broke, he was thrown into the torrent but managed to reach the bank safely.

Summing Up

Overall, due to the late August rains, more than 180 percent of the normal rainfall fell in August along the Rio Grande. September topped that with more than 290 percent of the normal rainfall in that same geographic area.[12] Seven flood peaks flowed through Rio Grande City in September and October. From September 5 through October 22, the Rio Grande River at Rio Grande City was in flood stage.

DEVIL'S RIVER AND RIO GRANDE RIVER FLOODS

MAY 1935

~~~~~~~

D'Hanis Flash Flood

THE MAY 1935 flash flood in D'Hanis is a classic in the Texas Hill Country. During this event, the monumental rainfall total was measured not in inches but in feet. The runoff tore down the streambeds and adjoining floodplains into a town built near the confluence of two creeks.

D'Hanis sits at the foot of the knolls of the southern Hill Country. Seco Creek meanders out of the region between Bandera and Utopia, and Parkers Creek heads in the country northwest of Hondo. The two streams flow southward and join just below D'Hanis. Flash floods had come down the creeks many times, with the most recent, significant one occurring in July 1932. But no flood in the history of D'Hanis could compare to the one that arrived in May 1935 because it was triggered by a rainfall that set a new world's record in a three-hour span.

Precedent Conditions

By the winter of 1935, the copious rains of 1932 had given way to harsh conditions. Drought had set in, accompanied by cold winters. During the last ten days of January 1935, cold temperatures persisted over the state, bringing the lowest readings in five years. A hard freeze reached down into the Rio Grande Valley.

In February, above-average rainfall brought some relief from the drought of the previous two years. In March and April, dust storms, the icon of plains weather of the 1930s, became the defining feature of Texas weather. The U.S. Climatological Data publication of March 1935 stated, "Dust storms were unusually widespread and severe during March 1935, there being only three dates on which dust was not recorded at some station in the state, namely the 2nd, 12th, and 24th." The storms were unusually severe in the western portion of the state.[1]

From April 10 to April 14 some of the worst dust storms on record struck Texas. In the northwestern sections, visibility dropped to almost zero, while in the southern reaches, visibilities shrank to less than a mile. Drought continued in the western and northwestern portions of the state.

In the Hill Country, rainfall totals at Blanco, Boerne, Kerrville, and Rocksprings were all 2–3 inches below normal. In the southern Hill Country, the first four months' rainfall was closer to normal. Uvalde was less than 1 inch below normal, thanks to 1.98 inches of rain in February and 2.49 inches in April. Deficits in Sabinal and Hondo were more than 1 inch below normal.

Other indications of a change in the droughty weather pattern included severe weather. On April 4 a windstorm developed near Eagle Pass, causing damage estimated at $500,000, killing 1 person, and injuring 139 others. On May 9 San Antonio was struck by a hailstorm. Nine days later the New Braunfels area reported a tornado. On the following day, May 19, storms dropped hail at Uvalde.

May's stormy weather chased off the dust storms and drought. The statewide rainfall average in May was 7.2 inches, nearly 3.5 inches above the monthly average. That total topped all but two prior May rainfall totals for the state.

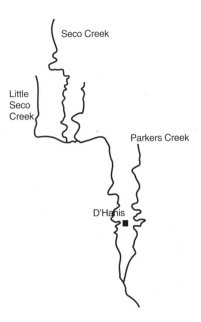

Seco Creek

Little
Seco
Creek

Parkers Creek

D'Hanis

Rainfall

Throughout the first three weeks of May, heavy rains fell in the Uvalde area. Uvalde itself received more than 12 inches, and Sabinal and Hondo reported more than 8 inches each. At the end of May, cloudbursts pounded the Sabinal, D'Hanis, and Hondo area. Hondo received more than 13 inches in four days, while Sabinal recorded more than 10 inches in the last five days of the month. The heaviest rains arrived on May 31, when Hondo and Sabinal received 9.15 and 7.70 inches, respectively.

As noteworthy as the heavy totals were at Hondo and Sabinal, the deluge near D'Hanis eclipsed the combined tally from its two neighboring towns. Near D'Hanis, precipitation started in the predawn hours (4–5 A.M.). As the rain poured down, some locations received almost their yearly average in several hours. Following an extensive study, J. H. Jarboe of U.S. Weather Bureau in San Antonio determined that 21.84 inches fell in only three hours at Woodward Ranch, ten miles northwest of D'Hanis. This total still stands as a U.S. record for that period.[2]

The *San Antonio Express* reported that, "while San Antonians were grumbling about the 'wettest' month in Weather Bureau history, a total of 14.07 inches having been measured here in the 31-day period of May, the Hondo-D'Hanis-Sabinal area had almost that much rain water dumped on it within a few hours time."[3]

Flood Results

The deluge quickly created a flash flood that came roaring down Seco and Parkers creeks into D'Hanis. The *Hondo Anvil Herald* stated, "Death rode on the flood tides Friday morning of last week when a cloudburst in the northwestern part of the county converted the usually dry creeks, sloughs and arroyos into raging torrents of muddy waters and tossing, battering drift." Furthermore, west of the Hondo Creek and past the Seco, every "draw became a flood area, and every arroyo a raging torrent."[4]

Seco and Parkers Creeks

Seco Creek left its banks eight miles above D'Hanis, flowing eastward and southward until it joined Parkers Creek, which was also flooding. The two streams covered the "entire valley as if it were a vast river pouring down its course." The *Hondo Anvil Herald* commented that it was "doubtful if there was an acre of this area that was not covered from a few inches to several feet in floodwaters."[5]

The floodwater overflowed into virtually every home in D'Hanis. The local school took in 2–4 feet of water. At 7 A.M. currents were flowing into basements and eventually reached a depth of 1–4 feet in buildings. Water reached its highest stage in the business district at 10 A.M. There, only three houses did not have water above floor level. Houses that had never before been threatened were now flooded. In D'Hanis, the water attained a depth of 13 feet, sweeping substantial homes off their foundations and carrying autos downstream. The railroad track washed across the highway, which became plugged with railroad ties.

One resident remarked that water from Parkers Creek reached his doorstep in the July 1932 flood. On the morning of May 31, he and his wife were using bran sacks to block the floodwater from Parkers Creek, which was lapping at their front door. Then he noticed the murky water of Seco Creek creeping over a cornfield northwest of his home. He said, "It seemed to come in great rolls and in a few minutes it crushed in the windows, flooded the room waist deep, and it was with difficulty that [I and my wife] could reach the second story up the stairway, so strong was the driving force of the current." After the flood, he pointed to a seven-foot-high watermark in the yard. He was the son of a pioneer to the area and said that there had never been such a flood since the late 1840s. He recounted a conversation with an old frontiersman who told of "seeing a drift high up on the side of Cross Hill, and he warned [me that] D'Hanis and the Seco valley might some day see another such flood."[6]

Aftermath

To help with the cleanup, the San Antonio Fire Department sent pumpers to D'Hanis to remove water from buildings and basements. For a few days, D'Hanis became the destination of sightseers. Castroville residents estimated that 5,000–7,000 cars passed through the town on June 2, presumably to view the damage to the west.

After the flood, D'Hanis residents expressed their thanks to all who helped restore the area, especially those citizens of Castroville who cleaned out the Holy Cross Church and Hondo residents who gave clothing and personal assistance. Josie Rothe, who wrote a column for the *Hondo Anvil Herald,* recounted a few sights from the flood that she would never forget:

• That last-of-the world feeling when you realize that you really were awake and that you hadn't lost your mind—it really was water.

• The Parkers [Creek] through the back of Joe Koch's field, whipped into six-foot breakers by the wind.

MAY 1935 DAILY PRECIPITATION DATA (IN INCHES)

	MAY 23	MAY 24	MAY 25	MAY 26	MAY 27	MAY 28	MAY 29	MAY 30	MAY 31	TOTAL
Austin	0.00	0.00	0.00	0.00	0.00	0.70	0.06	0.00	0.00	0.76
Blanco	0.84	0.00	0.00	0.00	0.00	1.36	0.69	0.00	0.03	2.92
Boerne	0.58	0.00	0.00	0.00	0.00	1.22	0.67	0.00	0.93	3.40
Brackettville	0.95	0.00	0.00	0.00	0.00	0.20	0.77	0.00	0.07	1.99
Del Rio	0.18				0.05	0.01	1.17	0.09		1.50
Harlingen	0.05						5.00		0.05	5.10
Hondo	0.95	0.00	0.00	0.00	0.00	2.67	1.45	0.00	9.15	14.22
Junction	0.40	0.00	0.00	0.00	0.76	0.00	1.10	0.00	0.00	2.26
Kerrville	1.30	0.00	0.00	0.00	0.00	1.89	1.65	0.00	2.38	7.22
Laredo	2.00	trace								2.00
Llano	0.00	0.00	0.00	0.00	0.00	0.46	0.46	0.00	0.00	0.92
New Braunfels	0.41	0.00	0.00	0.00	0.00	0.85	0.58	0.00	0.55	2.39
Rocksprings	0.00	0.00	0.00	0.00	0.60	0.80	0.60	0.00	0.54	2.54
Sabinal	0.52	0.00	0.00	0.00	1.75	0.00	0.83	0.00	7.70	10.80
San Antonio	0.64				trace	1.19	0.67	trace	0.43	2.93
Uvalde	1.15	0.00	0.00	0.00	0.00	0.16	0.52	0.00	3.70	5.53

Flood in the Seco
Valley

The corn grew green and tall
In the pleasant valley
Rich in its promise of golden grain.
The kine [cows] browsed on the luscious
　　grasses
In the sweetest of calm content,
And peace ruled in the valley
Where man's happy days were spent!

But clouds came over the valley
And the clouds by the thunders
Were torn and rent
And the angry winds
At their troubled fragments
Strove and whipped!

And the clouds out of their labor
Borned a Demon-
The Demon of Flowing waters!

And Death and Destruction
Rode the waters,
As they flowed
Down the valley,
Scattering Ruin where they went.

The Sun smiled through the Clouds
When their travail was spent,
And the Corn Plants
Lifted their heads from the mud and murk
At the Sun's gentle caress.

But Death—death even to man's Content-
Had ridden the Demon,
The Demon of unleashed Flowing Waters!

And worse
Than the ghastly ruin he had wrought
The Demon had left a Ghost-
A Ghost that will not down-
For it is an endless Fear!

And now when the clouds shall gather
In promise of refreshing rain
Each time the Ghost will stalk the valley,
Where once contentment dwelled,
Arousing an endless Fear
Along the track
Where the Demon of Flowing Waters
In his mad destruction went!

by Fletcher Davis, *Hondo Anvil Herald*,
June 7, 1935

• The first trip to town—waist deep—a rolling sea of water—and an anxious eye on what remained of a food supply in the grocery store . . .

• Matt Koch's family atop a mantelpiece.

• Quiet, encouraging voice of the Nuns.

• And the realization that all of these things were duplicated in each and every home for the length of forty miles . . .

• A clear Sunday morning—with EVERY-ONE in Church at eight o'clock—and as a Protestant you guiltily remember sleeping through an eleven o'clock service within two blocks of the church.

• Sightseers—with their skirts pulled high—as they smilingly remark "Isn't it terrible?" The quiet organized help of County officials, past and present, and of the Castro-

ville people who came in their work clothes and started putting our house in order.[7]

The flood damaged approximately twelve miles of roads and railroads. A railroad man inspecting the damage commented, "It looks like the Galveston flood."[8]

Area Reports

To the east of D'Hanis, a downpour in Hondo quickly filled the town's drainage ditches. As the water came down from the fields northwest of town via Hondo Creek, it had no place to go but through the streets. Locals called it the "highest water in the history of Hondo."[9] The *Hondo Anvil Herald* noted, "Probably for the first time in the history of the town, the draw which forms almost imperceptibly in the fields northwest of town and finds egress for its drainage through a culvert . . . at the foot of the hill in the western part of town, could not carry off its flood waters and the crest of the flood forced its way into town, along the railroad embankment, and converted North Front Street into a raging torrent for several hours."[10]

North of the railroad tracks that run east and west through town, water piled up against the railroad embankment, causing the water to back up into approximately twenty businesses. Fire trucks used their pumps to remove water from the basements of the stores. To the east of Hondo, the slough there "spread out like a vast lake, inundating many homes."[11] Because most of the houses were partially filled with water, the courthouse and the old Muennink gin were converted into refugee camps.

To the west of D'Hanis, the Sabinal River rose 30 feet to its highest level since 1919. A freight train was marooned in Sabinal, and floods damaged three miles of railroad line. Near Uvalde, the Nueces River rose 20 feet, and the Leona River 15 feet. Crystal City reported a 12-foot rise on the Nueces. The Frio River was 1.25 miles wide near Derby, where the track was being wired to limit its damage. On June 2 the Frio at Derby was 12 feet over the highway.

Turkey Creek twice washed away fences before the Smyth Ranch received even a drop of rain. Precipitation north of the ranch put the creek on a rise. Area ranchers could not recall another time when streams had been on so many rises in such a short period of time.

Talpa, Valera, and Sonora

On June 3 a ten-inch downpour was unleashed near Talpa and Valera. Near Sonora,

three men got out of their flooded car and waited on top of the vehicle. They summoned aid by "firing a very wet six shooter."[12]

July Rains

In July, from five to eleven inches of rain fell in the Medina County area, swelling the Seco and Parkers creeks again. Water once more filled basements. In D'Hanis, bridges over the streams had been improved, allowing water to pass more freely under them. In the Divide country, a storm dumped more heavy rains, which spread to nearby Tarpley and Utopia. The storm caused D'Hanis and Sabinal residents to listen to the rumbling thunder with apprehension. At Utopia, more than one inch fell within minutes with such noise that the telephone operator could not be "heard over the pounding of water on the roof of the exchange."[13] The *San Antonio Express* stated that D'Hanis residents were "looking the while askance as storm clouds were gathering on the horizon."[14] Hondo recorded four inches, and the Hondo Creek there reached a fifteen-foot level, as rainfall was heavier to the north.

May Rainfall Summary

Hondo's rainfall reports date back to 1880. Based on them, May's 22.40-inch total set a new record. The previous highest May total was 13.15 inches in 1913. The *Hondo Anvil Herald* noted that, "not only is the May 1935 record phenomenal in that respect, but it exceeds the entire annual precipitation over many years of record."[15]

In May 1935 San Antonio recorded its greatest one-month rainfall total so far—14.07 inches, approximately 11 inches over normal. Rain fell in the city on twenty-one days. For the year through May, San Antonio had gauged 22.08 inches, 10.74 inches above average.

Perspective

A week after the flood at D'Hanis, the *Uvalde Leader News* reported that "Ranchmen in country north of D'Hanis were warned 20 years ago that a flood, such as that which brought death and destruction in that town late last week would sweep the town, by C. J. Richarz, pioneer resident of this section." Richarz was born near D'Hanis eighty-three years earlier and had spent his entire life in Medina County. "Twenty years ago, I made a visit to that part of the country," he recalled, "and found places in the Seco Creek, where I had often fished as a boy, had grown up in trees and underbrush. I told some of my friends at that time that unless the creek bed was cleared of this obstruction that some day a rise would occur in the stream and send the water over the town. When such a great amount of water falls as it did north of D'Hanis last week, it should have an unobstructed flow in the stream, else there will be lots of damage."[16]

Richarz also added, "It might be a long time coming, but these cloudbursts often fall in this country, and if one should ever fall north of the city, you would see lots of the homes and business houses under water, unless the creek beds are kept clean so the water can rush through unimpeded."[17]

JUNE 1935

~~~~~~~~~~

Llano and Nueces Rivers Floods

FOLLOWING THE RECORD deluge at D'Hanis in May 1935, more heavy rain continued to fall in the Hill Country. Less than a month after the inundation in D'Hanis, another storm triggered multiple flash floods in the Hill Country. In June 1935 the bull's-eye of the heavy precipitation was in and around Edwards County in the Divide area, along the headwaters of the South Llano, the Frio, and the Nueces rivers. The upper reaches of these rivers have little stream-flow for most of the year, but in June 1935 the substantial rains in the Edwards County region triggered overflows that roared from the craggy canyons of the Hill Country to the flat plains of the Texas Gulf Coast. These flash floods and their subsequent inundations provided some of the most memorable photographs in the documentation of Texas rivers and weather events.

Spring Weather Conditions

The drought that dominated the Hill Country weather in 1933 and 1934 continued into the winter of 1934 and the early spring of 1935. In the spring of 1935, dust storms ravaged the Great Plains of the United States, and on April 14, 1935, infamously known as "Black Sunday," they blanketed the Texas Panhandle. Dust storms also dipped into the Hill Country that spring. The *Junction Eagle* reported that a "sandstorm swept down and brought misery to everyone" in March of 1935.[1] Relief from the drought and dust storms in the Hill Country began in April, when showers dropped more than two inches of rain in Hondo, Rocksprings, and Junction.

By mid-May, Hill Country newspapers were praising the change in the weather pattern. After more than two inches of rain fell in less than one hour on May 15 in Llano, the *Llano News* noted that "one of the hardest rains in many years fell."[2] Coupled with the rains of the previous weeks, the intense downpours pushed the Llano River to overflow the dam at Llano.

The May 23 edition of the *Junction Eagle* commented, "Good rains throughout the Hill Country during the month of May have put new life into farming and ranching interests of this section. It has been almost two years since enough rain has fallen in Kimble County to put a good season in the ground."[3] Junction's rainfall total through the morning of May 23 was 8.07 inches, which was more than 2 inches greater than its total from January through April of 1935. Areas north and northeast of Rocksprings reported 7 inches in late May.

For the first time in two years, muddy roads affected travel in the Hill Country. All over Texas, "dust bowls were turned into mud puddles," announced the *Fredericksburg Standard*.[4] Hill Country rivers sprang back to life after the rains. In late May high water on the West Nueces River blocked traffic between Rocksprings and Brackettville. Streamflow statistics from the Nueces River at Laguna reflected the change in weather conditions from March to May. In March the Nueces River at Laguna averaged

Llano River in flood at Junction (courtesy of the Kimble County Historical Museum).

Llano River in flood at Junction (courtesy of the Kimble County Historical Museum).

22 cfs per day; in May, it leaped to an average of 868 cfs per day.

Storm Characteristics

During the second week of June, the welcome spring showers ballooned into deluges. On June 14 torrential rains fell at Junction and Rocksprings. The latter, with an average yearly precipitation of 22.42 inches, received 9.50 inches on June 14, 1935, while Junction received 6.10 inches on the same date. The area southwest of Rocksprings, in the upper reaches of the West Nueces, received more than 16 inches of rain during the week of June 9–15. Representatives of the USGS, who were gathering data on the flood, discovered that the cans and buckets they ordinarily used to measure rainfall "were filled, running over, and some were washed away."[5]

The area southeast of Junction, near Segovia and Noxville, received more than 18 inches that same week. Those rains fell on the headwaters of the James River and Johnson Fork Creek. On the night of June 13 a location seven miles southeast of Segovia received 10 inches in twelve hours. Farther downstream, Mason, Castell, and Llano recorded between 6 and 10 inches of precipitation.

Flood on the Llano River

With heavy rains falling in the North and South Llano rivers' headwaters and two major tributaries, James River and Johnson Fork Creek, the Llano River rose to record levels. In Junction, the North Llano River reached 28 feet with a peak discharge of 46,700 cfs, while the South Llano River rose to 43 feet with a peak discharge of 319,000 cfs. The level of the latter was three feet higher than in the 1889 flood, its previous record flood at Junction.

The June 14 flood severely damaged tourist camps along the Llanos. Soldiers from Fort Sam Houston in San Antonio who were camping on the South Llano River rescued approximately thirty-five people at Kimble Courts in Junction. Judge J. B. Randolph, who owned a resort on the South Llano that lost seven cabins in the flood, worked with operators from Southwestern Bell to warn the residents of Kimble County. Thanks in part to their efforts, the Llano flood left no human casualties there.

Downstream of Junction, at Hedwigs Hill, the Llano River swept away a "new $115,000 concrete and steel bridge, the pride of the Hill Country." The peak occurred around 9 A.M., when the Llano River reached a stage of 43 feet.[6] At Camp Littlefield, which was owned by former University of Texas head football coach Clyde Littlefield, the flood left only three of twelve cabins intact.

At Castell the flood came in two peaks. One hit Castell at 1 P.M. on June 14, about the same time the Llano at Junction was peaking. The first flood wave washed out the bridge at Castell. The second peak arrived late at night, between 10 P.M. and midnight.

At Llano, the large, eight-hundred-foot bridge built in 1892 was in the path of the rising floodwaters. On the morning of June 14, police at Llano were permitting only one lane of traffic over the bridge as a precaution, although, as the *Austin Statesman* reported, "It was believed the bridge was not in any immediate danger."[7]

Like the bridges at Hedwigs Hill and Castell, the one at Llano did not survive the

Highway bridge at Junction after the flood (courtesy of the Kimble County Historical Museum).

Llano River Basin

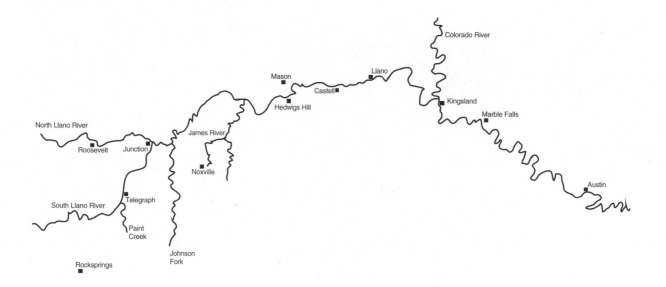

LLANO RIVER DISCHARGE, JUNE 14–15, 1935

DATE	TIME	NORTH LLANO STAGE	NORTH LLANO DISCHARGE	LLANO RIVER AT JUNCTION STAGE	LLANO RIVER AT JUNCTION DISCHARGE	LLANO RIVER AT CASTELL STAGE	LLANO RIVER AT CASTELL DISCHARGE
June 14	3:00 A.M.	2.44	474	3.33	1,400	5.4	
	4:00 A.M.	3.4	1130			8.6	11,500
	5:00 A.M.			4	2,150		
	6:00 A.M.	8.3	10,700	9	11,300	16	45,800
	7:00 A.M.	13.9	25,600	17	37,400		
	8:00 A.M.	15.35	30,000	29	123,000	25.4	149,000
	9:00 A.M.	16.3	32,800	37	221,000		
	10:00 A.M.	17.6	36,900	41	282,000	33.4	305,000
	11:00 A.M.	19	41,600	42.9	312,000		
	12:00 A.M.	20.5	46,700	43.3	319,000	36.8	383,000
	1:00 A.M.	20.5	46,700	42.8	311,000	37	388,000
	2:00 A.M.	19	41,600	41.2	285,000	36.3	371,000
	4:00 A.M.	14.3	26,700	36.6	215,000	33.4	305,000
	6:00 A.M.	12.35	21,300	29.6	130,000	30.6	243,000
	8:00 A.M.	12.5	21,600	22	65,200	31.4	260,000
	10:00 P.M.	12.2	20,800	17.7	40,600	35.7	357,000
	12 midnight	10.4	15,900	15.6	31,800	35.7	357,000
June 15	2:00 A.M.	9.1	12,600			32.6	287,000
	4:00 A.M.	8	10,000	13.1	22,900	28	192,000
	6:00 A.M.	6.95	7,700			21.7	98,200
	8:00 A.M.			11.4	17,800	18.7	66,900
	12 noon	4.72	2,860	10.2	14,400	15.1	39,700
	12 midnight	3.2	972	7.2	7,350	9.6	14,400

Stages in Feet
Discharge in cubic feet/second

incessant pounding of the waters. Residents lined up on both sides of the river to view the swell. They witnessed the power of the Llano River as it ripped away the steel spans of the bridge, creating a chasm in the community of Llano. Later in the day, a second flood wave, approximately three feet greater than the first, passed through the town, according to the *Llano News*. If the first wave had not already taken out the bridge, the second one would have.

The savage Llano emptied into the Colorado River at Kingsland. Fed by the enormous discharge from the Llano, the Colorado River followed the lead of the Llano River by wiping out a bridge. At 3:55 P.M. the bridge over the Colorado at Marble Falls tumbled into the river. Downstream on the Colorado, especially at Austin, the flood watch was on.

Nueces River Streamflow

While the Llano River was ripping away bridges and reaching record heights, the West Nueces River was setting hydrological records not only for Texas but also for the United States. The June 14, 1935, edition of the *Rocksprings Record* told of rises on nearby rivers and implied that conditions could be worse. The previous night, storms had knocked out telephone connections from Rocksprings to Camp Wood and from Rocksprings to parties along the Brackettville Road. The first news of the devastation along the West Nueces came from an area rancher who reported, as did others, that the West Nueces was anywhere from seventy to eighty feet high.

Ironically, the June 14 edition of the *Rocksprings Record* noted in its rain log for June 12

Bridge at Marble Falls col-
lapsed during the flood
(courtesy of the LCRA
Corporate Archives:
W00892, W00891,
W00893).

RAINFALL TOTALS (IN INCHES) DURING THE JUNE 1935 STORM

	JUNE 1–8	JUNE 9	JUNE 10	JUNE 11	JUNE 12	JUNE 13	JUNE 14	JUNE 15	JUNE 16	JUNE 17	JUNE 18
Austin	5.43	0	0	0	0.02	2.01	0.18	1.18	1.02	0	0
Blanco	1.99	0	0	0	0	1.42	0.76	2.11	0.76	0	0
Burnet	2.34	0	0	0.03	0.59	0.51	2.7	0.43	0	0	0
Cameron	1.11	0	0	0	0.23	0.32	0.27	1	0	0.47	0.94
Junction	2.66	0	1.55	0.76	0.4	0.1	6	0	0	0	0.85
Kerrville	1.27	0	0.68	0.48	0.12	1.79	2.47	3.9	0.03	0	0
Lampasas	2.66	0	0	0	0	0.56	0.58	1.46	0.47	0	0
Llano	2.8	0	0	0.16	0.02	2.15	1.3	3.23	0.03	0	0
New Braunfels	0.37	0	0.4	0.03	0.82	1.27	0.16	1.02	0	0	0
Rocksprings	1.6	0	0	1.3	0.5	0.75	9.5	0	0	0	0.45
San Marcos	2.12	0	0	0	0	0.85	0.95	0.51	0.35	0	0
Taylor	2.47	0	0	0	0	0.39	0.73	0.89	1.36	0	0.02
Temple	2.61	0	0	0	0	0.27	0.64	1.2	1.9	0	0
Uvalde	0.51	0.73	0.4	0.5	1.27	1.32	0.2	0	0	0	0

that "ranchmen report this to be the best rain that has fallen over the county in many years, coming as it has, slow and steady, soaking the ground thoroughly, and it is freely conceded that the best season in many years is apparent all over the range country in the section of the southwest."[8] A week later, the June 21 edition of the same paper encouraged area residents to persevere through the disaster: "No telling what the damage will amount to in dollars and cents in this prosperous ranching section, they all are glad that they got out with their lives, never thinking of the damage. They have the Western spirit, and will immediately get to work to remove all scars of the awful flood of 1935."[9]

Because there were no gauging stations on the West Nueces—and if there were, they would probably have been destroyed—the USGS performed a field study to gather basin information and apply the slope-area method to calculate the discharge. The results from the study were record setting. The USGS scientists computed the discharge at a point twenty-eight miles north of Brackettville to be 580,000 second-feet from an area of 402 square miles, or equal to a discharge of 1,440 second-feet per square mile. According to USGS Water Supply Paper 796, this computed discharge "exceeds any rates known previously for areas of similar size." It also reported that "No one could be found who had ever heard of a flood that was comparable in extreme magnitude with this one."[10] As the Nueces and its neighbor, the Frio River, tore through the remote canyons, neighboring towns feared for residents in Camp Wood, Barksdale, Reagan Wells, and Leakey.

West Nueces and Nueces River basins

Rebuilding bridges at crossing of Nueces south of Uvalde (courtesy of the El Paso Progeso Library, Uvalde, Texas).

When the Uvalde Chamber of Commerce appealed to military bases in San Antonio for assistance, Brooks Air Force Base dispatched a plane on June 15 to survey the area and drop supplies. The flight crew reported that the signals sent from the ground by residents of Leakey, Camp Wood, and Reagan Wells indicated "we need nothing."[11] An earlier report of eight people

dead at Reagan Wells was incorrect, as was a report that all residents of Leakey had to gather in the courthouse to avoid the rushing waters. On June 18 the Camp Wood area received an airdrop of food for fifty families who were isolated by washed-out roads.

On June 14 at 11 A.M., the Nueces River above the mouth of the West Nueces was flowing 26 feet deep with a streamflow of

Railroad bridge during flood in Austin (The San Antonio Light Collection, UTSA's Institute of Texan Cultures, No. L-0613-N).

213,000 cfs (about 3 feet under the flood level of June 1913). The record flood from the West Nueces then joined the near-record inundation on the Nueces. At its next gauging station (near Uvalde), the Nueces spiked from a 5.80-foot stage with a streamflow of 6,900 cfs at 4 A.M. on June 14 to a 36.9-foot stage with a streamflow of 616,000 cfs twelve hours later, including a 13.6-foot and a 461,000-cfs jump between 3 and 4 P.M. A highway engineer assigned to that section of the state said, "There is no possible way to describe the mountains of water rolling down the river. I believe every highway between Uvalde and the Texas coast will be swept away. The greatness of the flood is beyond imagination."[12]

The five-span steel railroad bridge eight miles west of Uvalde was swept away "like so much paper," according to the *San Antonio Express*.[13] Farther downstream, ten miles southwest of Uvalde, the Nueces took out the Uvalde–Crystal City highway bridge and the Missouri Pacific bridge. At a ranch twelve miles southwest of Uvalde, waters reached a house that was hundreds of yards from the river and had never been touched by floods in its sixty years of existence. The river carried away the house, barn, and animal pens. The only structure left standing was a windmill, which had a mark that "indicated the water reached a depth of 23 feet there, making the total depth 45 feet."[14]

At Cotulla, authorities removed the river-monitoring station to prevent it from being washed away. Observers monitored the flood discharge and stage readings by a staff gage and high-water marks. On June 18 the Nueces at Cotulla reached its all-time high stage: 32.4 feet. By the time it peaked at Three Rivers, it was within 1.5 feet of its record stage set in 1919.

Colorado River Streamflow

Following the news of the havoc in the Hill Country, the *Austin American* warned of impending currents "carrying the wreckage of at least three major bridges."[15] Authorities predicted the Colorado would rise to 35 feet, which was 8 feet shy of the record July 1869 flood. The floodwaters arrived late at night on June 14 and continued for several days. At 10 P.M. on June 14, the Colorado at Austin was 4.8 feet deep. Within two hours, it had risen almost 10 feet. By noon on June 15 the river had surpassed its predicted 35-foot level and was pushing the 40-foot mark.

The Congress Avenue bridge (or viaduct, as many people called it) was closed throughout June 14. The only means of shipping food and supplies across the river

Flooding in Austin: Two views, looking south on Congress Avenue (Austin History Center, Austin Public Library, Photo ID: C09065 [top]; LCRA Corporate Archives: W00894 [bottom]).

AVERAGE DAILY DISCHARGE, JUNE 1–20, 1935

	JUNE 1	JUNE 2	JUNE 3	JUNE 4	JUNE 5	JUNE 6	JUNE 7	JUNE 8	JUNE 9
Nueces River at Laguna	885	711	1,300	622	1,780	1,240	732	589	498
North Llano River at Junction	114	576	162	128	8,710	606	237	155	127
South Llano River at Junction	365	890	359	342	11,800	2,840	836	850	504
Llano River at Castell	752	752	752	752	3,270	10,600	2,690	1,380	562
Colorado River at Austin	7,630	8,440	7,900	14,000	14,600	25,400	43,400	29,800	20,500
Colorado River at Smithville	8,370	1,7800	8,540	7,280	14,900	16,600	27,500	36,500	26,700
Colorado River at Columbus	7,350	11,000	16,700	11,800	9,830	15,400	18,100	26,800	34,100

Discharge in cubic feet/second

AVERAGE MONTHLY DISCHARGE, JUNE 1934–JULY 1935

	1934						
	JUNE	JULY	AUG.	SEPT.	OCT.	NOV.	DEC.
Nueces at Laguna	27	16	11	9	9	8	10
South Llano at Junction	41	35	29	30	30	41	45
North Llano at Junction	3	0	0	0	0	0	1
Llano at Castell	40	22	12	33	25	43	52
Colorado at Austin	259	1,228	186	241	58	654	269

Discharge in cubic feet/second

Intersection of South Congress and Barton Springs Road, June 15, 1935 (Austin History Center, Austin Public Library, Photo ID: C090981).

JUNE 10	JUNE 11	JUNE 12	JUNE 13	JUNE 14	JUNE 15	JUNE 16	JUNE 17	JUNE 18	JUNE 19	JUNE 20
444	459	1,060	12,600	107,000	12,100	3,780	2,600	2,030	1,700	1,520
287	530	2,050	647	34,300	5,430	646	403	625	436	274
650	895	427	465	124,000	15,700	3,310	1,400	1,420	1,430	813
562	562	562	562	216,000	84,700	7,940	3,690	1,780	1,190	1,060
10,800	6,500	4,970	8,840	13,700	323,000	143,000	81,200	57,500	32,400	17,900
19,000	9,840	5,940	7,860	17,800	29,000	219,000	184,000	101,000	60,500	28,400
25,800	18,400	11,800	7,550	7,550	14,400	27,900	58,700	116,000	164,000	123,000

			1935			
JAN.	FEB.	MARCH	APRIL	MAY	JUNE	JULY
14	19	22	24	868	5407	392
45	50	52	61	414	5,797	251
6	17	11	20	78	1,938	75
56	133	72	74	2602	11,628	408
331	1,688	364	1,797	20,328	31,939	3,449

was via the railroad bridge, which spanned the river upstream of the Congress Avenue bridge and downstream of the battered Austin Dam. Railroad personnel accompanied the loads over the swirling, "nerve-destroying" waters, which had risen to a level only several feet below the tracks.[16]

Like their Hill Country neighbors, Austinites found flood watching a preferred pastime. On a day of "hazards and rumors," police struggled to keep bystanders out of situations "that meant certain death by drowning." Periodically, rumors that the Austin Dam had broken spread through the crowd. These reports were followed by a "wild reckless dashing of autos to the water front."[17] As it turned out, the Austin Dam did not collapse, as it had in 1900, but it did lose the western and center sections of its superstructure in the early morning hours of June 15. The water flowed 11 feet deep over the dam. The deep flow carried Armin Ritter's houseboat over the dam in one piece, pro-

viding the spectacular icon used for years to symbolize floods on the Colorado. Around 4 P.M. the river crested at 41.2 feet, just under a foot short of the record set in 1869.

In Austin the water carried away camp houses along the river's floodplain from Deep Eddy and Barton Creek to Montopolis. At the intersection of Riverside and Congress, the water carved out a 3-foot-deep section of pavement for 30–40 feet. At Zilker Park the flood deposited waist-deep piles of logs. In addition, while standing in waist-high floodwater at his house, the caretaker at Barton Springs reported, "Barton Creek is raging like a June bride who's just been stood up at the altar."[18]

Jack Specht, ace photographer for the *San Antonio Light,* recorded his impression of the flood in Austin: "A mighty yellow flood was sweeping over the dam, carrying away its super-structure and tumbling into a huge whirlpool just below. In the maelstrom were trees, logs, portions of dwellings and other

Houseboat over the Austin Dam (Austin History Center, Austin Public Library, Photo ID: C08484-A).

debris. There were waves six feet high and an awe-inspiring yellow spray was leaping 15 to 20 feet into the air."[19]

On its journey to the coast, the Colorado River threatened Bastrop, Smithville, La Grange, and Columbus. The Highway 71 bridge at Bastrop survived a 57-foot stage. At La Grange the river reached a stage of 51 feet, flooding the city to within half a block of the courthouse. The discharge of 255,000 cfs placed this swell behind only the mammoth 1869 and 1913 floods on the lower Colorado River. At Columbus the river broke through the levees, flooding ten square blocks of the town.

Hill Country Destruction

The June flood of 1935 extensively damaged the pecan-growing regions of the

Looking upriver from the fire tower (Austin History Center, Austin Public Library, Photo ID: PICA 04129).

From a Great Flood
Composed by Reverend
William Franklin
Saturday, June 15, 1935
514 West Annie Street,
Austin, Texas

I heard the people saying up in the tree,
Come somebody and save poor me,
From a great flood.

Chorus:
There was a great flood on the Colorado
    Stream,
The cattle was [sic] lowing, the children were
    crying,
Mother was saying my friends are dying,
From a great flood.

2.
I heard the people saying I thought it was a
    shame,
Look at the houses coming over the Dam,
From a great flood.

3.
I heard the women saying, we hafter cry,
Look at the people about to die,
From a great flood.

4.
I heard the laws saying I just declare,
We sent messages from everywhere,
About a great flood.

5.
I heard the women saying, I couldn't see but I
    ask the Lord to save poor me,
From flood on the Colorado stream.

6.
I heard the people saying I just say, I heard of
    a store called Cash and Carry,
And the Lord say I cash up and carry away,
In a great flood on the Colorado stream.

7.
I heard a great sound, I looked down the river,
And the Montopolis bridge went down,
From a great flood on the Colorado stream.

8.
I heard the people saying, I was warned, I was
    not at home,
But my house was gone,
From a great flood on the Colorado stream.

9.
I heard a woman say, all I have is gone,
But the good "Lord Is My Shepard and I Shall
    Not Want." [20]

Looking north on Congress Avenue (Austin History Center, Austin Public Library, Photo ID: PICA 20060).

watersheds. Llano County reported a $5 million loss to pecan timber and produce alone. Altogether Llano County's damage was estimated at $5.74 million. [21]

In the early 1930s the state of Texas began a multimillion-dollar program to build bridges above the average flood lines of streams. Unfortunately, the extreme overflows of June 1935 reached unprecedented heights and swept away two of the recently built bridges—the $203,000 structure outside Uvalde and the $115,000 Hedwigs Hill bridge. The *San Antonio Express* commented on the failed bridges in that flood:

In its consistent efforts to eliminate the notation, "Impassable on account of high water," from Texas road condition reports, the State Highway Commission has lately spent

many million[s of] dollars on new bridges all sturdily built and raised above the average flood line. . . . The outcome was a system of "high-water" bridges which, though still unfinished, was unsurpassed anywhere. Apparently Texas was well on the way to creating a system of roads which would be open when needed most—during a flood or in the wake of a storm. However, within the past few days, stages ranging from 20 to 50 feet have challenged the engineer anew. A 50-foot flood in the Llano River swept away the $115,000 steel and concrete structure near Mason. A 30-foot rise in the Nueces carried the steel span of the $203,000 bridge near Uvalde. The 550-foot steel railroad bridge there crumpled up.[22]

The *Dallas Morning News* used the flood as an opportunity to state its opinions on federal policy of that era:

It does seem as though the Weather Bureau at Washington, and its local representatives scattered throughout the country, should exercise more common sense and develop a better system in the regulation of rain. Last year the whole Nation besought Jupiter Pluvius to be kindlier and to let up on drouths and sand storms. No attention was given to those petitions. Under the new deal Washington had assumed control of the Nation's welfare and it was expected that this year at least its officials would dole out a due proportion of rain, fairly distributed over the whole of the United States. Instead of that, ever since the decision of the Supreme Court, the weather bureau has shown a vindictive spirit and has deluged the Middlewest and the Southwest with destructive floods. . . .

Congress Avenue viaduct during the flood (Austin History Center, Austin Public Library, Photo ID: PICA 13083).

Two views of the Congress Avenue viaduct (LCRA Corporate Archives: W00330 [top]; Austin History Center, Austin Public Library, Photo ID: C09066 [bottom]).

Secretary Wallace . . . should at once use his influence at Washington to have Jupiter Pluvius put under arrest for at least sixty days. Possibly Jim Farley reorganized the personnel of the weather bureau and mixed things up. If only he were in Uvalde at this time he would see the need of having experienced men in charge. Let him speak to Vice-President Garner about it.[23]

The 1935 flood prompted the federal government to accelerate the approval process for more flood-control dams along the Colorado River. Congressman J. P. Buchanan from Central Texas demonstrated that the losses from one flood equaled the whole cost of the Colorado River Authority con-

servation program. The price tag for completion of the Buchanan Dam was set at $4.5 million, $1.2 million less than the damage in nearby Llano County alone.

Summing Up

The recovery period for the flood-ravaged areas varied greatly. In Llano, a stressful fifteen-month stretch without a permanent high-water bridge in town forced residents from the two sides of the river to realize their dependence on one another. In Junction several weeks later, ranchers who were flooded out of their houses spoke fondly of the beneficial rains, which rejuvenated the rangeland.

DECEMBER 1935

~~~~~~~

Downtown Houston Flood

FOR TEXAS WEATHER, one of the wildest years ever was 1935. That spring, dust storms wreaked havoc on much of the state. A U.S.-record-intensity rainfall hit D'Hanis in May; the Colorado River Basin experienced record floods in June; and West Texas received more heavy rains in September. Nevertheless, the year still had another extreme event to unleash on the Lone Star State—this time it focused on the Houston area and the region well east of the Hill Country.

Six years earlier, in May 1929, floods gushed through the bayous that normally meander through Houston. Buffalo Bayou flowed three feet over the Waugh Drive bridge and reached out of the banks near Sam Houston Hall. White Oak Bayou lapped over the bridge on Heights Boulevard.

Rains

The December 1935 rains started on the night of December 6 and continued through December 8. The downpour covered all of Harris County and the eastern part of the state. The Houston area alone received between 5 and 17 inches. In northwestern Harris County, Satsuma reported 16.49 inches, while Hillendahl, approximately ten miles west of Houston, reported more than 10 inches. From December 6 to December 8, Richmond reported 10.25 inches, and Sugarland 9.41 inches.

Houston Bayous

With heavy rains pouring into the bayous and waterways above Houston, flood waves moved down Buffalo and White Oak bayous, steering the runoff from the west and northwest sections of the city toward central and downtown Houston. White Oak Bayou at the Yale Street bridge rose four feet higher than during the 1929 flood. After sheets of rain fell on the night of December 6, creeks and bayous inundated the low-lying areas west of Houston Heights and the Airline Farms community. When White Oak Bayou overflowed its banks, West Heights and Shady Acres were inundated.

Water usually flowed forty feet below the bottom of the Heights Boulevard and Yale Street bridges. During the flood, White Oak Bayou covered both of these bridges in addition to those at Shepherd Drive, Taylor Street, and Houston Avenue. As Buffalo and White Oak bayous rose beyond the 1929 marks, one flood refugee noted, "God only knows when the waters will stop rising."[1] Buffalo Bayou rose more than seven feet above previously recorded floods.

Director G. L. Fugate of the city's water department had surveyed earlier floods and said that the water level at 10 P.M. on December 8 at the Capitol Avenue bridge was rising at four inches per hour and was already six feet six inches deeper than during the 1929 flood. The inundation peaked at 40.3 feet between 3 and 4 A.M. on December 9. The flow exceeded that of any other flood in the city's history and was nearly twice as great as that of 1929.

More than fifteen blocks of the business district south of Buffalo Bayou were covered

Images from the 1929 and 1935 floods in downtown Houston (courtesy Houston Metropolitan Research Center, Houston Public Library).

with anywhere from a few inches to twelve feet of water. More than one hundred blocks of the residential section along Buffalo and White bayous were overwhelmed by the currents.

Downtown Houston

As the bayous rose, Houston's downtown merchants feared a repetition of the 1929 flood—or worse. Businesspeople along Commission Row moved their goods off the shelves and to higher ground. As the water climbed, the *Houston Post* reported that "Houston was left virtually an island in a vast inland sea."[2] The chair of the local chapter of the American Red Cross said, "It is developing into a disaster such as we have never known in Houston."[3]

At midnight on December 8, the floodwater was midway up Austin Street to Franklin Avenue. One area (Travis and Milam) near City Hall resembled "a millrace as the waters boiled with a swift current that reached within 30 feet of Travis Street."[4] Water was a foot deep at Texas Avenue and Travis Street, while four-foot-deep currents swirled in the fire station at Bagby and Walker. A veritable lake six blocks wide covered Sam Houston Park and the surrounding area. The basement of city hall was flooded, but the municipal records were removed to save them from damage or destruction. The *Houston Post* stated that floodwaters reached the northwest corner of the city hall apparently for the first time in the building's history. During the night, water was approximately 1.5 feet deep in the basement.

Even though Houston-area residents lived in a climate with more rain than their Central or West Texas counterparts, they participated in flood watching like their fellow Texans to the west. The Main Street viaduct was closed at 5 P.M. on December 8 because of congested traffic conditions, as police ordered the viaduct vacated. The December 9 edition of the *Houston Post* described the scene: "All Houston turned out Sunday afternoon and night to watch the waters of Buffalo Bayou creep steadily up-

ward. Thousands of automobiles and tens of thousands of pedestrians milled along the edges of the downtown flooded area, creating a traffic problem that at times defied all efforts of police to untangle." Police officers roped off the inundated streets, but the crowds pushed against the ropes. The *Houston Post* stated, "Houstonians apparently regarded the flood as a spectacle and all who could rode or walked to the edge of the inundated district, paralyzing traffic and hampering relief workers as well as creating the possibility of a real hazard in the event of a fire."[5]

Accounts

A Houston man rescued twenty-one marooned people from the second-floor windows of their homes in the Post Oak Road vicinity of Bray's Bayou. He said that one of the hardest things was to persuade a few of the stranded residents to leave their homes even though the water was creeping up to the second story. He told them, "Come with us or stay there and drown. . . . That usually brought them out."[6] He reported that grand pianos, radios, and tables could be seen floating around the houses.

One survivor recalled her experience: "I crawled across the board over the water. When I reached the other end of the board and got on firm ground I began walking away. I happened to hear a great rending crash and looked back. My house was shaking as though a giant was pushing it. Then, it suddenly slipped from its foundations and began drifting downstream."[7]

The flood presented an opportunity for some. A number of young boys swam into the water to retrieve objects—women's gloves, Panama hats, and so on—before the items floated away and then sold them to spectators. One recently transplanted Houstonian said, "I think I'll go back to

Oklahoma, where it never rains. I believe I can stand a drought better than a flood."[8]

Aftermath

High water, strong currents, and fire brought destruction to downtown buildings. The floodwaters undermined several structures, and a three-story brick edifice belonging to the Wholesale Specialty Company at 801 Commerce Avenue partially collapsed. The *Houston Post* reported, "No trace of it could be seen above the water."[9]

At 9:36 P.M. on December 9, police and workers in the lower reaches of Commerce Street were startled by a rumbling noise followed by a loud splash. Water cascaded high into the air when a building wall north of the Milam Street bridge caved in. Initially it was feared that the bridge itself had collapsed. At the Smith Street bridge, water over the structure "snapped off" light standards "like cheese straws." Two small frame houses were also lodged against the structure.[10]

The floodwaters found their way into three hotels: the Brazos, the Auditorium, and the Macatee. The Brazos and the Audi-

DAILY PRECIPITATION (IN INCHES) FOR DECEMBER 1935

	DEC. 1	DEC. 2	DEC. 3	DEC. 4	DEC. 5
Alvin					1.05
Beaumont				0.06	
Brenham				0.11	trace
College Station		0.32			0.33
Cuero				0.7	0.35
Freeport					
Galveston	trace		0.02	trace	trace
Hempstead					
Houston	trace		0.03		trace
Houston Airport				trace	trace
Richmond				0.05	
Sealy	0.02				
Sugarland			0.06	0.01	0.02

Will Houston Forget?

In 1929, when waters of a disastrous flood swirled through business and residential sections of Houston, driving people from their homes, exacting a toll of three lives and causing heavy property damage, there was an insistent demand that something be done to prevent similar disasters in the future.

Engineers and citizens interested in flood control warned against the danger of future overflows and pointed out that encroachment of business buildings along the banks of Buffalo Bayou had created new hazards which did not exist during the 20 years Houston was immune to floods prior to 1929.

But unfortunately the public outcry for flood prevention subsided almost as quickly as the waters receded. In a few months, the damage was repaired and the flood was forgotten.

Will Houston forget again?

If aggressive steps had been taken after the 1929 flood, the disaster from which Houston is emerging today might have been prevented. At least the damage could have been reduced greatly.

We should not forget that the elements were kind in the present emergency. Another day of heavy rainfall would have sent the flood water to Main Street. Two days of heavy rain probably would have inundated a large part of the principal business section.

Will we ignore this second expensive warning?

Houston is not the only city in Texas which has been menaced by floods or other acts of God, of course, but it is one of the very few which have failed to take steps to protect themselves against predictable disasters.

San Antonio was ravaged by a very serious flood some years ago. As a result of that disaster, a flood control system has been set up which has prevented similar overflows.

In 1900 Galveston virtually was wiped out by a hurricane. Its citizens, with the aid of the Federal government, built a seawall which has protected the Island City effectively against subsequent visitations.

Houston should delay no longer in making plans for flood prevention. It is a matter in which both the city and county governments must co-operate. It is not sufficient to widen the narrow course of Buffalo Bayou through the heart of the city, so that flood waters may drain more quickly. It is necessary also to work out a system of rural drainage which will carry off heavy rainfall without pouring the waters into the bayou inside the city limits or west of the city. This phase of the program must be handled by the county government.

The second Houston flood has demonstrated again how easily Houston's water system can be crippled by high water. It should be clear now that this vital part of the city's water system must be moved to higher ground.

Houston should not tolerate the flood menace longer. Steps should be taken immediately to work out a system of flood prevention and to provide water facilities capable of meeting the city's needs under any conditions.

We must not forget again, as we did in 1929. (*Houston Post*, December 10, 1935)

DEC. 6	DEC. 7	DEC. 8	DEC. 9	DEC. 10	DEC. 11	DEC. 12	DEC. 13	DEC. 14	TOTAL
1.96	2.1				1	0.32			6.43
	0.15	3.48			0.2	0.86			4.75
0.32	2.3	1.47	0.01	0.01	0.88	0.49			5.59
2.8	0.2		0.05	0.25					3.95
0.15	1.7	0.95	0.01	0.02	1.29	0.45			5.62
1.62	1.76		0.7	1.14	0.4				5.62
0.01	1.31	0.74		0.21	3.19			0.09	5.57
0.75	2.01	2.25			0.75	0.6			6.36
0.1	4.95	0.47		trace	1.24			trace	6.79
1.05	2.22	2.99		0.03	1.64	0.02		trace	7.95
trace	4.15	6.1		0.09	0.97	0.33			11.69
2.78	3.16				1.3			0.07	7.33
3.24	6.1	0.07		0.86	0.48				10.84

DOWNTOWN HOUSTON FLOOD

torium had four feet of water in their interiors, and forty-six guests found themselves marooned. On the night of December 8, Hans Nagel, the Hermann Park zookeeper, piloted a boat that was used to evacuate thirty-six guests. The receding waters revealed gaping holes that were three feet deep and twenty feet in diameter in the downtown streets.

Around 1:30 P.M. on December 8, a fire broke out at the Yellow Taxi Cab building at 510 Louisiana, when drivers attempted to move the cars out in order to escape the rising waters of Buffalo Bayou. Because of low water pressure, fire fighters were forced to use floodwater from the streets to douse the flames.

The flood made its way into the Sears Roebuck store to a depth of eight feet and caused damage estimated at $350,000. With Christmas season under way, the building was full of merchandise. Although many of the goods were moved out of the basement, some items remained there and on the first floor. A flood had hit the same location in 1929, when it created $250,000 worth of damage.

Two of the store's managers surveyed the destruction in a small boat and observed that water had come within two feet of the eighteen-foot ceiling. The field manager for the store said, "The loss to our store was great, but the loss to the city of Houston in prestige can hardly be estimated—I would place the loss at around $10 million. Unless something is done by the city and county to control future floods, large merchandising houses will hesitate to locate branches here in face of the adverse publicity which the city has received during the past few days. Few Northern or Western merchants know the true situation here and most of them think the whole town was flooded. A similar situation existed in San Antonio a few years back, but that city has put a flood

control project into operation. And it works."[11]

One of the managers—an engineer by profession—suggested that Houston dig a channel west of the city to link Buffalo Bayou with Chocolate Bayou; alternatively, he continued, the upper reaches of Buffalo Bayou could be dammed to control the flow. He criticized the city for building up a "bottleneck near the Farmers Market and Southern Pacific depot," which sent water into the vicinity of the Sears building. In addition, he commented about all of the drainage ditches: "For about 75 miles up the bayou there are many drainage ditches opening into it. Consequently flood waters pour into the bayou within 12 to 16 hours now, whereas they formerly flowed into the bayou in five or six days."[12] He added, "It would be impossible for us to construct a levee in front of the building for future protection, and unless the city does something to control floods in the future, we will be forced to move the present location and, perhaps, out of the city altogether." He added that Sears had not bought flood insurance after the 1929 inundation because the company had believed the city would undertake a flood-control project to alleviate the flooding problem.[13]

Comments on Flood Control

Like the Sears managers, Houston residents developed their own opinions on how to handle the flooding bayous. Most of them remembered the flood of 1929, as the *Houston Post* pointed out: "Constantly the warning has been sent out that what occurred in 1929 was likely to recur whenever the rainfall approximated that of 1929. And that's just what happened."[14]

One businessman said, "We are building a big city but unless some immediate atten-

	SEPTEMBER	OCTOBER	NOVEMBER	DECEMBER
Alvin	9.93	0	0	7.08
Beaumont	8.46	0.47	2.62	6.38
Brenham	5.65	1.4	4.03	6.97
College Station	5.98	2.03	3.04	4.83
Cuero	6.27	1.44	0.97	7.46
Freeport	12.36	5.39	1.37	9.03
Galveston	7.4	1.86	1.97	7.22
Hempstead	5.35	0.9	4.64	7.57
Houston	6.77	4.96	2.99	7.93
Houston Airport	6.62	3.25	1.46	9.59
Richmond	9.23	1.58	4.93	13.34
Sealy	6.36	5	4.35	8.75
Sugarland	7.51	6.98	5.35	12.24

tion is given to our water supply and flood control, the city can not continue to grow. This is the second big flood in six years and we certainly should not delay any longer." [15] Moreover, the Harris County auditor stated, "I have long thought that Houston's flood problem is related to drainage of the county as a whole. As the rural areas are settled and streams cleaned, the waters will be brought to Houston more quickly and with greater force than before." [16]

Mayor Oscar F. Holcombe proposed that the city study the feasibility of constructing a huge drainage ditch to connect Buffalo Bayou beyond the River Oaks addition and to circle the southern part of the city. Judge Ward criticized the restriction of the Buffalo Bayou channel by buildings and bridges: "When I was a boy there was sufficient low land on each side of the bayou to care for flood waters. While I'm not an engineer, it seems to me the congestion where downtown buildings have encroached on the bayou is responsible. The flood was a very deplorable occurrence and should not be permitted to happen again." [17]

One commissioner also weighed in on the discussion: "I think we ought to tear down the old brewery in the curve of the bayou, dredge out the bayou and straighten it in the downtown area, fill in the sinks along Buffalo Drive and dredge the channel in that area, and get the county to do something about the water which runs into Houston from beyond the city limits." [18]

One of the best-qualified Houston-area officials to express an opinion was the director of the City Water Department, G. L. Fugate, who recollected that, after the 1929 flood, he was laughed at for predicting a superflood such as the present one. He further commented on some of the flood-control proposals: "This flood was not unexpected. Information and rainfall and drainage conditions on Buffalo, White Oak and Bray's bayous, compiled several years ago, indicated that an 18-inch rain would result in a flood seven-feet higher than the 1929 disaster. I believe almost 18 inches of rain must have fallen on the Buffalo Bayou watershed because we certainly had the seven foot increase in the crest." [19]

Fugate added that diverting the water around Houston would not be feasible: "There isn't enough money in Texas to build a channel sufficient to carry off the flood waters that way. Besides, the water level in Clear Creek, which would be the only natural drainage into which the floodwaters of Buffalo Bayou could be diverted is very nearly that of Buffalo Bayou. You couldn't build a canal that would run only one way. There would be nothing to keep Clear Creek from draining into Buffalo Bayou in case of a flood of that stream. And the Clear Creek watershed is subject to the same rainfall as that of Buffalo Bayou." He recommended that the Buffalo Bayou channel be widened and straightened from San Jacinto Street to the ship channel and that a concrete channel be added, along with a terrace at the bayou banks west of the upper end of Memorial Park.[20]

In an editorial several days after the flood, the *Houston Post* urged the city to enact flood-prevention measures immediately: "Now is the time to push this project of flood control to a successful conclusion. The people right now are surely 'flood conscious.' If action is postponed, many of our citizens will be prone to forget the damage and the dangers of this disaster of 1935, just as they forgot about the losses of the 1929 flood."[21]

In another comment about the flood-prevention and monitoring effort, Houston weatherman C. E. Norquest said the city should erect a gage on Buffalo Bayou above downtown, possibly at River Oaks, to help give warning to the downtown area. He said, "I cannot understand why the city never has taken this simple precaution. There is no way of estimating how much good would have come of it if there had been such a gage at Buffalo Bayou which could have been checked Saturday [December 7]. It would be a simple matter for the city engineering department to erect an inexpensive gage—a wooden one would do—I am surprised that after the dreadful flood of 1929 it was not done."[22]

Houston Environs

North of Houston, a resident told the *Houston Post* that "flood conditions over the entire section with water from 10 inches to three feet deep prevailed over the entire section around Westfield, Spring and Aldine. I have lived here all my life and never have seen anything to compare with conditions here. Halls Bayou, Greens Bayou, Cypress Creek and Turkey Creek are spreading over many square miles as flood waters from the prairies of north Harris county came down these water courses tonight."[23]

At a sawmill near Cypress Creek (twenty miles northeast of Houston) thirty people were marooned. One man waded through waist-deep water from the camp and reported that everyone there was safe "They have ample lumber and workmen with which to construct a boat if needs be."[24]

Halls Bayou was almost a mile and a half wide over the Conroe-Houston highway near Little York. Greens Bayou, located a few miles farther north, was three feet over the road, forcing traffic to detour via Kuykendall Road. A resident of Little York said, "There is a solid sheet of water eight miles across reaching toward the Humble road. The roads are impassable. I have never seen anything like this before in my life."[25] Just south of Conroe, the San Jacinto River at the highway bridge was about two feet below the stringers of the new structure. Below Pasadena, the lowlands were inundated by floodwaters pouring out of Halls, Hunting, Greens, Carpenters, and Buffalo bayous. Ferry slips at Pasadena were under several feet of water. At the Market Street road crossing, the San Jacinto River was almost a mile wide.

South of Houston, a man died when he attempted to walk the railing of the West Bernard River bridge during a thirty-foot rise. He was swept to a tree and then drowned when he attempted to swim away from it. He had been on his way to visit his sweetheart near West Bernard, about two miles northwest of East Bernard. A man who saw the suitor clinging to the tree searched for a boat with which to rescue him, but the victim apparently tried to navigate the waters himself rather than wait for help. His clothes were found neatly tied to a branch of the tree.

~~

DOWNTOWN HOUSTON FLOOD

SEPTEMBER 1936

Concho River Flood

THERE ARE THOSE who might say that San Angelo owes some of its prosperity to a flash flood. In 1875 San Angelo was not chosen as county seat for Tom Green County. Instead, the smaller community of Ben Ficklin, five miles to the south along the South Concho River, was selected. On the night of August 23, 1882, heavy rains sent rising waters down the South Concho and its tributaries (Middle Concho River, Dove Creek, Spring Creek) above Ben Ficklin. The resulting flash flood destroyed most of the town and claimed the lives of sixty-five people. Following the event, the county seat was moved to San Angelo.

However, San Angelo's location caused it also to be prone to flash floods. The North Concho River winds its way from the northwest through the city, bordering the downtown area. At the southeastern edge of town, the South Concho joins the North Concho. In the 1930s only Lake Nasworthy had been built, and it was chiefly designed to supply water to the city, not to control floodwaters.

In September 1936 a series of heavy and sustained storms filled the San Angelo–area streams. Flash floods churned down the North Concho, Middle Concho, and South Concho rivers. San Angelo was unfortunately located in the path of all of these rises.

Precedent Conditions

Rainfall prior to the summer of 1936 for Central and West Texas was close to average. In June the central and western regions of Texas were 0.5–1.05 inches below average. In July, rainfall totals in most of the state were above normal. San Angelo, Paint Rock, and Substation 14 were all more than 1.5 inches above average for the month.

Texas' typical warm and dry August weather peaked on the twelfth. On that date, Seymour, in Baylor County, registered a 120-degree reading, which was the highest officially recorded temperature in the state's weather history. Throughout August, San Angelo recorded only 0.08 inches—1.90 below average. On September 13 a tropical storm moved inland over the lower Rio Grande Valley. Its slow northwestward trek produced a flow of moisture into the western half of the Lone Star State. Around September 15 the "gulf disturbance blew itself out" south of Corpus Christi.[1]

Rainfall

The big September rains began on the fourteenth in the San Angelo area and broke records that were more than fifty years old (many of which had been set during the 1882 Ben Ficklin flood). On the fifteenth, Veribest, Paint Rock, and San Angelo reported 10.1, 6.74, and 11.75 inches, respectively. Paint Rock added another 5.66 inches on the sixteenth. On September 17 and 18, another 4–8 inches fell in the San Angelo area, with the heaviest downpour unleashed north of the city. Water Valley reported 20.4 inches, while San Angelo received two heavy totals—4.64 inches on September 17 and 7.64 inches on September 18.

Deluges hit the Kerrville, Junction, Sonora, Menard, and Eldorado areas as well. Terrett Draw (ten miles south of Fort McKavett) received 21–25 inches between noon on September 15 and noon the next day. Kerrville reported more than 12 inches in the same period. Eldorado reported 14.2 inches on September 16. From September 14 to September 18 some locations near San Angelo exceeded their annual rainfall average. North of San Angelo, Carlsbad reported 28–30 inches, while Broome and Roosevelt tallied the same.

In January a San Angelo–area weather prognosticator had predicted that rains would fall on San Angelo between September 10 and 17. In the September 25 edition of the *San Angelo Evening Standard,* the forecaster was "ready to call off the rain dogs." He added, "There'll be no more flood here this year, despite the rumor that somebody else is reported to have said there'd be another one within 12 days of the first."[2] His second prediction missed as badly as his first prediction had been on target,

as rains fell in the San Angelo area and throughout North Texas during the last week of September. The precipitation was again heavy. Areas near Stiles and Sterling City reported more than ten inches on September 25 and 26.

More than 15 inches fell from September 25 through September 28 in North Central Texas at Kaufman and Hillsboro. Lampasas, Marble Falls, Burnet, and Fairland reported 6.5–10 inches over the same four-day span. Various locations in the South Plains were the targets of the downpour several days earlier, when Tahoka and Lubbock received more than 8 inches of rain (September 19–24).

Aside from the tropical moisture, area residents speculated on more imaginative causes. One resident claimed the reason for the flood-making rains near San Angelo was that some boys "killed too many green lizards and turned their bellies up to the sun."[3] Furthermore, although the September downpours were extraordinary in San Angelo, they failed to live up to all the hyperbole describing them. One Los Angeles, California, resident called friends in San Angelo to see whether the account of the rainfall she had read was accurate. She told her sister that a Los Angeles paper had reported that San Angelo received "99 inches of rain in 18 minutes." The *San Angelo Evening Standard* added, "Neither could understand how the rain had such unusual growth between here and there."[4]

For the month of September 1936, record rains over Central and West Texas propelled the statewide average to its highest ever for September—7.04 inches (4.15 inches above average).

San Angelo and Concho River Floods

The droughty conditions were evident in the water levels of area streams. The stage

Concho River Basin

North Concho River

Sterling City

Water Valley

Carlsbad

San Angelo — Concho River

Middle Concho

Mertzon

Spring Creek

Dove Creek

Christoval

South Concho River

LOCATION	9/13	9/14	9/15	9/16	9/17	9/18	TOTAL: 9/13–18	DATE TOTAL: 9/19–24
Austin	0.33	0.87	0.99	0.35	0.04		2.58	
Ballinger		trace	1.25	1.63	6.25	1.8	10.93	
Bronte							18.5	
Broome							30	
Brownwood			0.27	4.1	1.6	0.72	6.69	0.16
Carlsbad		1	3.2	3	6	0.1	13.3	1.1
Carlsbad 2.5 E							28	
Carlsbad 3.5 E							30	
Christoval				18	6		24	0.2
Coleman		0.97	1.93	4.03	2.7	1.2	10.83	trace
Comanche		0.1	1.22	3.79	2.73	0.04	7.88	0.04
Dallas	trace	0.7	0.2	1.24	0.29	trace	2.43	0
Eden		0.25	4	1.27	2.5	1.1	9.12	
Eldorado			14.2				14.2	1.4
Eola		8	1	5	2.5		16.5	
Ft. McKavett			4	3.5	2.5		10	
Goldthwaite	trace	1.1	1.7	2.89	1	0.4	7.09	0.4
Junction		0.69	5.22	1.39	0.23		7.53	0.33
Kaufman			0.21	0.13	0.2	0	0.54	0.15
Kerrville		0.56	6.42	5.95	0.95	trace	13.88	1.16
Llano		0.17	3.47	5.59	0.54	0.7	10.47	0.01
ubbock	trace		trace	0.09	0.02	2.53	2.64	8.32
Marble Falls		0.07	2.3	3	1.52	1.15	8.04	
Menard		0.18	1.6	6.03	1.14	0.31	9.26	0.64
Midland				0.43	1.45	1.1	2.98	2.02
Paint Rock			6.74	5.66	0.65		13.05	0.98
Robert Lee							15	
Roosevelt							16	
Roosevelt near							30	
San Angelo		trace	11.75	1.16	4.64	7.64	25.19	0.25
San Angelo 10 N							28	
San Angelo 11 NW			5.2		8.5	2	15.7	
Sonora			4.7	4	2.5		11.2	
Sonora		0.4	5.3	2.4	1.8		9.9	1
Stiles				1.2	2.2	0.8	4.2	4.2
Substation 14		0.6	2.98	2.13	2.08	0.03	7.82	0.11
Tahoka				0.14	0.7	1.04	1.88	9.39
Tennyson			7		12	3	22	
Veribest		10.1	1	5.7			16.8	0.1
Wall 4 e			9	1.5	5		15.5	
Wall SCS			7.5	0.8	4.1	2.4	14.8	
Water Valley		4.5	1.5		20.4		26.4	
Waxahachie		0.12	0.15	0.11	0.28		0.66	0.2
Weatherford			0.68	1.84	1.78	0.08	4.38	7.65

9/25	9/26	9/27	9/28	TOTAL: 9/25–28
0.35	0.85	1.38		2.58
	0.48	2.3	0.22	3
3.25				3.25
				11
0.08	0.07	3.2	0.35	3.7
0.3	1.7	0.2		2.2
				2.5
				5
		5		5
0.1	1.61	2.13		3.84
0.1	1.45	3.14		4.69
0.51	3.77	3.3	0	7.58
	2.75	1.15		3.9
2.4	1.9			4.3
	3.9	2.1		6
1	1			2
0.58	1.17	2.67		4.42
0.09	0.05	2.43		2.57
	0.21	13.9	1.04	15.15
trace	0.12	4.58	0.04	4.74
	0.44	3.25	0.25	3.94
0.15	0.18	0.13		0.46
	0.09	5	1.4	6.49
0.72	0.19	1.35		2.26
1.26	0.14			1.4
	2.76	0.99		3.75
				2.5
				1.5
0.08	1.11	0.88	trace	2.07
	2			2
1.5	1.9	0.3		3.7
	0.5	0.5		1
0.2	0.7	0.9		1.8
4.2	1.5			5.7
0.27	0.2	0.92		1.39
0.62	0.32	0.01		0.95
				2
	2.5	0.6		3.1
3.2	1.8			5
0.2	2.6	1.2		4
3.5				3.5
	0.73	8.5	1.02	10.25

at the Concho River at Paint Rock was one foot, and the flow was only 2 cfs before the rise on September 15, 1936.

The Flood of September 15

More than twelve inches of rain fell along the South Concho on September 14 and 15, driving the South Concho River up almost eighteen feet at Christoval. Prior to the downpour, the South Concho River there was flowing at only 3 cfs. Four hours later, at midnight on September 15, the river had risen almost 9 feet, with a 5-foot surge in the previous hour. In the next hour it rose another 5 feet. By 3:30 A.M. on September 15 the river was up to 18.48 feet and 58,500 cfs.

The South Concho River reached tourist cottages and washed one cabin away at Christoval. The floodwater was approximately 2.5 feet below the 1906 flood level. Spring Creek, a tributary of the Middle Concho River, hit an 18.7-foot and 19,900-cfs stage at 6 A.M. on the fifteenth. At 11 A.M. that day, the South Concho River at San Angelo reached a 20.6-foot stage at the gage one mile above the confluence with the North Concho. At 1 A.M. that morning, the river's stage was 2.08 feet. The flow had increased approximately 108,000 cfs in ten hours.

The Concho River gage, 1.75 miles below San Angelo and approximately 0.5 mile below the confluence, stood at 0.73 feet at 12:30 A.M. on September 15, when the streamflow was only 4 cfs. In the next hour, the river rose to 9 feet; by 2 A.M. it was up to 17.4 feet. From 5 to 7 A.M. the river rose more than 6 feet per hour. Around noon on September 15 it peaked at 43.6 feet.

September 17 Floods

Repeating the scenario of two days earlier, heavy rains fell in the Middle and

South Concho basins. Adding to floods on those rivers was a near-record surge down the North Concho. On September 17 the South Concho River at Christoval rose from 5.5 feet at 1 A.M. to 11.5 feet in a single hour (at 6 A.M. it peaked at 20.5 feet, with a flow of 80,100 cfs). Also at noon that day, the South Concho half a mile south of San Angelo peaked at 23.4 feet and 111,000 cfs. The river's stage stayed above 20 feet for nearly ten hours. The Middle Concho at the Twelve Mile Bridge reached 23.75 feet at 8 A.M. the same day. It began rising after 1 A.M., when it stood at 2.53 feet with a flow of 9 cfs.

As the South Concho and Middle Concho flood waves worked their way downstream, long-time residents wondered whether it would spur another disastrous inundation at Ben Ficklin, like the one fifty-four years earlier. This time Lake Nasworthy stood in the path of the currents. The lake level was held at six feet below the dam, and thirteen gates were opened in preparation for the expected swell. The dam moderated the South Concho flood wave into San Angelo, but the fish hatchery lo-

cated below the south end of the dam lost "untold thousands of bass, bream, and catfish."[5] Along the South Concho below the dam, boats were found "in an area which no person had reached since the [Ben Ficklin] flood."[6]

The rises on the South Concho affected San Angelo, but not the downtown area, where the North Concho flowed. The North Concho River runs from the northwest through downtown. On September 17 the heaviest rains fell with great intensity along the North Concho River basin, and the runoff produced a harrowing rise throughout the city.

At Water Valley on September 17, 20.4 inches fell. On the preceding evening at Carlsbad, the North Concho River began rising, pushing past 11 feet by midnight. At 2 P.M. on September 17 the river rose to a 15.8-foot stage and a streamflow of 89,000 cfs. Before the North Concho wave hit San Angelo, floodwater from the South Concho flowed into the city at midday on September 17 and backed up into the North Concho basin. The North Concho floodwaters then hit, bringing a flow of 184,000 cfs, its

AVERAGE DAILY DISCHARGE FOR SEPTEMBER 1936

| | | | | | | | DATE | |
STATION	14	15	16	17	18	19	20	21
South Concho River at Christoval	188	22,900	569	24,100	376	62	48	47
South Concho River at San Angelo		54,400	7,400	53,100	8,170	1,630	475	445
Concho River at San Angelo		82,300	14,700	131,000	17,000	3,040	594	1,280
Concho River at Paint Rock		52,600	61,900	134,000	90,500	26,600	6,070	1,090
Middle Concho River at Tankersley				7,650	921	445	64	114
Spring Creek near Tankersley		5,040	248	6,300	429	225	108	96
North Concho River at Carlsbad		238	820	62,900	4,170	560	84	971
Llano River near Junction		4,160	59,700	14,400	7,390	1,830	940	718
Llano River near Castell		15,200	93,000	46,000	14,100	4,730	2,580	1,540
Pedernales River near Spicewood	445	23,100	34,700	4,360	2,460	1,020	620	538
Colorado River at Ballinger		7,760	2,540	48,200	54,300	6,120	2,080	864
Colorado River at Austin		7,380	90,500	115,000	97,800	84,000	70,500	74,800

Discharge in cubic feet/second

greatest since at least 1853. Around 4 A.M. the Concho River gage (1.75 miles below the confluence of the South and North Concho rivers) began registering an increase. From 4 to 6 A.M. it jumped 9.3 feet, and from 6 to 7 A.M. it leaped another 8 feet. The peak flow of 230,000 cfs was recorded at 1 P.M. The peak stage was 46.6 feet—within a foot of the 1906 record.

At Paint Rock, the Concho eclipsed the 30-foot stage at 7 P.M. on September 15 and stayed above 30 feet for forty-five of the next sixty hours. It dropped to 23.6 feet before cresting at 43.4 feet and 301,000 cfs at 9 P.M. on September 17. At Paint Rock, the flood washed out the bridge housing the stream gage.

San Angelo Flood Tales

In the midst of the flood of September 17, Dean Chenoweth, editor of the *San Angelo Standard,* looked in the direction of his house and was "not able to see anything in that direction but acres of ugly, swirling water" and "big houses floating down the river."[7] At that time, only a small part of one of the three bridges across the North Concho was visible, so no one knew whether the three were still standing. The Chadbourne Street viaduct was closed shortly before 11:00 after a house was smashed to pieces against it and other buildings began piling up. The impact opened up an old crack in the structure.

Approaches to the bridges were also damaged. The Abe Street bridge lost thirty feet of its north approach. Reports outside of San Angelo speculated that the Sixth Street bridge had lost its approaches, but they appeared to be missing only because they had not yet been built. As the *San Angelo Standard* noted, "The 6th Street bridge has not carried a vehicle across it, yet it has already withstood a flood."[8]

Eyewitnesses said that "San Angelo looked like a seaport at noon today from the Western Reserve Building. . . . As you looked southeast toward the power plant, all was water." The South Concho River was lapping at the doors of Saint Mary's Church on South Chadbourne. The *San Angelo Standard* commented, "the Fort Concho addition stuck up like the inside of the letter

22	23	24	25	26	27	28	29	30
46	46	46	46	20,100	1,440	300	123	80
400	300	276	2,900	41,000	44,200	2,970	1,280	743
702	424	352	3,280	81,400	70,600	10,300	1,810	1,010
920	635	1,480	1,980	22,100	99,000	13,100	3,750	1,910
97	28	44	3,240	25,600	25,200	1,270	600	312
71	55	54	149	4,950	982	197	110	93
131	64	46	189	45,500	3,920	610	242	136
600	512	465	3,500	967	4,440	3,450	1,070	710
1,340	1,040	710	1,380	3,720	56,600	5,210	2,400	1,610
439	439	386	336	304	39,100	19,600	1,660	1,020
576	7,150	8,900	3,160	10,500	28,300	14,300	7,370	2,050
111,000	127,000	74,300	21,800	11,800	73,800	166,000	81,400	66,100

‘U’ with the North Concho on one side and the South on the other."[9] The paper added, "[It] will be a long time before people will see boats four blocks from the east end of the West Beauregard Street bridge."[10]

Many San Angelo businesses experienced heavy losses when the flood reached them before they could move goods out of their buildings. One florist lost one hundred birds, twenty-five hundred potted plants, and all of the store's flowers. Water filled the basement at the Cactus Hotel. At the Naylor Hotel, twenty-five to forty guests and employees were fed a "pork and beans and bread feast" as the flood filled 4.5 feet of the first floor, which required the guests to "wade in" to dinner.[11] The Casino lost its bathhouses and caretaker's house. Water at the Ritz Theater reached a depth of 3 feet in the lobby and 18 feet in the rear of the building, which ruined the screen. Water was 4 feet deep at the central fire station, whose basement filled with 10 feet of water.

In one residential section, a casket washed into a house at Abe and Twohig. At 215 Cottonwood, water was 8 feet deep and left 2½ feet of mud. One resident had a "flower garden that was the envy of San Angelo" and had recently hauled in six hundred loads of dirt. The currents washed away his dirt, "leaving that typical San Angelo rocky subsoil."[12] One woman's house floated away, and another landed at her lot briefly, prompting her to comment wryly, "Well, I just lost one house but I got another already."[13] One flood victim caught a ten-pound bass in the basement of a flooded building.

As the floods receded, the *San Angelo Standard* said, "The North Concho, like a skulking wolf in sheep's clothing, was back in its lair today, but it had made its kill . . . and left shambles of scores of houses, gaping holes in bridge approaches, uprooted trees, torn paving, [and] an obliterated park."[14]

The Flood of September 26 and 27

A day after the flood of September 17, the South Concho River at Christoval receded

Naylor Hotel on left, looking south down Chadbourne Street across the Concho River, San Angelo, Texas 1936 (West Texas Collection, Angelo State University 1989-9.1198).

Aerial view of the Concho River flood damage (The San Antonio Light Collection, UTSA's Institute of Texan Cultures, No. L-1255-S).

to a 3.5-foot stage. Two days later it settled at a 2.6-foot stage, where it remained until September 26, when heavy rains again pounded the San Angelo area. These downpours were centered farther upstream from Christoval, closer to the Eldorado region. In response, the South Concho again pushed well above flood stage, rising to a 19.94-foot level at 6 P.M.

This time the Middle Concho River, rather than the South Concho, carried the greater volume. The Middle Concho River at the Twelve Mile Bridge also rose dramati-

cally on September 26. At 3 A.M. it stood at 4.52 feet and rose 8 feet in the next hour. At 10 A.M. it peaked at 24.2 feet. The Middle Concho stayed above 23 feet for almost twenty-four hours. The flood on the Middle Concho created high drama at the Twelve Mile Bridge when seven people became marooned. Approaches on each side of the structure were covered with up to 15 feet of water for a quarter mile. Finding refuge in a small frame resort building, the stranded individuals were rescued after thirty hours. When one of them returned to his farm, he noticed that five of his pigs had survived the flood. He said they apparently took turns resting by biting the feed trough while the other pigs swam in the high water.

One farmer had worked a seventy-acre rented plot of land and was preparing to harvest his crops, but he was "swept clean" by the Middle Concho, which, according to the *San Angelo Standard,* was the "least troublesome of the three rivers that have kept a pistol cocked at the temple of this city for two weeks."[15]

Damage to San Angelo by the Concho River flood (UTSA's Institute of Texan Cultures, The San Antonio Light Collection).

On the North Concho River, the floodwaters at Water Valley were slightly higher than those of the flood on September 16 and 17. On September 26 the North Concho near Carlsbad peaked at 16 feet and 94,600 cfs. Because the extreme flooding ten days earlier had cleared the channel, this second inundation was "a flood without drift."[16]

The Concho River gage near San Angelo indicated that the rise on September 26 almost equaled that of September 15, when the river peaked at 42.6 feet at 5 P.M. The Concho River at Paint Rock stayed well above 10 feet from September 17 through September 27, peaking at 35.8 feet on the latter date, which was almost fifty percent greater than during the Ben Ficklin flood of 1882. From September 15 through September 30, the Concho at Paint Rock passed more than one million acre-feet of water.

San Angelo Area Flood Notes

San Angelo's parks were pummeled by the deluge. Santa Fe Park was completely covered by floodwaters, which washed away its restaurant and golf house and toppled numerous trees. The currents deposited a gas pump under a tree and a refrigerator in a bunker on the sixth hole. To describe the debris, the *San Angelo Standard-Times* evoked a festive image: "Christmas trees the day after Yuletide was what they looked like—those big pecans prostrate from Thursday's flood in San Angelo's City Park yesterday as workmen began reconstruction. For tinsel there was sheet iron, for presents there were torn dresses, even a red over-time parking tag high up 25 feet from the ground, a $2.50 necktie swinging around a twisted mesquite, fishing poles, a bursted electric refrigerator and two or three safes all guarded by special officers to prevent pilfering."[17]

After the repeated floods, residents were seeking humorous angles to lighten their moods. The *San Angelo Standard-Times* commented, "A new game has come

Cactus Hotel in center, view from southeast to northwest (West Texas Collection, Angelo State University 1989-9.1227).

Naylor Hotel on the southeast corner of Concho and Chadbourne (West Texas Collection, Angelo State University 1989-9.1219).

Railroad bridge across Concho River in eastern San Angelo, 1936 (West Texas Collection, Angelo State University 1989-0.1202).

to San Angelo called 'Watch the River.' It is less strenuous than bridge and football and it can be played only once every nine days since that is as often as the Conchos burst their bounds."[18] In spite of the bad situation, San Angeloans approached the clean-up duties with some optimism. The *San Antonio Express* stated, "There are compensations even in a flood as devastating as the one which visited this city during last week. . . . Today there are no unemployed here. Wages are higher than in the last 5 years. . . . With a building boom impending, San Angelo is all set for a return of the balmy days of 1929."[19]

A huge pile of debris stacked against the bridge across the North Concho River (The San Antonio Light Collection, UTSA's Institute of Texan Cultures, No. L-1255-A).

"Lake Eldorado"

Surface water is normally a good thing in West Texas, but a lake that formed on the highway between Eldorado and Sonora proved a major inconvenience. It reached a depth of seven feet, and travelers found no easy way to pass through the water. An enterprising rancher built a caliche road through his ranch and charged one dollar per car for passage around the lake. This "lake" provoked some insightful commentary from the *San Angelo Standard-Times:* "It takes nature herself to show up puny man. The flood here and all along the Concho and Colorado Rivers made a spectacle for and of man when it chased him like a rat from its normal banks." The lake "like a giant from the world of make-believe, told the motoring public it must travel all the way around by Barnhart and Ozona to get from Eldorado to Sonora." To explain why the highway had not been built higher, the editorial writer added, "Man just didn't think Nature would make a chump out of him. . . . The lesson to be had by many, who is [sic] intelligent even though sometimes made into a fool by Nature, is that what Nature did at Eldorado man can do all over West Texas. Scores of artificial lakes can be built to keep the streams of underground water more constant, the temperature moderate, the rainfall more regular. And that can make a better, more secure West Texas."[20]

San Saba River Flood

Between noon on September 15 and noon the next day the storms dumped 21–25 inches on Terrett Draw. The runoff "caus[ed] very high stages in all streams of that region."[21] Around 8 A.M. on September 16 the San Saba River at Menard peaked at 21 feet and 68,600 cfs. On September 27 it topped out at 16.6 feet and 33,100 cfs at 1 A.M.

Llano River Flood

On the North Llano, whose headwaters are adjacent to those of the San Saba River and near the South Concho watershed, rains up to 30 inches (with an intensity of 14 inches in 2½ hours) produced record stages on many small streams. Near Junction, the station on the North Llano was destroyed after experiencing its highest stage ever recorded. An estimated 24.9-foot rise was predicted to have occurred at midnight on September 15. In addition, Copperas Creek washed out the bridge between Junction and Sonora.

Farther downstream, the Llano River was well out of its banks. At Castell, the peak—22.9 feet and 153,000 cfs—hit at 3 P.M. on September 16. At Llano, the river swamped the temporary bridge within a week of the date the new bridge was slated to open. Initially it opened only for foot traffic, but officials opened it early to general traffic after the temporary bridge was washed away. Near Llano, the Sandy Creek bridge between Fredericksburg and Llano washed out.

Colorado River Flood

As the news of the West Texas floods died down, the next source of information would be the actual runoff data. The last major gauging station on the Colorado before its confluence with the Concho was at Ballinger. Even without any floodwaters from the Concho, Ballinger was in a bad situation. There the Colorado stretched a mile wide, and Elm Creek was in flood. The words of

Aerial photo of unfinished bridge. Initial reports from out-of-town newspapers indicated that the flood had washed out the approaches; in actuality, the approaches had not yet been built (The San Antonio Light Collection, UTSA's Institute of Texan Cultures, No. L-1255-X).

Night-time flood scene in Austin following upstream flooding along the Concho River Basin (The San Antonio Light Collection, UTSA's Institute of Texan Cultures, No. L-1322-D).

a long-time resident who helped in the recovery effort after Ben Ficklin in 1882 were recalled by his daughter: "If your children live long enough, it is my opinion that you will see both the low lands of San Angelo and Ballinger washed away by floodwaters of the Conchos and Colorado rivers and Elm Creek. Many early settlers who witnessed the [Ben Ficklin] flood believed that San Angelo was building too near the river."[22]

The floods on the Colorado produced swells at Ballinger on September 15 (to 13.75 feet at 14,900 cfs), on September 17 and 18 (to 28.58 feet at 75,400 cfs), on September 23 and 24 (to 12 feet at 12,400 cfs), and on September 26, 27, and 28, peaking at 22.73 feet on September 27 with a 33,500-cfs streamflow.

Fueled by the record floods on the Concho and upstream flooding in its basin, the Colorado below the Concho confluence rocketed to record-smashing highs. The most astonishing increase along the Colorado occurred in the Brown-Coleman-McCulloch county area. With the Concho flood wave coming down, floodwaters from north of San Angelo feeding into the Colorado, and heavy rains in Brown, Coleman, Concho, and McCulloch counties, the Colorado River stage at Rockwood attained an amazing 70 feet, some 14.5 feet (almost twenty-five percent) higher than the previous record. After being battered by debris, the bridge there gave way. At Winchell, the

flood stage reached 62 feet. Milburn was inundated with water and lost its bridge in the deluge. Near the Indian Creek community, the river was two miles wide. At the Brownwood-Brady bridge, the stage reached 72 feet—14 feet higher than ever before recorded.

In the Brookesmith-Winchell area, one couple fled to the roof of a barn and then to trees before they were rescued on September 19. A pastor from the area was stranded on a windmill tower near the Winchell community. The 65-foot stage at Regency knocked out the bridge there (it was later replaced with the current suspension bridge).

North of the Colorado, Brownwood dodged another deluge when Lake Brownwood corralled the floodwaters. On September 17 and 18 Lake Brownwood rose to its highest level in its short lifetime. The spillway passed more than 4.3 feet of water, only inches above the stage in September 1935. At Brownwood, Pecan Bayou was at 36 feet, the highest since the dam at Brownwood was built in 1933. As the flood wave moved downstream, the Coast Guard flew over the Colorado Valley to warn residents of the impending danger.

The massive influx of floodwaters from the San Saba, which set record levels in its upper reaches, had passed before the big wave from the Colorado arrived. At San Saba, the San Saba River rose to 30 feet shortly after midnight on the morning of September 17. Around noon that day, the Colorado just below San Saba exceeded 30 feet and remained between 31 and 35 feet as the next flood wave approached. In the early morning hours of September 20, the river finally dropped below 15 feet.

On September 21 the big wave from upstream hit in the San Saba, Lometa, and Bend areas. At the San Saba-Lometa bridge, the Colorado River peaked at 62 feet, 2 feet higher than ever recorded. At Bend, the high water reached the eaves of some of the houses and the lofts of local barns. The flood was described by the *Lampasas Leader* as "the most terrible disaster ever known" at Bend.[23]

Before Marble Falls and Austin, the one new obstacle in the river's path was the partially completed Buchanan Dam. However, nobody knew exactly how much it would attenuate the wave. At Marble Falls, Fire Chief John Luckey said, "This flood has even the most expert river observers guessing. Nobody here seems to know just what the crest will be, but most of them think it will be around 40 feet."[24] Speculating that it would reach Marble Falls by sunrise on September 22, he also noted that green pecan trees

40–50 feet long were bobbing in the currents. These, he feared, would pile up at the Kingsland bridge and send a wall of water 8–10 feet high down the river. He planned to send communications from higher ground, if needed, since Marble Falls was one of the last gauging stations before Austin.

At Marble Falls, the flood provided a test for the new highway bridge across the Colorado. The State Highway Department's resident engineer was "gratified to note that after the recent rise of 30 feet and higher in the river there is no doubt about the stability of the bridge."[25] Although not complete, the structure had sufficient flooring to make it suitable for pedestrian traffic.

Another bridge upstream at Tow was not so lucky: The flood of September 28 washed it away. Built in 1916, it was to be submerged by a filled Lake Buchanan. Until the dam or a new bridge was completed, the river would divide the community of Tow. The store, post office, school, and church were on the west side, while many residents lived on the east side. Their closest crossing was approximately seven miles down the river.

In Austin, the Colorado River prior to the rains stood at 0.28 feet on September 15. Before the Concho waters reached Austin,

Colorado River flooding in Austin along South Congress Avenue (courtesy of the LCRA Corporate Archives: W00890).

Flood in Lampasas square, September 27, 1936 (courtesy of the Keystone Square Museum, Lampasas, Texas).

Flood in Lampasas square, September 27, 1936 (courtesy of the Keystone Square Museum, Lampasas, Texas).

a 22.97-foot stage hit on September 16, and a 24.15-foot stage followed the next day. In Austin, little damage was done, but Deep Eddy and Barton Springs pools were inundated and filled with debris and sediment. With news of record floods and bridges being carried downstream, Austin wondered about its fate. The city prepared for a 30–35 foot crest, based on estimates using the 56.7-foot stage at Red Bluff (between San Saba and Lometa).

If the floodwater at Buchanan Dam rose no higher than 18 feet, the structure would not be damaged. One official of the Lower Colorado River Authority (LCRA) believed that the partially completed dam would "cause a material flattening out of the river below there."[26] One pilot said, "There is lots of water up there but it is running slowly, therefore, I believe it will rise very slowly and recede just as gradually. That will mean the river will be kept high here for several days. That will mean also that the crest will not be as high and the damage will be minimized."[27]

A 29-foot stage in Austin sent water into Congress Avenue. A state maintenance engineer recommended that residents be "prepared to negotiate with International Great Northern railroad for operation of a shuttle

September 27, 1936, flood in Lampasas square (courtesy of the Keystone Square Museum, Lampasas, Texas).

CONCHO RIVER FLOOD

train between the two sections, as was done last year."[28] Walter Seaholm, the city's electrical superintendent, advised Austinites not to worry about the light plant going out due to high water, thanks to a dike in front of the structure that could handle a 43-foot stage. Moreover, a county judge pointed out that tributaries in the Austin area would be able to take in backwater, unlike in previous floods.

The river in Austin remained steady at 15 feet for most of September 21. The following day, the river rose almost 6.5 feet, pushing it past the flood stage to a 24-foot level at 10 P.M. Large crowds of Austinites came out to observe the rise, lining the Congress Avenue viaduct. While they watched the rising river, anticipating a near-record swell, the unexpected happened—the flood wave went AWOL. "River flattens out somewhere but observers not sure where," proclaimed the headline in the *San Antonio Express* on September 23. [29] This situation caused some to revise the forecast for a peak of less than 30 feet. The *San Antonio Express* added, "Official observers admittedly were perplexed by the strange procedure of the flood."[30]

The weather bureau had used the USGS data to predict a 41-foot crest at Marble Falls and a 34-foot crest at Austin, but it later "announced it could not make an accurate prediction because of an apparent loss of the crest somewhere above Marble Falls."[31] They guessed that the peak that had ravaged the Winchell and Rockwood areas had spread over a fifty-mile stretch. The LCRA hypothesized that the partially completed Buchanan Dam had held back a large volume of water, thereby diminishing the peak.

On September 22 the Colorado River crested at 31 feet at Marble Falls and 18 feet at Buchanan Dam. At Tow, it peaked at 32 feet and 202,000 cfs—3.5 feet higher than previously recorded. On September 23 the river in Austin decreased slowly after peaking at 24.48 feet, slightly in excess of the flood level of September 17, which occurred with much less hoopla. As it passed, it caused little damage in the city.

By this time, praise for the Buchanan Dam was beginning to be heard. The *San Antonio Express* stated, "The half-finished Buchanan Dam . . . was credited as a major factor in flattening out the damaging crest of the flood. . . . Engineers said it held in check a large body of the slowly moving flood, while that which passed through a small opening was speeded, thus spreading out the water."[32]

While residents were voicing their approval of the dam, the highest peak of the flood arrived in Austin on September 27, when the river rose from 4 feet to more than 29 feet in less than twenty-four hours, closing the Congress Avenue bridge. At 4 A.M. the next day, the stage had reached 31.4 feet.

Following the flood in Austin on September 21 and 22, Deep Eddy pool was full of sand from the previous inundation, and clean-up operations were under way for the Barton Springs pool. With the heavy rains outside of Austin, Barton Creek itself was overflowing. The *Austin American* of September 27 commented, "a six-foot rise in Barton's creek Saturday may finish what city

September 27, 1936, flood in Lampasas County Courthouse and square (courtesy of the Keystone Square Museum, Lampasas, Texas).

workmen started two days ago—clean out the 12-inch deposit of mud left by the Colorado flood in Barton Springs pool. . . . Repeating history of the feud between the creek and the river, and experience has taught that the creek can rid itself of the river's silt deposits more effectively than a crew of workmen." Thanks to the help of the Barton Creek floodwaters, the pool was expected to open within a week.[33]

In Austin, the Colorado passed 3,288,000 acre-feet of water between September 15 and October 20. (The average yearly flow through Austin at that time averaged 1.96 million acre-feet for the thirty-eight years during which records had been kept.) On September 27 a rare situation occurred along the Colorado. With heavy rains in the country north of San Angelo on September 25 and September 27, the river was in flood in its upper reaches, as well as near its mouth. Floods were reported at Robert Lee (at 25 feet, the highest level since 1922), Ballinger (at 22.7 feet), and Wharton.

Lampasas Flood

One of the heaviest cloudbursts hit at Lampasas on September 27 and brought a powerful flash flood into the town. The

previous worst such event had struck there sixty-three years earlier—in 1873.

On the night of September 26, 4.33 inches fell, followed by 1.5 inches the next morning. Burnet received 10 inches in twelve hours on September 27, its worst downpour in thirty-six years.

At 3:30 A.M. on September 27, a siren was sounded in Lampasas after citizens along the Sulphur Creek called to say that the water was high and rising. By 10:30 A.M. the square at Lampasas was submerged. To keep the water from seeping in under doors, sacks of flour, sandbags, and cloth were stacked against and into openings. At Hancock Park, eighteen inches of water crept into the hostess house. Water flowed 1½–6 feet deep in the square. Afterward, one proposal for warding off similar events in the future was to build a levee along Sulphur Creek. The *Lampasas Record* stated, "The cost of such a levee for the two mile stretch would not cost a great deal compared to a real flood, provided a project could be worked out with the W.P.A. set-up."[34]

Other Flooding in Texas

Sonora flooded again. Floodwaters came down the Ben Meckel Draw and the Dry Devils River Draw, reaching 2.5 feet in several houses. Near Rocksprings, a downpour fed currents into the headwaters of the Hill Country rivers. As an excellent illustration of a Hill Country flash flood, the Frio went on an astonishingly high and brief rise. Although the Frio had a very high flood stage, its discharge was approximately sixty percent of the 1935 flood.

Following a downpour of 10–12 inches over Webb County, accounts noted that the "deluge broke practically every tank in that section, all of the water coming in a body, tearing out nearly two miles of the Asherton and Gulf railroad near Catarina. When it struck the Nueces River, witnesses said water 'flowed upstream' for 10 miles."[35]

Flood-Control Discussion

In reviewing the flood, Tate Dalrymple wrote the following in the Water Supply Paper: "The rivers of Texas are subject to great and frequent floods. Some of the maximum rates of discharge have exceeded any rates recorded from areas of comparable size elsewhere in the United States. The rivers of Texas are also subject to long periods of exceedingly low flow. Few people outside the state and probably not many of the residents of the State realize the great difficulties arising from these conditions that must be overcome in controlling and utilizing the flow of Texas streams."[36]

JULY 1938

~~~~~~~~~~

Brady Creek and San Saba River Floods

THE FLASH FLOODS of 1938 provided several tests for the flood-control efforts of the 1930s. Brady Creek presented another challenge to Brady and its low-lying downtown and courthouse. The San Saba River, into which Brady Creek flows, also rose quickly and threatened towns along its banks. In addition to the rises along the middle reaches of the Colorado River, the flows from these streams joined above newly built and functional Buchanan Dam. The flows into and out of Lake Buchanan contributed a timely lesson for those who were building subsequent flood-control structures downstream from Buchanan Dam. However, the lesson was at the expense of residents in that area, who believed that flood control had already been achieved.

Precedent

With generous rains falling over most of Texas, the year 1938 started out nicely for farmers. Monthly rainfall totals for January through April were above average for the whole state. May and June were both within one inch of their average rainfall. In the first two weeks of July, summer was accompanied by its usual hot and dry weather. San Angelo, Kerrville, Lampasas, and Llano all reported multiple days of triple-digit high temperatures. During the summer, the talk of many Texans focused on "Pappy" O'Daniel's run for governor. In Brady, following the primary election on July 23, a postelection party was planned, but, due to the weather, it was not held. As the *Brady Standard* noted, "Instead,

it was a party of a different sort, staged by Jupiter Pluvius."[1]

Rainfall

A change in the weather first appeared as showers dotted the Edwards Plateau on July 17. On July 18 Brownwood reported a 1.23-inch total. On July 19 the rains became more general and much more generous. Eden reported a 2.1-inch rain, and Paint Rock gauged almost 4 inches. The unusually timely summer rains prompted an excited headline from the *Brady Standard* on July 19: "Oh, Boy, Million-Dollar Rain in McCulloch." The article said that "A genuine 'Million-Dollar' rain—one of the kind that you read about but [do] not often actually see—has been visiting [the] McCulloch area throughout today—a slow, steadily-falling, dripping wet precipitation that is soaking old Mother Earth to the core. . . . The steady patter of rain drops spell[s] big crops and the turning of Prosperity Corner for farmers, stockmen and ranchmen of this section."[2]

With rainfall totals on July 20 and 21 reaching well above 2 inches, more praises for the rains surfaced in print. The *San Angelo Standard-Times* stated that the "moisture was a boon to rangeland vegetation and brightened feed prospects considerably."[3] By this point, Eden had received its fourth rain total of 0.4 inches or more in four days, pushing the four-day tally to 4.63 inches.

By July 22, Central Texans' attitudes about the precipitation had changed from welcoming to wary. The area between

Menard and Eden had recorded up to 10 inches of rain, and still the showers continued. The San Saba and South Concho basins received up to 10 inches of rain over another two-day period (July 22–23). Near San Saba, 8.47 inches fell at Sloan on July 23, adding to the 7.62 inches that had fallen on the two previous days, boosting its three-day total to 16.09 inches. After the big rains pounded the middle reaches of the San Saba Basin, the deluge moved downstream, and on July 23 the city of San Saba received 6 inches of rain.

During the rainy spell of July 16–25, Eden gauged 17.37 inches. As the welcome rains fell in various locations, the totals reached 10 inches and much more. Some of the greatest totals were recorded at Menard (14.13 inches), Brady (13.65 inches), and Sloan (21.49 inches). North of Menard, several 23-inch totals were reported. When USGS employees performed their detailed search for all rain-holding vessels, they found a location approximately 10 miles north of Eldorado that had caught 30 inches of rain. The same study yielded a 28-inch total at Melvin, as well as 24-inch totals 12½ miles east of Sonora and 18 miles north of Brady. The eastern portion of San Saba County also gauged 24 inches. On July 26 San Saba saw its first sunshine in a week.

The U.S. Weather Bureau noted the cause, as best as the agency could describe it, as follows:

The causes of this prolonged and torrential downpour are not readily discernible on the surface weather maps—no strongly developed center of disturbance crossed the country during this period; no tropical storm moved inland from the Gulf or was present on the Gulf; pressure gradients were for the most part very flat.

However, from July 18 to 22 a broad, rather shallow depression trough extended from the Middle Atlantic States southwestward across Texas into northern Mexico. At the same time a field of high pressure made its appearance in the Canadian northwest and moved slowly southward along the eastern slope of the Rocky Mountains. This combination set in motion one of the most efficient processes for the condensation and precipitation of atmospheric moisture about which anything is known—the raising of a mass of moist[ure]-laden air and thus reducing its temperature

Brady Creek flood in 1909 (courtesy of the McCulloch County Historical Commission, Heart of Texas Historical Museum, Brady, Texas).

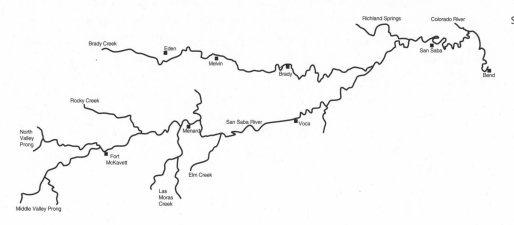

San Saba River Basin

and carrying capacity. Meteorologic observations indicate a persistent flow of tropical air for the period July 18–25 and soundings of the upper air show that this air was moist and convectively unstable.[4]

Streamflow

With the heaviest rains falling for days over the same area, the headwaters of the San Saba River, Brady Creek, and South Concho River produced record or near-record floods.

South Concho River

The South Concho Basin averaged 19.7 inches of rain. The resulting runoff drove the river to surpass the 1936 stage and to peak within 1.5 feet of the all-time record. At Christoval, the river had almost no flow on July 19, while staying at a stage of less than 1 foot. On July 20 the river experienced its first rise, peaking at 15.48 feet at 1:30 P.M. On July 21, following the second phase of the 10-inch rains that fell north of Eldorado, the South Concho rose again, this time to 12.74 feet at 10:55 A.M. The next swell began on the morning of July 23 and peaked at 21.95 feet at noon.

Park cabins along the river were swept away. The water covered a stob on a local farm that marked the high point of the 1936 flood. When the South Concho waters joined with the North Concho River in San Angelo, the latter was noticed to be flowing backward. The flow of the Concho River through San Angelo and Paint Rock was significant but caused no major damage. The river crested at 35.9 feet at its gage near San Angelo and at 31.95 feet at Paint Rock.

Brady Creek

The town of Brady had battled floods on Brady Creek for decades, primarily because the town's business section and courthouse were located near a bend in the creek and, at places, less than a quarter mile from the stream. In 1909 and 1930, floods propelled water into the courthouse square. In 1932 a levee was built to shield the downtown from such inundations.

In early July 1938 the Galveston office of the U.S. Army Corps of Engineers sent seven engineers to Brady to survey portions of Brady Creek, the San Saba River, and the Colorado River. They planned to be in the area for three months to compile data. Because they were in the Brady area from July 16 to July 23, the engineers received a bonus in data gathering—a record flood that materialized in front of their eyes.

After labeling the precipitation of July 19 as a "Million-Dollar Rain," the *Brady Standard*'s later headline indicated that the welcome showers had gone bad: "Tremendous Wall of Water Nears Top of Big Levee." On July 21 the rate of rise was estimated at one foot per hour throughout the morning, reaching within eighteen inches of the top of the levee. The article stated, "For the fourth time in a period of less than eight years, Brady Creek is making history by threatening to inundate the business section of the city. Only the big rock levee stretching from a point above the Brady Water and Light Works plant at the west city limits and extending through the business section to near the east city limits, so far has protected the business section from a devastating flood. The big 'sea wall' built in 1932 as a CWA [Civil Works Administration] project, and following the floods of 1930, is all that stands between the business section and threatened disaster."[5]

U.S. Army engineers reported that water rose at one foot per hour and crested shortly before noon. They stayed on the bridge

							DATE	
	17	18	19	20	21	22	23	24
Austin	0.00	0.00	0.00	0.00	0.00	0.31	0.96	0.10
Blanco	0.00	0.00	0.00	0.00	0.00	0.15	0.20	0.40
Boerne	0.00	0.00	0.00	0.00	0.00	0.49	0.35	0.09
Brackettville	0.00	0.00	0.00	0.00	0.00	0.37	3.69	5.92
Brady	0.00	0.04	0.02	1.42	2.63	4.39	3.54	1.10
Burnet	0.00	0.00	trace	trace	0.67	0.28	2.20	0.05
Cameron	0.00	0.00	0.00	0.00	0.00	0.00	0.48	0.05
Eden	0.48	0.45	2.10	1.70	1.58	1.39	6.89	2.86
Hondo	0.00	0.00	0.00	0.00	0.00	0.64	0.13	0.28
Junction	0.00	0.00	0.00	0.13	2.58	3.74	1.38	0.00
Kerrville	0.00	0.00	0.00	0.00	0.47	0.13	0.14	0.72
Lampasas	0.00	0.00	0.00	0.92	0.32	1.11	1.46	3.23
Llano	0.00	0.00	trace	0.13	2.00	0.51	0.10	0.70
Menard	0.00	0.00	0.00	2.02	4.40	4.00	1.93	1.59
New Braunfels	0.00	0.00	0.00	0.00	0.00	0.80	0.79	0.16
San Marcos	0.00	0.00	0.00	0.00	0.00	0.02	0.71	0.75
Sloan	0.00	0.25	1.37	0.70	3.70	3.92	8.47	0.22
Taylor	0.00	0.00	0.00	0.00	0.12	trace	0.43	0.41
Temple	0.00	0.00	0.00	0.04	0.10	0.40	0.53	0.47
Uvalde	0.00	0.00	0.00	0.00	0.00	0.00	1.45	2.48

Scenes along the square during the 1938 flood in Brady, Texas (courtesy of the McCulloch County Historical Commission, Heart of Texas Historical Museum, Brady, Texas).

25	26	27	28	29	TOTAL
0.05	0.00	0.00	0.00	0.00	1.42
0.10	0.00	0.00	0.00	0.00	0.85
0.00	0.00	0.00	0.00	0.00	0.93
0.08	0.00	0.00	0.00	0.00	10.06
0.51	0.10	0.00	0.00	0.00	13.75
0.27	0.00	0.00	0.00	0.00	3.47
trace	0.90	0.00	0.00	0.00	1.43
0.02	0.00	0.00	0.00	0.00	17.47
0.00	0.00	0.00	0.00	0.00	1.05
0.00	0.00	0.00	0.00	0.00	7.83
0.12	0.00	0.00	0.00	0.00	1.58
0.96	0.19	0.00	0.00	0.01	8.20
6.75	trace	0.00	0.00	0.00	10.19
0.19	0.00	0.00	0.00	0.00	14.13
0.00	0.00	0.00	0.00	0.46	2.21
0.00	0.00	0.00	0.00	0.00	1.48
2.86	0.00	0.00	0.00	0.40	21.89
0.06	0.00	0.00	0.00	0.00	1.02
0.01	trace	0.00	0.00	0.00	1.55
0.00	0.00	0.00	0.00	trace	3.93

throughout the day, watching the currents flow. Meanwhile, a large crowd gathered to watch the swirling, muddy waters at the Highway 9 bridge, which came within three feet of touching the "Welcome Visitors" sign at the east end of the Richards Park track. The CWA and local leaders who supervised the building of the levee were praised throughout the day for apparently saving the city from another flood.

The colorful "Sauce" column in the *Brady Standard* commented insightfully on the nature of the weather in this area:

This is a fast-moving country! We progress from dustbowl status to flood stage at a dizzy pace—or maybe it's a bedizzled pace. When The Standard *in its Tuesday [July 19] edition heralded a "Million" Dollar Rain for McCulloch, there were grumblings from the populace. Some said 'twas a "Two Million Dollar" rain and another averred it was a "Three Million Dollar" rain. And Sauce, kindly old soul that he is, had in mind today*

an issue to report the big moisture as a "Multi-Million Dollar" rain—just to meet all requirements—a-coming and a-going.

But alack and alas, here 'tis Thursday noon, and throughout the morning the floods have descended upon us—reminiscent of that first big flood which engulfed the business section on October 6, 1930. It will be recalled, too, that just a week after that first big flood, when merchants and business men had just about dug themselves out of the mud and water-soaked merchandise and debris, a second flood descended upon them—October 13 was the date.

There followed a period of apparent safety—the serenity afforded by Brady's justly famed "sea-wall," built with CWA labor. But that feeling was dispelled when on September 3, 1935, flood waters of rampaging Brady Creek overlapped the low spots in the wall and again invaded the business section. And today the heightened and straightened levee is again put to the supreme test, with flood waters seeking out fissures in the rock wall, and threatening any minute to go "over the top."

We live and learn. And the bitter lesson of the first flood in 1930, which caught most everyone unprepared, because everyone scoffed at the idea of Brady Creek ever in any measure proving a rival to the mighty Mississippi River, has taught the value of preparedness. . . .

Meanwhile, The Standard, *which has missed but one regular scheduled issue in all its twenty-nine years of operation—and that was when three feet of water seeped through the building back on that fateful October 6, 1930—is preparing to go ahead with its regular publication. This edition will come to subscribers in condensed form—if we are enabled to put out a paper at all before the threatened flood becomes a reality—but, rain or shine, flood or drouth,* The Standard *will carry on.*[6]

Late-breaking news noted that the flood danger on July 21 appeared to be over since

AVERAGE DAILY DISCHARGE, JULY 9–AUGUST 2, 1938

	JULY 9	JULY 10	JULY 11	JULY 12	JULY 13	JULY 14	JULY 15	JULY 16	JULY 17	JULY 18	JULY 19	JULY 20	JULY 21
Colorado at San Saba	332	360	385	301	292	265	229	208	194	181	178	10600	20700
Colorado at Austin	1,730	1,480	1,410	1,290	1,260	1,260	1,240	1,260	1,260	1,260	1,310	1,310	1,350
Llano at Castell	86	70	107	71	72	70	67	65	61	60	63	70	751
Pedernales at Spicewood	29	49	54	76	63	54	46	37	35	31	29	28	27
San Saba at San Saba	51	56	59	66	59	54	51	50	50	50	115	574	11,500
Concho at Paint Rock	35	18	14	13	12	14	14	12	8	27	598	1,140	8,120

Discharge in cubic feet/second

the creek had fallen three feet after cresting at 11 A.M. However, telephone reports from Melvin indicated that water was still rising there, but most people believed that much of that wave would be lost on the way.

With more rains coming down in the Eden-to-Eldorado area, Brady Creek rose again early on July 22, coming within nine inches of the high-water mark of July 21 before receding. No more than thirty-six hours after Brady nervously watched the second rise diminish, a swell that would eclipse the first two came roaring down from Eden and Melvin. At 8 A.M. on July 23, the town sounded an alarm to alert citizens that a flood wave was on its way. The water stood about a foot below the wall before the wave arrived. Country dwellers upstream reported the biggest increase in modern history, and officials and engineers believed the wall would not be able to protect Brady. On July 23 their fears proved well founded when, shortly after 3 P.M., the water topped Brady's big levee, flooding downtown.

The *San Angelo Standard-Times* called this event "Brady's most dreadful flood in modern history." The article described Brady Creek as "usually a shallow and innocent appearing stream, [which] Saturday blasted over the tops of its guardian dikes and smashed hellbent for the payoff in turmoil and destruction."[7] The paper added that the army engineers in the area "got an eyeful this weekend."[8]

The *Brady Standard*'s July 26 edition commented, "Swirling, derelict waters that

had menaced the town twice the past week made Brady Creek a veritable mad river Saturday [July 23] afternoon." Damage was estimated at $500,000, and the *Brady Standard* called it the "worst flood in the town's history."[9] At one point, up to fifty blocks were inundated. Water flowed six feet deep in the Brady Hotel and was within two or three feet of many business awnings in the downtown section. Power was shut down as the floodwaters overwhelmed the electric plant on the banks of the creek. When the water peaked in Brady, the levee could no longer be seen from the business district. Near the crest, water washed out the bridge on North Bridge Street. The flood stage was 14 inches higher than during the 1930 flood, when damage was estimated at $300,000. And, as before, the top spectacle in the land was flood watching. Authorities estimated that nineteen thousand visitors viewed nature's uproar in Brady during and shortly after the flood.

With the floodwaters inundating Brady, the *Brady Standard* could not be printed, so H. H. Jackson of the *Coleman Democrat-Voice* came to Brady to pick up the copy and print the newspaper. Other offers to do the same came from the *Mason News,* the *Eden Echo,* and the *Brownwood Bulletin.*

The flood caused the *Brady Standard* to speculate on the relative scale of natural disasters: "[A] big fire cannot possibly be worse [than] or as bad as a big flood." According to the article, silt covered everything and became a "sticky gumbo";

JULY 22	JULY 23	JULY 24	JULY 25	JULY 26	JULY 27	JULY 28	JULY 29	JULY 30	JULY 31	AUG. 1	AUG. 2
87000	191,000	186,000	175,000	122,000	88,800	61,600	28,700	8,580	9,190	7,500	4,100
1,390	53,500	209,000	254,000	202,000	119,000	93,400	67,300	48,900	45,700	24,400	
21,200	48,900	21,900	12,400	3,720	3,300	1,840	1,280	1,340			
29	731	1900	4810	251	122	70	51	66			
95,900	117,000	84,700	40,200	7,980	4,640	2,330	1,620	1,900			
4,980	40,400	42,600	4,270	4,230	1,040	575	318	200			

moreover, "every merchant carries fire insurance but not one in a thousand carries flood insurance."[10] No lives were lost in the Brady area, however.

Among the many anecdotes about the flood were reports of residents blaming an area preacher because he failed to cease praying for rain. The flood event was broadcast on KGKO of Fort Worth and KNEL of Brady on July 24 and July 25. Station KNEL sent out a warning before it went off the air on the afternoon of July 24.

San Saba River

The extremely heavy rains of July 20–23 fell between the main trunks of Brady Creek and the San Saba River, causing the runoff to fill both streams. Four rises advanced down the San Saba River at Men-

ard from July 20 through July 23. On July 20 the river reached 12.9 feet. The next day it hit 19.08 feet. On July 22 the river rose even higher, peaking at 20.9 feet. On July 23 at 9 P.M., the river topped that rise, too, as it peaked at 22.7 feet. The river was above the 10-foot stage from 5:10 A.M. on July 21 to 10 P.M. on July 24. From July 21 to July 24 the San Saba River at Menard passed more than 290,000 acre-feet of water, close to six times its average annual discharge. The stage of 22.7 feet was the highest since the 1899 flood.

One resident at Menard reported at 9 P.M. on July 23 that "our town looks like a river. It's still raining here and the water is rising fast. I can see folks now trying to wade in water on the main street. They can't do it—the water is too swift."[11] He added, "It's still rising here and the water is

Downtown Brady, Texas, during the 1938 flood (courtesy of the McCulloch County Historical Commission, Heart of Texas Historical Museum, Brady, Texas).

rising fast. . . . We only have this one telephone line left and it's liable to go at any second. The line stretches across the river and I can see fence poles and trees smashing into it now. . . . I don't know what we will do for drinking water—no one has had time to think about a drink for the last two hours."[12] Water reached a depth of five feet in the Mission Theater and one foot in the Bevans Hotel in Menard. The *San Angelo Standard-Times* remarked, "The San Saba River . . . made a war scene of Menard last night as citizens stacked sandbags as water barriers and then fled to higher grounds."[13]

At San Saba, the San Saba River began rising around 10 P.M. on July 20. The next day the river rose 20 feet (from 16.1 feet at 12:00 A.M. on July 21 to 36.1 feet at 12:00 A.M. on July 22). The *San Angelo Standard-Times* stated, "Fed with one mighty gulp from the rampaging Brady Creek, the San Saba River swelled to menacing flood proportions late last night as it swept toward the town of San Saba with a turbulent crest 35 feet high."[14]

In the morning of July 22, the San Saba River at San Saba dropped slightly before rising to 42.7 feet and retreating to 38.9 feet by midnight. The peak flow that day was 163,000 cfs at 2:30 P.M. The 42.7-foot stage was 0.1 feet above the previous high mark set in 1899. The river knocked out the bridge near Voca. One report from the air called the destruction at that spot so complete that it looked "as though no bridge had ever been there." Observers called to San Saba warn the town's residents that another rise (this one was 45 feet at Voca) was on its way. Aerial reports indicated that "San Saba presented a forlorn picture as water almost entirely surrounded the town and stretched out over fields as far as the eye could see." One block from the courthouse, water surged close to the business district, and approximately five hundred people were

driven from their homes as currents ran 2–3 feet deep through certain neighborhoods."[15]

On July 23 the San Saba River at San Saba paused in the early morning hours before surging to a 45.18-foot level at 11 A.M., which was accompanied by a 203,000 cfs flow. The *San Angelo Standard-Times* commented, "Derelict waters boiling along the tributaries of the Colorado . . . belched upon lowland country south and east of here . . . tossed homes like toy blocks into the surging brown fountains, and gutted a sector along the San Saba of its livestock and crops to match or surpass the loss of the unprecedented 1936 floods."[16]

On July 24 the river at San Saba lingered near the 37-foot level all day, rising to 39.32 feet at noon. As the currents surged in the town, motorboats from all over Central Texas were brought in to help rescue stranded citizens. In Austin, the chamber of commerce requested that motorboats be sent to San Saba. One Austin resident who was assisting in the rescue efforts at San Saba said, "I have never seen such a swift current. At one time in mid-stream, it was so swift that the 25 horsepower motor was unable to move us. The boat just sat there and quivered."[17] A Fox motion picture cameraman who made a three-hour trip to film

Brady, Texas, in the 1938 flood (courtesy of the McCulloch County Historical Commission, Heart of Texas Historical Museum, Brady, Texas).

the deluge at San Saba failed to return with footage because he had been so busy trying to save himself that he was unable to capture images.

On July 25 the San Saba River at San Saba maintained its 35-foot stage before dropping to 30 feet at midnight. Over the next two days, the river dropped from 29 feet to 21 feet and then to 17 feet. From July 22 to July 24 the river passed in excess of 690,000 acre-feet of water, more than four times its annual average discharge.

In the midst of the flood rescues, a small controversy developed. The *San Angelo Morning Times* headline of July 28 read, "Real Heroes of the San Saba Flood Were the Small-Town Boys Who Got There First and Stayed until Job Was Completed":

They talk about the "big-town" boys doing big things and broadcast it over a heavy net-

Aerial view of San Saba River flood at San Saba in 1938 (used with permission of the *San Saba News & Star*).

work of newspaper telegraph wires and blat it over the radio. The large cities have more facilities by which to tell the world about their heroes. But the unsung martyrs of no publicity fame are the spartan boys in the small towns who boast no agents. This weekend when San Saba was in the throes of its meanest flood disaster, by newspaper telegraph wires and by radio, tribute was paid to the rescue deeds of strong young men from Austin, the state's capital, and from other cities in the central and densely populated part of the commonwealth.

But permit me to inform you the REAL heroes of the war-torn sector were San Saba residents themselves and a galaxy of devil-may-care men and boys from Llano, 38 miles south of this stricken city.

Some of the bravest and most death-defying work done through the flood crisis here Saturday was turned in by a set of dare-

The San Saba River in flood at San Saba, 1938 (used with permission of the *San Saba News & Star*).

devil Llano men. This group sped into San Saba by the only open route during the city's four-day semi-isolation span."[18]

During their efforts, two rescuers "put their hands on every rooftop in that area" (under the railroad overpass east of San Saba)."[19] One of them tried to cross the violent San Saba River but was thwarted by the current, which was "so strong that it stood up the big boat at a 45 degree angle." He said, "Hell, they don't make a boat that can take that current!" He called these floods on "the sinister San Saba . . . the swiftest and most treacherous current he ever saw."[20]

Two of the stranded were stuck in a house west of San Saba. They slept in the attic one night and then cut a hole in the roof. For breakfast they cooked eggs and bacon on top of the house.

The San Saba River cut a path through the Riverside addition in the northwest part of town, then wandered through the northern sector and back up the south side. It carried away approximately twelve homes and damaged more than seventy others. One of those damaged had withstood three

floods and was among the oldest homes in town.

During the event, heavy rains in the San Saba Basin caused record rises on July 23 at three separate locations: on the San Saba River at San Saba at 11 A.M., on Brady Creek at Brady at 3 P.M., and on the San Saba River at Menard at 9 P.M. All of this water flowed unchecked into newly formed Lake Buchanan, presenting the Colorado River Authority (CRA) with it first critical opportunity to manage a flood on one of its reservoirs and to test its partially completed flood-control system.

Colorado River

Upstream of San Saba, the Colorado River was receiving early portions of floodwaters from the Concho River. Near San Saba, the Colorado started rising shortly after 12:00 A.M. on July 20. By 7 A.M. the river had reached a 10-foot stage, with 9,040 cfs. The Colorado continued on a slow, steady rise that day and the next, reaching 14 feet at 12:00 A.M. on July 21 and 18 feet twenty-four hours later.

July 22 saw the Colorado at San Saba rise 31 feet and reach 141,000 cfs. As the floodwaters from the San Saba began mingling with the Colorado, the latter turned "into a ribbon of dark brown, drift-covered water," which was clearly visible from the air as it penetrated the peaceful, clear waters. The big rise prompted river watchers to speculate that the newly completed Buchanan Dam, which was heralded for its help in limiting flood damage downstream in the 1936 flood, would be faced with its first chance to prevent similar destruction. The *Austin American* stated that Buchanan Lake "was reported as rising steadily Friday afternoon but flood-gate control at the dam will take care of the surplus water." [21]

As the record floods on the San Saba River from July 23 began feeding into the Colorado, record heights were reached that same day on the Colorado near San Saba, when the river hit 62.24 feet. This level exceeded the 1936 stage by more than 5 feet and the all-time record set on September 25, 1900, by 4.5 feet. The peak discharge on July 23 regis-

tered 224,000 cfs. For July 24 and 25, the river stayed above 51 feet before slowly dropping on July 26.

While preparing for the floods, the Colorado River Authority started releasing significant amounts of water from Buchanan Dam on the afternoon of July 22. A day earlier, the reservoir held 846,300 acre-feet of water while at a 1,013.42-foot level. At noon on July 22 the lake had risen to 1,015.38 feet and contained 888,500 acre-feet of water. At noon that day, the CRA began releasing water at 14,000 cfs, increasing the outflow to 28,500 cfs at 2 P.M. and 43,000 at 5 P.M.

That same day, Austin residents were expecting a rise on the Colorado, but, unlike previous swells, this would be a controlled increase from the releases at the Buchanan Dam. The *Austin American* predicted that "A man-made flood in the Colorado, held to harmless proportions, will reach Austin Saturday [July 23] as a substitute for what might have been a flood carrying considerable damage with it." [22]

As more water poured down the Colorado, Lake Buchanan kept rising—the

Looking downstream from Buchanan Dam during the release of water during the 1938 flood (courtesy of the LCRA Corporate Archives: W00889).

BUCHANAN DAM
7-26-38
LOOKING DOWNSTREAM FROM BRIDGE
FOURTEEN GATE SECTION

inflow jumped from 90,000 cfs at noon on July 22 to 154,000 cfs by noon on July 23 and 177,000 cfs by midnight on July 23. More water was released to make room for the accelerating inflow of floodwaters. On the morning of July 23 the release rate climbed from 45,000 at 12:20 A.M. to 64,000 at 6:40 A.M. and then to 84,000 at 8 A.M. At 11:20 A.M. the reservoir reached a level of 1,018.44 feet, which was within 2 feet of the spillway.

Around 12:20 P.M. water poured out of the dam at more than 100,000 cfs. Shortly after 12:20 P.M. the release rate jumped to 171,000 cfs for a couple of hours before dropping to 151,000 cfs. At midnight, the release rate was back up to 171,000 cfs.

In an attempt to manage the incoming flood, at 4 A.M. on July 24 the CRA released water at 189,000 cfs, which was 10,000 cfs above the peak streamflow of the Colorado River at San Saba in 1936. On July 24 the river's inflow into Buchanan ranged between 178,000 cfs and 186,000 cfs all day, so the dam was basically passing the full flow of water downstream.

On July 25 the release from the dam failed to keep up with the inflow, which reached 202,000 cfs at 1 P.M. The peak release rate was 192,000 cfs at 3:30 P.M. on July 25. At this point, the water was now approaching the spillway, reaching 1,019 feet at 11:20 P.M.

On July 26 the river's push into the Buchanan Reservoir decreased from 168,000 cfs at 3 A.M. to 106,000 cfs at noon. As the river slowed its flow into the lake, the release rate dropped from 165,000 cfs to 97,000 cfs by 1:30 P.M. Later that day, the release rate moved back up to more than 120,000 cfs before dropping to 100,000 at midnight. At 4:50 P.M. the lake level hit 1,020.16 feet.

Release rates ranged from 73,000 cfs to 97,000 cfs throughout July 27. The level of the lake peaked at 1,020.48 feet, Lake Buchanan's all-time high, and stayed above 1,020 feet all day.

In Austin, the river rose to 25 feet on July 23. At noon the river was flowing at 153,000 cfs, dashing people's hopes of a harmless rise, as even more water was charging toward Austin. The Colorado River in Austin rose from 26 feet at 1 A.M. on July 24 to its highest point of 32.1 at 6:30 P.M. on July 25. The peak discharge with the rise was 276,000 cfs, a streamflow surpassed only in 1869 and 1935. The daily discharge in Austin averaged 209,000 cfs on July 24 and peaked on July 25, when it averaged 254,000 cfs, before falling to 202,000 cfs on July 26.

The Colorado River at Smithville started to rise early on July 24. The river there shot up 18 feet that day and another 9 feet on July 25 before cresting at 36.02 feet at 4:25 A.M. on July 27. The maximum discharge reached 209,000 cfs. At Smithville, the river averaged 189,000 cfs on July 26 and 199,000 cfs on July 27.

While the unexpected flood in Austin caused minor damage, the deluge bearing down on the downstream communities and rural areas brought extensive destruction, especially since it struck the crops during a promising year. Farmers had predicted 3/4–1 bale of cotton per acre, and the picking would have begun in about two weeks. As the water swept over and ruined the crops, newspaper accounts chronicled how the "high water spread for miles over fertile fields. Refugees camped on hill tops and moved into the homes of friends in the higher places. Tearful women clutched frightened children and grim-lipped men stared absently at fields they had bent their backs over to stave off threatened bankruptcy because of previous floods. . . . Along the banks of the river, from Bastrop south, farmers moaned the loss of crops they said were the most promising since 1921."[23]

One reason the harvest prediction was so promising is that the floods of 1935 and 1936 had washed silt into the lowlands, depositing fertile soil in which farmers could plant their crops. Compounding the loss of the harvest was the financial scenario many farmers faced—they had borrowed money to plant their crops partially because previous floods had washed them away."[24]

With the river at its highest since 1935, the old La Grange bridge was swept away. The water level at La Grange was more than forty-four feet deep and reached within a block of the courthouse. The cotton and corn—the best in years—were both carried away.

Criticism of Buchanan Dam

Even before the flood had emptied into the Gulf of Mexico, Central Texans were talking about their false hopes of controlling the Colorado. On July 26, headlines in the *Austin American* stated, "Big Floods Are Blamed on Incompleted Central Texas

Brady Creek flood at the McCulloch County Courthouse several years before 1938 (courtesy of the McCulloch County Historical Commission, Heart of Texas Historical Museum, Brady, Texas).

Dams."[25] On July 27 the *San Antonio Express* headline said, "Colorado Dams Fail to Prevent Flood at Austin."[26]

Downstream residents were immediately critical of the 1938 inundation, labeling it a "man-made flood." One long-time Columbus resident commented that he had lived on the river his entire life and had never seen a flood like the one in 1938. In the "past the water all had been red, but now the back water is clear as crystal, indicating it came from a reservoir."[27]

The CRA responded to the criticism even before the lower Colorado communities began complaining about the management of Buchanan Dam. Fritz Englehard, chairman of the CRA, noted that "scant and sometimes tardy" river stage and rainfall information made the agency's job difficult. The CRA and flood control and electric power supporter Congressman Lyndon B. Johnson pointed out that, along the Colorado, not all of the dams were in place yet and that this was the main reason the flood could not be stopped."[28] Congressman Johnson commented forcefully about the capabilities of the Buchanan Dam versus the people's expectations of the lone dam to stop a major flood:

Anyone who would expect the Buchanan Dam to stop the present Austin flood all by itself would also expect his contractor to put up the roof of his house before he laid the foundations. If it hadn't been for Buchanan Dam two or three times the water flowing into Austin today would be on top of us for the simple reason that it will take the series of four CRA dams to provide complete flood-control insurance. Marshall Ford Dam will be the main flood control unit, and it is but partly finished. It will catch the Llano and Pedernales flood water. This is the reason we must get it built as fast as possible and as high as possible. Buchanan and Inks dams have done their work well and have fully proved their great value. Marshall Ford and Tom Miller dams will finish the job. The CRA is already taking steps to place flood gauges on all the creeks and tributaries of the Colorado so it will know exactly what to expect. At present, telephone and word of mouth are all that can be relied upon and they are unscientific.

It might be well for the critics who are tossing spears into the CRA and the builders of these great projects to remember that if the power companies had not blocked this progress with their ceaseless opposition from the beginning in the courts and out of them, we might now be far enough along with construction to prevent what we are going through. The sniping of these power companies and their hired legal henchmen scattered over our whole section, earning their high fees promoting the law's delays and undercutting everybody in the public service, should inspire all of us to fight harder to get this job done." [29]

Fritz Engelhard added that "as soon as the heavy rains were reported we began reducing the level of the dam to receive the additional water." [30] He stated that water coming into the Colorado "exceeds greatly that of the 1935 and 1936 floods." His view was that Buchanan Dam was to retard the flow and Marshall Ford Dam would "pinch it." [31]

By July 27 formal complaints from the downstream communities were being publicized throughout the state. The Columbus Chamber of Commerce wrote to Secretary of the Interior Harold Ickes: "The Buchanan flood control dam was being held full of water for purposes unexplainable. Rains occurred early in the week, and our information is the gates were not opened until Saturday, July 23, and when water was loosed it was discharged in such tremendous volume it is now approaching the di-

sastrous flood stage of 1935 which was the third highest in history." [32]

The Travis County agriculture agent noted that many farmers believed the water came down faster than in previous floods, carving out holes in the lowlands "as big as county courthouses" that would likely permanently damage the land." [33] Fayette County Judge E. A. Armin echoed the thoughts of many people who were living downstream of Lake Buchanan: "Was the dam full before the flood hit, and, if so, why? We will demand dams be used for flood control in part at least with power secondary and fishing and boating purely incidental." [34]

After making an investigation of his own, a Columbus resident stated that he couldn't "see that this flood was caused by anything but negligence." [35] A *San Antonio Express* article stated that, throughout the communities, men "stood in little groups on the streets and asked why Lake Buchanan assertedly was kept full of water to provide fishing and swimming and sailing for urban dwellers and then, they contended, allowed to ruin their farms when heavy rains came." [36] One farmer said, "Everyone said there would never be another flood. But now we find our corn and cotton washed away not by flood water but by clear water from Buchanan Lake." [37]

A Travis County farmer maintained that the Austin Weather Bureau told him "that any competent engineer should have known to open the flood gates at Buchanan Dam 48 hours before they were opened. . . . Every bit of the water that came through Austin as late as last Monday afternoon was directly from the dam." [38] In Washington, an initial response from Secretary of the Interior Ickes was that the law that authorized the building of Lake Buchanan required the conservation of water, which was as important as flood control. Attorney for the CRA A. J. Wirtz added that, "if there has been any negligence it has been because of the engineers' advice. The directors have operated the dam through technical advice given them by engineers whom they employed."[39]

Congressman J. J. Mansfield, chairman of the Rivers and Harbors Committee of the House of Representatives, added, "I've farmed on this river for many, many years. From my experience in Columbus and in Congress, I can say no one here will ever see complete control of the Colorado. It is impossible. The best we can do is to obtain a reasonable reduction of overflows. The Seine River in France has been flooding since the days of Julius Caesar in spite of all protection measures the French government had built."[40]

A subplot developed when E. J. Crofoot, president of the Gulf Coast Water Company in Bay City, produced a copy of a letter sent to Clarence McDonough of the CRA, dated June 24, 1938. In it Crofoot stated, "[T]here was considerable criticism of 'so nearly filling Buchanan Dam' and stating 'if you can by publicity or some other means in some manner counteract this feeling, I am sure it would be helpful to your authority.'" Crofoot added that McDonough's reply was, "We have worked this situation out and assure you that, with the greatest flood we have ever had above Buchanan Dam, such a flood can be controlled without producing any flood in the lower river."[41]

On July 7 Crofoot sent a second letter that addressed the needs of rice growers, who required more water from the Colorado for their crops. He wrote, "I cannot believe that it is profitable either for you or for us to experiment with flows in the river to the detriment of crops. We had given farmers to understand that we would have ample water at all times for as much acreage as we planted. . . . The river report this morning gives the stage at Austin as a minus 5 which is the same as it has been for several days." He added that, in 1937, his organization had

to secure an injunction to force the CRA to release water, which they did for three days—until the injunction was reversed. Crofoot's organization then paid the city of Austin $2,500 to open gates, he said. In 1934 they worked with Lake Brownwood to release water."[42]

Talk of the dam was also hot among Austinites. At a meeting of the Austin Rotary Club, Fred Adams of Adams Extract commented, "Our money is gone and so are the farmers' crops—gone down the river. . . . And there is no use blaming any one personally. They did not mean to do it. . . . But if it is possible by opening a few gates in one dam to cause such vast damage as is now being wrought down the river— is it not conceivable that with four dams above us they could wash the business district of Austin away? . . . We will only be safe when we can place dams in the hands of honest, practical men who will . . . not let the lakes fill up with floods even if President Roosevelt should want to sail his boat on them."[43]

The controversy prompted various U.S. agencies and the Texas state government to act. On August 1 H. W. Bashore of the U.S. Reclamation Bureau arrived in Austin to formally study the operation of the Buchanan Dam during the 1938 flood. On August 9 the Texas Senate began an inquiry into the operation of Lake Buchanan. Former governor Dan Moody represented Bastrop, Fayette, Colorado, Wharton, and Matagorda counties. University of Texas professor T. U. Taylor testified that the flood could have been prevented if the gates had been opened forty-eight hours earlier: "Until Buchanan Lake is kept empty there will be repetition of these floods. To afford flood protection, a dam must have its gates open and its lake full of air. As a reservoir for power production, it must be full of water. The two functions—power production and flood control—are absolutely antago-

BUCHANAN DAM INFLOW AND OUTFLOW, JULY 21–27, 1938

DATE	TIME	INFLOW	OUTFLOW
July 21	1:00 A.M.	16,000	500
	12:00 P.M.	28,000	500
July 22	4:00 A.M.	35,000	
	8:00 A.M.	42,000	
	12:00 P.M.	50,000	500
	2:00 P.M.		1,400
	2:30 P.M.		28,500
	3:00 P.M.	68,000	
	5:00 P.M.		43,000
	6:00 P.M.	67,000	
	9:00 P.M.	78,000	
	12:00 A.M.	90,000	45,000
	1:20 A.M.		51,000
July 23	3:00 A.M.	104,000	
	6:00 A.M.	119,000	
	6:40 A.M.		64,000
	7:15 A.M.		71,000
	7:40 A.M.		78,300
	8:00 A.M.		84,000
	9:00 A.M.	132,000	
	12:00 P.M.	144,000	
	12:30 P.M.		104,000
	2:40 P.M.		171,000
	3:00 P.M.	154,000	
	3:20 P.M.		151,000
	4:40 P.M.		135,000
	5:40 A.M.		153,000
	6:00 P.M.	162,000	
	9:00 P.M.	170,000	
	12:00 P.M.	177,000	171,000
	12:40 A.M.		171,000
July 24	3:00 A.M.	182,000	
	4:20 A.M.		176,000
	4:30 A.M.		184,000
	6:00 A.M.	184,000	
	9:00 A.M.	186,000	
	12:00 P.M.	184,000	189,000
	3:00 P.M.	180,000	
	6:00 P.M.		186,500
	7:00 P.M.	178,000	
	10:00 P.M.	179,000	
	12:00 P.M.	182,000	184,000
July 25	2:00 A.M.	188,000	
	4:00 A.M.	193,000	
	6:00 A.M.		183,000
	8:00 A.M.	198,000	
	12:00 P.M.		188,000
	1:00 P.M.	202,000	
	3:00 P.M.	200,000	
	4:00 P.M.		187,000
	4:20 P.M.		180,000
	5:00 P.M.	193,000	
	8:00 P.M.	184,000	
	9:30 P.M.		176,000
	12:00 A.M.	176,000	162,000

DATE	TIME	INFLOW	OUTFLOW
July 26	3:00 A.M.	168,000	
	4:00 A.M.		165,000
	6:00 A.M.	158,000	
	7:45 A.M.		148,000
	9:00 A.M.	145,000	
	10:00 A.M.		113,000
	11:00 A.M.	134,000	
	1:00 P.M.	128,000	
	1:30 P.M.		97,000
	2:20 P.M.		106,000
	3:00 P.M.		98,000
	3:45 A.M.		108,000
	4:00 P.M.	121,000	
	4:30 P.M.		102,000
	5:00 P.M.		121,000
	6:15 P.M.		128,000
	7:00 P.M.	116,000	
	10:45 P.M.		122,000
	12:00 A.M.	106,000	100,000
	1:45 A.M.		100,000
July 27	3:00 A.M.	100,000	
	3:30 A.M.		93,000
	4:15 A.M.		87,000
	6:00 A.M.	95,000	80,000
	9:45 A.M.		73,000
	10:45 A.M.		81,000
	12:00 P.M.	88,000	
	1:20 P.M.		89,000
	1:50 P.M.		97,000
	6:00 P.M.	82,000	89,000
	12:00 A.M.	77,000	86,500

Discharge in cubic feet/second

nistic. The choice must be made between the farmer in the valley or the money dividend in the hills. This disaster indicates that someone in the Lower River Authority should be elected to a life membership in the 'bonehead club.'" Upon cross-examination, Taylor admitted he had no specific data, as information was being gathered at the time of the investigation, but he prodded the CRA by stating, "Why don't you put your own engineers on the stand here and ask them those questions?" Taylor later amended his statement about the "bonehead club," saying the appropriate authorities should receive a suspended sentence instead."[44]

McDonough commented to the Texas Senate committee that more than two million acre-feet of water had come down the Colorado into Lake Buchanan. He added, "If the gates had been open since Christmas" and the lake was less than half full, water in Austin would have been one foot lower and less than that below Austin because of the "unprecedented quantity of water powered into the basin."[45] He said the CRA opened the gates at noon on July 22, six hours after receiving notice of a major inflow moving downriver. He maintained that, at the peak, Austin could handle 400,000 acre-feet of water per day without an overflow and that this flood exhibited a peak flow of 190,000 cfs for twenty-four hours.

On August 11 a preliminary version of Bashore's report was released. It contended that the dam had "actually reduced the recent flood in the vicinity of Austin by one foot and did not contribute to its inundation as charged."[46] The report also added that, if the dam gates had not been closed at the height of the flood, the stage in Austin would have been reduced three feet. Albert Stone, senator from Brenham, commented, "Three feet makes a lot of difference, especially in flat country."[47] Bashore's report concluded that, "while better preparation should have been made for emergency operation of the dam, it is doubtful if any careful forethought would have had much effect in reducing the damage caused by a flood having a peak flow and volume as great as that of July 1938."[48]

The controversy over the dam and the CRA's management spilled over into the editorial pages of the *Dallas Morning News* and the *Austin American*. On August 12 the *Dallas Morning News* repeated E. O. Taulbee's comments that, "From a study of the Lower Colorado River by the United States Bureau of Reclamation, they affirm that there are no locations for reservoirs below Austin, and for this we thank God, as any reservoir filled

Anecdote
According to an article titled "Flood Stocks Buchanan Lake with Young Fish," which appeared in the *San Antonio Express* on July 30, 1938, the flooding along the Concho curiously aided one local agency. When fish from the San Angelo–area fish hatchery were swept away during the flood, the game commissioner from the hatchery wryly observed, "We saved the costs of delivery, although the fish didn't go exactly where we'd have placed them."

with water, above the coastal Plain, is a direct menace to life and property here."[49]

The *Austin American-Statesman* commented on the article in the *Dallas Morning News:* "This continued attack upon the series of dam projects is unfair and unjust, by *The News*' own arbitrary foot rule. It is a malicious twisting of facts to suit a particular purpose and unfair journalism."[50]

On August 17 the *Austin American-Statesman* further remarked, "Those who tell you that our lakes should be yawing sun-baked mud flats—remind them that we do have drouths. And if there is anything more horrible than a flood, it is a drouth."[51] In response, McDonough added, "We cannot keep the reservoirs empty because we must conserve the water to repay Fed loans that have made flood control possible. We can empty the reservoirs before floods approach, hold down the overflow and store the water. It can then be used for power production and irrigation purposes."[52]

MAY 1949

~~~~~~~~

Downtown Fort Worth Flood

BY 1949 THE city of Fort Worth had been battling the Trinity River for decades. One of the most severe floods on that river ripped through Fort Worth in 1922. Twenty-five years after the event, a *Fort Worth Star-Telegram* article noted that, by improving levees and damming the river to create Lake Bridgeport and Eagle Mountain Lake, the city of Fort Worth had "pioneered in flood control while other cities awaited government aid."[1] The article also stated that more work was under way to provide additional protection.

In May 1949 floodwaters from the Clear Fork and the West Fork of the Trinity River surged into Fort Worth, and the flood-protection measures of the previous quarter century proved inadequate. The resulting flood stages exceeded those of 1922. Levee failure added to the destruction in the Fort Worth area.

May 1949 Weather

Texas weather news in May 1949 focused on a deadly tornado that hit Amarillo, the first destructive tornado in sixty-three years in that city. The typically active May weather pattern for North Texas continued in mid-May. On the night of May 16 a slow-moving frontal storm approached Forth Worth, traveling along the Clear Fork and West Fork river basins from the west. Around 12:30 A.M. it was near Wichita, Kansas, then moved to east of Wichita Falls and just west of Junction and Del Rio. Thunderstorms formed along its entire length. As

the front approached Fort Worth, it slowed, and the rain totals escalated. Between 6 P.M. and 3 A.M. rainfall topped 8 inches at Cresson and 7.5 inches at the Fort Worth courthouse. A large portion of the Clear Fork watershed upstream from Fort Worth received up to 6 inches in six hours.

By the end of the storm, 11 inches of rain had fallen at the junction of Bear Creek and South Bear Creek at the county line between Parker and Tarrant counties, nearly midway between Cresson and Benbrook. Southeast of Fort Worth near the Sycamore Creek watershed, 12 inches of rain fell. Kennedale received 12.8 inches in nine hours. From west of Aledo to just west of Dallas, the Clear Fork and then the West Fork of the Trinity after Fort Worth received more than 7 inches of rain.

Streams

The intense precipitation produced a flood wave along the Clear Fork of the Trinity River. Near Aledo, the Clear Fork peaked at both 3:45 A.M. and 8 A.M. with peaks of 25 feet and 12,400 cfs and 24.9 feet and 12,200 cfs, respectively. These stages were well below the 1922 record of 34 feet. Around 10 P.M. on May 16 the Clear Fork near Benbrook started rising substantially. By midnight it had risen 20 feet from its 6 P.M. level of 3.3 feet. At 3:30 A.M. on May 17 the river peaked at 82,900 cfs and 28.72 feet. It then receded before hitting a second, lesser peak of 28.51 feet and 78,000 cfs at 7:30 A.M.

The May 1949 flood in Fort Worth, Texas (courtesy of the Genealogy, History, and Archives Unit, Fort Worth Public Library).

At the Vickery Boulevard bridge in Forth Worth, water began rising on the evening of May 16. By midnight, it had risen more than 12 feet, to 15.1 feet, from a 2.8-foot level at 6 A.M. earlier that day. The river rose steadily throughout the morning of May 17. At 5:30 A.M. it surpassed its previous record stage of 27.4 feet, which was set in 1922, by hitting 28.2 feet. The peak flow was 107,000 cfs—almost 33,000 cfs greater than during the 1922 flood.

At the West Fork of the Trinity River gage in Fort Worth, located a quarter mile downstream from the mouth of the Clear Fork, the flood started early in the morning of May 17. At 12:30 A.M. the West Fork was at 9.28 feet. By 4:30 A.M. it was above 20 feet. The flood paused at 24 feet and a flow of approximately 51,000 cfs from 5:30 A.M. to 9 A.M. before rising again. It peaked at 12:30 P.M., reaching 25.91 feet with a flow of 64,400 cfs. The crests were affected by breaks in levees upstream from the gage and one break below it. On May 17 the average daily streamflow was 42,500 cfs.

At Dallas, predictions from the weather bureau prompted residents to prepare for a flood of 40–42 feet. The city's weather bureau stated, "A wall of water coming

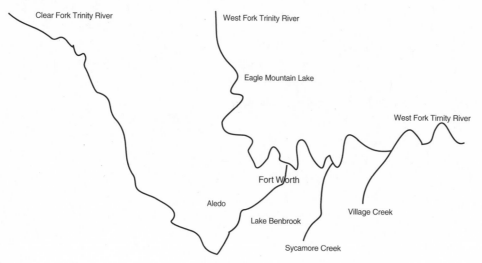

Trinity River Basin near Fort Worth

down from the West Fork of the Trinity from the Fort Worth area, merging with a flood crest from Carrollton on the Elm Fork, will bring a major flood to the Dallas area. Combining with flood waters from the East Fork of the Trinity, below Dallas, it will cause major flood conditions during the next eight to 10 days."[2]

Floodwaters from the West Fork and the Elm Fork propelled the Trinity River at Dallas to 46.93 feet on May 18 at 4:30 A.M. The peak flow of 82,500 cfs was less than half that of the 1908 record. A portion of the flood was absorbed by the wide flood plain, which was improved in 1930 to better accommodate flooding in Dallas.

Fort Worth Flood

Floodwaters reached Camp Bowie Boulevard, Seventh Street, University Drive, and Bailey Street. As the currents swept into Forth Worth, residents dealt with a familiar foe, which a caption in the *Fort Worth Star-Telegram* of May 17 colorfully characterized as the "Same Old Outlaw."[3]

At the west end of the Van Zandt viaduct on West Seventh street, floodwaters ten feet deep were flowing over the road. Homes ranging from shanties to a six-room house were washed against the viaduct there. The impact, which caused the concrete bridge to shake, smashed the homes to bits. One

count listed eight houses floating in the floodwaters between 4:45 A.M. and 7 A.M.

From Lancaster Street north to the West Fork and bounded by University Drive and the Clear Fork, a large area of about fifty city blocks was flooded. Livestock were driven from the riverbanks north of Belknap and wandered, bawling, down Henderson and Weatherford streets. Near a region nicknamed "Flood Bend," a break in the Samuels Avenue levee around 7 A.M. on May 17 flooded houses in the lowlands between Northeast Tenth Street and Northeast Fifteenth Street.

The residents of Crestwood and Linwood additions moved out after four levee breaks prompted police to use loudspeakers to urge them to evacuate. The first man to buy a house in Crestwood addition was one of the first to alert neighbors of the rising waters. After watching the water rise for two hours, he sent his wife out of the area around 3 A.M. He and his son returned to stack furniture after warning the neighbors. At 6 A.M., as he left his home in a rescue boat, he said, "I've suffered every flood, all five of them. The water is above my windows now."[4] One person was notified of the flood at 6:30 A.M. by a *Fort Worth Star-Telegram* photographer and evacuated in waist-deep water.

Trucks from the Carswell Air Force Base worked for hours pulling partly submerged trailers from the flooded Lazy

Fort Worth, Texas, in the May 1949 flood (courtesy of the Genealogy, History, and Archives Unit, Fort Worth Public Library).

DOWNTOWN FORT WORTH FLOOD

Land Trailer Court on White Settlement Road. And in Fort Worth, with residents trying to beat the floodwaters, the streets were hopping with activity. Dozens of young men helped by driving cars from used car lots. The roads were jammed early in the morning, but police kept the bumper-to-bumper traffic moving during the evacuation.

High water invaded the zoo, where, on May 17, currents flowed 2½ feet deep in the facility's offices. Water reached a depth of about 12 feet on Forest Park Drive, which runs through the zoo. At the height of the flood, the top of the merry-go-round was barely visible. The zoo director reported that he could see white deer swimming about their cage. He commented, "They could swim right out of their cage

if they had a mind to; the water is well over the eight foot fence there."[5] If the water had been 2 feet higher at the alligator cage, the zoo's 10-foot alligators might have gone swimming around Fort Worth, he added.

Floodwaters also caused major damage at the Colonial Country Club and Rockwood golf courses. (The 1949 Colonial golf tournament was canceled that year, following the May floods.) Boats piloted by firemen and police rescued the Colonial golf course caretaker and his family from their two-story stone home. The motorboats appeared to barely move against the powerful current as they headed upstream for a landing point about halfway between the first tee and the green. At the Rockwood golf course, the eighteenth green, the prac-

Fort Worth, Texas, May 1949. The top photo shows floodwater at the Montgomery Ward building (courtesy of the Genealogy, History, and Archives Unit, Fort Worth Public Library).

tice tee, and the clubhouse were the only points above water. The caretaker of the swimming pool was carried to safety in a boat after water reached a depth of four feet in his house.

At the La Grave ballpark, which was decimated by a fire two days earlier, water crept around the park. The groundskeeper evacuated his family from their home at 10 A.M., as water came through the levee and from storm sewers.

Montgomery Ward

One of the famous photographs of the 1949 flood was the high-water snapshot at the Montgomery Ward building, where the floodwater was ten feet deep at the building's west end and engulfed the first floor.

City Water Plant

The flood disabled Fort Worth's water pumps, as they were covered with water. In response to their failure, the Fort Worth City Council asked all nonessential businesses without a private water supply to close until the situation improved. To get the plant back in action, a new motor was sent from Indianapolis, Indiana. State highway patrols in Missouri, Oklahoma, and Texas were alerted

to locate a truck en route, carrying the electric motor destined for Fort Worth. Authorities feared that flooding in Oklahoma would slow down the shipment. After his 1,009 mile, thirty-three-hour journey, the driver of the truck carrying the motor was labeled "Fort Worth's own private Paul Revere." The *Fort Worth Star-Telegram* called the sounding of police sirens a message—"to faucets, to faucets, the water is coming"—to Fort Worth residents as the truck rolled into town at 12:40 A.M. on May 20.[6]

The driver had left Indianapolis at 4 P.M. on May 18 and stopped once—for 15 minutes on May 19. He commented, "It was the most important cargo I ever hauled. I tuned in my radio this morning and heard the announcer say folks in Fort Worth had no water, even for drinking. That's why I continued to shove it so hard. . . . . They asked me if I could get to Fort Worth in 48 hours. I told them under the circumstances I could do it in 32. I set out to make the trip in 28 hours and would have, too, except for heavy rain in Missouri."[7]

In Oklahoma he was stopped by a sheriff who believed he was driving too fast. The sheriff told him that "every patrol in Oklahoma was looking for him, to get the shipment through." He didn't stop again after the patrol picked up the truck ten miles north of McAlister, Oklahoma, until he reached Dallas, where he stopped for five minutes to unload machinery. A new patrol picked up the truck every twenty-five miles without slowing the vehicle.[8] He said, "You know, the folks down here have had so much trouble—storms and floods—that it just sort of did me good to get that motor here."[9]

Rescues

A woman who was caught in the current survived by swimming to a Ferris wheel in a nearby amusement park. She was tossed into the water again, though, when a tank

Fort Worth, Texas, in flood in the 1950s and early 1960s (courtesy *Forth Worth Star-Telegram*, Special Collections, University of Texas at Arlington Library, Arlington, Texas).

Flood scenes from the May 1949 flood in Fort Worth, Texas (courtesy of the Genealogy, History, and Archives Unit, Fort Worth Public Library).

hit the Ferris wheel. The water then carried her into a tree, where a rope was thrown to her to pull her to safety.

One man was running a boat up and down a flooded street, creating a wake that forced water into a grocery store and knocked merchandise off the shelves. When a patrolman told him to stop, the boatman replied, "Ha! Ha! Why don't you come and get me?" As he returned for another pass, his motor conked out. The patrolman then waded out to the man, whom he jailed for disturbing the peace.[10]

Follow-Up

In the days after the flood, the Fort Worth city health director urged people to not eat food that had been under water: "Some people seem to think that they can trim an inch or two off a piece of meat and that it will be all right to eat. It will not be fit for human consumption regardless of trimming."[11]

The Fort Worth city council speeded up work on flood control, including the Benbrook Dam project addressing inte-

rior drainage between the levees of the two forks of the Trinity River. In another step to accelerate flood protection and repair the levees, the Corps of Engineers planned to open bids on May 23 with the intention of awarding a contract in only a few hours. The agency added, "Red tape will have to take care of itself. We can not afford any delays in this work."[12]

Area

Around Fort Worth, floodwaters threatened a number of towns, and parts of White Settlement were evacuated. Near Hico, a man died when he drove a load of cattle

Photo used to encourage citizens to vote for additional flood protection in Fort Worth, Texas (courtesy *Forth Worth Star-Telegram* photograph collection, Special Collections Division, University of Texas at Arlington Library, Arlington, Texas).

Flood photo from the 1950s and early 1960s in Fort Worth, Texas (courtesy *Fort Worth Star-Telegram* photograph collection, Special Collections Division, University of Texas at Arlington Library, Arlington, Texas).

over a condemned bridge that collapsed. In West Texas, however, the rainfall was greeted with joy. The president of the First National Bank at Floydada said the region was experiencing its best season since 1941. The vice president of the Big Lake State Bank reported that the building had water to a depth of eight feet.

Summary

Damage estimates exceeded $15 million for the flood, with $11 million from the city of Fort Worth. In reviewing the flood, James A. Cotton of the U.S. Army Corps of Engineers said, "It was primarily a flood of the Clear Fork swelled by heavy rainfalls on the lower Clear Fork and the lower part of its watershed. It was simply too much water. It was too much for the levees." He added that Eagle Mountain Lake held up the West

Fork, which was a little over bank full in Fort Worth.[13]

Col. R. L. Robinson, head of the Galveston District Office of the U.S. Army Corps of Engineers, joined Cotton and said a thorough study was needed to see how runoff was divided above and below the Benbrook Dam site. He was sure that "if the Benbrook Dam already had been built on the Clear Fork and a proposed improved floodway system completed through Fort Worth, there would have been no real river flood for the city. Local overflow such as on Farmers Branch and Sycamore Creek would have resulted, but the main flood would have been eliminated."[14] Cotton added that theoretically a flood could still originate in the one hundred square miles between the Benbrook Dam and the head of the Fort Worth levees until additional work was done on the floodway program.

SEPTEMBER 1952

~~~~~~~~~

Pedernales River Flood

THE EARLY-TO-MID-1950S IN Texas are known for an oppressive and extreme drought. Even during this period, however, torrential rainfalls and flash floods did not cease in the Lone Star State. One of the most extreme flash floods in the history of the Hill Country struck in September 1952. The deluges of that month produced surges in the north-central Hill Country rivers, including the Pedernales, Blanco, San Saba, Llano, and Guadalupe, which changed from having no streamflow to registering near-record numbers in less than forty-eight hours. A month later, the drought continued its stranglehold, with no rainfall in much of the Hill Country throughout October.

Precedent Conditions

The previous two years were dry ones for much of Central Texas. In 1950, cities with deficits of at least 7 inches were New Braunfels (12), Llano (9), Austin (7), Boerne (8), and Kerrville (7). As bad as that year was for the region in terms of rainfall, 1951 was even worse. The deficits in inches for Central and West Texas were Boerne (14), Kerrville (11), Junction (12), Llano (10), Mason (14), Brady (12), Rocksprings (12), Sonora (15), Temple (13), Menard (15), and San Saba (17).

For the first six months of 1952, many Hill Country locations enjoyed a reprieve from the drought. Blanco registered above-average rainfall for each month in a March-through-July stretch, highlighted by a 6.19-inch total in May. Fredericksburg, Hunt, Kerrville, and Llano each recorded above-average precipitation from March through June.

July and August, however, brought their usual hot and dry weather. Tarpley, San Saba, Mason, Rocksprings, Austin, Boerne, Hunt, Blanco, and Fredericksburg all reported no rainfall whatsoever for August. Kerrville, Hondo, Brackettville, Llano, New Braunfels, San Angelo, and Temple all received less than a quarter inch of rain for the month.

Many Hill Country streams were at their all-time record lows. The Llano River at Llano had virtually dried up in August, requiring the city of Llano to ship in water in train cars. Lake Travis held only 374 acre-feet of water, which was only thirty percent of flood capacity. According to the records of the Lower Colorado River Authority (LCRA), Travis's all-time low is 619.06 feet, recorded on September 6, 1952.

In early September the federal government sponsored a program called "Operation Haylift" to ship hay from Iowa to Texas. Initially, seventy-three counties were eligible to receive these shipments. Three counties north of the Hill Country—Brown, Taylor and Erath—were the first to place orders.

Farther up from San Antonio and Austin, San Angelo continued its embattled relationship with water. The September 7 edition of the *San Angelo Standard-Times* summarized the synoptic weather scenario, noting the presence of a high-pressure system over the eastern United States and a low moving up from Mexico to Arizona and into Idaho. The article commented that

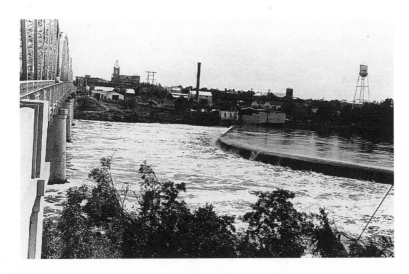

The Llano River at Llano was dry before the 1952 flood. This photo was taken after the flood moved through town (courtesy of the LCRA Corporate Archives: W00888).

rained again. . . . [The] bitter water shortage of 51–52 would not have occurred if gates had been closed. . . . This [lost water] will always remain one of the big question marks in San Angelo's history."[3]

The severity of the drought west of San Angelo was evident in the condition of desert plants—even cactus and yucca near Big Spring were dying from lack of water. A Central Texas resident said, "Dry and hot aren't enough to describe it. . . . Water in wells? We out here haven't seen any water in wells in so long that we have forgotten them."[4]

Rainfall

On September 9 an easterly wave moved into South Texas. A sounding taken that morning pinpointed the center of the wave just north of San Antonio. Over the next twenty-four hours, the wave moved to the west-northwest and encountered lift from the Balcones Escarpment and Edwards Plateau.

On September 9, as Operation Haylift was getting under way, rains began to fall. Initially they were slow and soaking, simultaneously earning the "dust-settling" and "million-dollar" rain labels from the Austin newspapers.[5] They worked their way up from the coast and into Central Texas, the Hill Country, and the edges of West Texas. Precipitation was reported from Austin to Uvalde and to Winters. In San Angelo the high temperature was only 81 degrees on the day the city banned the "water-using coolers."[6] In Johnson City, a partial total from September 9 and 10 recorded four inches of rain in twenty-four hours, prompting an area resident to remark that the moisture is "saving a lot of guys here."[7]

Then the gentle showers turned into deluges. Reports of 6–10 inches came in from San Marcos northwestward to Eden throughout September 10. As the rains came

this potentially promising pattern had not yet delivered: "The pressure systems weren't slammed right to stir up any moisture-laden clouds. . . . The most heartening statement was that the back of the real summer heat apparently is definitely broken."[1]

Two days after the *San Angelo Standard-Times* proclaimed that the summer heat was broken, the city of San Angelo announced drastic measures to conserve water. The city commission passed an amendment declaring a state of emergency and banning the use of air conditioners that used water. Sonora offered relief in the form of up to 1,016,000 gallons of water daily—if San Angelo supplied a means to transport it.[2]

San Angelo residents recalled that the inability to corral water from a 1951 rise on the North Concho River contributed to their need to ration the precious substance. In August 1951 the North Concho flowed from bank to bank for approximately twelve hours. The *San Angelo Standard-Times* commented on the frustrating situation: "It would not take more than a few hours to extend the line to the dam, but no responsible person was willing to assume the responsibility of ordering the gates closed and holding the water behind the dam. . . . No one had any idea it would be 13 months before it

138 down, LCRA officials noted, "it was a complete change from a short time ago when artificial rain makers were working to create rain."[8] These downpours soon became 10–20 inch rains. At Kerrville 12 inches fell, but a spokesman there maintained, "We can stand 12 more inches today and still not be in any danger of a flood."[9] In the Floresville area, the rain was considered a blessing. One resident remarked, "This is a lifesaver for us, and the finest rain in many, many years. We have no complaints, only happiness."[10]

The intense rains tallied up to 23 inches over an eight-county area, with the heaviest downpours hitting the San Saba, Llano, Fredericksburg, Blanco, Johnson City, Marble Falls, and Boerne areas. The drenching covered a 60-by-200-mile section near New Braunfels and Selma at the southeast tip, northwestward to San Saba and Paint Rock, farther west to Menard, east of Junction, and south to near Hondo. Extending from Hye to near Stonewall and north about 10 miles to Grape Creek,

the heaviest downpours loosed 26 inches of rain. Other high totals of 24 inches occurred between Bankersmith and Waring and between Cherokee and Llano, where a total of 18 inches was measured. Double-digit tallies for one day were also recorded at Blanco (17.47), Gold (13.8), Llano (12.53), and Hye (20.7).

The Brady Creek watershed gauged 14 inches at spots, and the rains in the Brady area were welcomed. One resident called the downpour the "finest rain he had ever witnessed since residing in Brady." Near Rochelle, one resident noted that precipitation fell for almost fifty hours. Another rancher from Melvin responded to the 10–12 inch tally by stating, "Miles and miles of smiles [are seen] on the farmers' faces around Melvin these days" as it has been a long time since "the farming Mecca of McCulloch County has had a grand soaker." A rancher from Mercury called it the "finest rain I have ever witnessed in my long ranching career in McCulloch County."[11] Rochelle's rains were labeled as

Scene from the washout of the Highway 281 bridge at Johnson City, Texas (courtesy of the LCRA Corporate Archives: W00727).

Washout of the Highway 281 bridge, Johnson City, Texas (courtesy of the LCRA Corporate Archives: W00728).

"one of those 'dream rains'—slow and easy with no wind."[12]

The bulk of the flooding rains fell in the Colorado River Basin. Lake Travis, the last large reservoir and one that would become the chief flood-control lake in the Lower Colorado River chain, was sitting at its record low for the next fifty years. Floods moved down the San Saba River, Llano River, and, most dramatically, the Pedernales River.

Brady Creek

The San Saba River flooded largely due to the rise on Brady Creek. With big rains falling in its watershed, Brady Creek again tested Brady's levee system. As precipitation in the upper section of Brady Creek at Eden was "knowing no curb," the *Brady Standard* noted that the downpour "continued to discourage Brady workers as they doggedly prepared for a crippling."[13]

Brady Creek was one of the first streams in the Colorado Basin to flood. Shortly after 6 A.M. on September 10, the creek surged from near zero discharge to greater than 32,000 cfs. With the rise coming down the creek that morning, Brady went into flood-prevention mode. At dawn, water had reached the bottom of the bridge on the San Angelo highway. The floodwaters rose approximately 6 inches per hour during the morning hours. It was evident that downtown Brady was going to trust again in "Fort Sandbag."[14] Brady High School students were dismissed from classes to help sandbag the downtown areas, and merchants moved their goods to second-story locations. Around 11 A.M., warning sirens sounded. The peak of the flood occurred at 12:10 P.M., reaching a 24.8-foot stage, falling some 20 inches shy of the top of the flood wall and 4.3 feet below the 1938 maximum. The creek peaked at 39,100 cfs.

Because the water did not eclipse the floodwall, most of the damage occurred away from downtown. At Richards Park,

Aside	On September 12, 1952, in an article titled "We Offer Our Thanks," the *Brady Standard* printed a list of things to be thankful for. Some of the items listed were the following: • Thankful that the flood commission did the flood control work during times of drought • Thankful for the spirit of the high school boys for their assistance • Thankful for the multi-million dollar rain, the finest we have had in the Heart o' Texas country in 14 years • Thankful that we are today doing business as usual

LOCATION	DATE 1	2	3	4	5	6	7	8	9
Austin	0.00	0.00	0.00	0.00	0.00	0.00	0.00	o	1.08
Blanco	0.00	0.00	0.00	0.00	0.00	0.00	0.00	0.00	o
Boerne	0.00	0.00	0.00	0.00	0.00	0.00	0.00	0.00	0.59
Brackettville	0.00	0.00	0.00	0.00	0.00	0.00	0.00	0.00	0.00
Brady	0.00	0.45	0.00	0.00	0.00	0.00	0.00	0.00	0.00
Burnet	0.00	0.00	0.00	0.00	0.00	0.00	0.00	0.00	1.30
Del Rio	0.00	0.00	0.00	0.00	0.00	0.00	0.00	0.01	0.03
Doss	0.00	0.00	0.00	0.00	0.00	0.00	0.00	0.00	3.25
Fredericksburg	0.00	0.00	0.00	0.00	0.00	0.00	0.00	0.00	0.77
Gold	0.00	0.00	0.00	0.00	0.00	0.00	0.00	0.00	2.63
Hondo	0.00	0.00	0.00	0.00	0.00	0.00	0.00	0.00	0.15
Henly	0.00	0.00	0.00	0.00	0.00	0.00	0.00	0.00	2.52
Hunt	0.00	0.00	0.00	0.00	0.00	0.00	0.00	0.00	0.00
Hye	0.00	0.00	0.00	0.00	0.00	0.00	0.00	0.00	0.00
Junction	0.00	0.50	0.00	0.00	0.00	0.00	0.00	0.00	0.16
Kerrville	0.00	0.00	0.00	0.00	0.00	0.00	0.00	0.00	o
Lampasas	0.00	0.00	0.00	0.00	0.00	0.00	0.00	0.00	0.00
Llano	0.00	0.00	0.00	0.00	0.00	0.00	0.00	0.00	o
Mason	0.00	0.13	0.00	0.00	0.00	0.00	0.00	0.00	1.10
Menard	0.00	0.00	0.00	0.00	0.00	0.00	0.00	0.00	0.00
New Braunfels	0.00	0.00	0.00	0.00	0.00	0.00	0.00	0.00	1.55
Richland Springs	0.87	0.00	0.00	0.00	0.00	0.00	0.00	0.00	2.35
Rocksprings	0.00	0.00	0.00	0.00	0.00	0.00	0.00	0.00	0.00
Roosevelt	0.00	0.00	0.00	0.00	0.00	0.00	0.00	0.00	0.22
Sabinal	0.00	0.00	0.00	0.00	0.00	0.00	0.00	0.00	0.00
San Marcos	0.00	0.00	0.00	0.00	0.00	0.00	0.00	0.00	0.35
San Saba	0.12	0.00	0.00	0.00	0.00	0.00	0.00	0.00	2.50
San Antonio	0.00	0.00	0.00	0.00	0.00	0.00	o	o	0.58
San Angelo	0.00	0.00	0.00	0.00	0.00	0.00	0.00	0.00	0.04
Sonora	0.00	o	0.00	0.00	0.00	0.00	0.00	0.00	0.00
Tarpley	0.00	0.00	0.00	0.00	0.00	0.00	0.00	o	0.15
Taylor	0.00	0.00	0.00	0.00	0.00	0.00	0.00	0.00	0.03
Temple	0.00	0.00	0.00	0.00	0.00	0.00	0.00	0.00	0.00
Uvalde	0.00	0.00	0.00	0.00	0.00	0.00	0.00	0.00	o

an amphibious vehicle was used to evacuate the park caretaker.

During the afternoon, a crew from Goodfellow Air Force base in San Angelo, led by a Brady native, brought fourteen trucks to help with efforts. One thousand workers from the Brady Aviation Corporation joined in the sandbagging work. During the night, another crest moved downstream, rising to a twenty-foot stage for two hours. As the water receded, Brady rejoiced in its successful flood-control strategy. On September 12 the *Brady Standard* stated that the "$300,000 federally constructed floodway bested a fluctuating crescendo of guideless waters from the rain-crazed Eden and Melvin watershed."[15] A headline from that same edition read, "Lesser of Two Evils . . . Thwarted Flood over Prolonged Drouth."[16]

Earlier in the year, work had been done to clean out the channel. In reviewing the flood at Brady, engineers estimated that the waters flowed through town at 8 mph, whereas

10	11	12	13	14	15	16	17	18	TOTAL
0.78	0.54	0.00	0.00	0	0.02	0.00	0.83	0.01	3.26
3.64	17.47	0.49	0.00	0.00	0.00	0.00	0.00	1.06	22.66
7.41	4.63	0.00	0.00	0.00	0.00	0.00	0.00	1.00	13.63
0.00	0.30	0.00	0.00	0.00	0.00	0.00	0.00	0.00	0.30
3.43	3.03	0.04	0.00	0.00	0.00	0.00	0.00	0.65	7.60
1.45	0.90	0.00	0.00	0.00	0.00	0.00	0.00	1.28	4.93
0.00	0	0.00	0.00	0.00	0.00	0.00	0.00	0.00	0.04
8.75	0.00	0.00	0.00	0.00	0.00	0.00	1.50	0.00	13.50
8.03	7.10	0.00	0.00	0.00	0.00	0.00	0.00	0.57	16.47
13.80	1.77	0.00	0.00	0.00	0.00	0.00	0.90	0.00	19.10
0.53	2.10	0.30	0.00	0.00	0.00	0.00	0.00	1.57	4.65
2.58	1.80	0.00	0.00	0.00	0.00	0.00	1.17	0.00	8.07
2.90	1.33	0.00	0.00		0.00	0.00	0.00	0.00	4.23
2.65	20.70	0.12	0.00	0.00	0.00	0.65	0.00	0.00	24.12
0.65	0.01	0.00	0.00	0.00	0.00	0.00	0.00	0.06	1.38
2.80	6.10	0.03	0.00	0.00	0.00	0.00	0.00	1.20	10.13
1.88	1.18	0.14	0.00	0.00	0	0.00	0.00	0.72	3.92
2.20	12.53	0.95	0.00	0.00	0.00	0.00	0.00	1.32	17.00
7.45	0.35	0.00	0.00	0.00	0.00	0.00	0.00	0.80	9.83
3.35	2.65	0.00	0.00	0.00	0.00	0.00	0.04	0.00	6.04
2.16	5.11	0.01	0.00	0.00	0.00	0.00	0.00	0.70	9.53
3.55	0.22	0.00	0.00	0.00	0.00	0.00	0.75	0.00	7.74
0.00	0.00	0.00	0.00	0.24	0.00	0.00	0.00	0.00	0.24
0.00	0.00	0.00	0.00	0.00	0.00	0.00	0.60	0.00	0.82
0.39	0.00	0.00	0.00	0.00	0.00	0.00	0.00	1.90	2.29
6.27	3.03	0.32	0.00	0.00	0.00	0.00	0.00	1.28	11.25
0.50	5.44	0.00	0.00	0.00	0.00	0.00	1.85	0.00	10.41
1.48	0.39	0.00	0.00	0.00	0.00	0.00	0.42	0.15	3.02
0.23	0.00	0.00	0.00	0.00	0.00	0	0.22	0.00	0.49
0.00	0.00	0.03	0.00	0.00	0.00	0.00	0.00	0	0.03
1.40	0.15	0.00	0.00	0.00	0.00	0	0.00	2.00	3.70
0.83	0.03	0.00	0.00	0.00	0.00	0.00	0.00	1.15	2.04
0.21	0.00	0.00	0.00	0.00	0.00	0.00	0.00	0.30	0.51
1.48	0.00	0.00	0.00	0.00	0.00	0.00	0.00	0.59	2.07

in the 1938 flood, water had moved at only 5 mph. The volume of water in the 1952 flood was not restricted in Brady as it had been fourteen years earlier. Commenting on the reason the channel had been cleared, former Brady mayor Earl Rudder said, "Brother, when you see something with your own eyes that perhaps could be prevented the next time, don't let any grass grow under your feet until you get the job done."[17]

When the rains did not bring another flood to downtown Brady, area residents and local officials showed their excitement at the ending of the drought. Brady's mayor, W. K. Cobb, in particular expressed his pleasure. He said that the people of the area "approved of the rain after such a long drouth 'but they just don't like to see so much of it at once.'" He added that there was little damage to crops because "there aren't many crops."[18]

Mayor Cobb offered San Angelo one million gallons of water as the flood started, but, after it had peaked at a near record, he

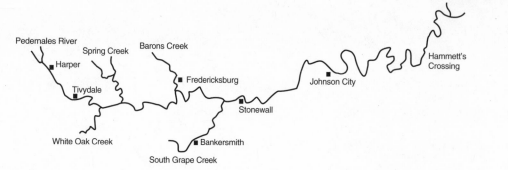

Pedernales River Basin

upped the offer to one billion gallons. The *San Angelo Standard-Times* wryly remarked, "Mayor W. K. Cobb showed his, uh, sympathy for San Angelo Wednesday."[19]

San Saba River

On September 11, floodwaters from Brady Creek contributed to a 36.9-foot stage on the San Saba River at 6 A.M. National Guard vehicles forded 6 feet of water to assist in rescue efforts in San Saba. Agricultural damage in this pecan-rich region was limited because crops were down due to the drought. Fueled by the 14-inch rains near Cherokee, Cherokee Creek south of San Saba rose to its highest level in fifty-two years. Floods coming down the San Saba into the Colorado were corralled by Lake Buchanan, which was down more than 50 feet and therefore had plenty of room to catch the water.

Llano River

The Llano River at Llano was in sad shape for the first nine days of September. The river had ceased flowing—its streamflow was actually at zero cfs. To meet its needs, the town of Llano had been shipping in water for two weeks.

As the rain fell on September 10, one long-time Llano resident commented, "This rain has been worth more to Llano County than any other rainfall in my life."[20] In a little more than one day, the Llano River rebounded from no streamflow to more than 200,000 cfs. On the morning of September 10 the streamflow at Llano was less than 10 cfs. From 1 P.M. to 3 P.M. the river's height fluctuated between 1.8 and 2.45 feet. When the flood wave hit in the next hour, the river spiked more than 12 feet in sixty minutes and pushed a volume of water almost eight hundred times greater than just an hour before (54 cfs at 3 P.M. vs. 42,800 cfs at 4 P.M.). From 4 P.M. to 5 P.M. the river jumped another 7.7 feet, to 22.6 feet and 106,000 cfs. The Llano continued to rise from 6 P.M. to 11 P.M., topping out at 32.6 feet, with a corresponding 232,000 cfs discharge. Rumors circulated that the bridge in Llano might go, as it did in 1935, but it held up to the 32.6-foot stage.

As an indication of which locations missed out on the rains, the streamflow for the Llano River at Junction barely budged. The river's daily discharge grew from 15 cfs (September 1–8) to 23 cfs (September 11–12).

Pedernales River

The torrential rains hit the bull's-eye in the Pedernales River basin. In Gillespie County, rainfall began around 7:30 A.M. on September 9. By the following morning, most locations around Fredericksburg had tallied 4–5 inches of precipitation.

The Llano River at Kingsland after the 1952 flood (courtesy of the LCRA Corporate Archives: W00887).

By the end of the day, another 10 inches poured from the skies and "had people measuring the rainfall by the foot instead of inches."[21]

The fifteen inches of rain in Fredericksburg brought high water into the town and its surrounding area. Barons Creek flowed 15 feet deep and broke a dam two miles outside of the city. South and west of town, the upper portion of the Pedernales rose mightily, too. At 8 P.M. on September 10 the river reached a 31-foot stage on Highway 87 and blocked traffic on Highway 16 to Kerrville. Old-timers debated whether the 1952 Pedernales flood was inches higher or lower than the 1900 flood.

Willow City reported 15–21 inches of rain. With 25 inches of precipitation in fewer than twenty hours, Pleasant Hill residents stated that the rain was "nice and slow" on September 9 and most of September 10; however, on the night of September 10 it was "the hardest rain anyone had ever witnessed."[22] Other communities also receiving heavy rains were Cave Creek, Rheingold, Bear Creek, and Wolf Creek. Flooding washed out bridges on Grape Creek and Rocky Creek, leaving gaps as large as thirty feet wide and twenty-five feet deep.

Stonewall Area

As the near-record flood on the Pedernales near Fredericksburg moved downstream, runoff from the more than twenty inches of rain near Stonewall added to the river's surge. The Pedernales cut across the bend west of Stonewall and flowed across fields to surround the town. There the river split, with one branch flowing south of Stonewall and merging again with the main branch.

School children who were stranded on

The Highway 281 bridge, Johnson City, Texas (courtesy of the LCRA Corporate Archives: W00813).

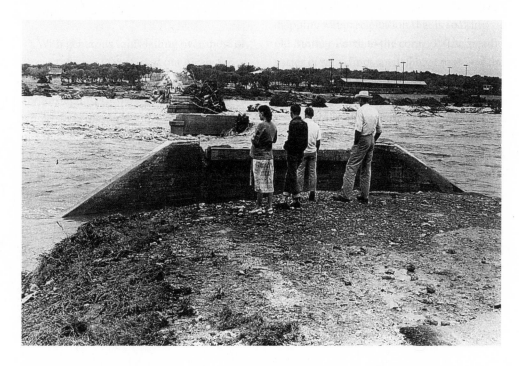

PEDERNALES RIVER FLOOD

	DATE									
LOCATION	1	2	3	4	5	6	7	8	9	10
Comal River	132	132	120	128	135	130	120	135	145	177
Frio River at Concan	1.80	1.40	1.40	1	1	1	0.90	1	1	2.20
Guadalupe River at Comfort	0	0	0	0	0	0	0	0	0	6,900
Guadalupe River at Spring Branch	0	0	0	0	0	0	0	0	0	3,100
Llano River at Junction	14	15	15	15	15	15	15	15	16	21
Llano River at Llano	0	0	0	0	0	0	0	0	0	52,000
Nueces River at Laguna	11	11	11	10	10	10	10	10	12	12
Pedernales River at Johnson City	0	0	0	0	0	0	0	0	0	54,300
San Saba River at Menard	0	0	0	0	0	0	0	0	0	85
San Saba River at San Saba	3	4	3.70	4.20	4.70	3.50	4.20	9.20	12	2,130

Discharge in cubic feet/second

the Stonewall side of the river could not return home until September 12. In the aftermath of the flood at Stonewall, the *Fredericksburg Standard* stated that the "beautiful tree-lined river bed resembles a wasteland with trees that withstood the ages broken, bent and reduced to kindling wood."[23] Moreover, the flood caused extensive erosion. One farmer in the Hye area, the location reporting an official 20.7-inch total for one day, had as "fine a field as to be found in Gillespie County before the rain. Now the field is just gravel and clay since all the topsoil was washed away."[24]

The flash flood near Stonewall proved to be an extreme demonstration of the might of fast-flowing water. The currents washed a tractor-trailer carrying nineteen tons of structural steel off Highway 290. The truck had a gross load of fifty-two thousand pounds and was carried four hundred yards downstream and then wrapped around a tree about one hundred feet from the pavement. Noticing a twelve-foot wall of water heading toward him, the driver fled. A car that was swept off the road nearby was found 1½ miles downstream.

At Lyndon Baines Johnson's ranch, the ranch foreman's car was overturned. When the flood hit, Johnson himself was hunting

Release of water at Starcke Dam along the Colorado River (courtesy of the LCRA Corporate Archives: W00246).

Pedernales River at Johnson City, Texas, after it washed out the bridge on Highway 281 (courtesy of the LCRA Corporate Archives: W00724).

11	12	13	14	15	16	17	18
13,900	988	202	180	192	195	197	196
3	2.60	2.60	2.20	1.80	1.40	1.40	2.20
2,810	292	105	65	55	60	87	176
44,600	10,900	892	528	382	318	286	414
23	23	22	20	20	19	19	19
51,400	3,000	1,070	582	386	288	384	5,120
12	11	10	10	10	10	10	10
129,000	2,190	661	387	292	244	329	962
11	3.60	2.20	1.60	1.20	0.90	0.70	0.40
36,300	3,840	799	436	295	200	650	1,510

in South Texas with Lloyd Bentsen Jr., while his wife, Lady Bird, was at the ranch. Johnson heard about the flood but was unable to reach anybody at the ranch via the phone. He was flown in his DC3 to within twenty miles of the ranch and went the rest of the distance in a small plane. After finding that his family was fine and visiting with them for a while, he attempted to depart in the small plane. According to Johnson, the aircraft hit a "washed-out chug hole on take-off and careened into a tree."[25] Johnson was then driven by car, which had to be pulled by tractor through high water, to return to his DC3.

Johnson City

With a twenty-six-inch downpour in the Hye and Stonewall area, the Pedernales River received the most intense runoff of this event. Like the Llano, the Pedernales River had no flow from September 1 to September 9. On September 10 the streamflow was 9 cfs. At 9 A.M. that morning, the river had started to flow, although just barely (the streamflow was 0.2 cfs). At noon, however, the river was at 137 cfs and a 3.0-foot stage. The flow and stage slowly increased through 5 P.M.

The Pedernales River flood began to show its power around 6 P.M., when the gage height was 9.2 feet with a 9,230 cfs reading. From

Lake Travis after floodwaters from the 1952 flood filled the lake (Archives Division, Texas State Library, 1978/23-263).

Lake Travis before floodwaters from the 1952 flood filled the lake (Archives Division, Texas State Library, 1978/23-238).

PEDERNALES RIVER FLOOD

6 P.M. to 7 P.M. the river rose 8.3 feet and to almost 33,000 cfs. From 7 to 8 P.M. the river surged another 7.7 feet and 59,000 cfs, up to 101,000 cfs. From 8 to 9 P.M. the flow more than doubled—to 218,000 cfs—prompting another 8.2-foot jump in the gage height. At 10 P.M. the flow had almost doubled the previous hour's reading once again, reaching 390,000 cfs, a new record discharge. The flood hit a new peak stage: 40.8 feet.

For the next four hours, the flood stabilized at 38–40 feet before pushing to a 42.5-foot stage at 3 P.M. on September 11. The new record flow rate was now 441,000 cfs, which was estimated to be twice that of the 1869 flood. During the rest of the day, the flood slowly died out, relaxing to a 7.3-foot stage and a 5,520-cfs reading at midnight. The average discharge for September 11 was 129,000 cfs, which, for a twenty-four-hour period, exceeded the previous flood's momentary peak discharge. The record flood obliterated the previous high-stage record of 33 feet, eclipsing it by 10 feet. The USGS noted that cypress trees 5 feet in diameter "were broken off like match sticks" and pecan groves were decimated as trees 2 feet in diameter were uprooted and washed away.[26]

The most prominent casualty of the flood in Johnson City was the bridge on Highway 281 over the Pedernales. The 441,000-cfs surge of water tore the roadway sections and beams from the piers supporting the road and bridge. As the swell moved downstream on the way to Lake Travis, the low-water bridge on Hamilton Pool Road over the Pedernales was reported to be covered by 60 feet of water.

Lake Travis

The record 441,000-cfs flood wave from the Pedernales and the 232,000-cfs surge on the Llano barreled into Lake Travis. Since no reservoirs were in place to catch either

rise, Mansfield Dam and Lake Travis would become the home for their floodwaters. Lake Travis holds 1,144,000 acre-feet when filled to the 681-foot elevation above sea level mark. The remaining capacity, at the 714-foot spillway level, adds another 778,000 acre-feet. In early September, the lake held 383,000 acre-feet of water. By September 9 it had dipped to 372,700 acre-feet, approximately one-third of the 681-foot level capacity.

Storage records for Lake Travis recorded the spike in inflow to the lake. At 2:15 P.M. on September 11, the inflow was 1,620 cfs (up from 600 cfs at 1 A.M.). In the next 15 minutes the inflow increased by more than 440,000 cfs. At 2:30 A.M. it shot up to 442,900 cfs. The flow into Travis continued to grow rapidly, surpassing 500,000 cfs at 3:15 A.M., 600,000 cfs by 5 A.M., 700,000 cfs by 7 A.M., and 800,000 cfs at 7:30 A.M. The flood spent itself over the next twelve hours, reducing its streamflow into Travis to 109,000 cfs at 7:30 P.M. By midnight the inflow had decreased to 26,000 cfs.

By the end of September 11, the lake held 1,073,000 acre-feet, a gain of 701,000 acre-feet in a single day; in other words, the lake's volume nearly tripled in twenty-four hours. From readings of the levels at Mansfield Dam, calculations indicated that the inflow averaged approximately 600,000 cfs for a ten-hour period. The massive increase in volume translated into a stunning rise in the lake level. Lake Travis rose 44 feet between 1 A.M. and 12 noon on September 11. Before the rains, the lake was at 619 feet. Afterward, the lake level stood at 676 feet, a gain of 57 feet in less than twenty-four hours. For the first time in seven years, the lake was full.

Guadalupe River

Like the Llano and Pedernales rivers to the north, the Guadalupe River at Comfort and Spring Branch had no flow prior to

Releasing flood water (Archives Division, Texas State Library, 1978/23-286).

the rains. Also, like the Llano and Perdernales, the torrential downpours of September transformed them in a matter of hours. The twenty-inch rains in the Bankersmith and Welfare area generated a flood wave at Comfort and points downstream. On September 10 the river's discharge at Comfort increased from a zero cfs flow at 1 A.M. to 38,600 cfs at 6:30 P.M., as a 25.4-foot rise came down the river.

At Spring Branch, September 10 also began with a zero cfs flow. At 6 P.M. a 434-cfs flow marked the start of the flood wave there. By midnight it had risen to 26.6 feet and 30,200 cfs. Over the next four and a half hours, the river pushed upward to 35.8 feet and 66,900 cfs and then stayed above 30 feet for most of September 11 and above 10 feet for more than ten hours on September 12.

New Braunfels had to deal with floods on both the Comal and the Guadalupe rivers. The Comal River's surge almost broke its all-time record. At 11 A.M. on September 11, it peaked at 36.14 feet, pushed to that level by a 35,000 cfs flow. The 36-foot stage was more than 5 feet higher than the 30.7-foot stage reached in 1935. (The Comal's record stage of 37.65 feet was estimated from flood marks in 1869 and 1870.)

In New Braunfels (above the Comal), the Guadalupe crested at 30.65 feet and 72,900 cfs at 1 P.M. on September 11. The

Landa Park in New Braunfels following flooding on the Comal and Guadalupe rivers in 1952 (Copyright 1996, Sophienburg Archives, New-Braunfels, Texas).

148

Aerial view of the Guadalupe River during the retrieval of trailers during the 1952 flood in New Braunfels (Archives Division, Texas State Library, 1978/23-264).

river stayed then above 20 feet for fourteen hours on September 12. The next day it fell to a 4.9-foot stage with a streamflow of 3,750 cfs. The *San Antonio Express* described the Guadalupe River as looking like "an octopus gone mad" from the air. It added, "The river's frothy tentacles stabbed across highways, snatched the ballast from railroad roadbeds and clutched at the eaves of riverside homes."[27] At Seguin, the Guadalupe covered Starke Park and the golf course. Houses at Lake Placid and Parkview were inundated with floodwaters up to their second floor. After rescuing flood victims, six National Guardsmen found themselves marooned on top of their truck.

Blanco River

The heavy rains near Bankersmith fed a flood wave that moved down the Blanco River on the night of September 10. High water stranded residents and travelers in Blanco. Approximately twenty area residents spent the night in the local bowling club, while some school children spent several nights away from home. The *Austin American* remarked, "This hill country town of 1000 has been deeply hurt by its old friend, the Blanco River."[28]

Retrieving trailers next to the Guadalupe River at New Braunfels during the 1952 flood (Copyright 1996, Sophienburg Archives, New Braunfels, Texas).

At Wimberley, the Blanco River had only 11 cfs flowing on September 10 at 4 A.M. At midnight, however, it was up to 1.25 feet and 166 cfs. The flood wave from upstream hit in the next hour. At 1 A.M. on September 11 the Blanco was at 15 feet and registered a flow of 24,000 cfs. Around 2 A.M. it added another 10 feet, reaching 25.10 feet and a flow of 64,600 cfs. At 8:30 A.M. the river crested at 30.10 feet and attained a peak flow of 95,000 cfs.

At San Marcos, the floodwaters from the Blanco caused the San Marcos River to flow backward. The backwater from the Blanco pushed the San Marcos River over the Highway 81 bridge at 1 P.M.

Cibolo Creek

The Cibolo Creek flood was spurred on not only by the runoff from the deluge but also by broken dams near Boerne. At 4 A.M. on September 11, Cibolo Creek at Selma rose from a 0.42-foot stage with no flow to 10.50 feet and 7,200 cfs at 5 A.M. In the next three hours it gained almost 9 feet and quintupled its flow, peaking at 19.37 feet and 36,400 cfs. After falling to just over 6 feet at 6 P.M., the stream experienced another rise, bringing it to almost 13 feet and 12,500 cfs at 10 P.M. on September 11.

Elsewhere in Texas

In other sections of Central and West Texas, the relief from the drought was spotty. San Angelo largely missed out on the rains, gauging only 0.27 inches on September 10 and 11. The city thus still faced a water shortage. Ballinger volunteered to let San Angelo use water since the town's new lake and old lakes were now full.

Elmer Kelton, a *San Angelo Standard-Times* reporter, commented on the rains: "From a farm and ranch standpoint, benefits from big rains far outweighed any damage done."[29] In the Eden area, many ranchmen who were prepared to sell off breeding stock because of the drought were "saved by the bell" of the rains. Since the rains brought a

Retrieval of trailers from land adjacent to the Guadalupe River during the 1952 flood in New Braunfels (Copyright 1996, Sophienburg Archives, New Braunfels, Texas).

renewed promise of better ranching conditions, they were able to keep the foundation animals they had planned to sell.[30]

Area ranchers and county agents from regions not flooded were overjoyed with the rains. A Goldthwaite resident remarked that it was the "most wonderful thing that's happened here in a long time." A Ballinger farmer said, "It's not going to hurt the little cotton crop we have left. It couldn't have been a more perfect rain. Everybody is happy." Coleman's county agent noted that it was the first "good general rain" in the county in about a year. Kerrville's county agent called the 2–7 inches in Kerr County "a dream come true," but he added, "We need another rain just as soon as it comes."[31]

The Texas Board of Water Engineers noted that millions of acre-feet of water flowed into the soil and underground reservoirs. They called the aquifer "nature's method of flood control."[32] San Antonio's aquifer observation well rose seven feet on the morning of September 12.

October 1952 Weather: No Relief from the Drought

As much as Texans had hoped for it, the September rains did not end the drought. The next month, October 1952, went down as one of the driest months on record. Austin, Rocksprings, San Angelo, Sonora, Sabinal, San Saba, Tarpley, Temple, Uvalde, Menard, Del Rio, Hondo, Brackettville, Mason, Junction, Llano, Hunt, Boerne, Kerrville, Blanco, and Fredericksburg all reported no rainfall for the entire month.

JUNE 1954

~~~~~~~

Pecos River's Eighty-Six-Foot Wall of Water

THE JUNE 1954 flash floods included one of the largest-scale inundations in Texas history. The heavy rains produced ferocious flash floods on West Texas creeks and draws, including Independence Creek and Johnson and Howard draws. These flood waves joined another one on the Pecos River to produce an astounding swell down the Pecos. This surge reached eighty-six feet along the Pecos River Canyon at Highway 90, validating the existence of the high railroad bridge over the Pecos just upstream of the bridge that was destroyed by the deluge.

Precedent Conditions

In 1953 the West Texas towns of Fort Stockton, Bakersfield, and Sanderson each received 5 inches of rain or less, a deficit of more than 8 inches for the year. Likewise, Ozona's rainfall was more than 8 inches below average. Closer to Central Texas, the shortfall worsened. Rainfall tallies in Sonora and Brady were more than 11 inches below average for that year, while Menard's total was more than 14 inches below average. San Angelo, which missed out on the 1952 rains, enjoyed above-average rainfall in 1953, thanks to a March total of five inches and an October tally of 4.95 inches.

For the first five months of 1954, rainfall in several West Texas locations was above average. Bakersfield caught 4.22 inches in May, pushing the town above average for the first five months of the year. Ozona was also above average due to a 6.05-inch total in

April. Pandale received a 5.34-inch total that same month and was almost 3 inches above average for the first five months of 1954.

Severe weather marked the first half of June 1954, when Bakersfield and various areas in Pecos County were hit with tornadoes and hail. In Cottle County, more than $6 million of hail damage occurred. On June 7 a storm created hail and wind damage totaling $1.5 million in San Angelo. Tornadoes and high winds struck Terlingua on June 11 and Big Spring on June 14.

Hurricane Alice

During the second half of June, Hurricane Alice dominated Texas weather. The first hurricane warning went out at 4 A.M. on June 25. The storm made landfall south of Brownsville, although earlier forecasts had predicted that it would move farther north. The air force base in Kingsville made plans to send 132 planes to San Angelo's Goodfellow Base to avoid the force of the hurricane. However, once it was learned that the hurricane had arrived south of Kingsville, the planes were not moved. On June 26 the weather bureau reported that the hurricane was "moving almost parallel with the Rio Grande."[1] By nightfall on June 26, rains were falling over the western Hill Country and Edwards Plateau. Precipitation reports from the San Angelo area showed that 19 of 21 gages had received some rain. Only Blackwell and Bronte missed out on the showers.

Rainfall

As the remnants of Alice pushed toward the northwest, the eventful weather of early June was about to become a lesser footnote in the history of West Texas weather following the rains of June 26–28, 1954. Near Laredo, Oilton reported 8.46 inches of precipitation on June 26, flooding two blocks of the town. A region from San Antonio to Uvalde and Pearsall gauged 1–2 inches, while Eagle Pass caught 3.8 inches. Other high totals were seen at Montell (6) and Camp Wood (6). One Edwards County resident noted that June of 1954 would be the region's wettest June since 1949. In Loving County, the showers were credited with spurring the growth of grass in the draws to be "as good as it ever was."[2]

On June 27 thunderstorms were spotted around Ozona and Langtry—one

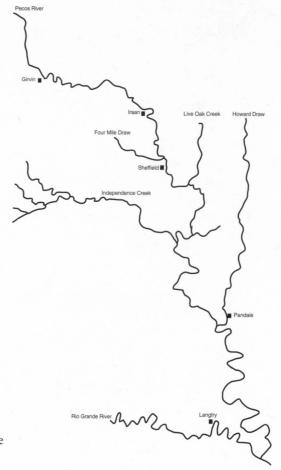

Pecos River bridge prior to 1954 flood (courtesy of the Texas Department of Transportation).

Pecos River bridge before the 1954 flood (courtesy of the Texas Department of Transportation).

Pecos River bridge before the 1954 flood (courtesy of the Texas Department of Transportation).

of them (around 20 miles north of Langtry) covered an area about 25 miles wide. These storms were hardly gentle sprinkles. Instead, they were the feared core rains from a dying tropical system that had proved capable of dumping rainfall measured in feet rather than inches.

Rainfall reports from June 27 indicated torrential downpours along the Pecos River watershed. Sheffield reported 9.1 inches of precipitation, while a Terrell County ranch reported 12 inches. The Vic Pierce Ranch near Johnson Draw, which had received no appreciable rain in three years, recorded 11 inches. A location south of the ranch reported 14 inches.

On June 28, reports from more remote locations indicated that the rains were even heavier than the previously reported totals. The highest totals approached the yearly averages for many West Texas locations. At the Del Rio Weather Bureau, H. B. Molyneaux reported that rains of 12–22 inches fell from Del Rio to Sheffield and Ozona. He

stated, "Black, ominous clouds continued to hover over the hilly, gully-marked wild country just below the foothills of the Big Bend mountains."[3]

A rancher in the Langtry and Dryden area reported 22 inches in 24 hours. Another ranch along Independence Creek in Terrell County reported 20 inches of rain in a 21-hour period. The intense downpours of the night of June 26 and morning of June 27 were highlighted by a peak rainfall of 27.1 inches near Pandale. Twenty-four inches of rain fell in an area approximately 50 miles long and 15 miles wide. The center of the system was located over the Pecos River near Pandale and Sheffield.

In analyzing the heavy rain event, the U.S. Weather Bureau noted that the showers were caused by the atmospheric circulation from dying Hurricane Alice, which remained over the Lower Pecos watershed for nearly three days. Upper-air charts showed a closed circulation up to a level of at least five hundred millibars.

PECOS RIVER'S EIGHTY-SIX-FOOT WALL OF WATER

Streamflow

The intense core rains from Alice generated some of the most powerful flash floods
in Texas history. Draws, creeks, and rivers
carried away houses and cars and obliterated major bridges.

Pecos River

The Pecos River watershed took a direct
hit from the formidable rains. Near Sheffield, at a fishing camp at the mouth of Independence Creek into the Pecos River, fishermen were stranded as a flood wave came
down the Pecos, and the camp buildings
were swept away. One survivor climbed to
the top of a cattle truck, where he stayed for
four hours, watching waves up to thirty feet
high. The flood washed another cattle truck
five miles downstream. A group of survivors
from the flooded camp organized a cara-
van to drive out and seek help. Because they
had to stop frequently to clear debris from
the road, it took them nine hours to travel a
mere thirty miles.

Much of the water came down from
Howard Draw and joined with the upstream
flood on the Pecos to propel the river to an
estimated fifty-five-foot stage at Pandale. A
pilot flying over the town reported, "Pandale needs help badly."[4] Four Odessa fishermen who had been fishing in Howard Draw,
10 miles north of Pandale, were believed
drowned. Five men were stranded, sitting on driftwood approximately one hundred yards from the bank, until it fell apart
and they headed to shore. One of the men
walked 4–5 miles looking for the other men.

Continuing one of the most amazing

Pecos River bridge prior
to 1954 flood (courtesy of
the Texas Department of
Transportation).

Grand opening celebra-
tion for the new Pecos
River bridge (courtesy of
the Texas Department of
Transportation).

Remnants of Pecos River bridge after the 1954 flood (courtesy of the Texas Department of Transportation)

Temporary Pecos River bridge (the structure was washed out in 1955) (courtesy of the Texas Department of Transportation).

Pecos River, looking up at the new bridge (courtesy of the Texas Department of Transportation).

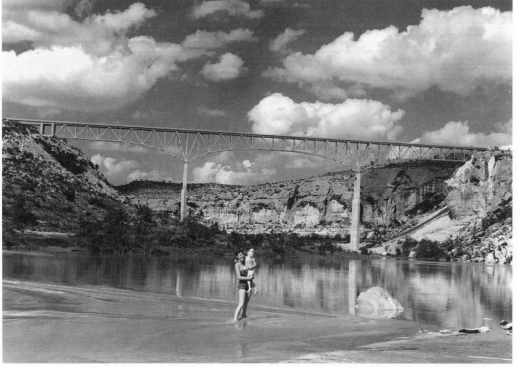

Scene from the Pecos River, looking up at the new bridge (courtesy of the Texas Department of Transportation).

rises on any river in the United States, the Pecos River churned down the canyon and took out the Highway 90 bridge. The thirty-year-old structure stood 50 feet above the normal water level. This clearance, however, was woefully insufficient to handle the rise on the Pecos. The first peak, estimated at 82 feet, hit on June 27 at 7:30 A.M. The second crest—an astounding 96.24 feet—came down about eighteen hours later, at 1:30 A.M. on June 28. (The steady-state stage was approximately 10 feet.) These peaks corresponded with discharges of 695,000 and 948,000 cfs, respectively.

The first wave took out the trusses of the Highway 90 bridge; the second washed out its center pier. The 948,000-cfs discharge distributed over the 3,504 square miles of the watershed between Comstock and Sheffield translated into a flow of 268.26 cfs per square mile. It was "probably the greatest rate of runoff for a watershed of this size in the United States," according to the International Boundary and Water Commission.[5]

Langtry

The high water not only took out the Highway 90 bridge but also destroyed

Devils River Crossing after the 1954 flood (courtesy of the Texas Department of Transportation).

railroad bridges near Langtry, where it stranded the prestigious Sunset Limited train from Los Angeles to New Orleans. When the Sunset Limited left Sanderson at 9:40 P.M. on June 26, it was informed of a possible washout at Castle Canyon. Then a second washout was reported at Osmund Draw. Railroad officials later said that three washouts of bridges over gullies occurred. The gaps in the bridges across the gullies created by the flooding ranged from 35 to 50 feet in width.

Passengers on the Sunset Limited were evacuated via buses and helicopters and carried to a point eighteen miles west on Highway 90, where five Greyhound buses were waiting to take them to their railroad connections. Governor Shivers authorized the use of helicopters from Laughlin Air Force Base in Del Rio. Officials at the base said it would take some time to evacuate the 262 passengers with the six helicopters available. Helicopters were also flown in from Corpus Christi and San Marcos to aid in evacuating the travelers. One passenger commented that he "looked into one ravine where 'the water was at least 40 feet deep' . . . [but] that was nothing compared to a spot we flew over."[6]

The passengers were taken to Langtry, a town whose population was estimated at 100. Because the town did not have enough supplies to feed the sudden influx of more than 260 visitors, the food from the train was put to good use. To ensure that no one went hungry, Southern Pacific arranged for the air force to drop a thousand pounds of provisions.

Another train, the Southern Pacific Argonaut, also found its path blocked in West Texas. Finding that it could not pass through an area near Sanderson, it backed all the way to Alpine, where it was switched over to Santa Fe tracks linking Alpine to San Angelo.

International Bridge after the 1954 flood (courtesy of the Texas Department of Transportation).

New bridge across Devils River (courtesy of the Texas Department of Transportation).

Ozona

With roads blocked to the west, many travelers waited out the floods in Ozona, whose residents helped put up those who could not find rooms in the town's hotels. But on the night of June 27, the floods focused on Ozona. Rains pushed Johnson Draw, which cuts through the western section of the town, to flood stage and beyond. By nightfall, the draw was reaching up to the highway bridge in Ozona. At midnight, local law officers warned residents in the eastern part of town that the Gurley Draw was on the rise.

In the early morning hours of June 28,

	DATE									
LOCATION	22	23	24	25	26	27	28	29	30	TOTAL
Bakersfield	0.00	0.00	0.00	0.00	0.00	0.00	0.00	0.00	0.00	0.00
Brackettville	0.00	0.00	0.00	0.75	0.70	0.60	0.06	0.01	0.00	2.12
Brady	0.00	0.12	0.00	0.00	0.00	0.31	0.00	0.00	0.00	0.43
Del Rio	0.00	0.00	0.00	0.00	1.68	0.54	0.31	0.01	0.00	2.54
Fort Stockton	0.00	0.00	0.00	0.00	0.00	0.31	0.02	0.00	0.02	0.35
Ozona	0.17	0.00	0.00	0.00	0.16	3.10	4.26	0.03	0.00	7.72
Pandale	0.00	0.00	0.00	0.00	0.55	16.02	7.50	0.00	0.00	24.07
Rocksprings	0.00	0.14	0.04	0.00	0.50	3.20	0.68	1.03	0.00	5.59
Sanderson	0.00	0.00	0.00	0.00	0.24	0.00	0.00	0.29	0.00	0.53
San Angelo	0.00	0.00	0.00	0.00	0.29	0.03	0.02	0.00	0.00	0.34
Sonora	0.26	0.00	0.00	0.00	0.70	1.07	1.73	0.00	0.00	3.76
Uvalde	0.00	0.00	0.00	0.00	1.10	1.58	0.02	0.00	0.00	2.70

the floodwaters of Johnson Draw pushed out of its banks and into the inhabited areas of town. The *Fort Worth Star-Telegram* noted, "Sirens screamed, church and school bells rang, and much of Ozona's population turned out to sight-see as Johnson Draw rose higher and higher at dawn Monday. Despite these warnings, lives were lost as the waters rose."[7]

The flood carried houses and trailers almost a mile. The *San Angelo Standard-Times* commented that "the west section of Ozona looks as if a giant hand had picked up everything and tossed it into the air."[8]

On June 27 a number of survivors spent the night on the roof of the Silver Spur Motel. Two oilfield workers borrowed a motorboat that was parked at the courthouse square to carry residents to safety. In his book *Ozona Country,* Allan R. Bosworth reflects on the flood: "Many an Ozona resident believes there was something more providential than coincidental about this, because the town can go a whole year without ever seeing a power cruiser of any kind. . . . Johnson Draw took its toll principally from the unknowledgeable, the outsiders who did not realize what a flash flood can do in the sharply tilted Southwest. It also struck at the underprivileged, because the small Negro settlement, in 1954,

was near its banks. At the time there was no other place where these people could live."[9]

In recounting the flood in Ozona, the *Fort Stockton Pioneer*'s "Baker's Dozen" column read as follows: "Nothing to compare with the Ozona flood has hit the ranch county of West Texas in modern times with exception of the Rocksprings tornado of 1927. The Rocksprings disaster claimed a great many more lives and inflicted tremendous property damage though probably not as great as the Ozona flood damage in dollars and cents loss. This week as in the days of the 1927 tragedy, the response of good neighbors was swift and decisive. Help was enroute to Ozona almost as soon as word reached the outside world of the desperate situation created by the rapidly rising waters of Johnson draw through the sleeping town. The death toll stood Tuesday night at 13 with the possibility of several additional fatalities when all the facts are revealed in more systematic search of the flood driven debris."[10] The final tally of the dead in the Ozona flash flood was sixteen.

Devils River

The floodwaters from Johnson Draw fed the Devils River, which in turn washed out the bridge at Seminole Canyon, five

miles west of Comstock on Highway 90. At 5 P.M. on June 28, the peak flow reached 585,000 cfs.

Rio Grande River

Fueled by the twenty-inch-plus rains from the Pecos and Devils rivers, the Rio Grande below Langtry and Comstock surged to record levels. At Del Rio, the river peaked at 1,140,000 cfs at 9:30 A.M. on June 28, sweeping away the approach to the International Bridge at Del Rio "like kindling wood."[11]

The initial forecast for the Rio Grande below Del Rio called for an increase less than that of July 1948. It predicted a stage of 41.5 feet at Laredo—just touching the bottom of the bridge. After the huge inflow at Del Rio was accounted for, forecasters admitted "they couldn't even guess what the climax might be. . . . The Weather Bureau at Brownsville said there is nothing on the records to compare with this flood—and the only comparison forecasters could make would be with legends about a great flood in 1835."[12]

At Eagle Pass, the Rio Grande took out the railroad and the International Bridge. At 6 P.M. on June 28 the swell hit 51.15 feet. The flood's crest reached 53.6 feet, almost matching the revised forecast of 54 feet. The peak flow of 964,000 cfs came at 5 A.M. on June 29. Across the river, the flood slammed into Piedras Negras, and many adobe homes disintegrated in the currents.

Laredo braced for a 60-foot stage, a level equal to 21 feet above the International Bridge. In preparation, customs officials removed everything they could. At 11 P.M. on June 29, water was halfway up the sides of the U.S. Customs House. Ten hours later, at 9 A.M. on June 30, the river peaked at 62.21 feet, surpassing the 1932 mark by 12.6 feet.

In Laredo, three 150-foot sections of the International Bridge were lost. Some of the flood watchers blamed debris from the Eagle Pass railroad and automobile bridge for knocking out the Laredo bridge. To facilitate travel across the river after the deluge, officials planned to erect a pontoon bridge as early as July 5. The bridge was delayed, however, when two pontoons were used instead to float water pumps at the crippled water plant. The bridge was finally opened to pedestrians on July 6.

Unlike previous inundations on the Rio Grande, a dam was in place to catch the currents before they swept down the Valley. Falcon Dam was completed in 1953. Prior to the flood, the reservoir held 520,000 acre-feet, although its capacity was 4 million acre-feet. By the time the flood wave subsided, Falcon Reservoir had taken in 2.1 million acre-feet.

In discussing the dam, the *San Antonio Express* commented that the structure had

cost $47 million, but "plenty of Valley peo-
ple . . . think it was a mighty good bargain
when they consider how much damage the
current flood could do to crops and property." Some Valley farmers pointed out that
the dam returned its investment after saving
the cotton crop, which was worth $60 mil-
lion.[13] Before the Falcon Dam corralled the
flood, the U.S. Border Patrol was credited
with warning residents in the area from Del
Rio to Falcon Reservoir and thereby saving
many lives.

Summing Up

The battle between the Pecos River and
the Highway 90 bridge continued for several years after the 1954 flood. While a suspension bridge was being considered, a
low-water crossing bridge was installed.
However, in 1955 floods ripped out this
structure. In 1957 the Texas Highway Department built a mammoth bridge across
the top of the canyon, similar to the famous
High Bridge used by the railroad.

~~~~~

Lampasas Mother's Day Flood

THE SPRING OF 1957 marked perhaps the most dramatic shift in Texas weather in the 1900s. The oppressive and unrelenting weather pattern that marked the 1950s as the drought years finally broke in April of 1957. As hallmark springs such as Comal Springs reached their lowest flows or ceased flowing altogether, 1956 became one of the driest years in Texas history. In the spring of 1957, residents' nearly decade-long prayers for rain were answered.

The established shift in the rainfall pattern began in April 1957. The apex of the reversal occurred on Mother's Day, May 12, 1957, when heavy rains fell throughout Central Texas, setting off flash floods throughout the region. The most spectacular one welled up in a familiar location—Lampasas. Twice during its history (in 1873 and 1936), Lampasas found itself in the path of major floods on Sulphur Creek. By 1957 a levee had been fortified to protect the town from floods on Sulphur Creek. In the spring of 1957 the Soil Conservation Service received approval to build flood-control structures upstream of Lampasas. Unfortunately, the Mother's Day flash flood that year proved the levee in place at the time was inadequate and that the planned flood-control structures were essential for protecting the town.

Precedent

The spring of 1957 marked the true ending of the severe drought of the 1950s. The previous year, 1956, was one of the driest in Texas history, and much of the state received less than fifty percent of normal rainfall. Austin and Waco were each more than 17 inches below average, Taylor was more than 19 inches below average, and Abilene failed to gauge even 10 inches of rain for the year, more than 13 inches below average.

The early 1957 weather pattern exhibited the same dry weather of the previous years. Rains in February and March were close to average and brought some relief from the drought. In April, heavy rains fell throughout most of the state, and Waco tallied more than 13 inches that month. For all of 1956, the city recorded only 15.1 inches of precipitation.

By early May, stories of dust and drought were being replaced by accounts of flooding and high water. Between Clifton and Meridian, the North Bosque River was out of its banks. Wichita Falls residents were evacuated due to high water. Flood-related damages in Bell County alone were estimated at $750,000. With heavy discharges in the Brazos River basin, the benefits of flood protection from recently constructed dams at Lake Belton and Lake Whitney were being estimated at around $23.7 million. (The actual damage totaled $27.5 million; damage estimates without the dams were as high as $51 million.)

Near the Texas coast, flood victims near Angleton survived for several days by consuming boiled armadillos and turnip greens. Angleton was located 12 miles from the Brazos, but water from the river, which was estimated to be 13 miles wide, spread out to within 2 miles of town.

By May 11 both ends of the state were dealing with inundations. In East Texas, Liberty

Sulphur Creek Basin

Lampasas River

Bear Creek

Lampasas

Espy Branch

Sulphur Creek

Manatt Creek

Pillar Bluff Creek

Looking north-northeast toward the Lampasas County courthouse from the East Seventh and South Chestnut Street intersection (courtesy of Gladden C. Corbin).

was expecting its biggest flood since 1942. In West Texas, heavy rains closed Highway 80 at Big Spring. Reports stated, "Jubilant ranchmen in the area, powder dry with President Eisenhower visiting in January, said that a seven-year drought may be broken."[1] In Central Texas, April's heavy rains produced significant rises on the forks of the San Gabriel. On the North San Gabriel

River near Georgetown, the river rose to within 3 feet of the 1921 flood. On the South San Gabriel near Leander, water was 6.4 feet higher than the 1921 flood, the highest since at least the 1869 deluge.

In Lampasas, the weather followed the statewide pattern of the first four months of 1957. At the start of February, the dry weather rendered pastureland almost useless. Reporting that they had less grass than ever, ranchers were burning cactus for their cattle to eat. However, after the rains of February and March, some of the residents commented that the "county looks better than it has in 15 years."[2] Despite that note of hope, they added that more rains would be required to rejuvenate the ground beyond the topsoil.

Like most of Texas, by the end of April, Lampasas was experiencing problems from too much water rather than too little. The

LAMPASAS MOTHER'S DAY FLOOD

Lampasas Dispatch stated, "April's drought-ending rains have brought problems along with the good." The showers brought high water that reminded area residents that dependable communication from the upstream watershed was needed. Residents and officials also recognized the need for the Soil Conservation Service (SCS) dams that had been proposed for area watersheds, including Sulphur Creek.[3]

At the end of April, heavy rains on the upper reaches of Sulphur Creek, Burleson Creek, and Cemetery Branch "gave Lampasas a bad scare."[4] Rainfall rates were estimated as high as 4.5 inches in forty-five minutes to 1½ hours. The minor damage that resulted was contained to the downtown square. Because of clogged drains, water from Cemetery Branch collected on the east side of town, while 15 inches of water pooled in a grocery store on the southeast side, damaging food and cooling equipment. Families living in low-lying areas near Sulphur Creek were evacuated to the First Baptist Church. On Highway 281, high water blocked traffic. Sulphur Creek peaked at 13 feet, just 5 feet shy of topping the levee.

May Rains in Central Texas

On the night of May 11 another wave of heavy rain swept over Central Texas. By early evening, Moody totaled 8 inches, Bruceville-Eddy 6.5 inches, and McGregor 4.5 inches. The Cow Bayou watershed received 5.2–8.34 inches.

The next day was Mother's Day. During the afternoon, storms popped up to the west of Lampasas, matching those high totals from the previous night near Waco, as Lampasas gauged 8 inches between 6:30 P.M. and 11:00 P.M. One resident stated that the rainfall was so heavy in the Lampasas area that "no one has been able to wade to the rain gages to see how much we got."[5]

Lampasas Area Runoff

Following the downpour on the evening of Mother's Day, May 12, the warning from late April proved prophetic. The items identified for improvement—better drainage, stronger and more extensive levees, the removal of obstructions—all contributed to the record flood on Sulphur Creek that night. The superintendent of Lampasas Waterworks reported that the creek rose 18–20 feet above normal; it also left a flood mark 3 feet up on the concrete settling tanks at the water plant, according to the

Cameron and Company building on the northeast corner of the intersection of Third and Elm streets in Lampasas (photograph by Gladden C. Corbin).

Reed Oil Company just north of Sulphur Creek on the west side of Key Avenue in Lampasas near where the Levee Broke (photograph by Gladden C. Corbin).

Inside the west entrance of the Lampasas County courthouse (photograph by Gladden C. Corbin).

U.S. Army Corps of Engineers. Downstream from Lampasas at Gunderland Park, Sulphur Creek rose 4.8 feet higher than the peak stage in 1936, and its maximum streamflow was 69,630 cfs.

Flood in Lampasas

As Sulphur Creek began to rise, one resident called the fire station and said, "Better get people to higher grounds, for it is coming." As the alarm was sounding, the levee broke upstream from Highway 281. In a matter of minutes, the section of the town from the creek to Fifth Street was under several feet of water. Shortly thereafter, a wall of water crashed into downtown.[6] The flood wave lifted the Santa Fe depot and rotated it ninety degrees. It also deposited a three-bedroom house in the middle of Highway 281.

Water flowed 6–10 feet deep in the courthouse square. The police station, sheriff's office, and fire station all found themselves flooded. Cars floated for blocks, including through the courthouse square. During the peak of the deluge, water was 4 feet deep in the courthouse. A reporter from the *Waco Times-Herald* wryly stated that, "as the water swirled six feet deep in the town square, the city's motto was tragically fulfilled within a single city block. Lampasas' motto is 'A place to fish, to hunt, to swim.'"[7]

Rescues and Accounts

As the flood hit, one man was looking at Sulphur Creek near his house. When a squad car pulled up and told him to get out of the area, he returned to his home and picked up his wife and grandchildren. Looking back while they were leaving, he saw "what looked like a wave eight feet high sweep his home from its foundation."[8]

One woman was rocking her two-and-a-

Looking north on Western Street toward the Lampasas County courthouse (courtesy of Gladden C. Corbin).

half-year-old daughter to sleep at her house (at 405 College Street) when, she said, "the creek went mad." She waded through waist-deep water to reach Spurlin Store on Ford Street and joined with another woman to make their way through shoulder-high water. She temporarily left her daughter atop an abandoned car to keep her above water.[9]

An eighty-one-year-old man survived the floodwaters at Gunderland Park by climbing a tree, even though he estimated it had been sixty years since he had last climbed one. He said, "A fellow named Standish kept me up in the tree."[10]

At Martin's Cafe, Delbert Martin stated that the only warning of the approaching danger came in the form of a wall of water. When it struck, he and his fifteen customers hacked a hole in the ceiling to escape. In one house, seven people who were watching the Loretta Young television show left the home and scrambled to Martin's Café, where they clung to the roof until help arrived.

Noticing the rising water, one man packed his family into their car. When he returned to the house to get their clothes, the water was already ankle deep. On his return trek to the car, it had risen to his knees. As he looked back while leaving, he saw the house float away and then splinter when it collided with a bridge.[11]

One of those who were caught in the flood at the *Lampasas Record* building noted, "In 1936 the water just came to a height of 23 inches in the building and I didn't figure it would come any higher." He and his grandson, who came to warn him, escaped by breaking a plate-glass window and then fleeing to the second story of an adjoining building.[12]

Another downtown businessman climbed to the highest shelf in his shop when the flood hit. Then, when the shelf began to float, he moved to the top of the doorway. While stranded by the currents, he received a phone call from his daughter in Cleburne.

He climbed down a ladder, answered the phone, and told her everything was all right.

The proprietor of the Lampasas Drug climbed onto the soda fountain, walked to the rear of the store, and knocked a hole in the back wall so that he could climb up to the roof.

One of the heroes of the flood was Dean Turner, manager of KCYL, the local radio station. Normally the station signed off at 6 P.M. on Sundays, which it did that night. But as the situation in Lampasas became life threatening, it went back on the air around 8 P.M. and operated intermittently throughout the night. Turner kept it running, even though his own house had five feet of water at the peak of the flood. The broadcasts

Lumber shed at the B. K. May Lumber Company (corner of Fifth and Live Oak streets) moved two blocks east and one block north to Third and Elm streets in Lampasas (photograph by Gladden C. Corbin).

Looking south on Chestnut Street from the Sixth Street intersection in Lampasas (courtesy of Gladden C. Corbin).

| | DATE | | | | | | |
LOCATION	9	10	11	12	13	14	TOTAL
Abilene	1.16	0.85	1.85	0.50	0.55	0.00	4.91
Arlington	0.23	0.00	0.00	0.22	2.75	0.13	3.33
Brownwood	0.00	0.00	0.00	1.53	1.65	0.00	3.18
Comanche	0.30	0.00	1.22	0.22	0.93	0.00	2.67
Dallas	0.20	0.00	0.12	2.09	1.00	0.00	3.41
Dublin	0.59	0.02	trace	1.40	1.23	0.10	3.34
Hamilton	0.22	0.08	0.00	1.00	2.42	0.00	3.72
Hillsboro	0.33	0.05	0.00	0.60	1.25	0.33	2.56
Lampasas	0.34	0.27	0.00	0.48	6.95	0.25	8.29
Marlin	0.95	0.00	2.93	1.65	0.75	0.00	6.28
Stephenville	0.83	0.00	0.03	0.93	1.13	0.00	2.92
Waco	0.48	0.00	2.22	0.02	3.04	0.00	5.76

from the station were credited with diminishing rumors.[13]

Another hero was Gracie Storms, who transported sixteen other residents, including a woman and her five-week-old baby, to safety. She and her children left their home as water began to seep into the house. Storms went through the streets honking her horn and picking up victims. She commented, "I knew some people had no way of getting out and I wanted to help if I could."[14]

Summing Up

As the reality of the devastation hit Lampasas, the *Lampasas Dispatch* summarized the situation: "Despair some people say is the one unforgivable sin. Residents and

The area northeast of the courthouse square and West of Hackberry Street in Lampasas (photograph by Gladden C. Corbin).

merchants had plenty of cause to despair. . . . [Lampasas was] a town virtually ruined by floodwaters the night of Mother's Day, May 12."[15] In town, the flood rampaged through sixty-eight blocks and destroyed thirty-eight houses and five businesses. Forty-six houses and forty-seven businesses sustained major damage. Ninety percent of the business district was affected. A joint study and an on-site inspection by the U.S. Army Corps of Engineers and the Soil Conservation Service determined that the official loss amounted to $5,485,210.

Assistance came from other Central Texas residents and from across the nation. Yuba City, Arizona, which was hit by a flash flood eighteen months earlier, organized a relief effort to aid Lampasas. Troops from Fort Hood helped extensively in the relief and recovery effort. Water had to be pumped out of the business district, and spoiled food had to be carted away before it created a health hazard. The 35th Engineering Group from Fort Hood brought in trucks to haul off five thousand loads of food, garbage, and moldy grain to a dump just outside the city. In all, more than 350 troops from Fort Hood assisted in cleaning and the prevention of looting.

The manager of one Lampasas company recalled the floods of 1936, 1937, and

Debris on street sign at the Sixth Street and Western Avenue intersection in Lampasas (courtesy of Gladden C. Corbin).

1944. This was the first time floodwaters had poured into the main floor of the business, indicating that it was 4–5 feet deeper than previous floods. Water pooled 2 feet deep over the main floor. The manager commented, "We had planned to go up with a new building. We have the green light to go ahead, but we are not going to spend a dime until Lampasas gets flood control and positive assurance that such a disaster as this will not happen again." The company lost eighty thousand pounds of dressed turkeys that were in storage.[16]

Another downtown business owner said, "There is no question about whether Lampasas will rebound. I think we will have a better Lampasas than we ever had. We have a common interest now to keep the water out of town."[17]

Lampasas River

The flooding on Sulphur and Burleson creeks combined on the east end of Lampasas, driving the Lampasas River out of its banks above Kempner. In the Youngsport area, the river ripped out four bridges.

The rise prompted a telephone operator

from Youngsport, known as "Mrs. Jodie," to leave the telephone switchboard for the first time in twenty-nine years. She said, "I hadn't been able to go to church for years because I always felt my duty was to stay with the switchboard in case someone needed me, but I had done all I could today, and I surely went to church and was glad to be there!" A call from Maxdale at 3:15 Monday morning (May 13) alerted her to the approaching floods. Mrs. Jodie responded by calling the area's residents and warning them all by 4:30 A.M.[18] About two and a half hours later the water arrived in Youngsport. Around 9 A.M.

Large tank toppled by the flood (courtesy of the Keystone Square Museum, Lampasas, Texas).

Debris caught at the Burleson Creek bridge at the Third Street crossing (photograph by Gladden C. Corbin).

it appeared the town might be overwhelmed with water "as the river threatened to overrun from both sides."[19]

To escape the currents, people gathered at residences on high ground and at the Baptist Church. The only people who chose to say in Youngsport were the owners of the general store, and Mrs. Jodie left a line open for them. The store owner took advantage of the connection to call the U.S. Army Corps of Engineers in Fort Worth to report the swell. The rising water cut off the store, but the proprietor was not worried. He said, "My wife and I weren't afraid,

we're not as young as we used to be, but we both figured we could still climb a tree if we had to." [20]

Shortly after 9 A.M. the group at the church heard the bridge west of town give way. It was a "crash so resounding that it could be heard even above the roar of the flood." [21] The operator of the Union Grove store said water was "all over fields and valleys and is running 12 feet deep over some river bottom fields." One area farmer stated that he had never seen the river so high. [22] At Highway 81 just south of Belton, the river "churned against stringers on newly con-

Flood debris in Lampasas (courtesy of the Keystone Square Museum, Lampasas, Texas).

	OCT. 1954	NOV. 1954	DEC. 1954	JAN. 1955	FEB. 1955	MAR. 1955	APR. 1955
Lampasas River at Youngsport	696	9,030	243	1,177	3,073	1,085	1,882
Lavaca River at Hallettsville	35	14	20	126	3,621	37	46
Leon River at Belton	93	32	21	70	259	79	177
San Gabriel River at Georgetown	58	58	64	151	555	562	181

	OCT. 1955	NOV. 1955	DEC. 1955	JAN. 1956	FEB. 1956	MAR. 1956	APR. 1956
Lampasas River at Youngsport	211	175	289	285	573	171	101
Lavaca River at Hallettsville	16	13	25	26	270	20	18
Leon River at Belton	132	111	188	242	228	204	141
San Gabriel River at Georgetown	17	29	39	73	84	64	31

	OCT. 1956	NOV. 1956	DEC. 1956	JAN. 1957	FEB. 1957	MAR. 1957	APR. 1957
Lampasas River at Youngsport	591	3,212	2,083	427	634	5,792	77,949
Lavaca River at Hallettsville	3	6	1,132	47	404	3,518	10,980
Leon River at Belton	657	26,177	10,711	83	106	148	4,331
San Gabriel River at Georgetown	497	1,554	1,167	130	341	920	45,018

Discharge in cubic feet/second

structed twin bridges just south of the present Highway 81 bridge." State highway department workers used a dragline to remove big logs and heavy debris to minimize the pounding on the structure.[23]

Flood Control

Lampasas then started methods of preventing another flood. Summarizing the situation with the dangerous creeks, Mayor Northington said Lampasas had two choices: Move the town from the Sulphur and Burleson creeks or control the streams. He added, "I don't think we're going to move the town. . . . In spite of Hell and high water, we're still here."[24] On June 6 the *Lampasas Record* referred to a report that was written "about 20 years ago" by the U.S. Army Corps of Engineers that predicted that a "flood of disastrous dimensions would probably happen at Lampasas once in a hundred years."[25]

As he had done after other Central Texas floods, Sen. Lyndon Baines Johnson pushed for the construction of dams, commenting that the Lampasas flood provided "convincing evidence that the federal government should push forward with construction of small flood prevention watershed dams as well as large flood control dams." He added, "In Texas, drought and flood too often follow one another in a distressing pattern of waste and loss. . . . I have . . . and shall continue to speak out in favor of building dams, big dams and little dams, on the river and streams in this community." He speculated that if a watershed project on Sulphur Creek had been in place, a good part of the damage would have been averted.[26]

The party surveyor chief with the Soil Conservation Service (SCS) estimated damage would have been $66,400 rather than $4–6 million if dams had been built. Outside of Lampasas, 2,645 floodplain acres were inundated. Dams, the experts contended, could have decreased this number to 914 acres. The surveyor added that drought conditions of the previous year had reduced

MAY 1955	JUNE 1955	JULY 1955	AUG. 1955	SEPT. 1955
26,644	11,528	4,977	2,299	4,015
5,931	615	16	1,148	64
264	172	153	226	173
4,692	2,506	1,343	1,600	132

MAY 1956	JUNE 1956	JULY 1956	AUG. 1956	SEPT. 1956
14,873	341	4	1,228	127
26	14	255	36	1
40,661	1,740	410	648	343
1,522	1	0	66	52

MAY 1957	JUNE 1957	JULY 1957	AUG. 1957	SEPT. 1957
96,573	17,647	1,761	566	886
3,165	1,962	26	19	3,226
121,775	180,058	194,900	20,709	832
17,899	23,078	1,923	669	1,148

High water in Williamson County (courtesy of the Taylor Public Library).

the landscape to minimal vegetation, and these "poor conditions caused very high rates of runoff and erosion and thereby increased the flood stages and sedimentation and scour damage downstream." Areas with good growth had moisture down to 4–5 feet, whereas those with poor coverage had deep moisture levels of only 19–29 inches.[27]

The acting state conservationist for Texas reported that, ten days prior to the Lampasas flood, his office had sent plans to Washington for approval. The proposals called for five flood-retarding structures at a total cost of $1.25 million.

In June, more rains around Lampasas prompted a small rise on the creek and caused a further awareness of the town's vulnerability. The editor of the *Lampasas Dispatch* wrote, "We feel very strongly that some work should have been started long before this, but since there wasn't, we think it should be started today."[28] By June 20 debris and silt had been removed from drainage areas and sewers in Lampasas.

By the fall of 1957, the federal legislative committees approved the Sulphur Creek Dam project. Construction was set to begin in January or February 1958, and the cost was estimated at $1,264,526. One phase was aimed at improving range and farmland to retard any runoff. The second phase called for the construction of five or more flood-retarding structures to store floodwaters temporarily so they could be released over an extended period of time.

Waco Area Weather and Runoff

Heavy rain in Central Texas caused other dangerous inundations as well. Floods caused by the intense eight-inch rain falling along Cow Bayou forced eight people to seek refuge in trees. Bullhide Creek swept over US 77. More than one hundred cars were trapped at one time early on the night of May 11.

In McGregor, Harris Creek was up, threatening the same cemetery in which some of the caskets had been exposed during the floods in April. In Killeen, water was four feet over low-water crossings. The Cowhouse Creek closed the west range road at South Fort Hood. Near Lorena, a man and a woman were marooned in a tree with one of two patrolmen who tried to rescue them, while the second patrolman clung to a traffic sign on Highway 81 during the night of May 11. In Falls County, every creek was reported to be out of its banks. At Marlin, the seven-inch downpour caused train track beds to soften, contributing to a derailment of twenty-five cars piled forty feet high. On Waco's east side, the storm sewers were closed so that water from the Brazos would not overwhelm the area. While the Bosque River flooded, Lake Waco passed water through eleven gates. The North Bosque rose nine feet at Meridian.

On May 15 the Belton Reservoir, whose conservation level was 569 feet, was rising at one inch per hour and was expected to surpass its record high of 610.68 feet, by reaching 612 feet by daylight. The resident engineer said, "The Leon River is the highest I have ever seen it. I don't know how much more water the lake will get."[29]

Water washed over the old highway bridge at Little River and the 6-foot gage, and old-timers believed this was the highest stage reached since 1936 or 1938. To match the level of the 1921 flood, the river would have had to flow 4 feet deep over the road at Thomastik's station on the highway, and it was still 1 foot shy of the road. The Little River at Little River was said to be within 6 feet of the 1921 high. Water was reported to be "hill to hill" in the bottoms and a mile across at its widest point.[30]

North of Lampasas, the city of Hamilton was struck by flash flooding. Flood control dams designed to prevent flash flooding on Hamilton's Pecan Creek are visible from the highways and Farm to Market roads leading into Hamilton.

West and North Texas Flooding Rains of 1957

In April and May, the San Angelo area experienced downpours and minor flooding, a more welcome set of problems than a nearly decade-long drought. By late April, residents of San Angelo and West Texas admitted they could "flick their thumbs at fast approaching summer." Lake Nasworthy was full.[31]

Area streams were pushing the limits of their banks. The South Concho River was at 16.8 feet, while Spring Creek was at 20.75 feet, its highest point in fifty years. Menard prepared to place sandbags along the San Saba River, if needed. In Brownwood, Adams Branch and Pecan Bayou were flooding. On May 25 and 26, Palo Pinto Creek, a tributary to the Brazos River near Santo, reached its highest stage since at least 1880. Farther west, Howard Draw near Ozona was on a rampage. In Ozona, Johnson Draw chased seventy-five families from their homes. The Pecos near Big Lake registered its biggest increase since 1941, and water poured over the spillway at Lake Colorado City for the first time since it was built in 1950. Between March 19 and June 6, 1957, Lake Texoma rose from its record low to its record high.

Summing Up

The incredible reversal of weather patterns and subsequent flooding prompted the Texas Water Development Board to publish a report on the springtime floods. It stated that the floods were outstanding in both the large area affected and the huge volume produced: "All streams in the State, from the Red River to the Rio Grande, were in flood much of the time during this three-month period. Excluding the Red River and the Rio Grande and considering only the interior streams in Texas, 38 million acre-feet of runoff, adjusted for storage in major reservoirs, was produced over the State during this three month period."

The report also stated that, from April to June 1957, heavy rains covered the eastern two-thirds of the state. Weather records do not "record a similar period when so much rainfall was experienced over such a large portion of the State in one continuing period." This was a "sudden switch from drought conditions which had prevailed over practically all of the State for many years."

JUNE 1965

Sanderson Flash Flood

THE IMAGE OF a West Texas flash flood is that of a wall of water thundering down a dry gulch. In 1965, just such a wall of water propelled the powerful flash flood that decimated much of Sanderson.

Two draws or canyons join at the western end (upstream) of Sanderson. The town sits below their junction, inside a curving canyon. It is a town sitting, as some have said, in a cup. On the night of June 10, 1965, strong thunderstorms stalled upstream of Sanderson and dropped intense rain. The deluges triggered flood waves that took out dams, railroad bridges, dozens of telephone poles, and everything else in its path. At dawn on June 11, 1965, the wave smashed into Sanderson.

This particular flash flood was a combination of the worst of multiple elements. The destructive wave rose in the dark, pre-dawn hours and, with little warning, struck the town at daybreak. The resulting increase was unprecedented, so even long-time residents would not have expected a rise to reach so far into town. The surge carried debris from miles above Sanderson and then added larger and more dangerous wreckage from the industrial sections of town. This was then thrust upon the residential sections of Sanderson hit by the flood. Overall, the Sanderson flash flood is one of the most scarring and prototypical inundations in the history of the United States.

Precedent

Sanderson's annual rainfall averages a little more than 13 inches. September is the only month that averages more than 2 inches (2.29). May and June average

Car behind Bart's Conoco station, Sanderson (courtesy of the Terrell County Historical Commission).

1.71 inches and 1.65 inches, respectively, and are the second and third rainiest months. In 1965 Sanderson received no rain in January and March. In February it gauged 1.31 inches and in April, 0.42 inches. May was a wet month for the town, as it received 2.15 inches. For the first five months of the year, rainfall was 0.04 inches below average.

Rainfall and Storm

Late on June 10 a storm moved into Terrell County from the west. A dispatcher at Marathon noted, "We were only on the edge of the storm, and it moved directly toward Sanderson." More big rains were reported from the Big Bend country to the Panhandle, following a cold front that dropped the temperature 15 degrees in Odessa. A weatherman at Odessa said the storm was "unusually calm considering the amount of activity in the area." The rains in Odessa dropped 3.1 inches in the northern portions of town.[1]

More stormy weather was reported at McCamey and near Rankin, where 0.8–1.6

inches fell. In the early morning of June 11 high water blocked Highway 329. Wink, Monahans, Snyder, Colorado City, and Midland all reported more than 1 inch of rain. The front that produced the precipitation hit Odessa and Midland around 3 P.M. on June 10. In the South Plains, near Lubbock and Plainview, the weather bureau said that funnel clouds that were "too numerous to accurately count . . . danced through the sky for hours." Evidence of the moisture in the system was seen in rainfall totals of more than 10 inches south of Muleshoe. Plainview's Running Water Draw, which was usually dry, ran five feet deep and fifty yards wide, while high water blocked traffic into Palo Duro State Park.[2]

Near Sanderson, the rains started falling at 4 P.M. on June 10. Between 6 and 9 P.M. the showers were well distributed over the Sanderson Canyon watershed. Hail fell on the southwestern edge of the area. Rain continued until 5 or 6 A.M. on June 11. At 4 A.M. the Three Mile Draw began receiving heavy downpours. Between 4 and 8 A.M. on

June 11, more than 5 inches fell in the watershed feeding Three Mile Draw. Official reports from the U.S. Weather Bureau listed rains up to 8 inches in two hours near Sanderson, with 6.3 inches reported in the north part of town, and 9.5 inches at Longfellow.

Streamflow

Fed by overnight rains that approached Sanderson's yearly average, the runoff down the dry canyons built to unprecedented levels in the town's history.

Upper Sanderson Canyon

The flood started in the upper reaches of Rattlesnake Draw during the evening

hours of June 10. The runoff breached a diversion dike, and water in the upper canyon washed out the area between the road and railroad embankment. Richard A. Crawley, a University of Texas student who studied the flood, stated, "A large trench, about 30 feet wide and 12 feet deep, and about one quarter mile long, was cut parallel with the railroad. Portions of the railroad were badly damaged."[3]

The flood topped the railroad bridge approximately fifteen miles upstream from Sanderson. After midnight, the pressure of the rising floodwater against a stock tank broke its dam. Crawley commented, "the breaching of the dam, which took place in the early morning, possibly initiated the flood peak which then moved rapidly

Possible grave sites at cemetery. (courtesy of the Terrell County Historical Commission).

Aerial view of damaged railroad tracks. (courtesy of the Terrell County Historical Commission).

Floodwaters undercut the rails and roads. (courtesy of the Terrell County Historical Commission).

Washed-out approach to railroad bridge. (courtesy of the Terrell County Historical Commission).

Ozona	0.00	0.00	0.68	0.30	0.98
Bakersfield	0.00	0.00	1.69	0.00	1.69
Fort Stockton	0.00	0.75	0.00	0.00	0.75
Sheffield	0.00	0.00	1.99	0.00	1.99
Eldorado 11	0.00	0.00	0.52	0.00	0.52
San Angelo	0.00	0.00	0.22	0.00	0.22
Del Rio	0.00	0.00	0.81	0.00	0.81
Marathon	0.00	trace	1.61	trace	1.61
Mentone	0.00	0.18	2.14	0.00	2.32
Odessa	0.07	0.08	0.99	0.00	1.14
Wink	0.39	1.32	0.18	0.00	1.89
Pandale	0.00	0.00	0.00	2.03	2.03
Sanderson	0.00	0.00	5.35	0.00	5.35
Monahans	0.22	0.22	0.80	0.00	1.24
Imperial	0.62	0.70	0.00	0.00	1.32
Girvin	0.04	trace	1.13	0.00	1.17
Sanderson 25W	0.00	0.50	2.50	0.00	3.00
Sanderson 16W	0.00	0.00	4.50	0.00	4.50
Sanderson 10WNW	0.00	0.00	5.00	0.00	5.00
Sanderson 1N	0.00	0.00	4.50	0.00	4.50
Sanderson 3N	0.00	0.00	4.50	0.00	4.50

downstream." Tree limbs and brush accumulated against wooden railroad trestles upstream of Sanderson, and at approximately 5 A.M. a bridge about seven miles above the town failed. After that point, trestles failed one after another down the canyon toward Sanderson.[4] Crawley noted that the "wooden beams from these bridges became effective battering rams against the buildings in Sanderson."[5]

Because Bob Mayo of the *Fort Stockton Pioneer* believed that most readers would have already picked up many of the details from daily papers about the "somewhat unbelievable cascade of water which swept down the normally dry bed of Sand-

erson Canyon," his report focused on what happened, where, and why.[6] Mayo said, "to much of the country, there is something incongruous about a severe flood in semi-desert country. But as a matter of fact sudden floods are more frequent . . . in the dry, mountainous West."[7]

Compounding the Sanderson Canyon floodwaters was additional water from Three Mile Draw. The water from the draw, merging with the Sanderson Canyon water, created "flood on top of a flood," causing a "turbulence and whirlpool effect which sent swirling, crushing waters in fantastic and terrifying currents . . . a veritable tornado of water." The force of this water smashed "high against the railroad embankment, rebounded in a counterclockwise swirl and smashed against the base of the mountain in the north side of US 90."[8]

The extent of the floodwaters' damage was evident by the destruction upstream of the town. More than eight miles of Southwestern Bell Telephone line and approximately forty telephone poles west of Sanderson were washed away in the deluge.

Sanderson Creek Basin

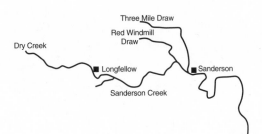

SANDERSON FLASH FLOOD

Sanderson

The flood waves moved toward Sanderson between 5 and 7 A.M. In town around 5 A.M. the storm was letting up. Because the creek there was beginning to fall, law enforcement authorities went home for rest. At 6 A.M., however, additional runoff from Sanderson Creek and Three Mile Draw arrived, producing the wall of water that battered the town. At 7:05 A.M. the crest swept through at a rate of 14.7 feet per second. The floodwater rose, peaking at 7:20 A.M.

As the wave destroyed warehouses and washed away the lumberyard, water also reached into the post office and Sanderson Bank. At the Southern Pacific rail yard, the water "bent miles of iron rail, twisting them like wet spaghetti."[9]

Reporting on the flood, a USGS agent from San Angelo said that the grade into Sanderson was 7 feet per 1,000 and Three Mile Draw, 10 feet per 1,000. (He added that the area around San Angelo was 4 or 5 feet per 1,000 and was considered a "pretty good grade.") His team determined that Sanderson "took on a high velocity of water." To calculate peak streamflow, the USGS studied high-water marks a mile upstream from the town and, on the Three Mile Draw, about three-quarters of a mile above the town. They did not study the marks in the town itself because the obstructions distorted the peak values.[10]

Peak discharge measurements were made on straight sections of the canyon and Three Mile Draw, using debris lines as the high-water marks. The peak discharge was 76,400 cfs for Sanderson Creek and 22,400–24,800 cfs for the Three Mile Draw. Combining these two revealed a streamflow of approximately 100,000 cfs into Sanderson.

On June 20 the *San Angelo Standard-Times* stated, "An earlier report indicated the Geological Survey team would determine the cause of the flood. Grozier said

this was in error, 'We can't determine what caused it.' He added, 'Or rather, everyone knows what caused it was a heavy rain in a short period of time.' . . . The wall of water which has been spoken of many times in news stories, Grozier said, resulted from a high intensity rainfall. 'It's not really a wall. It's just a large amount of water which comes down suddenly. It will carry pretty heavy rocks and boulders and when it hits a town will uproot trees."[11]

The U.S. Weather Bureau called it the greatest crest in the history of the area. The storm data summary described the resulting impact of the flood wave: "Houses, automobiles, and business buildings tumbled along like children's' toys in a drainage ditch. The complete destruction of the areas clos-

Building in Sanderson Courts (note pole thrust into building by the floodwaters). (courtesy of the Terrell County Historical Commission).

Debris that was carried for long distances at high velocities, creating a dangerous flood wave (courtesy of the Terrell County Historical Commission).

Aerial view of cemetery (courtesy of the Terrell County Historical Commission).

est to the banks of Sanderson Canyon re-sembled the path of a tornado."[12] Culverts that had existed for forty-five years were washed out.

Landmarks

The water left the channel at the con-fluence of Three Mile Draw and Sander-son Creek, running just south of Highway 90 and Oak Street in Sanderson. It jumped the channel just west of the Sanderson Wool Commission Company at the rail-road bridge and jumped again at the rail-road bridge just south of Oak and Fifth streets. The wave that followed the Fifth Street area path damaged Clymer Courts, Sanderson Courts, and houses on Legion Street. Caskets were washed out of graves at Panteon–Santa Rita Cemetery. A single

Deep erosion and flood damage to the road base of Highway 90 in Sanderson (courtesy of the Terrell County Historical Commission).

Asphalt was torn off the road base (courtesy of the Terrell County Historical Commission).

The flood tossed cars onto houses (courtesy of the Terrell County Historical Commission).

The flood scoured sections of the cemetery (courtesy of the Terrell County Historical Commission).

Close-up of ravaged grave sites at cemetery (courtesy of the Terrell County Historical Commission).

Debris from the flood (courtesy of the Terrell County Historical Commission).

tombstone remained erect. Headstones and markers were found as far as four miles downstream.

The Terrell County sheriff said, "The old timers told me they'd seen floods here before, but never like this."[13] A long-time Sanderson resident stated, "Nothing I've ever seen can compare with it. We've had floods up and down the canyon before, but it's never been from mountain-to-mountain before in the 34 years I have lived here."[14]

The churning water demolished one of Sanderson's landmarks, the giant Sanderson Wool Commission warehouse. As sacks of wool were ripped open, their contents were scattered and caught on poles and tree limbs.

As the flood wave hit the Oasis Restaurant, water shot through cracks in the wall. The owner of a nearby gas station recalled, "A deafening roar began thundering from outside as the building started shaking and water began spraying through cracks in the walls. [Customers] cleared out in nothing flat." Everybody in the restaurant escaped to higher ground.[15]

The Sanderson post office was left with prominent marks from the deluge. A 12 x 12 inch beam from the railroad tracks pierced the wall and was left protruding from it after the water level dropped. The post office was also left with knee-deep mud and sediment.

Sanderson Accounts

There was a warning that a wall of water was coming, but it did not arrive soon enough to alert all of the residents in the low-lying areas. South of the tracks and several hundred yards west of the depot, Judge Wilkinson's house, which stood some twelve feet above the creek banks, was surrounded by water. He and his wife narrowly escaped the surge as they scrambled to the roof of

their home. From there, they saw a railroad car float by only fifty feet away.

Near the Robertson Courts, one couple was staying at a house next to the Dairy King. When the man heard the gurgling of water, he thought the toilet was running, but then his hand moved down off the bed and felt the water there. As he arose and looked out the window, the flood wave hit the house, breaking it to pieces. The couple somehow grabbed on to the bumper of their car and then to a telephone pole to escape the onslaught.

The currents washed out the telephone lines. A railroad commissioner used a ham

Damage to the railroad yard in Sanderson (courtesy of the Terrell County Historical Commission).

The flood cut deep gullies in Sanderson (courtesy of the Terrell County Historical Commission).

Damage to the wool warehouse in Sanderson (courtesy of the Terrell County Historical Commission).

Sanderson Wool Commission Warehouse (courtesy of the Terrell County Historical Commission).

radio to send out a distress message: "Mayday, May-day. . . . Sanderson has been hit by a flash flood. . . . May-day, May-day. . . . Sanderson has been washed away. . . . We need assistance."[16]

A twelve-year-old boy was carried approximately a mile before being pinned against a utility pole. After holding on—with water up to his shoulders—for two hours, he was rescued. One of the rescuers saw the motel building that the boy's family was standing on. He said, "It started crumbling, and it went over and everybody was gone. Nobody could help them."[17]

One Sanderson resident ran both a motel and a store at that time. After the flood hit, only the walls of the motel were left standing. She then used flour sacks to build a

barricade against the currents. She said, "I started with the cheap stuff and worked myself up to the high price variety." The flood took its toll on her business, and she added, "I don't think I'm going to reopen—the bank just bought itself a grocery store. I'm just going upstairs to sit in my rocker and draw my poverty pay."[18]

One survivor rode out the water on top of his truck in the middle of Sanderson Cemetery. He commented, "I was on my way to town and the next thing I knew I was sitting in a cab full of water."[19] Terrell County's judge stated, "I've lived here about 45 years and I've never seen it this bad. It got three or four feet higher this time than I had ever seen it before."[20] After losing his four children in the flood, a father said, "I reckon I'll go back to Sanderson. I won't enjoy living there again, but I have a job and I've got to work."[21]

As the search for bodies continued, the power of the water was documented in the distance the corpses were carried. One was found twenty miles east of Sanderson. Since it had been carried so far, searchers began to wonder whether other bodies might have been washed into the Rio Grande. The sheriff commented, "If the bodies went into the Rio Grande, it will be just about hopeless." Rescuers decided to examine a dozen autos that were swept as much as three miles down the canyon.[22]

The fears that victims had been washed down the Rio Grande were confirmed. Two bodies were found in the river—one 300 miles downstream in Nuevo Laredo and the other 140 miles downriver about 18 miles up from Eagle Pass. Recovery crews also looked to the skies to help find flood victims. They would search where buzzards circled overhead. Usually they found only a dead animal. Once the bodies were located, it was a difficult task to identify them. One reliable method was to have the local barber look at their hair.

Aerial view of Sanderson after the flood (courtesy of the Terrell County Historical Commission).

Aerial view of Sanderson. Note damage to structures (Robertson Courts) in foreground, where the creek flowed over its banks (courtesy of the Terrell County Historical Commission).

Floodwaters flowed over bridges and deposited debris in bridge railings. This is the Highway 90 bridge on the edge of Sanderson (courtesy of the Terrell County Historical Commission).

One of the rescue workers said, "We're walking down the canyon turning over everything we see. There's so much debris you can't find anything. It's terrible."[23]

Damage

After the flood, the Terrell County commissioner called Sanderson "the damndest mess I've ever seen."[24] The deluge destroyed fifty-four houses, four motels, two drive-ins, and four service stations. A Red Cross survey estimated the flood covered thirty-five percent of the town.

"'They have our heart-felt sympathy,' said an Ozona resident. 'About half our town is already over there trying to get to them. All the medical supplies we had were sent down there. A truck was taken to help bring in water.'"[25] One unexpected relief effort came from Ector County, whose residents came in with a load of dirt and rebuilt the washed-out Little League field.

The sheriff of Terrell County observed, "People who live in West Texas get used to nearly every kind of disaster. This is a great disaster to our community, but I don't think that it will put us out of business. As soon as the water runs down, we'll be rebuilding."[26]

~~~~~~~

Dallas Flash Flood

IN 1962 AND 1964, significant flash floods ripped through the northern sections of Dallas. The peak flood events on Joe's Creek and Bachman Branch in northwest Dallas reached fifty-year recurrence levels. These floods in the rapidly growing metropolitan area seized the attention of the city's movers and shakers, who began implementing flood control measures along local streams. Nevertheless, in 1966, intense thunderstorms deposited high totals of rainfall in a short period of time. The result was another round of damaging flash floods that tore through some of the richest and stateliest neighborhoods in the Lone Star State.

Precedent

Late in April 1966, active weather focused on North Texas. A cold front pushed into the Panhandle and kicked up a blinding dust storm with 40-mph winds and temperatures in the 60s. On April 25 storms dropped golf-ball-sized hail, causing damage in Denton. In East Texas, high water hit Big Cypress Creek and Caddo Lake. Some counties in East Texas reported up to 22 inches of rain. In the Dallas area, almost 6 inches fell from April 22 through April 25. As the next round of storms approached the city, local streams and watersheds were already saturated.

Rains

In the early morning hours of April 28, around 12:30 to 1 A.M., intense storms began unleashing precipitation on north Dallas.

Moving in from the northwest, they brought a mix of hail and rain. Wind gusts up to 65 mph were reported at Farmers Branch. In north Dallas the rain was falling at greater than four inches per hour. The peak rainfall rates for thirty-minute and two-hour spans exceeded the one-hundred-year recurrence values.

The storm was centered in the northern part of Dallas on Cottonwood Creek and Floyd Branch, which both flow into White Rock Creek. They also affect other small watersheds. Joe's Creek, for instance, where 3.74 inches poured down within thirty minutes, received more than 4.4 inches throughout its watershed. Topping both the totals and intensity at Joe's Creek, Bachman Branch received more than 5.25 inches, with 3.86 inches falling within thirty minutes. Turtle Creek received 4.78 inches in its upper reaches and 2.49 in its lower reaches. The peak rainfall for the event, however, occurred in the White Rock Creek basin, which received 6.7 inches of precipitation.

Following the April 28 deluges, April 1966 was well on the way to surpassing the wettest April on record in Dallas, which had occurred in 1957. Following the rains on April 29 and 30, the 1966 total indeed eclipsed the 1957 tally of 13.85 inches. From April 22 through May 1 alone, 13.22 inches fell on Dallas. A sign at the Irving Chamber of Commerce pleaded, "We holler uncle to all rain gods."[1]

Streams

The small streams that were hit by the heavy rains all have similar features: Each has a wide flood plain on the upper reaches,

Cottonwood Creek along Forest Lane at White Rock Creek, Dallas, during the flood of April 28, 1966 (courtesy *Dallas Morning News* Archives).

Stream Response to the Flooding Rains

The heavy rains of April 28 produced a peak discharge of 6,350 cfs on Joe's Creek at Highway 114. As a result of the improvements made in the watershed, this volume was greater than or equal to that of the 1962 flood, even though the stage was lower.

In the 1966 flash flood, Bachman Branch produced a peak discharge of 3,160 cfs from Slaughter Branch at Walnut Hill Lane from a drainage area of 1.51 square miles. The peak runoff of 3,160 cfs per square mile over a 1½-mile area was the second highest peak-per-square-mile in the USGS records for Texas. The highest (3,350 cfs) was recorded at Bunton Branch near Kyle in 1936 and came from a drainage area of 4.12 square miles. As a result of that extreme volume, Bachman Branch at Midway rose 18 feet in a two-hour span.

Flooding Events

As the high water surged through north Dallas, the city's established neighborhoods were hit hard. Sinks, showers, lawn furniture, bicycles, and even powerboats were strewn throughout the creeks.

A fireman commented that he had halted his fire truck just before reaching the floodwaters from Bachman Creek, which was engulfing the bridge at Lemmon Avenue. He said, "I wouldn't have believed it, but we saw a pickup truck float by." For a while, it "looked like a barrel, turning over and over." The creek bent two-inch steel fence posts flat.[2]

Along the stream, lumber, a bench, clothing, and children's toys were deposited 15 feet up in trees. Other trees were not so lucky: A number of majestic oaks and elms, some 50–70 feet tall, were toppled when their roots were undercut by the currents.

Turtle Creek flooded the basement of a Highland Park police station, while along the creek north of Lovers Lane and south

as they start in fields and pastures, and then form deeper channels near their mouths. Their main channels extend down to limestone bedrock.

Following the floods of 1962, some of the Dallas-area watersheds were improved to permit a greater flow of water. On Joe's Creek, a low-water dam was removed below Royal Lane, parts of its streambed were channelized, and bridges and culverts were replaced or improved. However, by 1966, the expansion of Dallas meant that homes had been built in the floodplain where fields once fed the creek.

On Bachman Branch, a dam forming Bachman Lake (128 acres) was built in 1901 as part of the city's water supply. After the 1962 flood, several low-water dams were removed, and a bridge was rebuilt. The upper portion of Turtle Creek from Royal Lane to Walnut Hill Lane to the Lovers Lane portion was lined with concrete.

Bachman Creek, Dallas, just north of Northwest Highway (loop 12) during the flood of April 28, 1966 (courtesy *Dallas Morning News* Archives).

Bachman Creek at Park Lane and Audubon during the flood of April 28, 1966 (courtesy *Dallas Morning News* Archives).

of Northwest Highway, ten homes were inundated. A branch of Bachman Creek that ran behind Northwest Highway near Midway Road reached capacity within minutes. The floodwater lifted tables, appliances, and a boat and left them entangled in tree branches along the creek.

With the intense rains striking in the middle of the night, the police had a difficult time blocking off dangerous bridges and roads susceptible to flooding. As a result, a number of vehicles were washed into creeks, requiring rescues for the fortunate and recovery for the unlucky.

Two men clung to trees as their female companion drowned in their rented car, which was swept off Northwest Highway and into Bachman Creek about 3:30 A.M. After tumbling about four blocks, the car came to rest behind the "swank Guernsey Lane section beneath the towering Bluff View cliff." The powerful currents peeled

Looking southeast along the 2500 block of Eighth Avenue, April 29, 1966 (courtesy *Dallas Morning News* Archives).

White Rock Creek at East Grand and Garland Road, Dallas, April 28, 1966 (courtesy *Dallas Morning News* Archives).

the clothes off of one of the survivors, who was left wearing only his undershirt. The debris line indicated that water was fifteen feet deep through the area.[3]

On Guernsey Street a married couple reluctantly abandoned their house. The husband said, "I was awake doing some work in the house when it [the water] started to rise. I moved my car three times, then came back and we stuffed blankets around the door to keep the water out." When they fled, they waded through waist-deep water in their yard.[4]

Even the rescuers found themselves in trouble. Two firemen cheated death at 3:20 A.M. when White Rock Creek trapped them on a Greenville Avenue bridge, sweeping their boat, trailer, and station wagon away. For more than an hour they clung to trees before finally being rescued several hundred yards east of the 7800 block of Greenville behind Deuback Skating Rink.

					DATE			
LOCATION	21	22	23	24	25	26	27	28
Abilene	0.00	0.18	1.91	0.58	1.63	0.00	0.00	0.50
Albany	0.00	0.05	0.60	2.44	1.00	0.02	0.00	0.00
Arlington	0.00	0.03	0.87	1.82	2.10	0.18	trace	0.00
Benbrook	0.00	0.02	0.33	1.00	1.91	0.14	0.00	0.10
Breckenridge	0.00	1.72	1.03	0.63	1.49	0.03	0.00	0.63
Brownwood	0.00	0.37	0.50	0.85	1.41	0.00	0.00	1.26
Carrolton	0.00	0.02	1.07	2.20	1.00	0.90	0.06	2.60
Clifton	0.00	0.28	0.37	2.54	3.46	0.00	0.00	0.90
Dallas	0.00	0.49	1.86	1.25	2.33	trace	0.00	3.60
Denton	0.00	0.00	1.81	1.57	1.09	0.02	0.00	1.51
Eagle Mountain	0.00	0.08	0.35	2.27	1.07	0.70	0.00	0.12
Fort Worth	trace	0.38	1.10	0.91	1.41	trace	0.00	0.90
Hamilton	0.00	0.02	0.73	1.08	1.80	0.43	0.00	0.00
Hillsboro	0.00	0.02	0.42	2.20	3.10	1.32	0.00	0.00
Lawn	0.00	0.19	0.30	0.90	2.41	0.14	0.00	1.50
Marlin	0.00	0.30	0.48	2.33	1.51	2.91	0.00	0.00
Mineral Wells	0.00	0.93	0.35	0.67	1.38	trace	0.00	0.58
Roanoke	0.00	0.00	0.66	2.07	0.64	0.42	0.00	0.76
Waco	0.00	1.45	0.08	2.72	1.65	0.00	0.00	0.27
Weatherford	0.00	0.04	0.37	1.08	0.95	0.79	0.01	0.00

AVERAGE DAILY DISCHARGE, APRIL 21–MAY 3, 1966

				DATE			
LOCATION	APR. 21	APR. 22	APR. 23	APR. 24	APR. 25	APR. 26	APR. 27
Bachman Branch	4.6	9.2	86	130	319	56	26
Turtle Creek	3.8	27	247	119	531	26	12
White Rock Creek Keller Springs Road	1.4	1.5	333	304	654	77	24
White Rock Creek Greenville	13	34	1,020	985	2,880	285	129
White Rock Creek WR Lake	46	33	647	179	68	37	51
White Rock Creek Scyene Road	48	79	1,440	3,060	5,840	2,100	383
Duck Creek	6.2	17	1,010	1,260	2,300	180	38
Trinity River at Dallas	328	391	2,560	11,500	17,000	19,800	6,890

Discharge in cubic feet/second

Two teenagers driving behind the fire fighters watched the drama. One of them said, "We saw the red station wagon stall ahead of us and we put our bright [head] lights on them. It [the station wagon] tried to back up and the boat trailer turned crooked. The red light and siren came on. Then the current swept the whole thing off the road. We watched the car jam a minute against two trees and turn over. A fireman in a white shirt crawled out a window and stood up on the top. He yelled, 'Go back! Go back!' Then the water rolled the whole thing over and they were gone. It tumbled over and over."[5]

To reach the men, a rescue boat was launched. Although "bobbing like a cork in a millrace," it reached both firefighters, who had secured themselves by locking their arms around trees in the water. As the boat headed back to safety, its gas line was cut by a branch. One of the rescued firemen spliced the gas line, and the boat was able to continue back to shore.[6]

29	30	1	2	3	TOTAL
1.52	0.43	0.31	trace	0.00	7.06
0.69	1.92	0.92	0.01	0.00	7.65
0.56	0.75	3.11	0.00	0.00	9.42
2.58	0.87	3.95	0.02	0.00	10.92
1.25	0.78	0.67	0.00	0.00	8.23
0.23	0.85	1.50	0.00	0.00	6.97
0.93	3.71	2.47	0.07	0.00	15.03
0.27	0.59	0.39	0.00	0.00	8.80
1.84	1.02	0.83	trace	0.00	13.22
1.83	1.43	0.59	0.00	0.00	9.85
0.66	2.33	1.70	0.16	0.00	9.44
2.76	1.11	1.25	trace	0.00	9.82
0.86	0.20	0.81	0.11	trace	6.04
0.80	0.13	1.14	0.16	0.00	9.29
2.69	2.29	0.00	0.00	0.00	10.42
0.43	0.00	1.00	0.20	0.00	9.16
1.73	0.66	1.56	0.00	0.00	7.86
1.10	2.48	1.82	0.00	0.00	9.95
0.03	0.97	0.50	trace	0.00	7.67
1.20	2.00	2.47	0.01	0.00	8.92

APR. 28	APR. 29	APR. 30	MAY 1	MAY 2	MAY 3
1,250	822	454	350	56	39
695	385	178	229	21	12
1,940	1,900	1,300	402	86	56
5,980	5,310	3,490	2,010	451	331
908	2,450	3,720	3,940	709	237
13,000	6,240	6,450	8,460	3,000	584
2,330	2,030	1,960	2,890	84	48
12,000	14,400	23,800	38,100	25,200	16,400

Duck Creek

In addition to the creeks flooding in north Dallas, one of North Texas' most flood-prone streams, Duck Creek in Garland, also left its banks. It forced eighty people from their homes and damaged the Duck Creek Shopping Center on Garland Road.

Summing Up

Following the floods, Dallas officials received criticism for not having done more following the deluges of 1962 and 1964. Frank Randt, chair of the North Dallas Chamber of Commerce Flood Committee, blasted the civic leaders. After water entered his home, he strongly urged the city to do something about the flood situation. "There is a long history of flood here, but the city has never cooperated with the Corps of Engineers or the SCS to create a plan for flood control."[7] Moreover, Joe H. Golman, deputy mayor pro tem, stated, "people are dying and millions of dollars of property [have been] lost while we're waiting on studies."[8]

Anecdotes

Some odd moments from the flood included these two episodes in which people moved from danger to safety and then back to the danger of the floodwaters:

• One woman moved her car to a safe place and then returned through the floodwaters to her house while holding paintings over her head.
• One family drove their car to safety and then returned home through the swift currents. They then climbed into the attic to escape the rising water.

When Lawrence Welk's plane was unable to land in Dallas on the night of April 29, it detoured to Little Rock, but his fans were assured that he would still appear that evening. At 9:40 P.M. he arrived in Dallas, only 70 minutes late, as it turned out. The hall was practically filled with silver-haired ladies and bald-headed gentlemen rather than silver blondes and long-haired Beatles' cuts. "Even the Dallas deluge couldn't water down these fans' taste for champagne music," observed a newspaper reporter for the *Dallas Morning News* on April 30, 1966.

MAY 1970

〜〜〜

San Marcos River Flood

CERTAINLY THE HEADWATERS of the San Marcos River are among the most beautiful in Texas. Formed by the San Marcos Springs and several small creeks, the river originates at the edge of the Balcones Escarpment. The city of San Marcos and Texas State University have grown up around not only the river but also its contributing streams. A major road, Aquarena Drive, crosses the river just below the falls downstream of the springs and above Sewell Park. The striking scene of clear blue-green water belies the flash flood potential of the location, however. The bridge has a small gage along its base above the river. However, the best marker for the flash flood potential is not the six-foot gage on the bridge but the three-story apartment building, Clear Springs Apartments, that sits upstream of the bridge on the riverbanks.

The flash flood potential of the San Marcos River at San Marcos was recognized by some of the area's residents. One old-timer who remembered floods dating back to 1890 remarked, "Just you wait till the Blanco, Sink Springs and Purgatory all flood at the same time; then you'll see water in the courthouse."[1]

Precedent

In 1969 and the first four months of 1970, rainfall was close to average for San Marcos and vicinity (0.15 inch above average from January through April), and San Antonio's total was 2 inches above average for that same span. In May, Texas' usual stormy weather arrived on schedule. On May 11 Lubbock was devastated by a 1½-mile-wide tornado that ripped through sections near downtown, Texas Tech, and Lubbock Municipal Airport. Twenty-six people died, and more than $135 million in damages resulted from the twister, which traveled on the ground for eight miles.

Rainfall

In mid-May, heavy rains moved into central Texas and the Hill Country. The Sabinal and Knippa area reported 5 inches of precipitation. Farther south, Dilley gauged 3 inches. The storms then moved north, dropping 8.38 inches at Hondo and 6.9 inches at Fredericksburg on May 15.

The official total at San Marcos was 7.37 inches on May 15, but the unofficial totals near San Marcos were substantially higher. Locations north of the city had totals of al-

Aerial view of San Marcos River flooding (courtesy of the *San Marcos Record*).

San Marcos River Basin at
San Marcos

Blanco River

SinkCreek

Downtown
San Marcos

Purgatory
Creek

San Marcos River

Willow Springs

most 12 inches. San Marcos's radio station, KCNY, recorded 18.5 inches on May 15 and 16 during a thirty-hour period. The *San Marcos Record* noted, "Weathermen . . . called the hard, steady rainfall which spawned the flood a 'meteorological freak.'"[2]

Farther to the south, the upper watersheds of York and Plum creeks gauged 7.5–8.5 inches of precipitation. Buda reported 8 inches of rain, while above San Marcos on the Blanco River (in the Wimberley area), 5- and 6-inch totals were measured.

Streamflow

As the heavy rains poured down just outside of San Marcos, the small creeks that feed the San Marcos River there burst from their banks. Water rushed down Sink Springs Creek north of town, cutting off residents along Lime Kiln Road and engulf-

Aerial view of the San
Marcos River outside
the town of San Marcos
(courtesy of the *San Marcos
Record*).

ing Aquarena Springs, Travis Elementary School, the Clear Springs Apartments, and much of the northeast section of town.

When water from Sink Springs hit the front of their homes, one group of residents was absorbed in watching from their back windows as water flowed down the San Marcos River. A city fire marshal said, "It must have come down in a four to six foot wave of water—all of a sudden the water just went up that much." He said it began rising shortly after 8 A.M.[3]

At the same time, other torrents flowed down Purgatory Creek northwest of town, first striking a home at the end of Hopkins Street and then engulfing dozens of other houses along the stream. While people along Purgatory Creek were being rescued, residents at the Clear Springs Apartments climbed to safety as water inundated the first two floors of the buildings.

The flooding overwhelmed a third of the city. The only means of traveling from Interstate 35 to the western part of town was via boat. On many houses the watermark stood at six feet. At Aquarena Springs, the golf course, hotel, and grounds were all inundated, and up to thirty alligators were reported loose. The floodwaters hit several sporting venues in San Marcos, and debris covered Evans Field at the university, the golf course at Quail Creek Country Club, and the city park.

San Marcos

On May 16 the *San Antonio Express* described the situation in San Marcos: "If it wasn't so tragic, it'd almost be funny . . . record players in treetops, refrigerators atop railroad trestles, trailer houses turned into houseboats and alligators loose in the river. However, no one in San Marcos is laughing. Instead, they're attempting to straighten out [the] confusion caused . . . by the worst flood

in the city's history."[4] Fortunately, the water came down after sunrise; otherwise, the casualties would have been even higher. One official hypothesized that the rise "might have killed a hundred or more" if it had arrived at night.[5]

Rescues

Assistance came to the flooded parts of town "almost immediately" after the announcement of the overflow was broadcast on KCNY. Those who came to San Marcos to help with rescues included the National Guard, Seguin fire fighters, New Braunfels police officers, the Gary Job Corps, and students from Southwest Texas State University.[6]

After being rescued by helicopter from the roof of his car, a man answered a question about the whereabouts of his vehicle by replying, "I don't know where it is,

out there floating around somewhere, I suppose."[7]

The scene of "the most dramatic of the dramas," according to the *San Marcos Record,* was at Travis Elementary School, which was surrounded by water. Approximately 150 children were marooned in the building.[8]

Flood damage at Aquarena Springs (courtesy of the *San Marcos Record*).

Flooded golf course along the San Marcos River (courtesy of the *San Marcos Record*).

LOCATION	MAY 13	MAY 14	MAY 15	MAY 16	TOTAL MAY 14–15
Austin	0.02	0.96	3.65	0.00	4.61
Blanco	0.00	0.02	1.65	1.33	1.67
Brady	0.00	0.00	3.18	0.14	3.18
Burnet	0.00	0.10	2.45	0.00	2.55
Cameron	0.00	0.00	0.04	1.23	0.04
Del Rio	1.36	0.28	0.09	0.00	0.37
Fredericksburg	0	0.53	6.90	0.00	7.43
Henly	0.00	0.00	7.37	0.39	7.37
Hunter 4 NNE					11
Hye	0.00	0.00	4.60	1.72	4.60
Johnson City	0.00	0.00	2.22	1.00	2.22
Junction	0.06	1.34	1.73	0.00	3.07
Kerrville	0.00	0	4.93	0.48	4.93
Lampasas	0	0.00	0.84	1.62	0.84
Llano	0.03	0.00	3.42	0.20	3.42
New Braunfels	0.00	0.00	1.74	3.69	1.74
Richland Springs	0.00	0.00	0.00	0.00	0.00
San Angelo	0	0.64	0.31	0.00	0.95
San Antonio	0	0.72	0.44	0.00	1.16
San Marcos	0.00	0.00	7.37	0.39	7.37
San Marcos 2 ENE (KCNY Radio Station Estimate)					18
San Marcos 2 ENE (KCNY Radio Station measured but overflowed)					14
San Marcos 2.2 NE					13
San Marcos 4 NNW (courthouse)					12
San Marcos 8 NW					7.3
San Saba	0.00	0.00	3.04	0.20	3.04
Spicewood	0	0	2.98	1.30	2.98
Taylor	0.00	0.00	2.16	0.25	2.16
Temple	0	0.00	0.02	0.56	0.02
Uvalde	0.00	0.25	1.27	0	1.52

Summing Up

Flood damage was not as severe as it might have been in the worst-case scenario, which would occur if the creeks and the Blanco River flooded at the same time. In Wimberley, the Cypress Creek had a bigger rise than the Blanco. It rose 4–6 feet but did little damage because the Blanco was not flooding. The water upriver from Cypress Creek rose less than 2½ feet.

Titled "We Dam Our Streams—Too Late," the *San Marcos Record*'s editorial of May 21 stated, "Since the devastating flood of last Friday it become more apparent than ever before that we needed to have had dams on Purgatory, on Willow Springs, and on Sink Springs. . . . Only once in a great many years do all drainage channels converge at one and the same time to cause a major flood. And this time, if the Blanco River had flooded as it has many times in the past, the losses would have been astronomical—not just in property, but in lives as well." [9]

The 1970 flood accelerated flood-prevention plans in the area. The SCS supervisor noted, "It didn't take Lampasas or Sanderson long to get their dams built after the terrible floods they had." He added that the

Vehicle caught in the 1970 San Marcos flood (courtesy of the *San Marcos Record*).

survey for the upper watersheds of Purgatory Creek, Willow Springs (McKie) Creek, and Sink Springs Creek, which were scheduled for July, began in May instead.[10] (San Marcos and Hays County had applied to the Soil Conservation Board for a flood-control pan and flood-control structure in early 1969, but the response was delayed because of nationwide funding limitations.)

San Marcos 1970 flood damage to vehicle (courtesy of the *San Marcos Record*).

Anecdote

One of the stories of heroism during the flood involved Bill Veidt, the station manager of the San Marcos radio station. When Veidt woke up one morning, "little did he realize what the day held in store." He became an "essential link" between citizens as they listened to KCNY. Initially Veidt thought little about the reports of heavy rain. However, when he heard that water was washing over Lime Kiln Road at 8:15 that morning, he became concerned. Shortly afterward, he received numerous calls from worried listeners, so he and Ken Cumpton, the station's sales manager, decided to preempt the regular programs and switch entirely to flood coverage. While answering phone calls, Veidt heard that his apartment at Clear Springs was inundated by floodwater. Cumpton said, "[When Veidt]

Vehicle damaged in the 1970 San Marcos flood (courtesy of the *San Marcos Record*).

Vehicle damage, San Marcos flood, 1970 (courtesy of the *San Marcos Record*).

Bleachers at park caught debris during the 1970 San Marcos flood (courtesy of the *San Marcos Record*).

Watching the waters during the 1970 flood in San Marcos (courtesy of the *San Marco Record*).

claimed to be an Aquarena Springs employee and said that several alligators had escaped from the park.

In one of the curious stories that accompany floods, one woman left her house at 9:30 A.M., driving through two feet of water. She left in a hurry, leaving her dog asleep on its bed. When she returned at 4 P.M., the dog was still on its bed, which was floating in water that was fifty inches deep.

received a call that the first floor of the Clear Spring Apartments was under water, he kind of turned green."[11]

At 3:15 P.M. Southwest Texas State University journalism professor John Hobbs and a Southwest Texas student relieved them. Hobbs's usual stint was a Saturday morning show. He thought one of his students was pulling his leg when a caller

Aside

"This kind of thing happens only once or twice in a lifetime," according to an article titled "Folks and Facts" in the *San Marcos Record* of May 21, 1970, which compared the May 1970 deluge in San Marcos to that of 1921. The flood of 1970 inspired the career of one of Texas' top authorities on flooding. Roy Sedwick was attending Southwest Texas State University that year and watched the floodwaters tear through the edge of campus and San Marcos. For the next thirty-five

Flooding in downtown San Marcos during the 1970 flood (courtesy of the *San Marcos Record*).

years he researched floods throughout Texas and became the head of the Texas Floodplain Management Association.

Precursor to the 1970 Flood

On September 26, 1952, the *San Marcos Record* printed the following editorial:

Problem of Flood Control Is Evident
Not many people in San Marcos have realized, particularly during recent years, that we have a problem of flood control. Matter of fact, there had not been a flood of any proportions for so long that most everybody had forgotten that we ever had floods in the San Marcos and Blanco rivers. It will be remembered, however, that in 1921, there was a serious flood and again in 1929. In each of those instances, the floods occurred in both the San Marcos (with Purgatory Creek as a factor) and in the Blanco simultaneously. But good authority has it that the flood last Thursday was the highest in the Blanco in more than 60 years. That same authority warned that if the San Marcos and Purgatory Creek had also been at flood stage at the same time as the Blanco, we would have

Downtown San Marcos during the 1970 flood (courtesy of the *San Marcos Record*).

had a flood which would have dwarfed the Thursday flood. . . .

San Marcos can count itself fortunate last week that the flood was confined to the Blanco River. If the other rivers had gone on a rampage at the same time, it is a good bet that downtown San Marcos would have been flooded and there is strong likelihood that lives may have been lost. As it was, the water in the San Marcos River was altogether back water pushed up the stream by the Blanco.

It may be many years before we have another flood like that one of last Thursday. Again, it may happen again this year.

MAY 1972

~~~~~~~~~

New Braunfels Flood

MOST TEXANS ARE familiar with the natural beauty of New Braunfels. Sitting at the confluence of two of the state's most picturesque rivers, the Comal and the Guadalupe, and at the source of the state's largest spring, Comal Springs, the town has grown up along these waterways. Landa Park and vacation cottages along the Comal and Guadalupe rivers have been vacation destinations and recreation attractions for decades.

However, living in one of the most flash-flood-prone regions in the United States has presented a hazard for New Braunfels residents. By 1972, residents believed that this danger had diminished significantly with the creation of Canyon Dam. Indeed, Canyon Dam would now be able to handle flood waves from the Guadalupe River that had formed above Spring Branch and Comfort and surged through New Braunfels in 1921, 1932, and 1952. But the dam was miles above New Braunfels, and other, smaller streams and dry creeks still fed into New Braunfels. The May 1972 flash flood provided a chilling example of how a deluge placed between a large flood-control dam and a town can still decimate a municipality.

In the May 1972 flash flood, the small basins feeding into the Comal River produced a tragic rise. The Comal is the shortest river in Texas, traversing only three miles. On the night of May 11, 1972, a downpour just outside New Braunfels fed normally dry creek beds and transformed the shortest river in Texas into the mightiest and most destructive one in the Lone Star State.

Prior to the Flood

In 1972 South Central Texas suffered through a dry winter and early spring. From January through April, New Braunfels received less than 4 inches of rain (5.5 inches below average). Rainfall in San Antonio, Austin, and San Marcos also lagged badly, as each location was 4–8 inches below average.

The drought conditions translated into low streamflow in area streams. In April the San Antonio River was approaching a flow of zero cfs. In New Braunfels, the Comal River's streamflow was about twenty percent below its April average. After the first week in May, the weather shifted from dry and quiet to wet and stormy.

On May 7 San Antonio was hit by flash flooding that was precipitated by two thunderstorms—one in the early morning and the second at 8:30 A.M. The National Weather Service gage at the airport recorded 6.04 inches, while northeast San Antonio reported more than 7 inches of rain. The San Antonio Fire Department rescued thirty people, and the city's public works department barricaded 120 streets.

Several days after the deluge, the moist, volatile atmosphere over South Texas returned. On May 10 at Laredo, a downpour dumped 9.2 inches of rain in a two-hour period, flooding Zacate and Chaco creeks. Between 8 A.M. and 2:10 P.M. the Rio Grande River rose from 1.7 feet to 11.92 feet at the International Bridge. Closer to San Antonio,

DAILY PRECIPITATION (IN INCHES), MAY 5–15, 1972

	MAY 5	MAY 6	MAY 7	MAY 8	MAY 9	MAY 10	MAY 11	MAY 12	MAY 13	MAY 14	MAY 15
Blanco	0.00	0.28	1.50	0.43	0.00	0.00	1.74	1.50	Trace	0.49	0.00
San Marcos	0.00	0.16	1.73	0.28	0.00	0.00	1.67	4.05	0.04	0.05	0.00
San Antonio	0.55	1.58	5.34	0.00	0.00	1.79	0.41	0.13	Trace	0.09	0.00
New Braunfels	0.00	0.66	2.55	0.87	0.00	0.00	3.04	5.66	0.11	0.14	0.00

DAILY STREAMFLOW, MAY 5–15, 1972

	MAY 5	MAY 6	MAY 7	MAY 8	MAY 9	MAY 10	MAY 11	MAY 12	MAY 13	MAY 14	MAY 15
San Antonio River	35	313	1,510	997	31	262	199	288	65	58	52
Cibolo Creek	0	0	1,120	775	112	344	1620	13,300	670	362	276
Comal River	242	284	1,410	577	286	800	2430	14,400	595	534	484

Discharge in cubic feet/second

the National Weather Service issued a flood warning for the Sabinal River, predicting a 20-foot rise. Five inches fell on the Upper Guadalupe River, resulting in full banks at Comfort and Spring Branch.

May 11 Rainfall

On May 11 intense storms formed southwest of New Braunfels and moved northeastward to the city's westerly outskirts. Showers that began in the early evening intensified into unprecedented deluges. The storm lasted four hours and averaged eight inches over three hundred square miles. According to a report by Victor Baker, "Nearly 75% fell during the most intense hour, between 8:40 and 9:40 P.M. on May 11."[1] A rain gage on Trough Creek, operated by the USGS and the Texas Highway Department, measured 2.3 inches between 8 and 8:10 P.M. on May 11. By 8:20 the gage held 3 inches of rain.[2]

The most intense rain poured down in the Blieders Creek basin, and more than 10 inches fell along Mission Valley Lane. The deluge filled buckets nearly 12 inches deep at the T-Bar-M Tennis Ranch. Another resident reported that his gage filled to 8 inches in less than a single hour.[3] The Comal County sheriff commented, "We

had one area up there in the surrounding hills I know that had 10 inches of rain in 1½ hours."[4]

Several residents reported 12 inches of rain between 8:40 P.M. and 9:40 P.M. At the center of the storm, 16 inches fell within four hours. Postflood studies noted that this was 2½ times the four-hour, one-hundred-year-frequency rainfall. To the southwest of New Braunfels, 4–12 inches came down on the Dry Comal Creek basin. At Bulverde, a man reported that a 6-inch-tall glass filled to within half an inch of the top in twenty minutes. He then emptied the glass, and within forty minutes it was almost full again. Bulverde reported more than 7 inches with a peak rate of 4.5 inches in one hour. The deluge also caused Cibolo Creek to overflow.

Flood on the Comal and Guadalupe Rivers

The 16-inch rainfall in the Blieders Creek watershed fed the first flood wave on the Comal River, which struck at 11:45 P.M. on May 11. Its peak streamflow was 60,800 cfs. The second wave came down the Comal at 5:30 A.M. on May 12, largely due to the rise in Dry Comal Creek, whose peak stream-

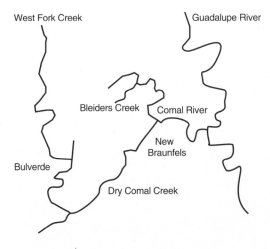

Blieders Creek and Comal River in New Braunfels

West Fork Creek

Guadalupe River

Bleiders Creek

Comal River

New Braunfels

Bulverde

Dry Comal Creek

flow was 55,800 cfs. One of the small creeks near New Braunfels set a new record during the flood. Trough Creek covers a drainage area of only 0.48 square miles. Its whole watershed received 10–11 inches, driving the creek to its maximum streamflow of 2,510 cfs, which was more than 5,230 cfs per square mile—a new Texas record.

The flood on the Comal River fed into the Guadalupe River, usually considered the culprit with regard to flooding in New Braunfels. After Canyon Dam was built,

many New Braunfels–area residents believed that the flood threat from the Guadalupe had been eliminated. In 1972, however, the area causing the flood was a mere eighty-six square miles—all situated between New Braunfels and Canyon Dam. At 12:30 A.M. on May 12, the flood on the Guadalupe peaked at 92,600 cfs, rising 12.5 feet in thirty minutes and 28 feet in two hours.

A construction supervisor at New Braunfels remarked, "Water had rushed like a tidal wave through the black night." He added, "They kept talking about a 30-foot wall of water that night, only they said it was coming down the Guadalupe . . . but, shoot, it all came across on Blieders Creek."[5]

The peak flow and stage level on the Guadalupe indicated a forty-year recurrence on the river. One study added, "The difficulties with such numbers is underscored by the fact that the Guadalupe flooding was produced entirely by runoff from only 86 square miles and the Comal peak was largely produced by runoff from the 15-square mile catchment of Blieders Creek."[6] The local sheriff described the flash flood as a "wall of water and rising at the same time."[7]

Decimation in New Braunfels

The multiple flood waves tore through New Braunfels in the dark hours of the night. The city's motto is "In New Braunfels ist das Leben schoen"—in New Braunfels, life is great. A *San Antonio Express* article on May 13 noted that, in New Braunfels after the deluge, it was "Leben Schoen No More." Even more, the article stated, for a time, New Braunfels was where the "living was sad."[8]

Around 11 P.M. the New Braunfels police department requested assistance from the National Guard because the rising water was making rescue efforts treacherous. Water was six to ten feet deep in many homes, and dislodged houses floated peril-

Weed skimmer at Landa Park (Copyright 1996, Sophienburg Archives, New Braunfels, Texas).

Car wrapped around tree following flood (Copyright 1996, Sophienburg Archives, New Braunfels, Texas).

ously in the currents. Six helicopters pulled people out of the water, while patients in a rest home were evacuated by boat. The local radio station, KGND, had signed off at sundown but returned to the airwaves to inform residents of the emergency situation.

New Braunfels residents fought the flood bravely and creatively. At 11 P.M. the Comal River ripped through Landa Estates. With water at her front door, one resident started toward her car at 11:15 P.M. Just seconds later the water rose four feet, and the surge carried her across the yards of two neighbors until she managed to take hold of a clothesline in the third yard down from her house. The water continued to rise. The woman lost her grip several times, sinking below the water and then grabbing objects such as trees and poles. Finally the water receded rapidly, and she was rescued.[9]

Downstream, a man left his house with his wife and child, but the floodwater washed them across the street into a vacant lot. The currents then carried various large objects in their direction. They were brushed by a pickup truck and then

dodged a camper. When they saw a sixty-foot travel trailer rushing their way, they jumped into nearby trees and rode out the flood there.

Elsewhere, a mother and son were having a snack when they noticed water bubbling up out of the furnace floor. When the son opened the door, he was thrown across the room by the force of the in-rushing water. They escaped by climbing on top of a car.

One of the saddest tales of survival and loss took place in the Rio Drive section of town. A husband and wife awoke to find two feet of water in their house. As the water rose another three feet, they hurriedly tried to escape. First they broke out a window, climbed outside, and grabbed the eaves of their house. Then, when the waters pried them from the eaves, they took refuge in a tree. However, that position, too, put them in jeopardy when the flood floated their house, which smashed into the tree. The husband then jumped onto the roof of his neighbor's house, but his wife was carried away. He knew that she would meet "sure death" at Lake Dunlap, so he attempted to swim to shore. After making no

Cars in Blieders Creek
(Copyright 1996, Sophien-
burg Archives, New Braun-
fels, Texas).

progress, he returned to his "roof raft." On the next attempt, he grabbed a tree branch and held on until he could jump first to shallow water and then to the bank. His wife's body was found the next day seven miles downstream.[10]

The flood deposited one car in the Landa Park swimming pool and lodged other cars twenty feet up in trees. The city manager's office estimated damages at $10 million. Of the 20,000 residents, approximately 4,500 fled their homes, forty-five of which were completely destroyed. Approximately four hundred homes were flooded with water up to ten feet deep.

The damage to Dry Comal Creek, Blieders Creek, and the Comal River amounted to nearly $3.3 million. Ironically, the proposed flood-control projects would have limited it to $180,000.[11]

Flood damage to train at
Landa Park (Copyright 1996,
Sophienburg Archives, New
Braunfels, Texas).

NEW BRAUNFELS FLOOD

After the Flood

New Braunfels had anticipated potential flooding from the Comal River. In 1954 local officials had appealed to both the U.S. Army Corps of Engineers and the Guadalupe–Blanco River Authority for help in constructing dams on Dry Comal and Blieders creeks. In his letter dated October 21, 1955, Chamber of Commerce manager A. D. Nuhn cited the flood of June 8, 1872, and said that the 35.8-foot rise on the Comal "could happen again."[12]

In 1957 and 1958, bonds were issued to build dams on Dry Comal Creek. Two structures were constructed, the Vogel Dam and the Eikel-Blank Dam, and both helped contain floodwater in the 1972 deluge. The Eikel-Blank specifically was credited with preventing more than four hundred acre-feet of water from sweeping through New Braunfels.

Other dams were proposed but not built. On Blieders Creek, funds to acquire the easements were available in 1959, but it took ten years for landowners and officials to find a mutually acceptable site. The easement was finally acquired in 1971. At the time of the 1972 flood, core testing was being performed prior to accepting bids for construction.

A Soil Conservation Service (SCS) agent said, "Had the Blieders Creek Dam been in place, it would have retarded about one-half the floodwater." He estimated that damage to Landa Estates, Landa Park, and the upper Comal would have been reduced by sixty percent.[13]

Before the 1972 flood, the dams were designed to handle 5¼ inches of rainfall in two hours, which was the value charted for a one-hundred-year flood. Close to twice that amount fell in the 1972 flood. The local SCS agent said, "We all should vow that we will be better prepared for floods in the future. Very few people of this community escaped the effects of the disastrous flood. If we were not in the path of the floodwater, we all had

friends who were. There are not words to describe what had happened. There are no records of this type of flood ever occurring before, and let us pray that it never happens again."[14]

Camp Warnecke after the flood (Copyright 1996, Sophienburg Archives, New Braunfels, Texas).

Downstream on the Guadalupe

Downstream from New Braunfels, the Guadalupe River ripped through sections of Seguin and flooded the Glen Cove subdivision. Residents were warned that a wall of water was coming, though the wave was greater than expected. The one that hit them was high enough "to float mattresses to within 1 foot of the ceiling."[15] To aid in the cleanup at Seguin, students from Texas Lutheran College were released from final exams.

Flood debris (Copyright 1996, Sophienburg Archives, New Braunfels, Texas).

MAY 1978

~~~~~~~

Canyon, Texas, and Palo Duro Canyon Flood

OUTSIDE OF CANYON, Texas, two small creeks join to form the Prairie Dog Town Fork of the Red River, which has helped to carve the spectacular Palo Duro Canyon. As the town of Canyon grew, housing developments sprang up along the two creeks, the Palo Duro and the Tierra Blanca. South of Amarillo, other housing developments, such as the Palo Duro Club, Timber Creek, Tanglewood, and Palisades, were constructed along the Prairie Dog Town Fork.

Living so close to these streams, even in the usually dry Texas Panhandle, brought risk. In both 1951 and 1968 floods hinted at the potential of the creeks to overflow near Canyon. Following the 1968 flood, the U.S. Army Corps of Engineers released a flood plain study in 1971 that concluded, "Only a few structures in the flood plains of Palo Duro and Tierra Blanca Creeks have been damaged by floods in the past; however, residential development has begun in the flood plains that have been inundated in the past."[1] The May 1978 flash flood confirmed the engineers' and hydrologists' concerns. Intense storms produced surges that ripped through the edge of Canyon and then into Palo Duro Canyon.

Precedent

At start of 1978, the Canyon area was dry. Going into March, Randall County had received only 1.1 inches of rainfall since September 1977, prompting area farmers to apply for drought assistance. In April, stormy spring weather brought some precipitation but also severe weather. Downstream from

the Red River, Hardeman County received grapefruit-sized hail. In late May a severe storm system formed over the South Plains and Texas Panhandle. On May 21 intense rains brought street flooding to Amarillo. On May 25 a tornado was sighted south of Lubbock, and wind gusts of sixty mph hit west of Canyon.

Rainfall

During the afternoon of May 26, the conditions at all levels of the atmosphere combined to form large thunderstorms and a squall line in the western Texas Panhandle. The jet stream was located across Mexico and Southwest Texas. In the middle levels of the atmosphere, the 200 millibar analysis showed evidence of divergence in the left exit region of the jet stream. At the low levels, a strong southeasterly flow approached the region almost perpendicularly to the jet stream flow.

A surface low-pressure system formed in southeastern New Mexico, and storms began developing around noon in the Tucumcari area. By 3 P.M. the storms were hovering between Tucumcari and Dalhart. The northern end of the storms then moved north and east, while the southern storms moved slowly to the southeast. The strongest ones appeared in the northeast quadrant of the surface low.

Two storm cells formed ahead of a squall line. Without competition from a line of storms for moisture, these two cells evolved into enormous cell storms. The easternmost of these bore down on Canyon around 7 P.M.

206 The main concern for this set of storms was tornadic activity. At 6:56 P.M. a tornado was sighted southwest of Canyon. At 7:24 P.M. 90-mph winds were clocked two miles southwest of Canyon. At 7:38 P.M. a funnel cloud was spotted east of Canyon. Near Buffalo Lake National Wildlife Refuge a motorist reported that golf-ball-size hail battered his car and broke its windshield.

The system prompted the National Weather Service to issue flash flood warnings for Donley, Collingsworth, Hall, Briscoe, and Childress counties as it moved east and north. Near the town of Dawn, the storms dropped six inches of rainfall between 5:15 P.M. and 9:15 P.M. Three inches had fallen there the day before. The heaviest rains began in the Hereford area and moved toward Canyon. Nearly ten inches reportedly fell in the Milo Center and Ford community areas in northern Deaf Smith County.

As the storms slowed, intense rains poured down near Canyon between 6:30 and 8 P.M. Two of the highest totals were 8 inches northwest of Hereford and 10 inches west and southwest of Canyon, just downstream of Buffalo Lake. The precipitation northwest of Hereford was fully caught by the totally dry Buffalo Lake, which had been drained five years earlier after a fish kill. The runoff filled the lake with 3,000 acre-feet of water, which was twice the lake's peak storage in the 1970s (1,500 acre-feet in 1973).

On the morning of May 27 the *Amarillo Daily News* summed up the weather of the previous night: "High winds, deep waters, pounding hail and funnels twisting like corkscrews from big, black clouds combined last night to pit nature against man in an atmospheric demolition derby."[2]

As the deluges fell and creeks surged with floodwater, the Canyon area was violently transformed. Carroll Wilson, editor

of the *Canyon News*, stated in the introduction of his outstanding report on the flooding, "Along with the sheer beauty of the setting . . . would come beauty's antithesis, that eventually nature, in its indifference, would show its ugliness, would threaten rather than embrace."[3]

Flood damage at a crossing near Camp Harrington downstream from Canyon (courtesy of the *Canyon News*).

Canyon Area

The strong rains near Canyon filled Palo Duro and Tierra Blanca creeks. In the northern section of Canyon, at Hunsley Hills, residents fled to the tops of houses and cars to avoid not only the currents of Palo Duro Creek but also the floating debris, including dumpsters and sofas. The two rampaging streams joined outside of Canyon and surged down the Prairie Dog Town Fork of the Red River, where the waters terrorized the residents of Palo Duro Canyon. At the Camp Don Harrington bridge, situated downstream of the Palo Duro Club, floodwaters rose thirty to forty feet above normal. Several residents of Timber Creek watched homes float by while sitting on their balconies. In some of these residences the water reached a depth of seven feet.

One husband and wife in Palisades were

Watersheds near Canyon,
Texas

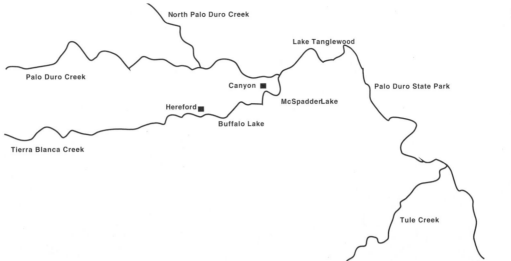

Flood damage near
Palisades (courtesy of
the *Canyon News*).

CANYON, TEXAS, AND PALO DURO CANYON FLOOD

relaxing at home after 9 P.M. Around midnight, however, the wife became nervous about the rains and began packing valuables and moving them upstairs. Her husband "scoffed at her midnight moving frenzy."[4] When the water advanced from the creek bed to their backyard, he stopped scoffing. The waters then surged higher and eventually broke down their back door. With water now four feet deep, they swam to higher ground to escape. The floodwater eventually reached a depth of eight feet deep in the house.

At the Lake Tanglewood Dam, floodwater peaked at 5 A.M., when it flowed six feet over the spillway. According to the *Amarillo Daily News*, as the overflow pushed through the usually tranquil creeks, the "sounds of whistling birds and chattering squirrels were replaced by the roar of rushing waters, the sputtering of rescue boats and the chop of overhead helicopters."[5]

Rescues

With the floods occurring unexpectedly in the middle of the night and with unprecedented ferocity, the people along Palo Duro and Tierra Blanca creeks and the Prairie Dog Town Fork of the Red River were startled to realize they would have to scramble for their lives. Southwest of Canyon at least 150 cars were stranded between Canyon and Happy. At a roadside park south of Canyon, a Randall Country sheriff's deputy used a boat to rescue trapped motorists who fled into the treetops at the rest stop. Near Canyon, a car was swept off the road, and the driver found temporary refuge atop the vehicle. Three others behind her also abandoned their vehicles and climbed onto her car. As it began to sink, a tool shed floated by, and the group clambered on top of it. Ninety minutes later a canoeist reached the group, ending their terrifying ordeal.

An eighteen-year-old boy staying at his grandparents' house in the Palisades that night called his grandparents, who were at their night-shift jobs, and told them of the flood at their home. He had been awakened by water smashing through the plate-glass window at the front of the residence. When he told his grandmother that he had to close the door to keep the water from rushing in, she thought he was referring to the front door. Instead, it was the door to the bedroom he was calling from. As the water rose, the boy had nowhere to go. About 3 A.M. he decided to straddle the door, standing on its doorknobs. He said, "I had

Watching high water near the Palisades community (courtesy of the *Canyon News*).

Palisades after the flood (courtesy of the *Canyon News*).

Aftermath at Palisades bridge (courtesy of the *Canyon News*).

Flood damage near Canyon (courtesy of the *Canyon News*).

about six inches of breathing space. That's all the room there was from the top of the water to the ceiling." He was rescued almost four hours later. When his grandfather looked at the house after the water subsided, he observed that his grandson had stayed in the only place in the house where he could have survived and pointed to a line of mud on the wall six inches below the ceiling.[6]

At another house in the Palisades, a couple was one week away from moving. When the pouring rain at night woke them up, they noticed an odd thumping sound. After getting out of bed to discover the source of the noise, they noticed that water was piling up against the side of the house. They quickly left, making their way through the rising water, which was still below their heads. The wife was wearing a heavy fur coat, which was almost a disastrous mistake. Her husband stated, "It got wet immediately and it soaked up so much water that it was extremely heavy. Fighting the swift current was hard enough but with that coat weighing her down, it was almost impossible." They both survived, though they lost many possessions, including the husband's thirty-year collection of technical research papers. This couple had also experienced two other severe weather events in the Panhandle area—the Lubbock tornado and the blizzard of 1971. The husband said, "I guess I should be getting used to things like this. The Lubbock tornado destroyed my business, but we survived it. We were moved in for three days here in February 1971 during that terrible blizzard. Now we are wiped out by a flood where floods aren't supposed to happen. But we're still here and that's the important thing."[7]

One of the most tragic events occurred when a teenage girl drowned after she returned to the flooded pickup truck she and her date had been traveling in. They had reached safety once, but she lost her grip on the trip back to safety the second time and was carried away by the currents.

During the flood, dozens of boats were swept out of Lake Tanglewood and over the dam, where they were carried into deep canyons. One observer noted, "They'll never find anything that looks like a boat in those canyons."[8]

Palo Duro State Park

Following the chaos and destruction outside of Canyon, the floodwaters poured over the dam at Lake Tanglewood, focusing their fury on the unsuspecting campers at Palo Duro State Park. One family at

Inspecting and cleaning a crossing at Palo Duro State Park (courtesy of the *Canyon News*).

Inspection and clean-up after the flood at Palo Duro State Park (courtesy of the *Canyon News*).

Flood damage at Palo Duro State Park (courtesy of the *Canyon News*).

Rescue during the flood along Palo Duro Creek (courtesy of the *Canyon News*).

Wreckage created by Palo Duro Creek in Canyon (courtesy of the *Canyon News*).

Flood damage from Palo Duro Creek in Canyon (courtesy of the *Canyon News*).

the Juniper camping area debated moving away from the river during the night. Later the wife woke up and asked her husband whether the sound she heard outside their tent was rushing water. He told her, however, that the noise was an echo off the canyon walls. When she woke him for the third time, though, he stepped outside the tent and into six inches of water. The cou-

212 ple then grabbed their two children and fled to higher ground as water rose up to their waists. They also tried to arouse other campers, but the sound of the gushing water eclipsed their shouts. Finally, "someone shot a gun, which aroused most people in time to make an escape."[9]

One camper described the flood: "About 90 seconds after I woke up, the water was already thigh high. Later, you couldn't see the tops of the cars. I would estimate the water here was about 20–25 feet above the creek bed and about 8 to 10 feet above the campsite. It began receding about 9 A.M." His car was filled with mud and debris up to the steering wheel. He managed to salvage only a pair of shoes, a basketball, and a sleeping bag.[10]

In the Sunflower camping area, the deluge also surprised campers, one of whom believed the law officers "certainly knew that the storm was moving from the southwest to the northeast and knew it was going to dump a lot of water into the canyon. Why didn't anyone drive down and tell those people to move their cars 25 yards? Why didn't they warn people in that five-hour span?" He reported that the waters did not hit the campsites and the canyon floor until 5 A.M., but the storms were raging nearby at midnight. He had listened to morning radio reports of the storm for several hours but was unaware that he was in harm's way. He said, "We were astounded that we didn't get any warning. . . . Inside of two minutes, the cars were covered with water."[11]

Two cross-country travelers survived by climbing on top of their van, then swimming from tree to tree until they reached safety. On the night of May 25, they heard tornado warnings at the Copper Breaks State Park, where park rangers wakened them with news of the approaching storms. One of the pair commented, "I felt quite secure with the Texas Park Rangers" when she went to sleep. Evidently the couple's van and all of their possessions disappeared in the torrents.

Following the Palo Duro Canyon flood, she said, "I'm just quite discouraged with the whole system at the canyon."

In explaining why campers were not alerted earlier, the assistant supervisor stated that high water over bridges and river crossings had kept him from reaching them. He said, "Everybody did everything they could, everything they could possibly do. I understand their feelings. I wish I could have done more."[12] The assistant park supervisor said, "I didn't know that water was coming. Of course we didn't know it was going to come a flash flood like that. We're not trying to drown anybody." He said that both the National Weather Service (NWS) and the Parks and Wildlife Department telephoned warnings of the impending flash flood to the ranger station. He said he thought the Parks and Wildlife warning came around 3 A.M. and the NWS warning preceded it. When he received the first alert, he went into the canyon and advised campers in the Hackberry Area to evacuate. He helped several groups of campers get started and even towed one with his truck. Then he noticed the water

Flood damage near Canyon (courtesy of the *Canyon News*).

Near Canyon (courtesy of the *Canyon News*).

Pole washed onto golf course near the Hunsley Hills area of Canyon (courtesy of the *Canyon News*).

in making twenty rescues. Its pilot carefully avoided blowing over picnic shelters that campers were perched upon.

A crew of boys from Cal Farley's Boys Ranch participated in one of the most outstanding rescues during the flood, saving the lives of a man and a woman. The couple had been camping and tried to flee through the high water but was swept against a juniper tree. The boys tied together several ropes and threw the line out to the couple. The woman wrapped the rope around her upper body and was pulled to safety. Three of the boys then waded into the water to rescue the man. One of the couple said, "We just feel like we owe them our lives, which we do." After being asked how difficult the effort had been and how they were responding to the ordeal of being isolated after the flood, one of the boys stated, "It wasn't too bad. I mean we weren't going potbellied or anything. But I'll tell you when I got to the top of the hill and saw the Red Cross guy with Coke and a hot dog, it was great."[13]

level had receded and thought "it was over with." He returned to the ranger station, where the second warning was waiting, but found when he returned to the canyon that water was already over the bridge. He then spent several hours trying to arouse campers by CB radio and reached the first around 6 A.M. The helicopter he had requested earlier arrived shortly afterward and assisted

Aftermath in the Hunsley Hills area of Canyon (courtesy of the *Canyon News*).

One member of a seven-family camping club from Borger endured the deluge at Palo Duro Park. "You know, you just don't plan on having this kind of weather in the Panhandle," he said while peering at his trailer and car, which were sitting in sand and water.[14]

On May 30 the sixth crossing in the park was still too high to be traversed, so the rangers used an alternate route around the Sunflower and Hackberry areas. Three cars were visible from the road—one was backed into a tree, the second was mired up to its doors in mud, and the third was stuck on top of campsite markers.[15]

After the flood, a park ranger said, "they'll [Texas Parks and Wildlife Commission officials] have to decide if they want to build over the damaged campsites or remove the sand—only I don't know where we'd put the sand and mud."[16] One park official estimated

that some areas would not be open to campers until the following year.

Follow-Up and Control

Following the overflow, the Randall County sheriff noted, "This is the worst disaster since the tornadoes of May 15, 1949."[17] A National Weather Service representative from Amarillo added, "It's the worst flood that's ever occurred. I think it passed all the previous highs." The worst flood on record took place in August 1968. The NWS noted that, in the May 1978 flood, water flowed as much as twelve feet over bridges. In commenting on the speed of the water, the NWS representative said, "The velocity was pretty fast. If you look at everything it washed away, I think you can determine it was undoubtedly pretty stiff."[18]

Few Canyon-area residents had flood insurance, even though many lived in areas that the 1971 study highlighted as being flood prone. The city manger of Canyon said, "Would you have flood insurance if you lived on the plains of West Texas?" He added, "Developers don't understand these things. [Floods] can and will happen. The potential is always there. You have to take the necessary precautions."[19]

Palo Duro State Park after the flood (courtesy of the *Canyon News*).

One of the most dedicated groups of rescuers and helpers was Canyon Boy Scout Troop 31. The youngsters were camping in New Mexico when they heard reports of the flooding and decided to cut their trip short. Around midnight on May 27, they came to the Canyon area, where they cooked and served hot dogs to the victims and kept sightseers out of damaged areas. The troop leader commented on their sentry duties: "The kids have gotten cussed out and threatened because they wouldn't let people in, but they stood up like Trojans." [20] Another Canyon-area troop, Number 132, also gave up its camping trip to help with cleanup.

Canyon's police chief said of the residents, "I can't over-emphasize the attitude of the people. We had people down there [in Hunsley Hills] who had their houses flooded but who put off their clean-up to go across the street and help someone worse off. People would be cleaning up and look up to find total strangers in there helping. . . . There was an unnamed man with a tractor who appeared in driveways clearing away the mud and piles of debris. He never gave his name or asked for a word of thanks." [21]

AUGUST 1978

~~~~~~

Hill Country Flood

IN LOOKING AT Hill Country river flooding during the mid-1970s, residents would acknowledge that they had missed some of the worst flash flood events, such as those in Sanderson, San Marcos, and New Braunfels. The Guadalupe River above Canyon Dam had not had a large rise since 1958 and 1960. With one of the most severe droughts since the 1950s under way in the summer of 1978, one of Texas' biggest weather dangers, a dying tropical storm, once again brought a world-class deluge and a set of flash floods to the Texas Hill Country.

The flash flood of August 1978 was one of the most staggering ever recorded. The slow-moving remnants of Tropical Storm Amelia produced the dreaded core rainfall during the middle of the night, sending walls of water down some of the Hill Country's most beautiful stretches, including the Medina River and the upper Guadalupe River. The lovely riverside settings outside of Bandera were home to some of the state's most popular summer camps and dude ranches. With the world-record-category deluge upriver, camp owners and campers had no idea that the unprecedented surges would rip through their camps. The scars of the 1978 flash flood left marks that will be remembered for decades.

Precedent

The spring and summer of 1978 were dry, causing most Hill Country and Central Texas counties to seek drought assistance. Cities with the largest deficits included Boerne (10.5 inches), Hondo (8 inches), Hunt (7.5 inches), and Brady (7 inches). Fredericksburg received boosts from stray showers in June and July, which dropped its rainfall deficit to only 0.18 inches. Streamflow in the Hill Country reflected the drought conditions. At the end of July, the Guadalupe River at Hunt was flowing at less than 20 cfs. Downstream at Comfort, it was flowing at less than 40 cfs. The streamflow for the Medina River at Pipe Creek was less than 10 cfs.

Rainfall

Late in July widely scattered thunderstorms formed in the Hill Country on several different days. On July 26 a tornado was spotted four miles west of Llano. A day later, sixty mph winds were reported at Lake Travis, and a day after that, a tornado was reported near Thrall. While these storms brought some violent weather to parts of

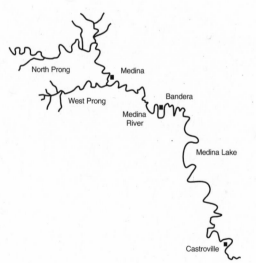

Medina River Basin

Damage to the bridge over the Medina River at Bandera's city park (Austin History Center, Bandera, 100327, Neg. 16, 19).

Central Texas, a much larger system was needed to break the drought.

That system would come from the Gulf of Mexico. In the last week of July, a tropical wave approximately 200 miles south of Brownsville briefly intensified as it approached the Texas coast, where it was upgraded to a tropical storm and named Amelia; its winds officially peaked on July 30 at forty-five mph. Amelia hit the Texas coast 40 miles north of Brownsville. During the night it moved northwesterly, passing approximately 50 miles west of Corpus Christi. The storm was officially designated as a tropical depression or tropical storm for less than two days, prompting the *San Antonio Express* on August 1 to comment, "Amelia's rapid ascent and demise caught many unaware, touching off a controversy about the reliability of weather forecasters."[1]

By nightfall of July 31, the center of Amelia's remnants was west of San Antonio. Moist air flowed into Texas from the Gulf of Mexico—the dew point stood at 79 in Corpus Christi that night. Rains associated with the fading storm began falling in

South Texas that day. Totals were light, most of them less than 0.5 inches. San Antonio managed to break a fifty-day rainless streak.

At 6 A.M. on August 1 forecasters reported a vorticity center near Del Rio. (On July 29 Del Rio received 0.23 inches of rain, followed by 1.73 inches on July 30.) The storms from the previous day dissipated in the afternoon, but the threat of heavy rain was developing as the remnants of Amelia settled over the Hill Country. The National Weather Service issued a flash flood watch on the afternoon of August 1. At 7 P.M. the NWS raised the watch to a flash flood warning for Bandera, Kendall, and Kerr counties. Showers in the Medina area and the Guadalupe River basin intensified rapidly near midnight and moved slowly through Bandera, Kerr, Gillespie, and Kendall counties. These were the core rains from the dying tropical storm in action. Massive totals of more than 20 inches of rain fell in the early morning hours of August 2. The highest totals were at Medina (20.2 inches) and north of Medina at Manatt Ranch (31 inches). Others included Kerrville (18 inches), Vanderpool (11 inches), and Fredericksburg (7.5 inches).

With the moist air and triggering mechanisms still in place, the forecast was for 6 inches of rain on the night of August 2. The downpour continued, as predicted, with the main concentration falling north and northwest of the upper Guadalupe and Medina basins. By 7 P.M. convective showers started again in Bandera County. Around 10:30 cells intensified and expanded into central Kerr County, as well as western Gillespie and southeastern Mason counties. The center of the rain, which again exceeded 20 inches, was located in west-central Gillespie County. Parts of the Guadalupe basin were hit once more, with the peak rain falling at Ingram (almost 16 inches). Hunt logged 7.5 inches that same night.

The Medina River basin again received heavy rains, as Manatt Ranch gauged another 12 inches. The total at the ranch was 48 inches, a new record for a seventy-two-hour period in the United States. Incredibly, the rainfall averaged almost an inch per hour, as most of the 48-inch total fell within fifty-two hours. The city of Medina received only 0.6 inches during the night of August 2, indicating how abruptly the heavy rain subsided.

Gillespie County's rains focused on the western portion of the county and fed the Pedernales and Llano rivers. The greatest total was in the Spring Creek area, where 21 inches fell. Harper, White Oak, and Pilot Knob each tallied close to 20 inches. The Doss area gauged 10–13 inches. The Kerr County agriculture agent remarked, "For the first time since I have been here, I hope it does not rain tonight."[2]

As the storms pummeled the Hill Country, additional concern for disastrous downpours arose due to a cool front that was expected to push south from the Texas Panhandle.

Streamflow

At Manatt Ranch, the 30-inch rains on the morning of August 2 fell in the headwaters of the Medina River. At the headwaters of Verde and Turtle creeks, which flow into the Guadalupe near Center Point, 15–20 inches fell. USGS gauging stations were active on the Medina at Pipe Creek, well below the origin of the flood, on the Guadalupe above Center Point at Kerrville and below it at Comfort. Because the streamflow gages were not distributed throughout the rivers, the official records did not chronicle the flood wave as it moved down the Medina River or Verde and Turtle creeks.

The downpours on the night of August 2 were centered at the headwaters of Spring Creek, which feeds into the Pedernales River southwest of Fredericksburg. Only the section of the Guadalupe above Kerrville received significant rain in the second round, with sixteen inches falling at Ingram.

Pavement peeled off bridge and roadway over the Medina River just south of downtown Bandera (Austin History Center, Bandera, 100327, Neg. 9A).

LOCATION	AUG. 1	AUG. 2	AUG. 3	AUG. 4	AUG. 5	AUG. 6	TOTAL
Blanco	1.05	2.22	0.05	0.00	0.00	0.00	3.32
Boerne	1.45	3.98	0.05	0.00	0.00	0.00	5.48
Brackettville	0.2	0.00	0.00	0.00	0.00	0.00	0.20
Brady	0.05	3.25	5.6	0.02	0.00	0.16	9.08
Burnet	0.64	0.57	0.25	0.00	0.00	0.14	1.60
Crider Ranch	1.45	3.98	0.05	0.00	0.00	0.00	5.48
Camp Wood	0.18	4.05	0.00	0.00	0.00	0.00	4.23
Del Rio	0.00	0.00	0.00	0.00	0.00	0.00	0.00
Doss	0.00	2.27	0.03	0.00	0.00	0.00	2.30
Fredericksburg	2.67	7.5	0.14	0.00	0.00	1.5	11.81
Gold	0.00	1.55	1.70	1.26	0.00	0.00	4.51
Hondo	1.32	3.14	0.00	0.00	0.00	0.00	4.46
Henly	1.91	1.43	0.00	0.00	0.00	0.00	3.34
Hunt	5.05	6.85	7.60	0.00	0.00	0.00	19.50
Hey	0.40	4.48	0.15	0.00	0.00	0.00	5.03
Johnson City	0.61	1.80	0.04	0.00	0.00	0.00	2.45
Junction	0.00	1.38	0.00	0.00	0.00	0.00	1.38
Kerrville	4.20	11.60	0.78	0.00	0.00	0.00	16.58
Lampasas	0.15	0.39	0.35	0.00	0.00	0.33	1.22
Llano	0.03	1.80	1.75	0.00	0.00	1.12	4.70
Mason	0.00	4.45	1.20	0.00	0.00	0.60	6.25
Menard	0.00	3.29	0.21	0.00	0.00	0.15	3.65
New Braunfels	2.39	0.00	0.00	0.00	0.00	0.00	2.39
Prade Ranch	0.06	3.07	0.19	0	0.00	0.07	3.39
Rocksprings	0.74	0.20	0.20	0.00	0.20	0.65	1.99
Roosevelt	0.00	1.38	0.00	0.00	0.00	0.00	1.38
Sabinal	0.00	2.94	1.02	0.00	0.00	0.00	3.96
San Marcos	1.91	1.43	0.00	0.00	0.00	0.00	3.34
San Saba	0.03	1.03	3.28	0.00	0.00	0.30	4.64
San Antonio	3.87	0.13	0.00	0.00	0.00	0.16	4.16
San Angelo	0.00	0.00	1.27	0.00	0.17	0.00	1.44
Sonora	0.00	0.12	0.00	0.00	0.00	0.03	0.15
Spicewood	1.30	0.85	0.00	0.00	0.00	0.00	2.15
Tarpley	1.05	2.22	0.05	0.00	0.00	0.00	3.32
Temple	0.00	0.81	0.02	0.00	1.00	0.00	1.83
Uvalde 1	0.00	2.27	0.03	0.00	0.00	0.00	2.30
Uvalde 2	0.00	2.94	1.02	0.00	0.00	0.00	3.96
Vanderpool	11.53	1.12	0.00	0.00	0.00	0.00	12.65
End of World Ranch	4.00	15.20	3.90	0.00	0.00	0.00	23.10

Medina

At Medina, the Medina River encircled the town, overflowing its banks by six hundred feet in places. As the flood grew in the early morning hours, the numerous camps nestled against the river were in its direct path. At Peaceful Valley Ranch, one family was awakened by floodwaters at 4:30 A.M. The "roaring was like nothing I'd ever heard before," said the father. When the family members awoke, water was almost up to the window of their cabin. They tried to reach their car, but the door of the cabin would not open. They then climbed onto the roof of the cabin. When the waters covered the roofline, they moved to nearby trees. Once the water receded, they returned to the roof and watched the flood carry away trees and houses.[3]

220   Another trapped camper at the Peaceful Valley Ranch was Miss USA 1977, Kim Tomes, who clung to a tree to escape the currents. The owner of the dude ranch said, "She was really lucky. She was actually in the water and managed to catch the last tree before she would have been swept away."[4] An elderly ranch hand sleeping in his trailer at the Mayan Dude Ranch when the flood hit at 5:30 A.M. "lost all his worldly possessions, including his teeth." Although everyone assumed he had drowned, he was actually clinging to a sixty-foot-tall oak tree. He credited his four-month-old Doberman puppy with saving his life by waking him when the flood arrived. When he opened the door, three feet of water poured in. After escaping from his trailer, he still had to deal with the ten-foot-tall deer fence, all the while navigating with water up to his neck. After negotiating the fence by climbing through a hole that had been made when his trailer started to float away, he grabbed a tree limb. He lost track of his puppy, which he said was a "better pal than his last wife." Later he found his puppy, safe in a nearby tree.[5]

The late Grace Kitzman of the Peaceful Valley Ranch described the horrible event: "The water was rising so fast that Art, the last to leave had to float out the window. By this time, other guests aroused and were screaming. There was nothing we could do. . . . Very soon the roof on which we stood began to move and Art started shoving us up into trees that overhung the house. These trees were not very large but they were oaks, and we straddled little wet limbs, with the water roaring just under our feet. The force of the flood was so great there were white caps on the water and the rain continued to fall in torrents. . . . It was like sitting on a very skinny wet horse with no saddle."[6]

The *San Antonio Express* described the scene at Peaceful Valley: "Almost everything but the buildings' concrete founda-

tions was washed away." The ranch's airplane was contorted into a twisted mess in a tree downstream. About twenty staff members and campers survived by clinging to trees or rooftops for six hours.[7] Tourists who had visited Peaceful Valley Ranch for more than twenty-five years donated money and offered to spend their vacations helping to rebuild the ranch. About 6:30 A.M. the director at Camp Serendip in Bandera County heard the river roaring and watched it take all of the lower cabins within three hours. After

Searching through flood wreckage in Bandera (Austin History Center, Bandera, 100352, Neg. 20A).

Guadalupe River at Kerrville (Austin History Center, 8/2/78 Kerrville flood; Neg. 8).

Damage to Bandera's city park (Austin History Center, Bandera, 100327, Neg. 16, 19).

the flood, the owner of the Twin Elms Guest Ranch said, "That river was worth millions of dollars to us. We had a beautiful riverfront. It will take a while to clean it up. . . . It's taken years to build up our businesses, but it'll all be back. It'll be in full swing next year."[8]

Bandera

The Medina River flood at Bandera began at 6:30 A.M. on August 2 and peaked at fifty-six feet at 1 P.M. that day. The town re-

ceived only 3.5 inches of rain, but the huge runoff from upstream pushed the river to record heights. Fire sirens and loudspeakers awoke Bandera residents at 3 A.M., warning them to evacuate to higher ground. Along the horseshoe bend of the river, at least twelve buildings were swept away. One woman survived after being carried eight miles downstream, riding the roof of her home until it fell apart.

A report from an aerial flyover of the flood yielded these comments: "From 250′ in the air, there was a strange, unreal beauty in the rain-swollen Medina River . . . until you looked closer. . . . New and used cars twisted and bobbed in the water, floating by at strange angles as if thrown down by a giant's hand."[9]

One old-timer said, "I remember the 1919 flood. I was 12 years old then. This one was nearly as bad. I knew it was going to be a bad one when I saw the water rising so fast. That ole Medina did it again. It just keeps trying to destroy this town."[10] One Bandera resident followed his grandfather's advice and built his house above the water line of the 1919 flood. In the 1978 flood, the house

Wreckage at a car dealership on Highway 16 in Bandera (Austin History Center, Bandera, 100314, Neg. 14A, 18).

221

LOCATION	JULY 24	JULY 25	JULY 26	JULY 27	JULY 28	JULY 29	JULY 30	JULY 31
Medina River at San Antonio	63	62	63	60	60	139	68	68
Medina River at Pipe Creek	9	9	9	9	10	9	9	9
Johnson Creek at Ingram	9	9	9	9	12	12	11	11
North Fork Guadalupe River at Hunt	11	11	11	11	12	13	12	12
Guadalup3 River at Hunt	18	19	20	21	21	23	23	23
Guadalupe River at Comfort	37	40	42	47	50	53	52	48
Guadalupe River at Spring Branch	24	26	25	24	38	43	39	36
Comal River	234	234	234	234	226	242	242	246
Blanco River at Wimberley	19	19	18	19	19	21	23	26
Blanco River at Kyle	0	0	0	0	0	0	1	1
Beaver Creek at Mason	0	0	0	0	0	68	14	2
Llano River at Junction	78	77	93	91	100	100	92	93
Llano River at Llano	47	47	47	49	51	54	85	112
Llano River at Mason	70	70	71	72	84	103	94	96
Pedernales River at Johnson City	2	2	2	2	3	42	51	54
Dry Fork Frio River at Reagan Wells	1	1	1	1	1	1	1	2
Frio River at Concan	23	23	21	21	24	26	26	26
Frio River at Uvalde	0	0	0	0	0	0	0	0
Sabinal River at Sabinal	0	0	0	0	1	1	1	1
Sabinal River near Sabinal	7	7	7	7	7	7	7	9
Nueces River at Laguna	25	24	24	24	25	28	28	29
Nueces River belowUvalde	22	22	22	22	22	22	22	22
Hondo Creek at Tarpley	1	1	0	0	0	1	1	0
San Saba River at Menard	24	25	23	22	23	24	25	26
San Saba River at San Saba	14	13	16	15	12	13	20	22
Colorado at San Saba	12	16	18	18	21	20	18	18
Colorado at Austin	1,800	1,480	1,140	1,400	1,240	1,280	1,280	1,330
Cibolo Creek at Boerne	1	1	1	1	1	2	2	1
Barton Creek at 360	0	0	0	0	0	0	0	0
Brazos River at Waco	77	83	55	42	39	37	37	41
Brushy Creek at Round Rock	0	0	1	1	1	1	1	1
Lampasas River at Youngsport	0	0	0	0	0	0	1	2
Onion Creek at Driftwood	0	1	1	2	1	0	0	0
Bull Creek	0	0	0	0	0	0	0	0
Cibolo Creek	0	0	0	0	0	0	0	0
Onion Creek nr Austin	1	1	1	1	0	0	0	0

Discharge in cubic feet/second

was covered by eight feet of water. In a lower part of town, an automobile dealership lost 125 vehicles and sustained more than $500,000 in damages.

Three days after the deluge a local Red Cross officer noted, "Everything is still a mess. A quarter of the town is gone. Water got up a mile and a half wide at some spots and covered things we never thought of."[11]

After examining the flood marks, the USGS calculated the peak discharge on the Medina River as 123,000 cfs, based on a drainage area of 67.5 square miles on the North Prong Medina River, approximately ten miles upstream from Medina. The peak discharge probably occurred just downstream from the confluence of the North Prong and the West Prong. On August 2 the flood surge on the Medina River near Pipe Creek topped the previous maximum set in 1919, when the peak discharge was 281,000 cfs. This station had a recurrence interval of more than one hundred years.

The August 2 gage record for the Medina

AUG. 1	AUG. 2	AUG. 3	AUG. 4	AUG. 5	AUG. 6	AUG. 7	AUG. 8	AUG. 9
788	434	7,760	6,250	3,370	2,320	1,890	1,720	1,300
41,700	15,000	3,680	2,870	2,030	1,420	776	816	581
3,710	17,200	215	130	106	97	87	79	73
6,370	5,870	194	135	120	109	95	86	79
16,300	9,460	687	424	342	324	234	189	171
74,200	55,100	3,820	1,800	1,270	1,330	936	772	695
6,730	76,500	46,300	4,290	2,550	2,280	2,020	1,500	1,240
340	286	266	309	335	335	330	330	335
94	63	45	41	39	37	35	33	37
107	52	32	22	18	18	17	14	12
616	12,800	73	35	29	25	22	18	16
14,800	6,030	610	338	258	226	200	173	160
233	54,300	6,000	2,090	1,760	949	618	399	314
4,430	30,300	2,240	947	647	526	362	295	255
22,400	30,100	2,580	743	451	1,230	455	277	220
136	68	46	36	32	32	29	27	25
834	616	415	280	207	184	165	151	139
480	249	144	44	2	0	0	0	0
4,590	1,660	506	209	113	80	64	53	41
5,710	1,480	331	186	135	111	96	86	78
419	265	184	148	135	128	119	112	108
2,670	275	109	75	59	52	48	44	42
3,270	488	234	152	114	97	82	70	62
5,240	5,460	315	151	113	103	97	97	87
34	8,620	8,520	1,020	601	470	376	298	256
41	3,020	19,700	11,400	17,700	9,060	1,820	1,160	836
82	1,100	1,440	2,170	1,920	2,140	2,130	2,220	2,150
97	5	2	1	1	3	2	1	1
0	0	0	0	0	0	0	0	0
38	32	34	95	101	61	759	1,070	2,710
1	2	4	2	2	1	1	1	1
4	6	10	10	9	9	10	9	8
0	0	0	0	0	0	0	0	0
1	0	0	0	0	0	0	0	0
0	0	0	0	0	0	0	0	0
19	0	0	0	0	0	0	0	0
21	5	2	1	1	1	1	1	1

at Pipe Creek showed an astounding rise from the Manatt Ranch rains. That day, the Medina at Pipe Creek started out at 4.2 feet and 57 cfs. Only eight hours later, at 11 A.M., it had risen to 49.6 feet, with a flow of 281,000 cfs. The stage remained above 25 feet until 4 P.M. and later decreased to 15 feet between midnight and 2 A.M. A secondary rise hit at 4 A.M. on August 3, when the river reached 23 feet and 30,400 cfs.

Medina Lake peaked at 1,076.67 feet, causing a 4-foot flow over the spillway. Its volume increased from 188,200 acre-feet to 281,000 acre-feet in less than thirty-six hours from August 1 to August 2.

Rescues

An eighty-year-old woman lived around seven hundred yards from the Medina in a rock house built in 1934. In the 1978 flood, water reached almost to her ceiling. She said, "My mouth was against the ceiling and my hair was in the water. I only had 6 inches of

Large cypress trees washed out by flood (Austin History Center, 8/3/78 flood, 100322, Neg. 21A).

air to breathe." She was rescued after an exhausting two-hour ordeal in the currents.[12]

Military Assistance to Safety and Traffic (MAST) flight crews estimated that they airlifted about forty people to safety. Four crews worked out of Fort Sam Houston all day, plucking victims from treetops or high ground.

Awakened at 4 A.M. a grandmother called her neighbor after the water began creeping under her back door. Shortly afterward, water poured into the house, quickly reaching up to her neck. She escaped through the front door but was unable to see in the darkness. Her leg caught on a fence wire, and she went under water a few times before breaking loose and making her way to higher ground.

Bandera lawyer Rein J. Vander Zee commented, "A lot of us, including me, thought it was a physical impossibility for that much water to enter the watershed in that short a time. You have to remember that we went from just short of a disaster area by drought—we've had 18 months of drought—to being a disaster area by flooding in just a few short hours."[13]

Guadalupe River

With talk of mammoth rains only fifteen to twenty miles away near Medina, some Kerrville residents expected a torrent down the Guadalupe River at Kerrville. The first rise on the Guadalupe, however, came largely below the town from the Center Point area near the Verde Creek and Turtle Creek confluences.

Cars piled on top of one another by the flood in Bandera (Austin History Center, Bandera, 100341, Neg. 3A).

Flood damage along Highway 16, entering Bandera (Austin History Center, Bandera, 100327).

Verde Creek

Picturesque, cypress-lined Verde Creek meanders from Camp Verde to Center Point. Fed by the fringe of the record Manatt Ranch–area rains, the creek rose like it never had before and obliterated several residential areas along the way. The *Kerrville Mountain Sun* described the damage: "An entire village of houses were [*sic*] swept away leaving only shards of aluminum hanging from the trees."[14] One man,

who estimated that the stream was twenty feet deep, woke to the sound of Verde Creek rampaging through his mobile home subdivision at 6 A.M.

Another person living near the creek was awakened at 5:30 A.M. by a sound he thought was that of hail falling, but then he saw his grandmother standing at the door with a flashlight and yelling. He said, "I went to put on my shoes and get over there, and before I could get my shoes on, my grandmother's house had crashed into ours." After the water knocked down a wall, his family escaped through the roof of their mobile home. They sought refuge in a tree from 6:30 to 8:30 A.M., climbing higher as the water rose.[15]

One long-time Center Point resident stated, "The river wasn't so bad. We knew about the river in time. But the creeks—we never had the creeks flood out at the same time as the river."[16]

Comfort

Fed by the rains upstream of Kerrville and by the huge runoff from Verde Creek, the Guadalupe River was transformed from

Aerial view of damage at a car dealership along Highway 16 in Bandera (Austin History Center, Bandera, 100314, Neg. 14A, 18).

having almost no flow into a record-setting river gone berserk in less than twenty-four hours. Prior to the rains, the Guadalupe at Comfort at 9 A.M. on August 1 stood at 4.1 feet and had a flow of 50 cfs. At 4 P.M. the flow was beginning to increase (4.36 feet and 103 cfs). For the next three hours the river gained nearly 2 feet every sixty minutes and slowly moved up to 11.25 feet at midnight on the night of August 1–2. It rose slowly to 15.85 feet around 5 A.M., before the big rise started. The surge down the Guadalupe then met a "simultaneous rise on Cypress Creek at Comfort."[17]

At 6 A.M. the river reached 22.97 feet and 36,000 cfs. At 7 A.M. it was at 30.98 feet and 99,500 cfs. In the next hour, it came close to its all-time high, hitting 37.55 feet and 183,000 cfs. At 9 A.M. it exceeded the previous record stage set in 1869 by 0.6 feet, peaking at 40.9 feet and 240,000 cfs. The river remained above 30 feet until after 3 P.M. and above 15 feet throughout the following night (August 2).

Following the second big rain of the August 1978 event, the river gained more than 10 feet, rising from 19.38 feet to 30.76 feet between 5 and 6 A.M. on August 3. By 8 A.M. the river had taken on another 4.32 feet, cresting at 35.08 feet. Throughout the day it slowly receded and by noon on August 4 was back to a 10.88-foot level.

A Kendall County judge stated, "Neither Comfort nor the Hill Country has seen a flood this bad since the 1930s."[18] One old-timer in Comfort remarked that it was the "worst flood I've ever seen and I've been here since 1899."[19] Recalling the rise of the river, one survivor said it "came all of a sudden. There was just no time. . . . We saw it coming but we just didn't think it would get any higher." Her family found themselves standing in water that came up to their chins. They eventually climbed into the attic of their one-story framed house. Relief

Guadalupe River at Comfort (Austin History Center, 8/3/78 flood, 100322, Neg. 23A).

came when rescuers chopped an exit in the roof.[20] Another flood survivor was rescued from his attic, which was filled with water up to chin level. In a different instance, at 7 A.M. firemen warned a man living near the river about the impending overflow, but he replied that he would wait until he finished his cup of tea. When the water hit, it reached chest high, but he submerged himself to keep his wife, who was on his shoulders, above water. Together they managed to climb onto the roof.

Law enforcement officers alerted residents to the approaching flood by sounding their sirens. Unfortunately, one family did nothing because they "thought they [the police] were after somebody." At 7 A.M. they saw Cypress Creek rising rapidly and fled to the Turn Verein Tavern and Bowling Club, which was also eventually flooded, requiring them to find refuge on top of the bowling club building.[21] After the flood, 4–6 inches of mud remained in the structure. Noting that the hall had withstood the inundation, one Comfort resident was not surprised: "After all, this was built by Germans."[22]

The record flood invaded various historic structures in Comfort. Water reached a depth of eight feet in the Gladdis Me-

Car swept away by flood in Comfort (Austin History Center, 8/3/78 flood, 100322, Neg. 24).

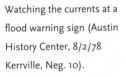

Bridge over the creek along Highway 16 entering Bandera (Austin History Center, Bandera, 100352, Neg. 14A).

Watching the currents at a flood warning sign (Austin History Center, 8/2/78 Kerrville, Neg. 10).

down from the guy wires of power lines. At least two cars were left dangling precariously from the sides of utility poles after the floodwaters receded. The Department of Public Safety estimated that $2.5 million damage was done in the Comfort and Center Point area.

Canyon Lake and New Braunfels

The Guadalupe River at Spring Branch rose from a 2–3 foot level early on August 2 to 10.95 feet at 6 P.M. and to 17.7 by 8 P.M. At midnight, it surged to 34 feet. In the early morning hours of August 3, the river crested at 45.25 feet at 3 A.M. and registered a streamflow of 160,000 cfs. At its peak, the river was lapping at the base of the Highway 281 bridge. At Spring Branch, a secondary rise came at 2 A.M. on August 4, when the river peaked at 40.60 feet and 118,000 cfs.

Residents of New Braunfels and Seguin braced for floods after hearing predictions that the Guadalupe floodwaters would pour over the Canyon Lake spillway. The *Austin American* of August 4 reported, "By late

morial Methodist Church and seven feet at Saint Bonisface's Episcopal Church. At the high school stadium, water splashed over the top of the bleachers. The field house at the school was found twisted and smashed against a pecan tree. Remarking on the damage in town, one resident said, "It's hard to believe that this is usually a paradise." [23]

During the cleanup, the National Guard used heavy equipment to pull automobiles

DRIVE WITH CAUTION
STREAM CROSSINGS ON
THIS ROAD SUBJECT TO
FLOODING IN WET WEATHER

today, a 4 foot stream will pour over the lake's 1260 foot-wide spillway and send the river on a rampage of destruction, perhaps reminiscent of the 1972 flood that took 16 lives and caused an estimated $15 million in damage."[24] The U.S. Army Corps of Engineers estimated that the river would grow by 20–25 feet at New Braunfels, where it brought in more than 150,000 sandbags to help flood-proof the town. Nevertheless, residents believed the Corps of Engineers had not done enough to prepare for the overflow. An owner of a small camp said, "Just tell them that they are a bunch of SOBs. . . . It seems damn funny to me that they couldn't get a little word out that the river was going to go over the tops of people's houses."[25] "In this case they should have been letting the water go 3 days ago," said another camp owner, adding, "In 1972, the flood was an act of God, this is an act of man."[26]

Fortunately for New Braunfels and Seguin, the prediction of water flowing over Canyon Dam proved to be a false alarm. On August 4 the Corps of Engineers announced that the river would not spill over and that the gates would be opened gradually until a flow of 4,500 cfs was reached by the end of August 4, producing only a 3–4-foot rise at New Braunfels.

Floodwater from the Guadalupe River filled Canyon Lake, which grew from 362,200 acre-feet on August 1 to 588,400 acre-feet on August 4, the maximum storage since the dam was completed in 1962.

Pedernales River

The second storm's big rains spurred the Pedernales and every stream in the western and southern sections of Gillespie County to rise to their highest stages in history. The dry conditions before the flood are reflected in the streamflow of the Pedernales at Johnson City. On July 24 the river was

down to 1.5 cfs. At the end of the month, rains boosted this to 54 cfs. The heavy totals of August 2–3 along the Pedernales occurred well above Johnson City, centering on the Spring Creek basin west of Fredericksburg.

The twenty-inch deluge drove Spring Creek into a deadly rampage. Two men driving in a cattle truck drowned when their tractor-trailer rig was washed off a bridge over Spring Creek. The truck was washed downstream and smashed by the currents. After a rancher found cattle in his fields that weren't his, officials began searching for the truck's occupants. One of the men's bodies was found 1½ miles downstream; the other was found 2½ miles downstream. The watch of one of the victims had stopped at 3:22 A.M., approximately twenty minutes after the flood wave hit their vehicle.

Veteran river watchers said the Pedernales River along Highway 87 was five feet above the high set in 1900. It was the first time since the bridge was built in the 1930s that water had covered it. At Highway 290 east of Fredericksburg, water seeped over both approaches. Many people believed the flood of 1900 would not be exceeded, but the river eclipsed that mark by five feet at a

Watching the Pedernales River flood (Austin History Center, 8/3/78 Pedernales, Neg. 8A).

Boiling floodwaters of the Pedernales River (Austin History Center, 8/3/78 Pedernales flood, Stonewall, Neg. 19).

Pedernales River flood approaches statue of LBJ (Austin History Center, 8/3/78 Pedernales, Neg. 28A).

point four miles south of Fredericksburg. A German tourist took photos of the Highway 87 bridge. He had been in Mexico City attending college and decided to visit Fredericksburg after seeing a film that mentioned Walkfest. He said, "I was told it was hot and dry in Texas and now all I see is oceans of water, everywhere."[27]

One family was holding its family reunion in a pecan bottom four miles south of Doss. A crowd from the reunion was still there when the high water arrived, forcing them to scramble up a bluff for safety. Several vehicles were washed down the creek. A deputy sheriff taking inventory of cattle on Highway 16 heard that a tractor-trailer had been washed off Highway 290, prompting him to venture downstream to Stonewall to warn residents. He said, "I had difficulty in convincing those people of the rise that was coming because they had very little rain there that night." When he tried to return to Fredericksburg, he was cut off by the currents on Highway 290 at the river.[28]

Stonewall and Lyndon B. Johnson State Park

The Pedernales River rose to a twenty-four-foot stage at the Lyndon B. Johnson State Park, where it reached the swimming pool and recreation buildings. Longtime residents in the Stonewall area say that the 1952 flood was higher, however. Fort Hood sent sixteen soldiers to LBJ Park to help pro-

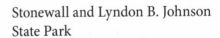

230 tect the former president's gravesite with sandbags. In Stonewall the floodwaters spread out all the way to the front steps of the Lutheran church.

Lake Travis

With the Pedernales tearing downstream, people with interests in Lake Travis started speculating on how high the lake would rise. On August 1 the lake was at 646.65 feet and was predicted to surge another 40 feet, reaching 686.4 feet, the next day, some 5 feet above normal. The news was greeted with both cheers and tears. Those who were expecting only a 10–12 feet rise responded to this prediction in "stunned silence or said, 'You've got to be kidding' before they rushed out to recruit extra help." Many lake-area businesses and dock owners had recently extended their docks and put in additional stairs and walkways to accommodate the lower lake level.[29]

A marina boat serviceperson remarked that the additional water was great, but it was "heartbreaking to be tearing down all the things they just put in." Ann Richards, Travis County commissioner, issued a statement advising people along the Lake Travis shores to take precautions.[30]

As the floodwaters entered, though, the lake started to level off at 670 feet, well below the 686-foot mark predicted. A week later it settled at 662 feet.

Llano River Basin

In the Llano River basin, Bear Creek northwest of Junction surged to an 81,000-cfs flow from its 155-square-mile basin. At Bear Creek, Interstate 10 was inundated for several hours. On Beaver Creek near Mason, the peak stage hit 24 feet and 66,900 cfs, a level 10 feet greater than the previous maximum set in 1965.

Summing Up

President Jimmy Carter granted Dolph Briscoe's request that Bandera, Kerr, and Kendall counties be designated major disaster areas. It was the twenty-eighth time in twenty-five years that portions of Texas had been declared disaster areas as a result of storms and flooding. When Briscoe toured the region, he called the flood "the worst in the history of Texas."[31]

An account in the *Austin American-Statesman* documented some of the sights from Bill Kreuger's and Briscoe's trip to review the flood damage: "Utility poles . . . scattered about the flooded area like broken match sticks, crushed automobiles [that] lay around as though dropped from the sky, and homes [that] were reduced to unrecognizable rubble." They also witnessed a thirty-foot cypress tree jammed into the limbs of another tree about twenty-five feet above the ground.[32]

Earl Estelle, head of the National Weather Service Disaster Survey Team, maintained that the "reason for [the] increasing death toll and escalating property damage is increased development on flood-prone land. . . . People are building in places

Pedernales River flood approaches LBJ State Park (Austin History Center, 8/3/78 Pedernales, Neg. 5).

Pedernales River flood approaches Lutheran church at Stonewall (Austin History Center, 8/3/78 Pedernales flood, Stonewall, Neg. 21A).

where—if they had the facts—no one in their right mind would build."[33]

Following the disastrous inundations, the National Weather Service visited the area to ascertain how well warnings were issued and heeded. Its report on the flood and the staff's handling of the event concluded, "The death toll in last week's tragic Hill Country flood could have been reduced if the National Weather Service had provided better warning . . . [b]ut NWS forecasters . . . were hampered by a shortage of monitoring systems in the Hill Country. . . . Consequently, the NWS had little idea of the magnitude of the record flood. . . . We knew something was going on, but, only after the fact did we realize we had a monster of a storm on our hands. . . . Although NWS issued a flood warning for the Hill Country

on August 1—just hours before the Guadalupe, Medina, Frio, Pedernales and Sabinal rivers surged from their banks—the danger was not adequately stressed. As a result, Hill Country residents 'did not feel sufficiently threatened.'"[34] The investigation found that many people simply did not believe the flood was going to be severe; it also contended that additional reporting and recording stations were needed throughout the Hill Country to gather more data.

Another report stated that the long-distance telephone service failed around 5:45 A.M. on August 2. Moreover, lightning knocked out the Department of Public Safety's radio transmitter tower, and the Bandera County sheriff's radio transmitter also went out that same day.

AUGUST 1978

〜〜〜〜〜

Albany, Texas, Flood

THE ALBANY, TEXAS, flash flood of August 1978 was the second chapter in the distastrous path of dying Tropical Storm Amelia. Forecasters—well aware of the havoc wreaked near Medina and the Hill Country—feared for the next area along Amelia's route. The remnants of the tropical storm moved north into the heart of the drought-stricken Texas Big Country.

Residents there had resorted to cloud-seeding experiments. As the storm parked itself north of Abilene and dropped dozens of inches of rain, one participant in the experiments had to wade to through several inches of standing water to turn off the cloud-seeding devices. However, cloud seeding was not to blame; instead, it was again a dying tropical storm letting loose moisture on dry, hard-packed terrain. The unfortunate town that was hit by the resulting flash flood was the picturesque Big Country town of Albany.

Precedent

By late summer 1978 the Big Country was suffering through another hot, dry season. Rainfall was well below average: Abilene was more than seven inches below normal, and Albany more than nine inches below normal.

Shackelford County residents had been hoping for a good rain for more than a year. For the previous twelve months (August 1977–July 1978), Albany had been more than fifteen inches below normal; actually, below-average rainfall had fallen for that entire pe-

riod. The Soil Conservation Service (SCS) director reported that the last decent rain had fallen in May 1977. At the start of August, his office was processing drought-relief applications.

As the remnants of Tropical Storm Amelia pushed their way northward from South Texas to the Hill Country, Big Country residents were hoping that drought-relieving rains would soon visit them. The headlines of the August 3, 1978, edition of the *Abilene Reporter-News* illustrated the paradox of tropical storm rains: One recapped the Hill Country flooding ("Texas Floods Kill Eight"), while another welcomed the rains, even with all of the attendant danger ("Thank You, Amelia, Rain Finally Arrived").[1]

Rainfall

The traces of Amelia mixed with a cold front and associated trough over the Big Country. Watching the drought coming to an end before their eyes, residents were at first excited about the precipitation, which Nolan county's SCS agent described as "the greatest thing that has happened." The initial giddiness changed to dismay, however, when six to eleven inches poured down on the Abilene area. Another SCS agent noted, "There's water running uphill."[2]

On August 4 the headline of the *Abilene Reporter-News* announced, "Drought Ends, Floods Begin."[3] High rainfall totals were reported at Scranton (8.7 inches), Abilene (6.3 inches), Lawn (9.19 inches), and Throckmorton (17 inches). But the most remarkable

Road signs attest to the damage caused by flooding in and near Albany (courtesy of the *Albany News*).

Highways into Albany sustained flood damage (courtesy of the *Albany News*).

numbers came from Albany, where residents recorded 20 inches—and the storm showed no signs of letting up. The *Abilene Reporter-News* sent a reporter to Albany, but he had to turn back because of the intense rain and hail, which reduced visibility to only a "couple of yards."[4] Soon it became apparent that Albany was receiving more rain in a single day than the 22 inches it had averaged for an entire year.

For the twenty-four-hour period ending at 7 A.M. on August 4, 29.05 inches fell at the NWS gage in Albany, while various locations in Shackelford County received more than 25 inches. The maximum tally of 32.5 inches fell three miles west of Albany, where 23 inches came down in an eight-hour period ending at 2 A.M. on August 4.

Albany

The deluge fell on dry, hard ground, so the runoff was rapid and violent and created a mighty flood in local creeks. The North Prong of Hubbard Creek normally creates at most a pool at Albany, whose southern edge is bounded by the stream. The creek's basin encompasses 393 square miles. The rains drove the stream to crest at a devastating 103,000-cfs flow through town. When the North Prong joined other tributaries in extreme flood stage, the stream receiving the runoff, Hubbard Creek, peaked at an enormous 330,000 cfs at its gage below Albany. Hubbard Creek surged to a 41.41-foot stage with a flow of 330,000 cfs at 7:30 P.M. (The second greatest flow on the creek in the previous thirty-three years amounted to only eleven percent of the 1978 flow—36100 cfs on October 13, 1981.)

The unprecedented increase prompted most of Albany to flee, as the flood-waters covered eighty percent of the town. The operator of the Hereford Motel, south of downtown, was warned by one of her tenants that the creek was rising. He said,

ALBANY, TEXAS, FLOOD

234   "I don't want to scare you, but this is worse than in 1946 when the dam burst."[5]

One resident went down to the creek to watch the swell. He said, "I set a marker at the edge and went to tell one of my friends. When I came back in 15 minutes, a 20-ft wall of water came down that creek washing trucks off the road, houses off their foundations and tearing the highway all to pieces."[6] In much of Albany, water was up to the rooftops. Ham radio operators estimated that downtown Albany had five feet of water flowing through the streets.

One Abilenian who made it out of Albany said, "I never realized it could rain so much. It was unbelievable. There was just water everywhere. . . . We saw campers floating downstream and [oil] tanks bouncing up against the bridge in the current." To escape the waters, he and his friends drove to a location near the courthouse in Albany, where they parked their car and waited for the water to recede.[7]

The Schackelford County sheriff reported that Albany became an island: "I sat there yesterday and watched three pickups go under that bridge. And one of them had a man in it." He called it a "nightmare for 12 or 15 hours."[8] The sheriff added that, at 7 P.M., "water was coming up fast. Here came a truck tumbling down the creek . . . then a red and white pick-up. . . . Much as we tried we couldn't get to him. He rode right under the bridge." He had called the Anson sheriff, who sent a bus to evacuate people, but the bus stalled in the waters. A little after 7:30 P.M. a mobile home came down the creek, but the sheriff was also unable to help the man who was trapped in it.[9]

An area rancher who approached Albany at 6 P.M. remarked, "One look showed [me] Albany was in trouble. Water was more than 100 feet wide and rising. Never had seen it that high." He saw the sheriff's son in the

Highway Department park, "hanging onto something for dear life." (He was clutching a historical marker for the Cook Ranch oilfield.[10])

Another rancher who was caught in water that was within a block of the post office sought safety on a carport. Lights were off all over town, so he used his flashlight to signal whenever he saw car headlights in the night. He said, "I'm going to put my flashlight in a museum somewhere because it never gave out." Around 3:30 A.M. he was rescued by a four-wheel-drive, front-end loader driven by a fireman from Graham.[11]

At 6 P.M. another Albany resident approached the town from Abilene. Shortly

Wrecked car in Albany (courtesy of the *Albany News*).

Debris and damaged road sign near Albany (courtesy of the *Albany News*).

LOCATION	AUG. 1	AUG. 2	AUG. 3	AUG. 4	AUG. 5	AUG. 6	AUG. 7	AUG. 8	AUG. 9	TOTAL
Abilene	6.30	0.10	0.01	0.00	0.00	0.00	0.00	0.00	0.00	6.41
Albany	1.20	NA	0.00	0.40	0.00	0.00	0.00	0.00	0.00	1.60
Breckenridge	1.6	2.68	0.14	0.00	0.00	0.00	0.00	0.00	0.00	4.42
Brownwood	2.08	0.31	0.06	0.00	0.00	0.00	0.00	0.07	0.00	2.52
Dallas	0.00	0.41	1.70	0.00	0.00	0.00	0.00	0.00	0.00	2.11
Dublin	1.73	0.08	0.07	0.00	0.00	0.00	0.00	0.00	0.00	1.88
Hamilton	0.84	0.00	0.18	0.00	0.00	trace	0.00	0.00	0.00	1.02
Lawn	3.52	9.19	0.11	0.00	0.00	0.00	0.00	0.00	0.00	12.82
Mineral Wells	0.80	0.00	0.75	0.00	0.00	0.00	0.00	0.00	0.00	1.55

NA = not available (More than 20 inches of rain fell between August 2 and August 4. For the twenty-four-hour period leading up to 7 A.M. on August 4, 29.05 inches fell.)

after 7 P.M. he was at Nine Mile Hill, where "water was everywhere." When he came down the hill, he saw "oil field tanks floating on water spilled over from Hubbard Creek." He was able to get across the bridge even though water was spilling over it.[12] He added, "That Thursday night was nothing but a bad, bad dream. After I couldn't call my wife, I got in my pick-up and started to see what I could do. I was over near the highway barn when a surge of water came, and my pick-up was suddenly in water up to its headlights. I was rescued by a highway fellow in a front-end loader. . . . I never did see any '30-foot wall' of water. But the water would go up and down."[13]

The floodwaters invaded the home of

Flood wreckage in Albany (courtesy of the *Albany News*).

Shackelford County's agriculture agent, where currents swirled around the first story. His wife said, "It just became a wall of water, and we just started getting out." They moved to the Bluebonnet Village nursing home but had to leave there, too, as the water continued to rise. Residents of the nursing home were evacuated in high-clearance, heavy oilfield trucks.[14]

A bus from Illinois with a teenage church choir was in town for a concert at the time. After dropping off the choir members at a church north of the bridge, the bus driver went to a motel on the south side of the bridge. When he noticed that the water was coming up over the highway, he fled to the bus along with the motel manager, his wife, and two guests. They escaped just in time.

Following the battering of tanks, trucks, buildings, and other debris brought downstream, the Hubbard Creek bridge buckled but did not collapse. Help arrived in stages, when volunteers navigated as best they could. The Department of Public Safety (DPS) arrived at 11 P.M. with six units, and a group from Dyess Air Force Base in Abilene was headed by a son of an Albany couple. They reached the west bank of the North Prong at 2 A.M. on August 5. The National Guard brought in six-wheel-drive vehicles and a thirty-foot boat. Guard members mobilized at 1:45 A.M. but could not get into

town because the roads and bridges were washed out. Four men were stranded at the oil rig they were working on near Hubbard Creek east of Albany. They remained marooned for more than twenty hours before being rescued by a DPS helicopter.

Assessing the damage to houses in Albany was a sobering task. One volunteer noted, "With some of them, there is nothing to assess. The house is gone; in some cases even the foundation is gone."[15] Highway 283 required 14 miles of repair north toward Throckmorton and 12 miles south toward Baird. On Highway 6, one account stated that "damage extends from about the courthouse to Moran" (about 15 miles).[16] Six-

Debris on bridge over North Fork Hubbard Creek in Albany (courtesy of the *Albany News*).

Flood damage in Albany (courtesy of the *Albany News*).

Flood-damaged car in Albany (courtesy of the Albany News).

reported that thousands of tons of valuable topsoil had been carried away. The floods affected sixty-five homes, of which ten rural residences were completely destroyed. Five hundred miles of fences were destroyed. Overall, the county sustained $16 million in damage. One farmer looked out at his pasture covered with crumpled mesquites, dead cattle, and 150-foot sheets of asphalt and remarked, "I'd hate to give $5 an acre for that and expect to get any money out of it."[17]

One of the tragedies of the flood occurred when a fifty-year-old man and his companion were swept off the Hubbard Creek bridge. One witness said, "[He] was sightseeing like everybody else." His truck was carried downstream, but his companion was rescued fifteen hours after being swept away by the currents. She said, "We held on to each other as long as we could. I lost him when we came to a barbed wire fence."[18]

Another flood victim was found buried under six feet of gravel. His sister hired two bulldozers to dig and search for her broth-

inch-thick chunks of asphalt that had been ripped off the roadway littered Highway 6 and adjacent fields. Five bridges near Albany were washed out—two on Highway 6, one on the county road at Fort Griffin, one on U.S. 283, and one on FM 601.

Agricultural losses in the county amounted to $3.5 million, and the SCS

Bridge over North Fork Hubbard Creek in Albany (courtesy of the *Albany News*).

Floodwaters on North Fork Hubbard Creek in Albany (courtesy of the *Albany News*).

Aerial view of bridge over North Fork Hubbard Creek in Albany (courtesy of the *Albany News*).

Looking upstream from bridge at the North Fork Hubbard Creek in Albany (courtesy of the *Albany News*).

er's truck, which had been swept under the bridge.[19]

Summing Up

Following the flood, Albany's Dairy Queen and High Chaparral restaurants had no bread and water but stayed open. The owner of the High Chaparral said, "We couldn't turn the needy away." They served cookies as long as they lasted.[20] As an indication of the independent nature of the local residents, a Red Cross volunteer said that some of them tried to pay the Red Cross for the sandwiches and coffee they received.

Nobody in Shackelford County carried flood insurance. One resident quipped, "I imagine when Noah got his flood, we only got a half-inch in this part of the county. You either burn up or freeze out, but you never think of washing away."[21] The *Abilene Reporter-News* commented, "Most residents here who lost everything to the high water say they'll stay and rebuild. Albany is their home and a little thing like a flood can't drive them away."[22]

An example of the hidden dangers of such an inundation came two weeks after the event. An explosion that shook the town was blamed on a butane tank or a case of

Looking downstream from bridge at the North Fork Hubbard Creek in Albany (courtesy of the *Albany News*).

Washout on highways leading into Albany (courtesy of the *Albany News*).

Spectators watching flooding on North Fork Hubbard Creek in Albany (courtesy of the *Albany News*).

dynamite that had been carried away and buried by the floodwaters.

A highly publicized relief effort was undertaken in Albany, New York, where radio station WOKO organized a relief drive for Albany, Texas. A week after the flood, the station's news director accompanied a flight that landed at Dyess Air Force Base to deliver the money and goods that listeners had contributed. WOKO had to stop accepting donations because there was not enough room on the plane to carry everything. At a news conference after arriving in Abilene, WOKO's news director told the audience, "I'd heard of Albany, Georgia, and Albania but never Albany, Texas."[23] The well-received response from New York prompted a DPS sergeant to say, "There's no such thing as the Mason-Dixon line anymore."[24]

An editorial in the *Abilene Reporter-News* described the water and weather situation in the Big Country:

The paradox of feast-or-famine water is perhaps unique among the weather conditions which shape the destiny of man. Tornado is all bad. Typhoon and hurricane are all bad.

Blizzard is almost all bad. Unrelieved sunshine brings the dry suffocation of drought. And rain, the essential factor without which there would be no life, breeds both prosperity in generous moderation and quick misery in overabundance. . . . For most, the steady rains have replenished dry stock tanks, soaked parched soil—money in the bank for future crops and refilled water supply reservoirs after prolonged 100-degree days had caused water shortage. . . . But for some, the curse of Amelia has brought death and sorrow. . . . This sort of ravaging disaster brings out the best in most people. They involved

Backhoe at the bridge in Albany (courtesy of the *Albany News*).

Intersection at southern end of Albany, near North Fork Hubbard Creek (courtesy of the *Albany News*).

Flood debris and wrecked vehicle in Albany (courtesy of the *Albany News*).

themselves to help those in need. They go sleepless to lend a hand. And government often battered by criticism, responds at all levels.[25]

Lake McCarty

One of the boom-and-bust stories came from Lake McCarty, ten miles southwest of Albany. A week before the flood, the lake was drained. During the flood, the surge filled the lake, eventually breaking the dam and creating a thirty-foot rupture. The county's agriculture agent said, "I can't imagine the wall of water that came in to fill up the lake because it was plumb empty Wednesday."[26]

Lake Hubbard

The record overflow coming down the creek pushed the Hubbard Creek Reservoir near Breckenridge from 185,800 acre-feet on August 2 to 401,500 acre-feet at 8 A.M. on August 5. Strategic releases of water from the dam limited the flooding downstream on the Clear Fork of the Brazos River. Downstream of the reservoir, the creek peaked at only 14,600 cfs.

Brazos

The Clear Fork of the Brazos was hit by flooding from above Hubbard Creek. At Fort Griffin the river crested at 149,000 cfs and exceeded the previous known maximum stage by 0.88 feet. At South Bend, 1.8 miles downstream from the Clear Fork Brazos River, the peak discharge was 78,100 cfs—less than during the 1941 flood there. The Brazos River at Fort Griffin State Park

	JULY 24	JULY 25	JULY 26	JULY 27	JULY 28	JULY 29	JULY 30	JULY 31	AUG. 1
Hubbard Creek below Albany	o	o	o	o	o	o	o	o	o
North Fork Hubbard Creek near Albany	o	o	o	o	o	o	o	o	o
Clear Fork Brazos River at Fort Griffin	o	o	o	o	o	o	o	o	o

Discharge in cubic feet/second

Dam break at Lake McCarty near Albany (courtesy of the *Albany News*).

The dam at Lake McCarty near Albany was breached by the pressure of flood-waters (courtesy of the *Albany News*).

AUG. 2	AUG. 3	AUG. 4	AUG. 5	AUG. 6	AUG. 7	AUG. 8	AUG. 9
0	2,150	94,700	6,400	333	175	98	64
0	6,760	13,100	67	31	15	7	7
0	988	72,800	67,900	19,800	7,430	4,090	2,880

Washout near Albany (courtesy of the *Albany News*).

Bridge washout near Albany (courtesy of the *Albany News*).

was usually 2–3 feet deep and 100 yards wide. While in flood it was 35 feet deep and 2–3 miles wide. Possum Kingdom Lake, 26 miles from Graham, "seemed to merge with the flooded areas into one huge, shimmering puddle."[27] One man who was concerned about his lake house at Possum Kingdom piloted his boat downstream for 26 miles "over normally dry highway and ranchland to his cabin, without touching bottom."[28]

Graham

Graham was the largest town just after the point where the Clear Fork joined with the Brazos River. Salt Creek in Graham also overflowed. Although the creek was usually 20 feet deep, it was estimated to be running some 70–80 feet deep in parts of the county. The western third of Graham was inundated, and water also threatened the town square.

Millers Creek Reservoir

Millers Creek Reservoir was full for the first time since its completion in 1974. During the flood, the reservoir caught 25,500 acre-feet, compared with its normal 1,200 acre-feet. (The reservoir had a controversial history since it was first proposed in 1957. The project was challenged in courts for five years, and members Rochester, Rule, and Seymour withdrew from the North Central Texas Municipal Water Authority before the reservoir was finished.[29])

Cloud Seeding

The biggest controversy after the Big Country flood was whether a cloud-seeding operation near Albany had intensified the rains. After the floods swept through Albany, newspapers reported that a cloud-seeding project in nearby Breckenridge was under way on the day of the storm and even while the storm was raging at Albany. At least one of several private cloud-seeding experiments aimed at curbing the drought was still in operation at the height of Tropical Storm Amelia's downpours. The project was centered in Breckenridge and used nineteen ground-based generators throughout a twelve-county area to shoot silicon-iodide crystals into clouds. Generators in the Breckenridge area were in operation through August 3, and one was running as late as 9 P.M. that night, two hours after the flooding had started in Albany.

A meteorologist at the NWS forecasting center in Fort Worth stated that scientific data on cloud seeding is "not conclusive enough to say whether the Breckenridge operation had any effect on the torrential rains there. . . . We don't have any way of knowing whether what one man has done to the atmosphere has changed it. But rainfall from tropical origin is much more intense than other rains, and the rain that fell over West Texas and caused the floods was tropical."[30]

An Albany resident who was one of about twenty private citizens monitoring the cloud-seeding project was supposed to turn on her seeding gun at 9 A.M. on August 3 and leave it on until 9 P.M. At 7 P.M. the generator was standing in water, so she turned it off.

John Carr, chief of the weather modification section of the Texas Department of Water Resources, stated that the state's primary cloud-seeding project is strictly controlled by federal regulations, which mandate that the operation shut down when a severe weather watch or warning is issued.[31] There is no such stipulation for private operators, however. Carr said, "Since it rained as much or more for a 200-mile area, I doubt seriously that the cloud seeding aggravated it."[32]

A professional paper published by the

USGS and the National Oceanic and Atmospheric Administration (NOAA) analyzed the weather conditions. On August 1 the warm, moist air mass moved into North Central Texas, and the dew point in Abilene rose on August 2 and 3. Strong vorticity was situated over the area. Moving in from the Texas Panhandle and adding to the mix was a cold front, ahead of which a trough developed. The interaction between the front/trough and the remnants of Amelia brought torrential rain to Haskell, Throckmorton, and Shackelford counties beginning early in the morning of August 3. The most intense downpours came during the evening and night of August 3 and 4, and many portions of the counties received more than ten inches of precipitation within two days.[33]

MAY 1981

~~~~~~~~~~

Memorial Day Flood in Austin

IN APRIL 1915 a harrowing flash flood roared down Shoal Creek in Austin. Most of the damage along the creek occurred near downtown, in the vicinity of Fifth and Sixth streets. In the sixty-five years following the deluge, Austin grew northward along Shoal Creek. It advanced along Lamar Boulevard, which bounded Shoal Creek from Eighth to approximately Thirty-fifth streets. The city also expanded farther north along Burnet Road and Loop 1 (MoPac Expressway), which bounded a large residential section bisected by Shoal Creek.

When the flash flood of April 1915 struck the Shoal Creek Basin, development was limited to houses along the lower reaches of the stream. As the city spread, Austin residents recognized the peril of building along the creek, yet little had been done to restrict construction or reduce the effects of flooding along the channel of Shoal Creek. In the Memorial Day inundation of 1981, Austin residents would endure another tragic flash flood. This one was exacerbated by multiple factors: swells that overtook the advanced development in the flood plain; storms that hit the city on a holiday weekend and knocked television stations off the air; and an overflow that struck at night.

Precedent

Late spring in Central Texas and the Hill Country was accompanied by unusually wet weather in its southwest reaches and somewhat dry conditions near Austin and to the northeast. In April, Austin re-

ceived 0.81 inches of rain, 2.68 inches below average. Areas south and west of San Angelo were the recipients of a rainy spell, with many locations receiving rain on nine of eleven days from April 14 to April 24. Brackettville recorded 7.14 inches for the month, 5.15 inches above average.

In April, brief, intense storms produced flash floods that closed roads near Uvalde and Rocksprings and washed a car off a crossing near Harper, drowning the driver. Early in the morning of April 23, a line of storms dissipated as it approached Austin, but its southern flank intensified as it passed San Antonio. This lower section brought hurricane-force winds from La Grange to Columbus to Houston, as it traveled along Interstate 10 all the way to Beaumont, where a tornado was spotted.

In May, Austin missed out on a line of destructive storms. On May 8 hail the size of softballs tore through roofs and even the interior ceilings of houses in Fort Worth and Arlington. The month was a wet one for South and East Texas and spots in North Central Texas. Goliad and Bridgeport both received more than a foot of rain for the month.

In Austin, during the first five days of May, light precipitation fell. The highest one-day total was 0.68 inches. On May 15 and 16 a total of 1.57 inches of rain fell, while Leander and Lake Travis reported a tornado. A week later, on May 23, the Saturday of Memorial Day weekend, the weather service office in Austin gauged 0.84 inches. A National Weather Service spokesperson

Flood debris on bridge along Shoal Creek in North Austin (*San Antonio Express-News* Collection, UTSA's Institute of Texan Cultures, San Antonio, Texas, No. EN 5/25/81 #13A).

said, "It's just the kind of hard, soaking rain we need."[1]

The storms that night were much heavier in the Hill Country, as three-to-five-inch rains fell in the Llano area and baseball-sized hail came down between Menard and Mason. On the morning of May 24, the weather observations and soundings indicated that thunderstorms might develop later that day, and, if they did, they would have little movement due to weak steering winds. Moisture was abundant in the low and middle levels of the atmosphere, while soundings showed that, if the moist lower-level air were heated, it would produce deep convection.

Rainfall

During the daytime hours of May 24, a front stalled northwest of Austin, and heavy thunderstorms began to form. At 3 P.M. the National Weather Service issued a flash flood watch for the Hill Country, includ-

ing Travis County. At 5 P.M. the precipitation probability was set at eighty percent. At 5:37 P.M. severe thunderstorms were forming southwest and west of Austin, near Dripping Springs and Marble Falls, which prompted the issuance of a severe weather statement, warning specifically of heavy rains.

At 7 P.M. the National Weather Service issued a severe thunderstorm warning for Travis County and counties to the north and west. A thunderstorm producing hail and heavy rains with cloud tops to 52,000 feet was spotted near Liberty Hill, and the Stephenville radar indicated a hook-shaped echo, which indicates a possible tornado, near Liberty Hill. At 7:20 P.M. a storm with tops of 40,000–45,000 feet was located over the Shoal Creek watershed. Rainfall rates were initially estimated at 1–2 inches per hour but were later gauged to be twice as high. At 9 P.M. torrential rainfall was centered in north and west-central Austin, producing 4.5 inches per hour over a two-hour span.

At 10:36 P.M. the National Weather Service issued a flash flood warning for Travis County. Records at automated gages indicated that the peak hour of rain occurred between 10 and 11 P.M. At the gage at the airport, the most intense downpour began at 10:30 P.M. and lasted for two minutes, when two inches fell.

In the upper reaches of Walnut Creek, 10.12 inches fell, with a 5.41-inch peak from 9 to 10 P.M. Bee Creek in the Westlake area gauged 8.82 inches, with 5.5 inches falling in one hour. Shoal Creek at the Balcones Research Center, the head of the stream, received 7.55 inches, with 4.44 inches falling in one hour and 5.59 inches in ninety minutes. In the Round Rock area, Lake Creek received almost 9 inches of rain.

The National Weather Service in Austin stated, "We can expect one of these every 10–20 years."[2] During the storm, the NWS there took a direct hit by lightning, which knocked out the radar and other equipment shortly before midnight.

Shoal Creek

Fed by the intense storms and a previously saturated watershed, the usually peaceful, puddle-filled Shoal Creek went out of control. One of the first people to respond to the deluge was Austin's public works director, who walked outside his northwest Austin home between 8:30 and 9:30 P.M. Recounting the situation, he said, "I was standing there in the rain, getting wet and realizing that the last time we had a rain like that we had a helluva flood." He then alerted the bridge and street supervisors.[3]

The first accounts of flooding came in around 9:30 P.M., when a car was swept off the road in Jollyville. The first call to the fire department came at 9:32 P.M. Water was reported coming into houses at Danwood and Oak Knoll, near Jollyville. By 10 P.M. Koenig Lane was under siege by the Shoal Creek. At 10:10 P.M. Jefferson Street reported flooding. The flash flood warning was officially given at 10:26 P.M., but flooding had already been raging for at least thirty minutes. Between 10:30 and 11 P.M. the area from Twelfth Street to Town Lake was inundated. Around 11 P.M. debris from Shoal Creek started flowing into Town Lake, including automobiles and pianos from the South Lamar section along Shoal Creek. Peak stages along Shoal Creek occurred at Steck Avenue at 10:55 P.M., at Northwest Park at 11:15 P.M., and at Twelfth Street at 11:30 P.M. Many houses adjacent to the creek from Forty-fifth to Seventh Street were flooded. Dwellings along the bends of the creek were especially vulnerable.

All available City of Austin Electric Department employees were called in. All three television stations and cable TV were

People viewing cars washed into Shoal Creek (*San Antonio Express-News* Collection, UTSA's Institute of Texan Cultures, San Antonio, Texas, No. EN 5/25/81 #30).

knocked off the air. The superintendent of the energy control center of the electric department said, "Our people out in the field tell us they've never seen anything like this before." The center received 700–800 calls from customers.[4] Several homeowners tried to flee their houses but were trapped when the water forced their exterior doors shut.

Northwest Austin

Northwest Austin was pounded hard by the storm. The fire department counted more than forty calls from residents who reported 3–6 feet of water in their homes. Sections of Highway 183 and Loop 1 were closed due to high water, while firefighters waded through 4 feet of water in the 6000 block of Bullard Drive just after midnight to evacuate residents. The currents propelled trees through dining room windows. The neighborhood between Northcross Mall and Shoal Creek experienced heavy damage. One resi-

Cars swallowed up by raging Shoal Creek (*San Antonio Express-News* Collection, UTSA's Institute of Texan Cultures, San Antonio, Texas, No. EN 5/25/81 #24).

dent noted that the creek rose so rapidly that "there was really no time to move. Or get out. Or anything."[5] A family living less than a block from the creek was driven out by 5–6 feet of water. They said they had "lived here 22 years, and it's never even gotten out of the creek bed here before." The water came into the garage, under the front door, and under the kitchen cabinet. The family was unable

Flood recovery in North Austin (courtesy of the Austin History Center).

to escape through the back door because the "waves were roof-high."[6]

Austin American-Statesman writer and film critic Patrick Taggart was caught in the flood at Anderson Lane. He recalled that, "Just after I came off the Anderson Lane overpass, my car collided with what seemed to be a wall of water. I had not seen it coming. The engine died and I realized that I was in about a foot of water. . . . Almost immediately a man in a yellow slicker staggered toward my stalled vehicle. 'Get out!' he yelled. 'I thought I'd just stay here 'til it let up,' I replied. 'Well, I've been here two minutes and the water has already raised a foot. You better get out. You can replace that car—you can't replace you.' The man made sense." Taggart found the car "or what was left of it," the next day at 4 P.M.[7]

One police officer saw the floodwaters carrying a car off the road and called it the "most heartbreaking feeling he's ever had." In other rescue situations, another police officer had to swim for safety when his own car was swept under water in north Austin. Yet another officer was stranded on top of a patrol car.[8]

What the creek took in from various houses, it spat back out along its banks: grandfather clocks, rolltop desks, groceries, and lamps. More than ten cars were swept into the creek itself. Northwest Park was covered with rocks washed up from Shoal Creek. The force of the floodwater was evident in a two-inch-diameter steel post that was bent parallel to the ground. The bridge at Shoal Creek and Northwest Park was destroyed, and four cars were fished out of the stream in the park.

One resident said he had tried to get city authorities to widen and deepen the Shoal Creek channel but received no support because, he believed, Shoal Creek had never invaded the city officials' own homes. He

said, "People just don't believe it can happen." He called the Woodhollow Dam in northwest Austin an "unsung hero." Built in 1977 to hold forty acre-feet at spillway level, the structure was designed to allow a portion of a one-hundred-year flood to go over the structure. The basin it regulates covered the area between Spicewood Springs Road, Greystone Drive, and Woodhollow Drive. On the night of May 24 floodwaters up to four feet flowed over the spillway. The high-water marks indicated that water was within six inches of the top of the dam—representing a five-hundred-year flood.[9]

Jefferson Street

Approximately thirty blocks downstream from Northwest Park, the Jefferson Street neighborhood experienced unprecedented flooding from Shoal Creek. Richard Abrams of the *Austin American-Statesman* called it a "street with two dead and a washed out dream at every doorstep."[10]

Recounting his own experience, a resident on Pete's Path stated that he had grabbed his dachshund and waded through waist-deep water to a neighbor's house. He said, "I knew a little rain put water up to my curb. I knew someday we'd get flooded if we got a gully washer. I wasn't a bit surprised." He was one of the few people in the area who had flood insurance.[11] At another house, a family escaped by breaking out a window. The children were floating on a mattress in the bedroom, where their heads touched the ceiling. The water line was six feet high in the house.

Also on Jefferson Street, a woman and

Vehicles washed into Shoal Creek near downtown Austin (*San Antonio Express-News* Collection, UTSA's Institute of Texan Cultures, San Antonio, Texas, No. EN 5/25/81 #23A).

her son drowned when they chose not to evacuate when warned of the flood. According to a neighbor who called her, she said she was going to stay because "she's never left during a flood."[12] Ironically, the woman who drowned was quite concerned about the creek's potential to overflow and had sent a letter to the Austin Planning Commission on May 3 protesting town house construction along the stream. She had lived on Jefferson Street since 1951 and had commented, "I've watched the water rise anxiously during and after many rains." She recalled that water rose to a 2½-foot level in her house during the 1960 flood.[13]

One flooded-out resident had been in a car accident two weeks before the deluge. He said, "I've been saying for two weeks [since the accident] that things couldn't get any worse. I'm going to quit saying that. I expect to break out in boils any minute."[14] During the late-night hours of May 24 he spent 1½ hours hanging on to the posts of his front porch, where he watched cars and other debris float by.[15]

Lamar Avenue—Downtown

The business section that was hardest hit was along and east of South Lamar, south of Martin Luther King Blvd. Some Austinites had been expecting the creek to invade the area during a major flood. One resident claimed he was told in the 1960s that a large quantity of water dumped on Shoal Creek in northwest Austin would cause water to "stand 6 feet deep in Louis Shanks' Furniture Store."[16] Another Austinite commented on the northwest Austin drainage plan: "The idea was to get rid of the water as quickly as possible. Those caught in the torrent downstream know now that the plan works."[17] Both Strait Music and Louis Shanks's furniture store were battered. Furniture floated out of the latter and into nearby businesses and the creek. At the 7-Eleven convenience store at Ninth and Lamar, the overnight attendant said of the flood, "It was quick, it was quick." Water rose to a six-foot level in the store.

Car washed between houses along Shoal Creek in North Austin (*San Antonio Express-News* Collection, UTSA's Institute of Texan Cultures, San Antonio, Texas, No. EN 5/25/81 #20A).

Damage at car dealership along Shoal Creek (*San Antonio Express-News* Collection, UTSA's Institute of Texan Cultures, San Antonio, Texas, No. EN 5/25/81 #44).

One of the most spectacular rescues occurred near Tenth and Lamar. A passerby saw a man clinging to the top of a "No Parking" sign at approximately 11:30 P.M. They watched couches, a Volkswagen, and other flotsam float by in the currents. The stranded man held on to the sign until he saw a camper top coming toward him, which knocked the sign over. He then moved to the top of the camper shell. The passerby-turned-rescuer said that he "couldn't turn my back on the old boy. I would have felt like a heel."[18] When the passerby told police he was going to rescue the victim, he said the police "at first . . . thought I was just some fool. I looked like Darth Vader because my wet suit is all black and my ski vest is black." But they helped in the rescue. First, the rescue party "threw a rope down from Strait," and the rescuer managed to make his way across Lamar. He said, "I had to dodge telephone poles that were floating my way." When he reached the victim, he tied a rope around him. When the police pulled on the rope to retrieve the two men, they both shot straight to the bottom. After a couple of seconds the rescuer popped up, whereas the victim "took a little while" to surface because the current was "so swift and his sodden cowboy boots weighed him down." The victim was sore but not seriously injured.[19]

A portable office that housed the *Austin Business Journal* at 800 North West Street, was washed down the creek. Hundreds of cars from the Toyota, Chrysler-Plymouth,

Damage inside convenience store on Lamar Boulevard near Shoal Creek (*San Antonio Express-News* Collection, UTSA's Institute of Texan Cultures, San Antonio, Texas, No. EN 5/25/81 #10A).

Subaru, Volkswagen, and Ford dealerships were also swept away, and the dealerships reported losses of at least $2.9 million. The flood damaged or destroyed 565 new and used cars. One dealership estimated that fully half of its stock ended up in the creek. One owner said that "some cars . . . are just flat gone. We have no idea where they went."[20]

At Tenth and Lamar, across the street from the 7-Eleven, the newly opened

Whole Foods Market estimated its losses at $250,000–350,000. John Mackey, president of Whole Foods, said, "Our inventory is in the river right now."[21] Luckily, sixty volunteers helped clean up the store, and one of the four owners added, "We'll be back."[22]

In commenting on how Austin's famed music industry survived the flood, the *Austin American-Statesman* noted that, as "much as the image of the piano several people saw floating down Fifth Street during the storm Sunday night might be an attractive metaphor, it appears that, for the most part, Austin's music business didn't go down in the flood."[23]

At 609 Wood Street, the office of Joe "King" Carrasco and the Crowns took on three feet of water, destroying the band's entire file of press clippings, as well as most of the record collection of manager Joe Nick Patoski.

A few blocks north of Twelfth Street, the flood destroyed a bridge over Shoal Creek at Pease Park, where the swimming pool filled up with mud. The deluge also invaded the

Flood cleanup at Whole Foods on Lamar Boulevard near Shoal Creek (courtesy of the Austin History Center).

LOCATION	MAY 20	MAY 21	MAY 22	MAY 23	MAY 24	MAY 25	MAY 26
Austin WS	0.00	0.00	0.00	0.84	3.88	0.06	0.00
San Antonio WS	0.00	0.00	0.00	0.23	2.09	0.00	0.00
Burnet	0.00	0.00	0.00	0.04	0.91	4.02	0.00
Blanco	0.00	0.00	0.01	0.03	2.08	0.88	0.00
Johnson City	0.00	0.00	0.00	0.00	0.10	1.41	0.00
Taylor	0.00	0.00	0.00	0.01	0.80	1.60	0.00
Hye	0.00	0.00	0.00	0.00	0.00	0.83	0.00
Spicewood	0.00	0.00	0.00	0.00	0.50	1.75	0.00
New Braunfels	0.00	0.00	0.00	0.00	1.26	0.52	0.00
Lampasas	0.00	0.00	0.00	0.00	1.28	1.47	0.00

LOCATION	JUNE 1	JUNE 2	JUNE 3	JUNE 4	JUNE 5	JUNE 6
Burnet	0.00	0.00	0.34	5.15	2.44	0.00
Fredericksburg	0.00	0.65	0.03	5.45	0.00	0.00
Temple	0.00	0.00	0.74	0.86	3.21	0.03
Hye	0.45	0.00	0.02	0.00	3.31	0.00
Taylor	0.00	0.35	0.34	0.60	2.40	0.01
New Braunfels	0.00	0.38	0.33	2.19	0.55	0.00
Austin WSO	0.62	0.26	0.55	0.06	0.16	0.00

LOCATION	JUNE 10	JUNE 11	JUNE 12	JUNE 13	JUNE 14	JUNE 15	JUNE 16
San Marcos		0.80	2.54	0.96	13.98	0.09	1.07
Austin WS	0.03	5.66	0.21	4.50	0.75	0.12	2.02
San Antonio WS	.	2.13	0.99	1.22	0.89	0.18	2.32
Burnet		1.34	0.34	0.02	0.67	0.36	2.16
Hye		0.22	0.28	0.09	0.28	2.60	2.66
Junction			2.00	0.13		0.04	3.07
Del Rio			0.45			2.90	1.05
Taylor		0.95	3.87	0.13	3.62	0.35	2.00

Austin Recreation Center, covering its basement and first floor. The currents heavily damaged the field at House Park.

Other Austin Creeks

Tragedy struck at various locations along other Austin creeks. Two men were drowned when their car was swept off the road at Bull Creek near the County Line restaurant. A friend of the drowned pair said that they had been at the County Line restaurant when the lights went out and the floodwaters arrived. He said, "They told us the place had to be evacuated, and the waiter said [Ranch-to-Market Road] 2222 was impassable." He himself drove east, but

Child investigating car demolished by the flood (courtesy of the Austin History Center).

MAY 27	MAY 28	MAY 29	MAY 30	MAY 31
0.00	0.00	0.22	1.38	0.00
0.00	0.00	2.72	0.57	0.00
0.00	0.00	0.00	0.02	0.23
0.00	0.00	0.00	0.32	1.16
0.00	0.00	0.00	0.31	2.15
0.00	0.00	0.00	0.66	0.51
0.00	0.00	0.11	0.21	2.10
0.00	0.00	0.00	0.00	0.70
0.00	0.00	1.12	0.01	0.00
0.00	0.00	0.00	0.00	0.05

JUNE 17	JUNE 18
0.39	0.01
0.00	0.00
0.02	0.00
0.03	0.00
0.08	0.00
0.63	0.09
0.00	0.00
0.48	

his friends drove west and into raging Bull Creek, where they perished.[24]

Bee Caves and Westlake

The torrential rains in the western sections of Austin also brought on violent flash floods west of the Colorado River. Bee Creek and Dry Creek in Westlake and Rollingwood took several lives and tore away buildings. The police chief in Rollingwood said he was told that the flood was "a wall of water, not a gradual rise." A police officer reported that the water was "tossing a Volkswagen around like a Tinker Toy."[25]

Along Bee Caves Road, the flash flood blasted into Rollingwood Plaza, where a restaurant had opened a few days earlier. It closed early on May 24, however, due to the weather. Water surged out of the banks of Dry Creek and smashed into the complex and the restaurant. The last three people leaving the establishment had to wade through thigh-high water.

Watermarks were four feet high in the shopping complex, which was only two feet above the flood plain of the creek. The backs of the stores adjacent to the stream were torn out, and a wall of an unoccupied building collapsed. The currents smashed plate-glass windows and deposited three inches of mud on the sidewalks outside the stores.

One tragedy occurred at 10:15 P.M., when a man who was taking his family's baby-sitter home drowned after his car was swept away by Bee Creek on Westlake Drive. The baby-sitter jumped into a tree, where she found refuge. The Westlake police chief said the tree was not big enough for both, however. The man grabbed a branch, which broke, and was washed away.

Rollingwood's mayor noted that, regardless of the flood's origins, the U.S. Army Corps of Engineers' flood-plain map "is no longer appropriate because every flood changes it."[26] Victimized business owners blamed impervious cover from a new shopping center and housing subdivision upstream. Runoff from nearby housing and highway projects deposited large amounts of sediment into the creek at Wild Basin.

Flood Damage

Of the thirteen people who drowned in the flood, six died in cars that were swept off low-water crossings, five were in cars swept off bridges, and two perished in a house when they failed to evacuate after being warned. The U.S. National Research Council's report on the flood stated, "The high mortality rate was almost certainly due to the fact that nothing in recent experience had prepared people to anticipate and respect the violence of the rapidly rising waters."[27] After the deluge, the City of Austin issued a bond proposal to buy lots prone to flooding, including sixteen residential lots on Jefferson Street, four homes on Silverway Drive in northwest Austin, and twelve properties on Elm Parkway.

Summing Up

With devastation throughout the heart of Austin, residents rallied to help one another. As the *Austin American* pointed out,

"Nature on a rampage serves as almost nothing else to focus people's minds on the basics."[28] The city began to work on getting relief aid to help repair and rebuild. Although Sen. Lloyd Bentsen stated that the chances of obtaining federal aid were slim, Gov. Bill Clements said he was "certain President Reagan will issue a disaster declaration that would allow federal grants to the city."[29] However, the Federal Emergency Management Agency (FEMA) informed Austin that its grant request was rejected. Some believed the aid was denied because the city overstated its losses. In response, the city lowered the damage estimates, but FEMA did not change its ruling.

Two weeks after saying that he was certain that President Reagan would issue a disaster declaration for the city, Governor Clements said that aid was not needed after all. He also claimed that the aid request was turned down because the city had overestimated the damage. Clements pointed out that it was FEMA that declined the assistance, not President Reagan. The *Austin American-Statesman*'s editorial of June 3 commented that it was disappointing that Austin did not gain full disaster declaration from the White House. Most Austin residents, however, shrugged off the matter.[30]

Warnings and Studies before May 1981

Following the flood, authorities reviewed Austin's preparedness for flooding and the ways in which the city handled the Memorial Day flood. Residents and city officials remarked that the city had previously used a weather warning system that utilized sirens. Austin discontinued this system around 1972 because of "frequent false alarms" and the need to update it to keep pace with the city's growth.[31] The decommissioned system

Texas Department of Water Resources vehicle damaged in the Shoal Creek flood (courtesy of the Austin History Center).

was criticized because citizens did not know whether they were hearing a false alarm or a warning of a nuclear attack, tornado, or flood.

Furthermore, Shoal Creek had recently been studied to determine how well it would transfer a one-hundred-year flood. The report claimed that many houses and businesses would be hit by floodwaters in such a deluge. The one-hundred-year flood marks from the study closely matched those of the May 24 overflow.

Some citizens focused their blame on new development in the upper watershed as a major cause of the flooding. Others blamed environmentalists who opposed widening and channelizing the creek. The city had considered improving the carrying capacity of the creek, but Austin residents protested this action, stating that they did not want Shoal Creek to become "Shoal Ditch." An editorial in the *Austin American-Statesman* said that the next one-hundred-year flood could actually be a ten-year flood made worse by impervious cover. It added, "Austinites likely won't stand for channelization of creeks. A channelized creek is no longer a creek, but an ugly, concrete funnel."[32] One resident attributed the flood to development in northwest Austin and suggested that Shoal Creek land should be a greenbelt. "Mother Nature is going to kick you in the teeth if you don't do it," she warned.[33]

The USGS and a private hydrology firm did not agree that either scenario was the direct cause of the overflow. They stated that rains had saturated the soil, that Shoal Creek was hit with a one-hundred-year flood (which closely followed the predicted levels of such an event), and that many of the damaged homes and businesses were within the one-hundred-year flood plain. Their studies showed that the heavy precipitation would have caused extreme flooding without the added impervious cover because the soil was soaked after the first few inches of rain.

National Research Council's Assessment of Austin's Warning System

In its formal report on the disaster, the National Research Council (NRC) stated, "In Austin, as in other cities, a sizable segment of the public does not really know where flooding can be expected to occur or how serious it can be when it happens. Although the problem may have been investigated and may be understood by some departments of the city administration, that insight is not necessarily shared by the community at large."[34] The agency added that a "false sense of security based on the limitations of one's own experience may have been a factor" in the deaths of eleven people in automobiles. The report highlighted the fact that no deaths occurred outside of the urban areas around Austin, even though those locations received heavy rains, too. One factor, according to a county engineer from a rural area was that "rural people know the hazard of low-water crossings during a storm and act prudently." The NRC report added that "not only had the people of Austin little or no experience with flooding in their city as great as that of May 24–25, but probably few knew how easily an automobile can be floated and moved by a high-velocity stream of water. The size of objects movable by a stream is a function of its velocity, more than its discharge, a fact probably contrary to popular impression.

Brushy Creek north of Austin flooding in June 1981 (Austin History Center).

Truck and debris along Shoal Creek near Fifteenth Street (*San Antonio Express-News* Collection, UTSA's Institute of Texan Cultures, San Antonio, Texas, No. EN 5/25/81 #19A).

Any educational program on flash-flooding should stress that shallow fast streams can move large objects a much deeper but slower stream couldn't budge."[35]

With regard to the effectiveness of warnings for the flash flood of May 24 and 25, the National Research Council's report found that, "For a variety of reasons, the information in these [weather warning] statements does not appear to have stimulated responsive action by the city or its residents. It was the Sunday evening before the Memorial Day holiday. The television and radio stations, as well as city offices, were minimally manned; indeed, most of the stations were being operated by a single person. Later in the evening, many of the stations were knocked off the air by lightning. And the citizens were not alert: They were in the middle of an enjoyable holiday; most of them had been through many thunderstorms, including the one of the previous evening; many had seen heavy rainfalls in Austin, preceded or accompanied by weather service 'statements,' that had resulted in inconvenience but not loss of life or significant property damage; and few had weather radios and even fewer were listening to them."[36]

A National Weather Service official in Austin issued the flash-flood warning, but one weather specialist maintained that, "on weekends, radio and television stations don't seem to be able to get the information to the public very fast.... A lot of people in the Austin area were unaware of the danger unless they had their own NOAA weather radios and were picking [the warnings] up from there."[37] The National Weather Service team from Fort Worth studied the response made by the Austin NWS team and found that they had performed up to standard.

Area officials then began scrutinizing Austin's warning system. A San Marcos city official observed, "When the creeks in San Marcos begin to rise, lights flash and bells ring in the San Marcos Fire Station and duty officers can trigger sirens to alert the public of flood dangers.... We have an hour, maybe two hours advance warning in a flash flood." Kerrville and New Braunfels also had similar warning systems at the time, while both Dallas and San Antonio had gauging systems linked to warning units.[38]

One Austin official said, "We probably have one of the best early warning systems around, and it's not based on blinking lights and computers. It's based on individuals calling to the police, fire and EMS saying, 'Hey, the water is coming up.' The early warning system is ideal to predict what might happen if you get one, two or three hours lead time. But with our terrain, the creek system, the rain and flood could be over in an hour's time."[39]

Postflood Rains in May

Unfortunately for Austin, rainy weather continued to plague Central Texas for several weeks after the May 24–25 flood. On May 30 a thunderstorm drifted into Austin in the mid-afternoon and dumped close to two inches of rain in parts of the city, while pea-sized hail fell in the downtown area. The National Weather Service at Austin said the storm was almost as potent as the flood-producing storm a week earlier, but this one did not become stationary.

The rains caused residents along Jefferson Street to be evacuated, as fire fighters went door to door to evacuate the 3900 block. The National Weather Service reported, "We've been getting 30 to 40 calls an hour from people every time any clouds appear in the sky. But they shouldn't get so worked up. All we expect in the near future are a few garden variety summer thunderstorms."[40] On June 4, however, another storm caused brief flooding at low-water crossings in Austin, when 1.8 inches fell in one hour.

Postflood Rains in June

On June 11 heavy rains fell in Williamson, Travis, and Hays counties. Williamson Creek flooded more than twenty houses, and residents along the creek evacuated quickly because they "didn't want . . . what happened at Shoal Creek."[41] Shoal Creek overran its banks and again flooded some of the businesses on Lamar Street. In Williamson County, the San Gabriel River north of Leander flowed over the Highway 183 bridge.

The rainy pattern continued down to the coast, where, through June 12, sections of Victoria County had received twenty-six inches of rain since May 1. As intense and impressive as the earlier June rains were, the storm on June 13 topped them all, dumping more than thirteen inches of rain on San Marcos. The NWS said that a front had stalled over Texas and served as a trigger. The rain was caused by an "almost tropical upper air disturbance that drifted north from Mexico and was not expected to reach Austin."[42] The prediction that the upper-air disturbance would move into Southwest Texas was incorrect, however; instead, it moved into Central Texas. Following the June 13 deluge, an NWS meteorologist said he was "well aware of" the disturbance but did not think it would move that way. He added that Austin was "supposed to be out of the rainy season. . . . [We] get one day of rain now and everybody is up in arms." He said he would make the same prediction if he had to do it again.[43] A member of the Austin NWS commented, "When you're standing there in the water, it doesn't matter where it came from."[44]

San Marcos

With the thirteen-inch rainfall in San Marcos, Purgatory Creek rushed over its banks and covered more than half of the south side of town, including four lanes of Interstate 35. "Every creek, every river, everything with water in it is over its banks," said a Hay County sheriff dispatcher. A

Houstonite bound for Wimberley said, "This is unbelievable. I lived in Houston for 48 years and we went through hurricanes and high water and all kind of bad weather. But I've never seen anything like this."[45]

Fourteen hundred residents had to be sent to emergency shelters. At the Clear Springs Apartments, water lapped up to the second story. The San Marcos River crested at a level one foot below the peak of 1970. For the month of June 1981, San Marcos received 22.96 inches, more than 19 inches above average.

Onion Creek

On June 13 Onion Creek hit 31.26 feet, a new official record (the unofficial record was 38 feet in 1869). Flood stage was 21 feet. The streamflow was 46,000 cfs, the highest since May 28, 1929, when it reached 76,000 cfs, according to a USGS hydrologist. Onion Creek's floodwaters crushed several mobile homes.

Westlake

In Westlake, Dry Creek tore large sections of pavement from Bee Caves Road. One man escaped the flooded 2600 block of the road at 3 A.M. while returning from his job at Chelsea Street Pub. His car floated into a tree, and as the tree began to give way, he bodysurfed to the bank.

Miscellaneous Incidents in Austin

Williamson Creek flooded at Oak Hill after nine inches fell and fed the stream, which was table-top high in the 5300 block of Meadowcreek Circle. Near the main campus of the University of Texas, the Villa Capri was damaged by high winds. The Travis Country subdivision tallied ten inches, which fed into Barton Creek. The surge there brought out the thrill seekers, several of whom had to be rescued by helicopter after becoming stranded during their treks down the flooded stream.

Following the floods, the manager of a Christian radio station in Austin wondered aloud whether Austin was being punished for being a modern-day "Sodom and Gomorrah." He said, "I guess we're not too far from that."[46]

Pedernales River

In another tragic event, four people were swept away at Pedernales Falls State Park near Johnson City on June 16. As a rise came down the river, the victims were trapped on the rocks above the falls. Park rangers repeatedly threw inner tubes to them, but the current carried the tubes downstream. A helicopter that had been called to rescue them arrived ten minutes too late.

North of Austin, a Fort Hood soldier was swept away while trying to reach others in a hilly area twenty miles south of Killeen, near Mountain Creek, seven miles east of FM 440. Maneuvering through the currents on foot, he was trying to check on an elderly couple when he was pulled under.

Near Lake Travis, eight feet of water flowed over RR 1431 west of Cedar Park. Three men rode inner tubes down Sandy Creek into Lake Travis. When asked why they wore life jackets when going out in the dangerous currents, one man answered, "We're crazy, but we aren't stupid."[47]

AUGUST 1998

~~~~~~~

Del Rio Flood

WHEN A TROPICAL storm approaches the Texas coast, residents throughout the state pay attention. When one approaches the middle to southern Texas coast, residents, especially of the Hill Country, know their worst fears may be realized.

In August 1998, Tropical Storm Charley formed with little fanfare in the Gulf of Mexico. As it moved toward shore, the southern Hill Country became a target for the deluges it could unleash as it slowed and lost its guiding upper-air winds. Charley's remnants produced strong rains over a small area. This is the story of what happens when intense precipitation falls directly on a small basin and then flows through a populated area. This worst-case scenario came to pass at Del Rio's San Felipe Creek, one of the most beautiful and life-giving streams in the Lone Star State. One of the richest creekside communities was decimated by an old friend when a year's worth of rain fell in one evening. This is one of the saddest weather-related tragedies in recent Texas weather history.

Precedent

The year 1998 was marked by extreme drought during its first six months. Especially unusual was a smoky haze that blanketed much of Texas from drought-driven fires in Mexico. May and June saw extremely high temperatures. On June 14 high temperatures throughout Texas approached or exceeded 110 degrees. Lamesa reached 109 degrees, and Monahans 110 de-

grees. Near the Gulf Coast, Goliad recorded 112 degrees. Two weeks later, the high temperature in Monahans peaked at 115 degrees. Boquillas topped that at 116 degrees.

Along with the scorching temperatures came stifling drought, and May 1998 turned out to be the driest May in 104 years. During that month, fewer than ten of the more than four hundred weather stations in Texas reported above-average rainfall.

The late spring and early summer heat charged the Gulf of Mexico for tropical storm development. In mid-August, Tropical Storm Charley formed in the gulf and, on August 21, was given a name. It was forecast to strike the Texas Gulf Coast on August 22, bringing winds of 60 mph and four to eight inches of rain. As Charley approached the shore, Bob Rose of the LCRA commented on the dangers of tropical storms, even during drought periods, when streams and lakes are low. Rose said, "A lot of rain in a short time could still cause dangerous flooding."[1]

Charley made landfall in Port Aransas at 5 A.M., when winds topped at 49 mph. The storm moved northwestward and dumped 13 inches of rain in Refugio County. Other amounts in the area ranged from 4 to 9 inches. A Woodsboro rancher characterized the scenario by saying, "This is a typical Texas end of drought—a flood."[2]

As with other tropical storms that buffet the South Texas coast, the steering winds pushed this one toward the Hill Country. As Charley skirted south of San Antonio, it reached the Uvalde area, which had already received heavy rains on August 19. On the night of August 22, rains totaling up to eight inches fell in the Frio River basin. In the early morning hours of August 23, the ensuing flood inundated Garner State Park, where one man died while being evacuated. The waters caused approximately $500,000 in damage to the park. One restroom building was completely demolished. Pieces of the porcelain toilets and sinks were found downstream months afterward. Along the river, water was eight feet deep in the campgrounds.

After deluging the Uvalde area, the Charley's center moved to the Del Rio area, about eighty miles to the west of the Garner State Park area. The center settled just northeast of Del Rio on the evening of August 23. At this location, the tropical storm remnants shrank in coverage but set up to produce the dreaded core rains. In the twenty-four-hour period leading up to 8 A.M. on August 24, 17.65 inches fell in Del Rio. From 1 to 3 A.M. that day alone, 7 inches fell.

Del Rio's yearly average rainfall is 18.24 inches. For 1998 Del Rio had received slightly more than half its usual total for that time of the year—5.61 inches of 11.14 inches up to late August.

Forecasters from the NWS said that

Damage to a pedestrian bridge in a park along San Felipe Creek just south of Highway 90 (photo by Jonathan Burnett).

Park land next to San Felipe Creek (photo by Jonathan Burnett).

	AUG. 16	AUG. 17	AUG. 18	AUG. 19	AUG. 20	AUG. 21	AUG. 22	AUG. 23	AUG. 24	AUG. 25	AUG. 26	TOTAL
Del Rio 2 NW		1.08	0.69	1.41	0.22	0.64	0.17	6.12	11.47	0.40	0.25	22.45
Del Rio Airport	trace	0.06	1.23	0.66	0.06	0.70	0.01	-	0.72	trace	0.38	3.82
Lake Amistad		0.19	0.46	1.86	0.03		0.07	0.15	7.10	0.35	0.10	10.31
Brackettville		1.20	1.37	0.89		0.60	4.85	2.45	0.20			11.56
Brackettville 22		0.48	1.23	0.69		1.45	4.27	6.51	0.16			14.79
Carta Valley		trace	0.49	1.13		0.45	0.25	0.80	10.75	1.40	0.21	15.48
Camp Wood		0.08	0.47	1.75		0.60	0.08	4.75	2.00	1.75		11.48
Prade Ranch		0.90	0.58	0.58		0.50		7.25	0.64			10.45
Rocksprings		0.67	0.52	0.94		0.02		2.37	1.67	1.49	0.71	8.39
Sonora	0.69	0.58	0.05	1.07	0.17	0.15	0.10	1.27	0.97	0.95		6.00
Uvalde		1.07	1.10	1.73			0.30	3.70	0.10	0.51	0.10	8.61
Sheffield			0.08		0.76				0.47	5.06		6.37
Leakey		0.40	0.73	0.16	0.40		1.24	5.65	1.50			10.08
Vanderpool 4N	0.96	0.81	0.51	0.51	0.02	0.31	0.93	6.40	0.58			11.03
Utopia		0.20	0.67	0.27		0.05	1.02	7.05	0.21	0.20	0.20	9.87

A sentiment seen throughout Del Rio after the flood (photo by Jonathan Burnett).

San Felipe Creek at Del Rio, August 1998

San Felipe Creek

Del Rio

Rio Grande River

DEL RIO FLOOD

dying tropical storms and core rains are "one of our nightmare scenarios."[3] For residents along San Felipe Creek in Del Rio, the rains indeed produced a horrifying nightmare.

Del Rio Flood

The heavy rains brought a flood wave down San Felipe Creek from northeast of Del Rio, much of which is built around the stream, and the city has created scenic parks along the creek. Farther downstream, one of the city's main cultural centers was built around Brown Plaza, which was being renovated prior to August 1998. The flood wave engulfed all of these landmarks and much more.

As seventeen inches fell, much of it in a two-hour period while Del Rio residents slept, the massive amount of rain transformed into a flood wave that exceeded the one-hundred-year flood. Water reached a depth of seven feet in houses located hundreds of feet from the creek. The recreational water park at Moore Park near U.S. Highway 90 was strafed by the floodwaters. At Brown Plaza, an approximately twelve-foot wall of water and debris hit in the early morning hours.

Flood damage to vehicles (courtesy of the *Del Rio News-Herald*).

Many vehicles were carried away by the floodwaters (photo by Jonathan Burnett).

The flood height of the San Felipe Creek is evident by the debris on the stone foot-bridge south of Highway 90 (photo by Jonathan Burnett).

The flood tore through park land along San Felipe Creek (photo by Jonathan Burnett).

Vehicles destroyed by the flood (courtesy of the *Del Rio News-Herald*).

Even heavy older cars were toppled in the flood (photo by Jonathan Burnett).

The force of the floodwaters bent this metal beam around the stone and concrete approach to a bridge over San Felipe Creek (photo by Jonathan Burnett).

Looking upstream from below the bridge and its approaches on Bridge Street (photo by Jonathan Burnett).

As the floodwaters reached unheard-of heights, residents found themselves in great danger. Compounding the peril was the time the core rain arrived—in the middle of the night. As water filled their homes, residents took extreme measures to survive. One woman tied her bedridden husband to the bed and then held on to a five-gallon bucket full of chains to keep from floating away.[4]

The high water and extreme velocity made rescues dangerous. One would-be rescuer wanted to launch his boat but found it bumping against the roof of his

Destroyed vehicles (courtesy of the *Del Rio News-Herald*).

Vehicle damage (courtesy of the *Del Rio News-Herald*).

shed. He went out with others and said that what he had thought was the bleating of goats was actually people screaming for help.[5]

Families took drastic measures in order to survive. Parents let their children go with rescuers while they themselves waited for the next round of rescues. With the rising waters and hazardous conditions, one rescuer said he would ask for the parents' last names in case they perished before he could return to rescue them.[6] The same rescuer stated that one father slid his three-month-old infant down a piece of sheet metal to the waiting rescuer.

Flood damage at Brown Plaza (courtesy of the *Del Rio News-Herald*).

Wreckage at Brown Plaza (courtesy of the *Del Rio News-Herald*).

Extensive flood damage to the Moore swimming pool adjacent to San Felipe Creek (Photo by Jonathan Burnett).

Community Center at Bridge Street was decimated by San Felipe Creek (Photo by Jonathan Burnett).

A van was washed into the community center (Photo by Jonathan Burnett).

A van inside the community center (Photo by Jonathan Burnett).

Residents and rescuers dodged floating cars, houses, and refrigerators in the dark night. One survivor said, "You could hear the roar of the water rushing by. You could hear the bubbling of the houses sinking."[7] One house had watermarks at a height of seven feet. The clocks in the house had stopped at 1:10 A.M. and 1:25 A.M.[8] Following the flood, "the area resembled a washed-out ghost town."[9]

Aftermath

Rescue efforts quickly came together in Del Rio, and the destruction wrought by the flood astounded many. The logistics coordinator of the American Red Cross said, "This is exactly what a lot of those bombed-out European cities looked like during World War II."[10] Aid came in all sorts and from all directions. Water arrived from as far away as Kentucky. General Mills sent 8,400 boxes of Cheerios in an eighteen-wheeler tractor-trailer. A railroad car filled with orange juice arrived "uninvited, no note attached, just a rail car of orange juice."[11]

Following the catastrophe, residents

This old hotel at Brown Plaza was being renovated before the flood struck (courtesy of the *Del Rio News-Herald*).

Examining the destruction at Brown Plaza (courtesy of the *Del Rio News-Herald*).

Looking along Bridge Street at the approach to the bridge (Photo by Jonathan Burnett).

Close-up of the remnants of the approach to the bridge (Photo by Jonathan Burnett).

wondered about their fate and whether anybody was to blame for the calamity. One priest stated that residents had been praying for rain, and now "we're trying to figure out what to tell God."[12] A U.S. Border Patrol agent added, "We wanted [a tropical storm] to fill up the lake, but not in one night."[13] A judge in Terrell County, home to Sanderson, stated that the citizens of Sanderson were "very sympathetic to their problem."[14]

Residents and officials wondered why flood-control measures were not in place along San Felipe Creek. In a letter to the editor of the *Del Rio News-Herald,* the former head of city planning for Del Rio in 1976 wrote that the city had looked into building dams, but complications ranging from uncooperative landowners to a lack of leadership on the council to endangered species had bogged down the endeavor.

Texas agencies with ties to the swift-water rescue teams discussed ways to involve their teams in the future. For the August 1998 flood, teams were on alert in Austin, Houston, and Dallas. The director of aviation of the Texas National Guard said, "There's no way anybody could have gotten to Del Rio to save anybody. They were all dead before we got there."[15]

Rio Grande

With the huge swell of water from the Del Rio area, the Rio Grande responded with its biggest rise in years. Lake Amsted gained approximately 350,000 acre-feet from the runoff. As the water moved past Del Rio and into Eagle Pass, it spread approximately a mile wide. As the currents approached Laredo, residents there prepared for the worst. One woman who had witnessed the 1954 flood as a girl said, "All this is in the Bible: the drought, the floods, the volcano in Mexico. But we don't want to believe it. It's a shame."[16] Another resident said, "We've never seen anything like it. It's like the end of the world. It's like a potential flotilla of death."[17]

On August 26 the river crested at noon at the Colombia-Solidarity bridge, thirty miles upstream from Laredo, at a stage of about 45 feet, some 5 feet above expectations. At Laredo, the flood was expected to hit 38 feet. At 5:20 A.M. on August 27 the river peaked at 35 feet. Flooding was not as bad as expected in Laredo, partly because the floodwaters flowed into area creeks that were not in flood and could therefore absorb water from the river, rather than add to it. Laredo's city manager acknowledged, "Just a little [more] rain would have changed everything."[18]

Following the flood, George Bomar, author of *Texas Weather* and meteorologist at the Texas Natural Resource Conservation Commission (TNRCC), commented, "Droughts have a way of creating a day of reckoning." In stagnant weather patterns, hot and dry weather creates a humid atmosphere. Bomar added, "When you introduce a gulf storm into this environment, it feeds on the low-level moisture and it doesn't go anywhere fast so you get rainstorm after rainstorm in the same area, creating heavy runoff in a very short time span. . . . The landscape is like concrete."[19]

Park land next to San Felipe Creek (Photo by Jonathan Burnett).

Wreckage at Moore swimming pool next to San Felipe Creek (Photo by Jonathan Burnett).

OCTOBER 1998

~~~~~~

Hill Country Flash Floods

THE FLASH FLOODS of October 1998 demonstrate what happens when scientists' worst-case analysis is realized. They have called Central Texas "Flash Flood Alley." Three of the atmospheric factors contributing to this label are the ready supply of moisture from the Gulf of Mexico to the southeast, moisture from the Pacific Ocean from the southwest, and the presence of triggering mechanisms in the upper atmosphere. In October 1998 all of these aspects converged over the region just north of San Antonio. This convergence was further enhanced by the orographic lift of the Balcones Escarpment. The resulting storm was another extremely efficient rainfall machine that dropped huge amounts of water for a prolonged period.

The resulting deluges struck areas that had been hit several times in the previous decades. But by 1998, additional development in the Hill Country meant that more

Wreckage at Schlitterbahn (photo by Jonathan Burnett).

people and additional structures lay in the path of the runoff. In particular, this was the second time that the perceived protection from Canyon Dam did not prevent New Braunfels from being flooded. That wave down the Guadalupe River was joined by others along the river, creating an unprecedented inundation along the river at Luling, Gonzales, and Cuero.

Precedent

Following the Del Rio floods of August 1998, Texas Hill Country residents knew they had been spared the catastrophe created by the dying Tropical Storm Charley. In September, the coastal regions of Texas were battered by Tropical Storm Frances. The Gulf of Mexico continued its storminess, producing Tropical Storm Hermine in late September. By October, the threat of Gulf Coast storms was beginning to diminish.

Rainfall

By the middle of October, hurricanes Lester and Madeline had formed off Mexico. Madeline was officially designated a hurricane on October 17 and moved northward into the Bay of California before dissipating. On October 17 Hurricane Lester was south of Madeline but still close enough to Texas to affect its weather. Moisture from both Madeline and Lester began streaming into Texas that day. Adding to the mix were a strong upper-level trough and an approaching cold front.

The forecast for Saturday, October 17, called for cloudy skies with showers turning into thunderstorms. Precipitation models for the six-to-ten-day outlook showed chances for heavy rain, exceeding five inches for much of the Hill Country. At 5 A.M. on October 17, showers began to form near San Antonio and grew in coverage and intensity throughout the morning. In addition, the storms followed a training-effect pattern over the southern Hill Country.

Official tallies for October 17 and 18 exceeded 20 inches in New Braunfels and 12 inches in San Marcos, Lockhart, Gonzales, San Antonio, Luling, and Wimberley. Unofficial totals exceeded 30 inches in the San Marcos and New Braunfels vicinity.

Gruene, October 1998 (photo by Jonathan Burnett).

Runoff

Rains produced record floods in the San Antonio River, San Marcos River, and Guadalupe River basins. As the precipitation cascaded over San Antonio and its rocky soil, a National Weather Service spokesperson said, "Every creek and river and drainage system and road and highway in the city of San Antonio is either flooded or about to be flooded."[1] Two creeks hit by extreme high waters were the Olmos and the Salado. The former brought in enough water to fill the Olmos reservoir and require floodgates to be opened. Water nevertheless backed up from the dam and blocked part of Highway 281.

Gruene after the October 1998 flood (notice the doors deposited in the tree and the debris mark on the road sign) (photo by Jonathan Burnett).

Damaged building at Garden Street bridge (photo by Jonathan Burnett).

proposed for years, it was determined after the flood that it would have been breached by the currents anyway. Water was 2.4 times greater than during the second largest official flood on record (1961, which does not take into account the 1921 and 1946 floods).

In San Antonio, overflows shut down Interstate 35. One resident along Perrin Creek said that the water rose eight feet within a few minutes. Another resident near the creek said, "One minute you worry about your rugs, and the next you worry about your life. That's how fast it happened."[2]

Part of the story of the San Antonio flooding was that two of the city's flood-control projects worked well. The Olmos Dam held a great volume, and the San Antonio River tunnel diverted water that would have inundated much of the San Antonio River Walk. The volume of water carried by the tunnel was estimated to be enough to fill the Alamodome within three hours. When debris caught on the grate at the entrance of the tunnel, city workers risked their lives to clear it. San Antonio's Public Works director called the tunnel a "godsend." He said, "If it weren't there, we would be in big trouble."[3]

The Salado caused extensive flooding, highlighting the continued need for flood prevention along its basin. At one campground, the rapidly rising water trapped campers and recreational vehicles before they could be moved to higher ground. Although a levee along the creek had been

DAILY PRECIPITATION (IN INCHES), OCTOBER 16–21, 1998

LOCATION	OCT. 17	OCT. 18	OCT. 19	OCT. 20	OCT. 21	TOTAL
Aransas Refuge		2.13	3.5	0.01		5.64
Austin Airport	6.24	1.46	1.02	0.1	0.15	8.97
Blanco	3.63	3.25	0.43	0.21	0.08	7.6
Burnet	2	1.6	0.1	0.4	0.1	4.2
Cuero		3.37	3.05			6.42
Goliad		5.52	1.04	0.03	0.05	6.64
Gonzales		11.83	1.62	1.93	0.56	15.94
Hallettsville	5.75	3.76	1.88	0.02	0.08	11.49
Johnson City	3	2.6	0.22	0.41	0.12	6.35
Lockhart		13.38	0.78	2.45		16.61
Luling	trace	10.53	1.8	2.07	0.74	15.14
New Braunfels		18.35	2.6		2.3	23.25
Refugio 3 SW			9.5	0.12	0.16	9.78
San Antonio Airport	11.26	3.16	1.19	0.03	0.02	15.66
San Marcos	15.78	2.86	2.02	1.84	0.06	22.56
Seaworld	8.2	2	0.95	0.01	0.01	11.17
Temple	9.62	0.02	0.53	0.22		10.39
Victoria ASOS	0.35	3.27	0.15	0.06	0.01	3.84
Wimberley 2ESE		12.5	0.52	0.98	0.06	14.06

Cibolo Creek

North and northeast of San Antonio, Cibolo Creek took a direct hit from the torrential rains. Some Bulverde residents were rescued from rooftops, while at LaVernia, water from the creek stretched two miles wide. Jet skis and front-end loaders rescued stranded residents. Cibolo Creek reached a flow that was greater than its one-hundred-year peak rate and was the mightiest since before 1869 in Selma and before 1890 at Falls City.

San Marcos River

Above San Marcos and along the Blanco, a dramatic situation similar to that in San Antonio played out along Cypress Creek in Wimberley. Around 8 A.M. drizzle began falling, and thirty minutes later a flood struck along Cypress Creek. At 9 A.M. four-foot-deep currents were swirling inside condos and buildings along the stream. One long-time resident said, "I've known Wimberley 71 years and this is some kind of rain. I've never seen it over the high water bridge."[4] Another resident added, "No one ever thinks it's going to happen. You look out there [at Dry Cypress Creek] and it's all rocks and dry."[5] The heavy precipitation also hit in the San Marcos area, where floodwaters reached into Strahan Coliseum, depositing two feet of mud.

Looking upstream from the Garden Street bridge (photo by Jonathan Burnett).

Upstream from the Garden Street bridge (photo by Jonathan Burnett).

276

Gruene after the flood of October 1998 (photo by Jonathan Burnett).

Gruene, October 1998 (photo by Jonathan Burnett).

Austin Area

The rains in Austin pushed Shoal Creek out of its banks and into businesses between the eighth and twelfth blocks of Lamar Boulevard. Elaborating on the Whole Foods Market's newly acquired moniker, "Whole Floods Market," the current owner commented, "There was a reason no one moved in here earlier." The owner of the property said, however, "We fully disclose to everybody that this place floods. It's not that it might flood. It floods." [6]

The worst damage in Austin was not along Shoal Creek. In south Austin, Williamson Creek and Onion Creek hit high levels. Houses along the former were inundated with several feet of water. Residents said it was the most water they had seen in twenty years. Onion Creek was thirty feet above normal levels, which was second only to the flood in 1929.

Guadalupe River

The heavy rains north of San Antonio on October 17 created an extreme runoff in the Guadalupe River basin near New Braunfels. The Guadalupe then sent savage floodwaters through Gruene, devastating the riverside recreational businesses. Water along River Road rose ten feet in only thirty minutes.

Heavy rain in New Braunfels brought high water to small streams in the area. Many city streets were flooded by 10:30 A.M. By 12:30 P.M. houses were seen floating down the Guadalupe along Rio Drive. Half an hour later, water was entering homes along Rio Drive.

The Comal River rose to its highest level since before 1869. Landa Park was flooded, and the waters damaged the facilities at Schlitterbahn water park, rearranging picnic tables and damaging the Surfenburg area. The current also ripped away several cabins along the bend of the river from San Antonio Street to Garden Street. The currents and debris also knocked out portions of the concrete bridge rails and reached into the lower floor of the condominiums next to the Garden Street bridge.

Several blocks down from there, the Guadalupe and Comal rivers met. Above the convergence, the Guadalupe tore houses off their foundations. One man living near Common Street said, "I had my grandkids, and the water was in the back yard and rising fast, so we got out fast. I know this river, and I know it's nothing to toy with."[7] In the Guada-Coma community, the floodwater covered houses that, in the 1972 flood, had water almost to their rooftops. One home on steel stilts was "cut off like a razor blade" when a neighboring house slammed into it.[8]

The flood, as in 1972, wreaked havoc on Rio Drive, where residences were wrenched from their foundations once again. Water reached a depth of eight feet in homes that were left standing. One person who had bought a house on the street eight months earlier said, "I don't want to live on the river anymore."[9]

One of the most noteworthy businesses inundated by the flood was the *New Braunfels Herald-Zeitung,* whose newspaper offices were located near Dry Comal Creek, upstream from Landa Park. In the afternoon of October 17 water threatened the building, prompting the publisher and workers to move computers out of the building around 4 P.M. By 8 P.M. water was chest deep in the building. The staff then moved into the publisher's house and finished preparing the paper, which was printed at the

Schlitterbahn (photo by Jonathan Burnett).

Seguin Gazette-Enterprise. Publisher Doug Toney stated, "Come hell or high water, we promise to do whatever it takes to keep the HZ coming to your doorstep."[10]

Casualties would certainly have been higher if the flood had not developed in the daytime hours. (In 1972 it arrived in the middle of the night.) The assistant to the city manager said, "When you think of the magnitude of what rolled through the city, the loss of life was amazingly low."[11] As New Braunfels residents recovered from the shock and dealt with their grief, they called on the same resolve that had helped them cope with the devastation wrought by the 1972 flood and implement flood-control measures along Blieders Creek. Publisher

Flood debris and damage at Schlitterbahn (photo by Jonathan Burnett).

Gruene, October 1998
(photo by Jonathan Burnett).

Garden Street bridge and
damage to adjacent building
(photo by Jonathan Burnett).

Foundations where cabins
once sat at Schlitterbahn
(photo by Jonathan Burnett).

Foundations of cabins washed away at Schlitterbahn (photo by Jonathan Burnett).

Common Street bridge in New Braunfels (photo by Jonathan Burnett).

Flood damage at Schlitter-bahn (photo by Jonathan Burnett).

Tables carried away by currents at Schlitterbahn (photo by Jonathan Burnett).

Debris at Comal River near Landa Park (photo by Jonathan Burnett).

Toney of the *Herald-Zeitung* said, "We will not just survive; we will prosper. That's our history. And it will be our future." [12]

The flood that battered New Braunfels also churned its way to Seguin. One subdivision there, Glen Cove, was warned at 1:36 P.M. that the flood would reach 25 feet. At 5 P.M. the river was 28 feet. At 5:07 P.M. a pickup truck came floating down the river. Glen Cove, Elmwood Village, and Parkview were the hardest-hit subdivisions in Seguin. At Starke Park, the office was inundated with 5–6 feet of water, and boats were strewn about the greens of the golf course. The Guadalupe at Seguin peaked at 36.5 feet at 1:10 A.M. on October 18. Flooding along Geronimo Creek also damaged houses and threatened lives.

Following the initial deluge on the Guadalupe River on October 17, floodwaters were predicted to reach the forty-five-foot level in Gonzales on October 20. Gonzalez City Manager Andy Rodríguez said, "We knew we were going to get a flood, rain or not." However, torrential rains started falling at 3:30 P.M. on October 17. As water from the San Marcos River met with Guadalupe water upstream of the city, the flood wave rose higher and picked up speed as it charged through Gonzales.

The publisher of the *Gonzales Inquirer,* Charles Wood, recalled his first sight of the deluge and his immediate recognition of its magnitude, both in flood stages and the impact on the community. The flood ended the giddiness of the previous night, when Gonzales upset Cuero in a key district football game. Wood said that he was "on top of the world yesterday because Gonzales upset Cuero. That was the number one story in town. Not any more." While driving, Wood was worrying about the deadline for the newspaper. At Luling, he "couldn't get out on 183 because the Guadalupe was over the bridge." He switched to Highway 80 in the hope of getting to Interstate 10 but then saw "what [he] was getting into. The San Marcos River was about to rise over the bridge." As he saw a road sign that was completely under water, he noticed that Highway 183 south of Interstate 10 looked like "Lake Amistad. . . . The thought occurred to me: I could get killed driving in this."[13]

At Luling, the San Marcos River and Plum Creek created quite a mess. Homes hundreds of yards from Plum Creek were inundated with several feet of water. Round hay bales were slammed into the fencing along Highway 183 south of Luling. Between Luling and Gonzales, Palmetto State Park was also overwhelmed by the water, as was the neighboring Warm Springs Hospital, where helicopters removed patients to safety.

The flood wave from the two rivers rushed toward Gonzales, devastating the Lake Wood Recreation Area outside of town. Cabins on an island in the lake were demolished or went missing, and the office at the park was washed off its foundation. The camping area remained submerged for more than a week.

In Gonzales, water reached to the southern edge of the city's residential area and also engulfed Green DeWitt village on Sunday afternoon, October 18. One resident of the village said, "I was looking at the water coming up from the back window. But I didn't ever think it would come in from the front."[14] The floodwaters smashed into Independence Park as well, knocking over the baseball field fences, gutting the golf course sheds, and washing away the golf carts. Just south of Gonzales, floodwater from the river, which is one to two miles away, covered Highway 183.

Cuero Flood

On the way to Cuero, the Guadalupe River crosses Highway 183 at Hochheim.

Garden Street bridge (photo by Jonathan Burnett).

Water there covered all of the lowlands, washing hay and hay bales over the road and into fences. An eighty-year resident of Hochheim was evacuated at 8:30 A.M. and stated that that was the first time his house had ever been flooded. The crest did not occur there for another 5½ hours.

The predictions from the Western Gulf River Forecast Center and National Weather Service indicated that the peak would arrive in Cuero on October 20. As more data came

October 1998 flood in Gruene (photo by Jonathan Burnett).

into the prediction centers and were verified by eyewitnesses, forecasters accelerated the flood's arrival and peak stage. Still, residents and officials in Cuero were not expecting the rise until October 20. On October 19 the city's situation went from near normal to unprecedented crisis as water covered half of the town, approximately one day earlier than townspeople expected. Homes floated onto major streets, bodies of cows were deposited in bridges, and livestock sought shelter on the tops of houses. An estimated four thousand of Cuero's seven thousand citizens sought shelter. The peak stage, which occurred at 7 P.M. on October 19, was measured at 48.89 feet.

One man commented that he had "raced from tornados in the Katy area, experienced the destructive force of a hailstorm at Arneckeville, and worked day and night at an evacuation shelter in Houston during Hurricane Carla. But nothing I had previously seen or experienced had prepared me for the soul wrenching sights I observed as my wife and I drove into Cuero this past weekend." [15]

Victoria Flood

As the flood sped toward Victoria, officials prepared for the worst. They knew the flood had beaten the estimates of its arrival time at Cuero. Victoria residents heard that part of the flood was caused by a break at the small dam outside of town, but, as officials noticed, the volume of water coming through that opening would hardly affect the volume of water rushing down in the flood. At Victoria, the Guadalupe River peaked at 34.2 feet, and the zoo was forced to release the animals and perform emergency evacuations.

JUNE 2001

~~~~~~~

Tropical Storm Allison Flood in Houston

THE SHOWERS AND thunderstorms that follow the outer "pinwheel" bands (called feeder bands) of hurricanes and tropical storms and precede the eye flow counterclockwise into the center of low-pressure systems. If one of these tropical systems stalls over the Texas Coast, its feeder bands can tie into the copious moisture in the Gulf of Mexico. In such cases, it is possible for torrential rains to continue for hours and hours without interruption.

In 2001 Tropical Storm Allison came ashore near Houston and moved northward before looping back and parking itself over east-central Houston. While sitting there, the unlimited moisture from the Gulf of Mexico fed into the storm and turned into a sheet of rain falling over the city, with its flat landscape and bayous. Tropical Storm Allison's multiday deluge over Houston produced flood stages in several streams that exceeded the five-hundred-year flood levels. Streets were inundated, and concrete-lined creeks and drainage ditches overflowed. The resulting surges of water overwhelmed the engineered solutions that had been established to guard against inundation.

Tropical Storm Allison

The origins of Tropical Storm Allison, the first tropical storm of 2001, were linked to a tropical wave exiting Africa to the west on May 21. The disturbance moved westward and migrated into the Pacific Ocean before heading north. In early June the National Weather Service Office in Houston was waiting for replacement parts for its radar. On June 4 the parts arrived, and the radar was operational once again. Nobody knew that in the next five days the radar would be heavily relied upon to document and predict one of the great rain events in North America.

On June 4 the disturbance was located in the Bay of Campiche. At 9:55 A.M. on June 5, the National Weather Service labeled the storm system "the Blob."[1] Forecasters did not believe they were dealing with a tropical storm until the reconnaissance airplane flew through the center of the disturbance. The aerial measurements recorded a core temperature that was warmer than expected, indicating more of a tropical system than anyone had anticipated. Thereafter, the storm developed rapidly.

By the afternoon of June 5, the system officially became a tropical storm approximately eighty miles south of Galveston. The National Weather Service commented, "The tropical season is under way . . . and we have the misfortune of having to deal with the first one . . . Allison."[2] Allison moved inland that evening. At that point, the NWS reported that it would be dealing with "a precipitation engine."[3]

The steering winds over southeast Texas were controlled by one high-pressure ridge west of Texas and a second one east of Florida. In the morning update, the NWS stated, "We had been complaining lately that we needed more rain. The last 24 hours should keep us happy for a while."[4] Later, on June 6, the NWS stated that Allison's center was difficult to locate, adding that it "looks more like a trough."[5]

On June 7 the ridge over Florida weakened, and the one to the west strengthened. The center of Allison responded by moving in a clockwise loop and then drifting to the southwest. Water vapor images showed two moisture axes to the south—over the Gulf of Mexico. They were aligned to be injected into Allison's flow, potentially bringing torrential rain. At 1:44 P.M. the National Weather Service warned, "The remnants of Allison will continue to be a serious and dangerous weather player for southeast Texas on into the weekend."[6]

Weather models were predicting that the system would move to the west, perhaps bringing another catastrophic Hill Country flood caused by another dying tropical storm. Instead, the meandering system stalled and drifted toward Brenham. On June 8 the center was located between College Station and Huntsville. The National Weather Service's update at 3:37 A.M. on June 8 warned, "Precipitation efficiency will be extreme tonight through Saturday [June 9] night. . . . Extreme rainfalls will not be out of the question and look out for Saturday!"[7] As the forecasters feared, Allison now was close enough to the gulf to funnel another series of disastrous downpours onto Houston.

The National Weather Service's 9:45 A.M. update on June 8 advised, "Despite the current lull . . . this heavy rain event is nowhere near from being over!"[8] That afternoon, the NWS was confidently predicting that isolated areas would receive more than ten inches of rain overnight. By June 9, the center had moved to the south near Brenham in the morning and near Palacios that evening. The deluge that devastated central Houston struck during the night of June 8 and the morning of June 9. At 2:45 A.M. the NWS called the unfolding event "a bad night indeed."[9]

Allison moved sharply southeast, skirting the southwestern side of Houston. By 10 A.M. on June 9 Allison was near the coast again. Within the next twelve hours, Allison exited Texas less than fifty miles from where it had entered. In doing so, it became the first tropical storm to enter Texas from the Gulf of Mexico and to exit the state in the same location.

Even after leaving Texas, Allison's effects were far from over. As the storm moved across the coastal regions of Louisiana, Alabama, and Mississippi, it spawned deadly tornadoes and flooding. Areas near Gulfport, Mississippi, and Tallahassee, Florida, received 10–12 inches of rain. As it moved over North Carolina, it dumped 8–21 inches. Before dying out, Allison dropped 8–10 inches in southeastern Pennsylvania on June 16 and 17, more than a week after it had dropped 28 inches in Houston.

Rainfall

Allison delivered heavy rains to Houston, southeast Texas, and south-central Louisiana in three episodes. First, when it moved northward on June 5, it dropped ten to twelve inches over the area. A second, less severe round for Houston hit on June 7 and poured down on southwest Harris County, flooding Sims and Keegans bayous. In Beaumont, up to a foot of rain fell on June 6 and June 7 before noon on June 7.

Allison's biggest blow, however, known as its "knockout punch," was delivered on the night of June 8, when the central portion of Harris County received more than 10 inches. Sections of Houston northeast of downtown recorded more than 25 inches. The twelve-hour total was more than 15 inches for most of central, northern, and eastern Houston. Rainfall rates were as high as 5 inches per hour.

Several rainfall totals were "off the charts," as a local flood district official described them. The recurrence interval for the rainfall at Greens Bayou at West Mount Houston surpassed the five-hundred-year storm for 2-, 6-, 12-, and 24-hour intervals. The recurrence interval at Hunting Bayou at Interstate 610 exceeded five hundred years for the 12- and 24-hour intervals, as did the 6-hour interval for White Oak Bayou at Ella Boulevard.

Locations with intervals calculated at one thousand years were Hunting Bayou at Interstate 10 for its 22.59-inch total in 12 hours and Greens Bayou at Mount Houston Parkway for its 21.19 inches in 6 hours, 28.33 inches in 12 hours, and 28.49 inches in 24 hours. Allison's rainfall ranked as the fourth highest total in Texas, falling behind only Tropical Storm Claudette's 43 inches in Alvin in 1979, the 40-inch total of the 1921 Thrall storm, and the 48 inches recorded at Medina in August 1978. The director of the Houston Weather Research Center said, "These slow-moving storms are always the ones that seem to give us the most trouble. They're just mean." [10]

Runoff

The June 5 rains affected mostly the southern areas of Harris County. Clear Creek, Sims Bayou, Brays Bayou, Armand Bayou, and Vince Bayou were hit the hardest. A resident in Pearland who was victimized by flooding for the fifth time said, "I'm leaving this time. I've had all of Pearland I want." [11]

Two residents in the Pasadena and Spencer Village area rode out the flood in their house—one clung to a floating mattress and the other a drifting dresser. Their house had flooded fifteen times in almost thirty years. An assistant to the mayor of Pasadena commented that many people in Spencer Village had more flooding than other residents living in the flood plain. One house in the Pearland and Friendswood neighborhood had been flooded eight times in five years.

On June 5 it took on four feet of water and then eight feet three days later.

The major flooding occurred after the deluge on June 8 and 9. After the rains of the previous three days, the soils were saturated. Allison's heavy rains produced runoff equal to 70–95 percent of the total rainfall and runoff values of 50–70 percent. The executive director of the Harris County Flood Control District said, "We don't design for that kind of water. So many aspects of Allison were just off the chart." [12]

Almost all of central Houston was flooded. When ditches and bayous overflowed, the streets and sewers were unable to contain the water. Runoff spilled into downtown tunnels. After the flooding, studies determined that 46 percent of central Houston was deluged when the rainfall surpassed the drainage capacity of the streets and sewers. In other words, almost half of central Houston was flooded not by rampaging streams and bayous but by water coming down faster than streets and storm sewers could carry it away.

The floods resulting from Allison exceeded historic peak levels in seventeen of forty gauging stations in Harris County. The most extreme flows and stages were recorded at Greens Bayou and Hunting Bayou. Greens Bayou at Mount Houston Parkway received more than twenty-eight inches in twelve hours. At Hunting Bayou, 28.65 square miles out of 29.77 square miles of total drainage area received flood damage. At Greens Bayou, 142.09 of 210.63 square miles were impacted.

Six stations recorded peak streamflows that exceeded the one-hundred-year interval: Sims Bayou at Telephone Road, Berry Bayou (a tributary of Sims Bayou) at Forest Oaks Street, Brickhouse Gully (a tributary to White Oak Bayou) at Costa Rica Street, Cypress Creek at Westfield, Halls Bayou at Jenson Drive, and Greens Bayou at Ley Road.

Bayou Flooding

With precipitation falling at the rate of almost 5 inches per hour, Greens Bayou at Mount Houston Road recorded 28 inches in 12 hours and then 12 inches in 3 hours. The peak streamflow for Greens Bayou at Ley Road more than doubled the previous record value (69,700 cfs versus 32,500 cfs on June 27, 1989). Rainfall rates exceeded the 100–1,000-year probabilities for Greens Bayou, whose 70,000-cfs peak flow was 115 percent of the previous high and also the highest peak streamflow of any creek in Harris County for the 2001 flood.

At Greens and Halls bayous, 22,000 residences were flooded, and local drainage overflows affected 6,400 properties. In many areas floodwaters were ten feet deep. The runoff produced overland flow that crossed from one watershed to another. Officials who were studying the inundation remarked, "This deep overland flow contributed substantially to the massive flood damage."[13]

The largest emergency shelter in northeast Houston was Lakewood Church (at 7313 Houston Street). Lakewood spokesman Donald Iloff said, "Everybody's swimming for the island. God is good, and he's going to help us through this."[14]

During the night of June 8 Hunting Bayou received 17–23 inches of rain, 14 of which fell within six hours. Major flood damage occurred all along the bayou, and deep overland flooding struck especially hard in the area west of Loop 610. Hunting Bayou at Interstate 610 bested its historic peak value as well when it reached a peak streamflow of 4,400 cfs (versus its previous high of 3,470 cfs).

Sims Bayou topped its historic peak streamflow values at Hiram Clarke Street and Telephone Road. At Hiram Clarke, the peak streamflow was 9,030 cfs (compared to 7,510 cfs in the October 18, 1994, flood). Sims Bayou's streamflow at Telephone Road more than doubled its previous record, which was the peak flow for a period of forty-nine years. The previous peak streamflow was

Floodwaters block the I-45/ I-10 interchange north of downtown Houston (Copyright 2001 Houston Chronicle Publishing Company, reprinted with permission, all rights reserved).

11,400 cfs on August 18, 1983, while the peak in the 2001 flood was 25,800 cfs. Although Sims Bayou was situated in the middle of its $320 million flood-control project, flood-control measures were partially in place only for the upper basin—not the lower.

White Oak Bayou meets up with Buffalo Bayou just northwest of downtown, and its streamflow records date back to 1935, the year of the flood in downtown Houston. During that event, the bayou's peak streamflow was 28,100 cfs, which was 3,000 cfs more than the previous peak. On the night of June 8, between eight and fifteen inches of rain fell within twelve hours. Record flooding was recorded at stations at Heights and Alabonson. Tributaries Little White Oak Bayou, Brickhouse Gully, and Cole Creek also recorded new records. Three thousand buildings were flooded by local drainage. White Oak Bayou overflowed and filled Interstate 10 west of downtown to create the incredible scenes of eighteen-wheel tractor-trailer rigs floating in the water. In the morning of June 9, the National Weather Service commented, "I-10 looks like a bayou with semi tractor trailer tops scattered about."[15]

A resident of Bliss Meadows near Armand Bayou said, "When we first came out here, we never had water in the neighborhood. There was nothing between Spencer Highway and Interstate 45 but Ellington Field. There were chickens and horses on the corner from us. There was nothing there, just wetlands. In the 28 years we lived there, Spencer Highway was redone and raised. . . . Eighteen buildings were put up in 28 years, all 2 feet higher than we were. When we moved out here, we weren't required to have flood insurance. Now I wouldn't live on top of Pikes Peak without it."[16]

In June 2001 modifications to Buffalo Bayou were being considered, and consultants were brought in to study the proposals. They had considered trying to make the bayou a constant-level body of water like the

San Antonio River in San Antonio. After the flood hit, however, those plans changed as the consultants "came to have a healthy respect for what bayous can do."[17]

Flooding in Brays Bayou was largely concentrated from Loop 610 downstream to Buffalo Speedway and from the state highway to Calhoun. Thirty-five hundred residences were reportedly flooded by local drainage or minor tributary overflows. The flooding at the Texas Medical Center was largely caused by an overflow along a tributary, Harris Gully.

Flooding at the Texas Medical Center of Houston

At St. Luke's Episcopal Hospital in the Texas Medical Center , an employee arriving on the afternoon of June 9 said, "I was com-

Semi-trailers and cars float on I-10 west of downtown Houston (Copyright 2001, Houston Chronicle Publishing Company, reprinted with permission, all rights reserved).

pletely unprepared for the devastation within the hospital. As daylight faded, the only lights remaining on the hospital's 25 floors were beams from flashlights. Without power, the usually cooled air was becoming hot and humidity-laden. . . . Without elevators, bottled water and ice were relayed 25 flights up to each patient-care area to assure hydration and hygiene for staff and patients."[18]

Memorial Hermann Hospital lost electricity, evacuated six hundred patients, and remained closed for more than a month. Researchers at Baylor College of Medicine lost thirty thousand lab animals. The University of Texas Medical School sustained $100 million in damage. The interim executive vice president for research affairs at the University of Texas said, "In terms of our medical school, everything was affected. Everything. Period."[19] The medical center's executive vice president added, "We are still collecting our thoughts, thinking about what we should have done differently. There's no passing the buck. We just didn't recognize how fast the water could come nor the impact it would have."[20]

Security videos recorded footage of manhole covers "bobbing on geysers of sewer water." Memorial Hermann's vice president for construction, engineering, and support services said, "It was a hypodermic effect. It wasn't just rising water but the pressure of 20 million gallons. It just literally blew out the walls; basically exploded the pathology lab and pharmacy."[21]

Thanks to the "submarine-style flood doors" that had been installed in the tunnels of Texas Children's Hospital, the building averted extreme flood damage. It was estimated that the flood doors kept out more than six million gallons of water, which was instead contained in the parking garage.[22] Following the flood, all critical operations were moved out of basements, prompting the University of Texas' interim executive vice president of research affairs to say,

"Heaven forbid that we ever have another flood. But if we do, we're just going to lose folding chairs."[23]

One family member accompanying an evacuee from the Texas Medical Center to a hospital in Katy said, "I feel this is out of a movie or TV. This cannot be real life."[24] In 1999 the medical center was warned that its drainage system could adequately handle only a 10-year flood. With Allison dumping a 100–500-year event on Houston, the devastation was nearly unimaginable. Reflecting on the destruction, Phil Bedient, at professor at Rice University, said, "It's the flood of the century. You've got the bayou way up, you've got this huge amount of rain hitting Rice and the Medical Center, and it's basically just a wall of water. I don't know if we can ever be prepared for a storm like this."[25]

Theaters

Some of the most startling flood damage came from runoff from the streets and involved downtown Houston's art and theater district. The overflow, in excess of 250 million gallons, swept into the City of Houston's underground parking garage at Tranquility Park and Jones Plaza, where the water blasted into the tunnels and found its way into the basements of numerous buildings.

At the Alley Theatre, cast members returned from a visit to a neighborhood bar about 1 A.M. Due to the ongoing deluge, they stayed at the theater. At 3 A.M., the sound of rushing water awakened them as water filled the lower levels of the building. One stage filled with eight feet of water. The theater's managing director, Paul Tetreault, said, "Set pieces were bobbing around. It was like something out of Titanic or The Poseidon Adventure." It took two weeks to pump all of the water out of the theater. Phones were down for four weeks, and the air conditioning was inoperable for six weeks.[26]

One member of the Houston Symphony Orchestra lost his two-hundred-year-old double bass to the deluge. The symphony's library was in the basement, where hundreds of thousands of musical scores were soaked in floodwater. Many scores were freeze dried, and conductor's notes were handwritten. The orchestra's spokesperson said, "This is a catastrophe for us." One of the losses was a grand piano donated by Ima Hogg.[27]

Downtown Tunnel System

Flooding from the tunnel system under the Bank of America building was blamed for the drowning death of a woman in an underground parking garage. Initially, it was believed the elevator had flooded. Later, "workers, who themselves narrowly escaped the water, theorized [she] was swept away as she dashed for the elevator."[28]

Basement Flooding

One builder said, "We need to rethink the use of basements. We're not going to change our topography, and there's only so much we can do about flood control."[29] Some garages contained up to 30 feet of water.

Highway Flooding

Area residents gathered to watch the flooding of their landmark highways. One resident at the Mandell Bridge of U.S. 59 said, "We saw it on TV and on TV it looks fake." Another spectator said, "I can't believe 59 is a river."[30]

Miscellaneous

The deluge placed a premium on rental cars, and at local offices, waiting lists fre-quently contained a hundred names. In ad-dition, downtown flooding knocked out the primary and secondary power supplies for the Pulse network of automated teller machines (ATMs). The power outage was expected to affect 76,000 ATMs in twenty-two states. At the University of Houston, the law library lost 250,000 books worth $35 million. It was estimated that the floodwater dumped on Houston could have filled the Astrodome 5,600 times.

Total Flood Damage

Allison's flooding damaged 73,000 homes and caused more than $5 billion in damage. More than 95,000 vehicles were flooded.

Category 5 Hurricane

Scientists and planners looked into the consequences of the most intense hurricane, a category 5 storm, hitting the Houston area. One study predicts that a dome of water up to fifty miles wide and thirty feet high would invade Galveston bay toward Houston. Storm surges from the event would inundate twenty-five percent of Harris County. Whereas Allison's runoff blocked most roads for about half a day, this storm would prevent travel for several days. Rice University professor Phil Bedient, an expert on hydrology, especially that of the Houston area, stated, "In Houston and Galveston, we really haven't been hit as hard as we could be."[31] Moreover, Harris County Judge Robert Eckels said that, in such an event, "We're not going to tell people to leave their homes for no reason. If they stay behind, they're going to see something of a scale that is almost unimaginable."[32]

JULY 2002

~~~~~~~~~~

Guadalupe River Flooding

THE JULY 2002 flash floods marked an unprecedented event for the Guadalupe River Basin and Canyon Dam. Multiple rises from the river into Canyon Lake eventually topped the large flood-control dam and cut a new channel below the emergency spillway. These events provided data that have enabled scientists to study the formation of channels. Unfortunately for one of Texas' most water-oriented cities, New Braunfels, this translated into one the town's worst deluges. For residents living above New Braunfels, the flood wave from the spillway overflow meant that the land they believed would never be flooded was covered with many feet of water. This set of flash floods devastated Hill Country residents who had withstood the 1998 floods and rebuilt, often in the same areas that were flooded in 1998.

Rainfall

Prior to the flooding rains, all of South Central Texas was dry. At Edwards Aquifer, the water level for San Antonio dipped below 650 feet on June 26, triggering stage 1 restrictions. The day before (June 25), showers began falling in South Texas and spread farther west over the next four days. The first rounds of heavy rain on June 30 hit the San Antonio and Austin areas. During this time, tropical moisture stretched from Tampico, Mexico, to Oklahoma. A trough that was forecast to move westward interacted with an upper-air disturbance to produce the rains. However, because an upper ridge over West Texas kept the trough nearly stationary, it did not move west as predicted. Instead, it parked itself over South Central Texas and siphoned tropical moisture into the region. In early July this moisture hit the orographic lift of the Balcones Escarpment, focusing heavy rains along the escarpment's southern edge.

On July 2 and 3 the showers and heavy rain started and spread northward. By July 5 San Angelo's forecasters were commenting on the unusual weather pattern: "So this is July in West Texas!" More rain is on the way!"[1] They added, "It may be our chance to fill some reservoirs. May not be a drought buster . . . but it ain't going to hurt."[2] By July 8 forecasters were quipping, "Where is our usual summer upper-level high when you need it?"[3]

June 30 marked the beginning of the torrential rains. At Hye, 8.8 inches fell, and nearby Bankersmith received 5.2 inches. Burnet and Dripping Springs tallied nearly identical amounts: 5.65 inches and 5.64 inches, respectively. On July 1, 9.52 inches fell in San Antonio, the city's second highest daily total and a new monthly record for July. Rainfall rates up to 4.5 inches per hour were recorded over north San Antonio. Bankersmith, near Luckenbach, recorded

Aftermath of Guadalupe River flooding at Common Street (photo by Jonathan Burnett).

the highest official rainfall for that day: 10.9 inches. South of San Antonio, Dilley and Tilden received more than 9 inches of rain in storms that were identified as producing rainfall rates up to 6 inches per hour. Three sites with heavy rainfall in the first six days of July received some of the highest totals on July 1. Comfort, Camp Verde, and Sisterdale all recorded between 6 and 8 inches that day.

After the July 1 rains, the National Weather Service forecasters were still focused on the extended drought: "To the question about the drought . . . Is it over? No. It is only momentarily suspended until it stops raining and then the drought will return."[4] The next day, a downpour struck Uvalde. For the first six months of 2002, Uvalde had received only 5.47 inches of rainfall. From 9:30 A.M. to 10:45 A.M. on July 2, the town received 7.75 inches of precipitation. To the north, Leakey recorded 7.9 inches. Other sites with heavy rains on July 2 were Comfort (7.43 inches), Vanderpool (6.3 inches), and Boerne (6.13 inches).

On July 3 the heavy rains continued over South Central Texas but also stretched farther north. Hill Country locations that received more than 5 inches that day included Boerne, Kerrville, Camp Verde, Kendalia, Sisterdale, Comfort, Bankersmith, and Utopia. To the north, Coleman recorded almost 5 inches. From July 4 to 6, the rains were less extreme but still excessive in several areas. The peak rains for this period hit the Abilene area, Boerne, Camp Verde, Tarpley, Utopia, and Vanderpool. Throughout the latter part of the deluges in Central Texas, West Texas and the Panhandle also received heavy downpours. On July 5 both Alpine, Texas, and Carlsbad, New Mexico, reported street flooding. Roads near Marathon and in parts of Terrell County were closed briefly in the next two days. For the first ten days of July 2002, the rainfall total made that month the third wettest in San Antonio history.

San Antonio Area Runoff

In San Antonio, the heavy rains on July 1 created a flood situation similar to the one that plagued much of Houston as a result of Hurricane Allison. The runoff overwhelmed the local drainage system. Near Woodlawn Lake, houses were inundated as water came in through doorways. One homeowner had been protesting the city's recent designation of his house as lying in the one-hundred-year floodplain. After water broke through his door and flooded his home, he was glad he had paid the premium for flood insurance.[5]

San Antonio's city engineer said, "The magnitude of the flood was far beyond what the drainage system in the district was de-

Flood in Sabinal River Basin, July 2002

Bandera after the flood, July 2002 (photo by Jonathan Burnett).

Guadalupe River flooding at Highway 281 bridge (taken at peak of flood, photo by Jonathan Burnett).

Guadalupe River flooding at Highway 281 bridge (photo by Jonathan Burnett).

GUADALUPE RIVER FLOODING

Luckenbach

A furious flash flood tore through historic Luckenbach on the night of July 1, and a long-time resident described it as the worst flood since 1952, when the water was only knee deep in buildings. In the 2002 flood, water was eight feet deep in the general store and demolished the cotton gin, where machinery weighing 5,000–8,000 pounds was toppled. During the cleanup, friends of Luckenbach arrived from all over the country to help. One Louisiana businessman offered a high-power vacuum for free, explaining, "This is not about business. It's about Luckenbach."[9]

The flood also demolished a mobile home whose occupants escaped at 4 A.M. after hearing creaking sounds that "sounded like a boat dock." Despite having to wade to their truck, where the water was up to the door handles, they managed to get away. They stated that "within three minutes . . . the lights were out . . . and it [the mobile home] was gone."[10]

Frio River

The Frio River rose abruptly throughout its picturesque Leakey-to-Concan stretch. The Leakey correspondent for the *Uvalde Leader News* described the scene there: "The water just flowed through the downtown area of Leakey. It came off the mountains and springs and the gorges just filled up."[11] With reports of "sheets of water" drenching the town and tallies of nine inches within two hours, area camps were on the alert. The swell came suddenly, and campers had only fifteen minutes to seek higher ground or safety in trees and rooftops. One camper said, "I thought we were going to get washed away. I haven't been this scared since I was in Vietnam."[12]

This rise, more than any other in recent history, startled long-time residents. An

signed for."[6] During the peak of the flash flood, one resident commented, "I think it was a Cadillac that I saw floating down the street there like a boat."[7] The heavy rains in the northwest section of the city produced runoff that again flooded Rudy's Barbecue and the original location of the Macaroni Grill. With the repeated showers, San Antonio's chief engineer said, "In an event like this one, the ground gets saturated and sheds water just like concrete."[8] Olmos Dam caught 38.59 feet of water, approximately 10 feet less than during the 1998 flood.

294 Uvalde architect who built above the one-hundred-year flood line found three feet of floodwater in his home. One long-time resident along the river had been measuring floods for more than sixty years. His son noted, "Daddy has been making a mark on a metal tank in front of the house for years—the flood of 1966, 1973, 1998. This one was taller than the tank itself."[13]

The owner of Neal's Lodge said, "This has never happened before, even in the 1930s when my grandmother was here."[14] The Dry Frio and other tributaries also raged through the basins, destroying the Happy Hollow Grocery along tiny Pecan Creek. After the flood, a steakhouse run by a local camp owner served as a makeshift shelter.

Sabinal River

With the heavy rains at Vanderpool, the Sabinal River rose swiftly on July 2 and July 5. On July 2 a man was washed off his tractor by the currents and swept to his death. As many as four houses were also carried away in that rise, and Utopia's park and several campgrounds were devastated as well. On July 5 the river rose again, cutting off Utopia. The owner of the Lost Maples Cafe in the center of town said, "You can see the river from the cafe. I've never seen it like this before."[15] The general store in Utopia took on six inches of water, and the store owner said, "We can't evacuate anywhere. When you stand in the middle of the road, you can see the river."[16] One Utopia resident added, "It was a good blessing for us that people at the headwaters were calling down the river to warn us of the impending danger."[17]

Medina River at Bandera

On June 29 the Medina River at Bandera was trickling past the gage at 15 cfs, just a few days before the floodwaters surged through town. On July 2 water invaded the shops in

Bandera Village, and front-end loaders and large trucks were brought in to evacuate people. When two of the trucks stalled, rescuers formed a human chain to get people to higher ground. The county judge commented, "I've lived here 56 years. The last time I saw this much water was in 1978, when we had a major flood. . . . This one isn't as bad."[18]

The highest water was recorded on July 5, when the flood wave carried away buildings and the mascot of the Jellystone RV Park on the shore of the river. Water invaded the buildings along Highway 16 southeast of downtown and reached well into the Bandera Village, where it rose to a depth of three feet in the Dairy Queen. Upstream from downtown, the river spread well across Highway 16, into the co unty maintenance

Bandera flood damage, July 2002 (Photo by Jonathan Burnett).

Remnants of gin at Luckenbach along Grape Creek (Photo by Jonathan Burnett).

Guadalupe River flooding at New Braunfels on July 6, 2002 (photo by Jonathan Burnett).

seventy-seven-year-old resident said, "I've never seen water like this before. I've seen a lot of flooding but nothing this bad since 1935 when the water washed out the train tracks in D'Hanis."[19] The river flooded a dance hall and an outdoor patio at Koenig Park with six to eight feet of water.

Guadalupe River Runoff

The multiple totals of more than five inches at Comfort, Sisterdale, and Camp Verde all flowed into the Guadalupe River. On July 3 the bridge over the Guadalupe near Bergheim was closed as the water neared the bottom of the structure. The peak stage at the Highway 281 bridge was 43.75 feet at 12:15 P.M. on July 3.

Despite the heavy runoff along the Guadalupe, local authorities and the U.S. Army Corps of Engineers did not anticipate an overflow at Canyon Dam. An overspill there had never happened before, even though it had been feared in both 1981 and 1987. As the inflow from the Guadalupe into Canyon Lake increased, the Corps of Engineers could not release water because its protocol prevented doing so when the flow at Gonzales exceeded 12,000 cfs (it had reached 17,000 cfs). But as the rains continued to pour down in the Kerr County area, sending the Guadalupe at Comfort to its highest levels of the event, authorities were concerned that the lake might overflow the spillway for the first time in its history. While monitoring the streamflow at Comfort, Comal County's engineer said, "Some of these numbers are looking pretty scary."[20]

At 1 A.M. on July 4 local officials issued warnings that the Canyon Dam would be topped for the first time ever. At 6 A.M., structures that would be affected by a flood of 28,000 cfs were evacuated. Only five hours later, the Corps of Engineers notified local authorities that the flood wave could reach 50,000 cfs. When water began pouring over

yard and up to the rodeo arena. Surprisingly, throughout the exceptional and extended flooding in Bandera, no lives were lost.

The currents of the Medina River charged south of Bandera and poured into Medina Lake, which rose quickly, especially on the morning of July 5. Water poured over the spillway at a record depth. In its prior peak overflow, in the record rainy year of 1919, water topped the dam by 6.9 feet. In this flood, the peak depth over the spillway was 10 feet, 4 inches.

The unprecedented overflow gouged the Medina River basin downstream of the dam. Trees that were more than one hundred years old were torn out of the earth and carried away. Castroville experienced its worst Medina River flood ever, and one

After the flood in Bandera, July 2002 (photo by Jonathan Burnett).

the spillway at 4:28 P.M., the Comal County judge soberly noted, "The thing you have to remember is that, once it goes over the top of the spillway, we have no control over it. We can't stop it . . . [or] slow it down."[21]

The flow over the spillway peaked on July 7. During the eight-hour period of maximum flow, more than fourteen billion gallons of water gushed over the spillway. The peak depth there was 7.32 feet. The torrent gouged out a new canyon downstream of the dam, decimating the bridge there.

Downstream at New Braunfels, the flood again ripped through much of the riverfront property that had been victimized in the 1998 flood. One resident said, "I can't believe it's happening again. It's like a dream. A bad dream." The county judge added, "I've been here my entire life, and I've never seen anything close to compare with what I saw today."[22]

Predictions mentioned numbers as high as 85,000 cfs. Fortunately, the actual streamflow fell well short of that estimate, topping out at 69,300 cfs at 10 A.M. on July 6. (My photos of New Braunfels were taken at 7:30 A.M. that morning.)

One New Braunfels resident who lived along the river (even though she had told herself she never would) said the river reminded her of a nursery rhyme about a little girl: "When she was good, she was very, very good. And when she was bad, she was horrid. That's what this river is."[23]

Perhaps the most reprinted image of the flood was the photograph of the nearly intact house floating down Common Street. When the owner of the house rebuilt on her river-front lot following the 1998 flood, she had constructed the new residence on a metal platform and steel stilts. As the water pounded on the home, it broke free from its supports and was gently launched down the river. Pictures remained on the walls, and flowerpots stayed in place on the porch. The owner said that, in the 1998 flood, her "house

didn't float, it was totally ripped apart." She had no plans to leave the river, however: "I would have no problem going back there. Your home is your home. Everyone knows that is where I live. My grandchildren say to people, 'That's granny's river.' "[24]

Brownwood

The July 3 rains caused water to cover Highway 67 near Brownwood and Coleman, while the DeLeon area was flooded by the

Flooded area of Guadalupe River near the "horseshoe" below Canyon Dam (photo by Jonathan Burnett).

Guadalupe River flooding at Bergheim near peak stage there (photo by Jonathan Burnett).

Flooded Guadalupe River Bergheim (photo by Jonathan Burnett).

Sabana River. The Cross Plains and Oplin area north of Brownwood recorded up to 11 inches of rain. On July 7 water flowed 7.7 feet over the spillway at Lake Brownwood. In the town of Brownwood, a two-square-mile section was covered with 3–4 feet of water. Although the commercial district near Pecan Bayou and the former traffic circle was again submerged, officials stated that the flooding would have been worse if the U.S. Army Corps of Engineers had not improved the channel for Adams Bayou, which flows into Pecan Bayou.

When the residents at the Day's Inn near Pecan Bayou were evacuated, the manager of the hotel noted that exaggerated reports contributed to a small-scale panic: "People come from the outside and tell crazy stories to the customers." One woman who was working to sandbag property commented, "I never thought we'd ask God to stop the rain in July."[25] The heavy rains north of Brownwood and south of Abilene pushed Lake Coleman over its spillway as well, and the overflow added to the rise at Lake Brownwood.

Abilene

Early in the morning of July 6, the storm system expanded and dropped heavy rains in the Abilene area. The southern and central sections of Taylor County (Buffalo Gap,

Lawn) received up to a foot of precipitation. Peak rainfall rates topped four inches at the Abilene airport and five inches on the south side of Abilene. A National Weather Service forecaster from the San Angelo office commented, "That storm Saturday just sat over Abilene and stayed there."[26]

The downpours from south of Abilene, near Buffalo Gap, flowed into Elm and Cedar creeks. Closer to Abilene, they also filled Cat Claw and Lytle creeks. Their floodwaters moved through Abilene, as did the overflow on Elm and Cedar creeks, filling Kirby and Lytle lakes. The inundation from Elm and Cat Claw creeks invaded sections of southwest Abilene that were not expected to flood. An Abilene police sergeant said, "We're going to have something that we didn't anticipate."[27]

Flooding hit Buffalo Gap, Tuscola, and Lawn especially hard. In Tuscola the postmaster was unable to reach the post office due to high water, so a mail carrier ran the office on July 6. Some sections of Buffalo Gap had water flowing several feet deep, and water was knee deep at the town hall.

Abilene Area

At 10 P.M. on July 6, Hubbard Creek at Albany was at 16.4 feet and expected to reach 31 feet by 1 A.M. and 32 feet by 7 A.M. the next

ABILENE AREA	JULY 1	JULY 2	JULY 3	JULY 4	JULY 5	JULY 6	JULY 7	JULY 8	TOTAL
Abilene 2	0.15	0.09	0.03	2.37	trace	3.54	5.03	0.14	11.35
Abilene Regional Airport	0.33	0.01	0.36	1.41		5.67	0.02		7.8
Aspermont				0.12	3	3	0.85	0.44	7.41
Coleman	0.24	0.03	4.72	1.26	0.22	1.85	0.32	0.02	8.66
Lawn	0.37		1.65	2.32	0.05	5.51	0.75		10.65

HILL COUNTRY									TOTAL
Blanco	2.88	2.52	3.5	1.13	2.27	0.29	0.02	0.05	12.66
Boerne	2.95	6.13	6.76	4.58	5.05	0.48			25.95
Brady	0.24	0.18	0.71	1.47	0.25	0.14			2.99
Burnet	0.4	0.5	3	0.8	2.1	0.1	0.52	0.02	7.44
Camp Wood	0.26	0.04	3.3	0.25		0.59			4.44
Del Rio	0.18	0.04		0.13	0.03	0.01	0.07		0.46
Fredericksburg	2.74	0.86	4.81	1.98	1.62		0.14		12.15
Johnson City	3.93	1.85	4.55	0.7	1.6	0.03		0.11	12.77
Kerrville 3 NNE	2.46	2.6	5.13	2.26	3.15	1.87			17.47
Lampasas	4.07	0.4	0.88	1.77	2.36	1.99		2.06	13.53
Uvalde 3 SW	0.88	7.22	1.2	trace	3.8			0.12	13.22
Canyon Dam	1.15	4.05	2.45	0.02	2	4.56	0.16	1.05	15.44
Dripping Springs 6E	0.87	3.12	4.46	0.63	0.47	0.06			9.61
Karnes City 2 N	1.29	3.34	0.38		2.91	0.37	0.52		8.81
Lytle 3 W	4.18	1.07	2.18	2.15	2.78	0.02			12.38
San Antonio Airport	9.52	2.01	1.25	0.89	1.36	0.02	0.12		15.17
San Marcos	1.28	3.49	1.09		0.6	0.02	0.43		6.91
Charlotte 5 NNW	5.5	0.03	1.25	1.95	2.3				11.03
Choke Canyon	4.45	0.52			1.2	0.06			6.23
Dilley	10.5	0.37	2.43		1.18	0.15			14.63
Fowlerton	4.2	1.36	2.93	0.45	1.5	0.2			10.64
Poteet	3.1	3.7		2	1.54	0.35			10.69
Tilden 4 SSE	9.13	1.65	0.73		1.05				12.56
Camp Verde	7.87	4.85	5.4	6.33	3.01	3.71			31.17
Kendalia	4.16	4.45	6.18	3.21	3.8	0.23			22.03
Sisterdale	6.5	4.6	8.75	3.5	4.2	0.55			28.1
Leakey		7.9	0.89	2.78					11.57
Comfort	8.09	7.43	6.04	3.05	2.44	0.69			27.74
Bankersmith	10.9	1.21	6.95	4.5	0.62				24.18
Tarpley	1.5	1.8	3.42	4.82	7.5	2.4	0.05		21.49
Utopia	0.7	4.55	5.99	6.44	2.55	3.79			24.02
Telegraph			0.82	0.13	2		0.06		3.01
Vanderpool 4 N	2.76	6.3		2.3	4.81	0.33	0.02		16.52

morning. Though the downpour approached a year's worth of precipitation, the Hubbard Creek Reservoir was still only half full.

Choke Canyon

Flows along the Nueces River were topped only by the June 1935 flood and the one following Hurricane Beulah in 1967. Those down the Atascosa River, which

peaked on July 2, ranked fourth in its history. At Tilden, the Frio River set a new record high when it hit 30.06 feet on July 10. By July 9, as floodwaters from the Nueces, Frio, and Atascosa rivers converged on Three Rivers, the area was swamped. The NWS at Corpus Christi stated that, at the approaching 40-foot level on the Nueces, "massive flooding reaches miles from the main channel."[28]

APPENDIX

~~~~~~~~~

Overview of Significant Texas Floods

START DATE	END DATE	LOCATION 1	LOCATION 2	DESCRIPTION
July 5, 1819		San Antonio		The 1819 flood reached levels similar to those of the 1921 flood in San Antonio. Houses at the Main and Military plazas were washed away. Other floods in the 1800s noted in the research of the 1819 flood occurred in 1852, 1865, 1866, 1868, and 1880.
June 1853		Concho River		The exact date of the flooding is not known. Reports indicate that the 1853 flood would have brought a flood depth of six feet at the courthouse in San Angelo.
July 3, 1869	July 6, 1869	Austin		The 1869 event is the flood of record for the Colorado River at Austin. A marker indicating the river level of that event is located along the hiking trail on the north shore of Town Lake near Congress Avenue in Austin. Rain fell for sixty-four hours, driving the river to a stage of forty-three feet.
May 27, 1880	May 30, 1880	Coleman	San Saba	High flood along the Colorado River. Near Coleman the river exhibited a thirty-foot rise.
August 14, 1880	August 17, 1880	West Central Texas	Fort McKavett	Streams were impassable from San Antonio to the Rio Grande. Fort McKavett near San Saba and along the San Saba River reported a rise to ten feet within ten minutes. At Horsehead Crossing, the Pecos River rise washed away the bridge.
August 27, 1880	August 30, 1880	Brackettville		Heavy rain produced a flood that covered the main street in Brackettville with eight feet of water. Reports indicated that more than twenty people drowned.
September 1880		Hill Country	West Texas	The Frio River near Uvalde was higher than ever before known.
February 1881		North Texas	East Texas	A week's worth of heavy, constant rainfall produced significant flooding along the Trinity River. Streams in the river basin reached their highest stages since the floods of 1852 and 1866.
November 1881		Rio Grande River		The southern portion of the Rio Grande River was reported to be higher than at any time since 1848.
August 23, 1882		Ben Ficklin		Torrential rains produced significant flash floods along the Middle Concho River, South Concho River, Dove Creek, and Spring Creek and inundated Ben Ficklin, the county seat of Tom Green County at that time. Sixty-five people drowned. The flood wiped out the town and prompted the relocation of the county offices to San Angelo.
April 28, 1884		Dallas		Intense rainfall produced runoff that caused the Trinity River to flow upstream, a condition last noted twenty-five years earlier.

START DATE	END DATE	LOCATION 1	LOCATION 2	DESCRIPTION
May 20, 1884	May 21, 1884	Statewide		Railway travel in Eastern Texas suspended due to washouts and damage to the tracks. Trinity River at Fort Worth was more than a mile wide and higher than in 1866. At Corsicana, Chambers Creek was more than 1½ miles wide. Flood rise on the Rio Grande at El Paso began on May 10 and reached Brownsville on May 26. The unprecedented event caused extensive damage and loss of life in El Paso.
May 27, 1885	May 31, 1885	Waco	Calvert	Heavy rains near Valley Mills helped to fuel the most destructive flood at that time at Waco. At Calvert, the Brazos River rose five feet above the previous highest flood mark.
August 29, 1887		Buffalo Bayou		Buffalo Bayou floodwaters claimed eleven lives.
June 3, 1889		Denton		Heavy rain caused the highest local flood in memory.
July 31, 1889		Fort Worth		Downpours produced the highest flood since 1866.
June 27, 1899	July 1, 1899	East Central Texas		One of the greatest rainstorms in Texas and U.S. history. Near Turnersville, more than thirty-three inches of rain fell over a three-day period, while an average of seventeen inches fell over an area of seven thousand square miles. The Brazos River reached a record high, and flood damage was estimated at nine million dollars. After unparalleled rain totals on June 28 and 29, all of the tributaries to the Brazos River from McClennan County to Brazos County were higher than ever before known. One long-time farmer stated that the Brazos flood was greater than those of 1885, 1852, 1843 and 1833.
April 1, 1900		South Concho River		The South Concho River reached a stage of approximately forty-five feet, which would roughly equal that of the 1882 flood.
August 1, 1900		San Angelo		An intense rainstorm directly centered on the Concho River basin produced a flood that was higher than the 1882 event in San Angelo but not as great as that of 1853 (fourteen years before the founding of Fort Concho).
September 20, 1900	September 24, 1900	North Texas	Central Texas	More than eleven inches fell in North and Central Texas. Flooding was reported on the Brazos, Trinity, and Colorado rivers. (This storm was not the Galveston hurricane of 1900.)
July 20, 1902	July 30, 1902	northern half of Texas		Up to seventeen inches fell in the region extending from Mitchell County (in West Texas) to western Louisiana. Extensive flooding in the Brazos River basin damaged large areas of cotton.
March 3, 1905		Junction	Castell	North Llano River near Junction reported a 22.9-foot stage. The Llano River at Castell reached 28.4 feet.
August 5, 1906		San Angelo	Ballinger	Rainfall estimated at 8½ inches fell on the Upper Colorado River. Flooding at San Angelo and Ballinger reached near-record stages.
May 22, 1908	May 25, 1908	Dallas	northern half of Texas	A large area of rain was produced by storms throughout Texas. Abilene received 6.78 inches in a twenty-four-hour period between May 22 and May 23. Flooding occurred from the Trinity River basin to the Nueces River basin. The most noteworthy event was the significant flood in Dallas, where the Trinity River peaked at 52.6 feet and was estimated to be two miles wide. The memory of the 1908 flood spurred Dallas's civic leaders to build the massive flood-control system the city now has.

START DATE	END DATE	LOCATION 1	LOCATION 2	DESCRIPTION
June 27, 1913		Uvalde	Laguna	Montell received 20.6 inches of rain. The Nueces River rose to 29 feet at Laguna and 26.4 feet near Uvalde.
October 1, 1913	October 4, 1913	San Antonio		Heavy rains in South Central Texas produced floods on the Colorado, San Antonio, Guadalupe, and Rio Grande rivers. A major flood moved down the San Antonio River. The San Antonio flood of October 1913 motivated city leaders to start considering flood protection. However, plans were not implemented until after the massive flash flood of September 1921 in the city. The San Antonio River rose to 28.35 feet, and the Cibolo Creek rose to 38 feet at Falls City.
December 1, 1913	December 5, 1913	Central Texas		A slow-moving winter storm system dropped more than ten inches over Central Texas after the wet autumn, including the October 1913 flood. Flash floods tore through Belton along Nolan Creek, and the Little River fed a large flood on the Brazos River.
April 22, 1914	April 28, 1914	North Central Texas		A rainstorm centered over Knox County fed floods on the Red, Trinity, and Brazos rivers.
August 5, 1914	August 9, 1914	South Texas		Thirteen inches of rain fell over Bee County, and the storm also dropped 5½ inches over an area of forty-eight thousand square miles. Flood damage was minimal due to prior dry conditions throughout the region.
October 21, 1914	October 25, 1914	West Texas	Coastal Texas	Up to fifteen inches fell in the West and Coastal Texas regions. Flooding was reported along the Rio Grande and the Guadalupe rivers.
April 20, 1915	April 26, 1915	Central Texas		Heavy rains produced flash floods on Waller and Shoal creeks in Austin, while flooding was reported on the Colorado, Brazos, Trinity, and Guadalupe rivers.
August 17, 1915	August 20, 1915	Eastern Texas		Remnants of a hurricane dropped 18½ inches at San Augustine.
November 5, 1918	November 8, 1918	North Texas		Stephenville received more than sixteen inches of rain, while area rivers flooded after the downpour.
June 21, 1921	June 25, 1921	East Texas	North Texas	Rainfall of as much as fourteen inches produced flooding on the Red and Sulphur rivers.
September 6, 1921	September 10, 1921	Central Texas		The great 1921 rainstorm produced rainfall rates at Thrall that approached world-record intensities. The storm also produced downpours in the headwaters of the San Antonio River, triggering a violent surge through downtown San Antonio in the middle of the night.
April 23, 1922	April 28, 1922	North Texas		More than twelve inches of precipitation fell over North Texas. Intense rains caused a rise on the Trinity River that flooded Fort Worth. The 1922 flood there precipitated the implementation of expanded flood control and levee systems in Forth Worth.
May 27, 1929		Blanco	Hays County	Localized, heavy precipitation fell in the Hays County area, producing sharp rises on Barton, Miller, and Onion creeks and on the Pedernales, Blanco, and San Marcos rivers. The Pedernales River rose to a 40.4 foot stage and discharged 155,000 cfs.

START DATE	END DATE	LOCATION 1	LOCATION 2	DESCRIPTION
May 31, 1929		Houston	San Jacinto River	Heavy rains in East Texas resulted in floods throughout the region. The San Jacinto River near Humble recorded its highest-known stage at that time. At the confluence of Buffalo and White Oak bayous, the waters rose to a stage of 34.3 feet. In 1879 flooding there produced a similar stage. Another high stage occurred in 1854.
October 6, 1930	October 14, 1930	Central Texas		Pecan Bayou at Brownwood peaked at 16.9 feet and discharged 52,700 cfs, the highest marks there since 1908. Brady Creek at Brady set a peak stage of 29 feet and inundated downtown Brady and the McCulloch County courthouse (see photo in Chapter 12). Brady Creek rose three times in eight days to invade or threaten downtown Brady.
June 30, 1932	July 2, 1932	Hill Country		Deluges fell in the upper reaches of the Guadalupe, Frio, and Nueces river basins. Peak totals fell along Johnson Creek above Ingram.
July 1, 1932		Hill Country		Downpours occurred in the upper reaches of the Guadalupe River and Nueces River basins.
August 26, 1932	September 8, 1932	West Texas	Rio Grande River	Sustained heavy rains fell over West Texas and Mexico. Extreme rises moved down the River Grande and Pecos rivers.
July 22, 1933	July 27, 1933	East Texas		Large rain-producing storms began over East Texas and then moved northeasterly out of the state. Seven inches of rain fell over 94,000 square miles, while fifteen inches fell over 10,000 square miles (including areas outside of Texas).
May 31, 1935		D'Hanis		One of the most intense rainstorms in Texas history. Twenty-two inches of rain fell within 2¾ hours. The two creeks that flow from north to south through D'Hanis went on a rampage and flooded the town.
June 15, 1935		Hill Country		Heavy rains in the headwaters of the Llano and Nueces rivers produced unprecedented rises in those two river basins.
December 6, 1935	December 10, 1935	Houston		In response to rainfall totaling as much as sixteen inches, Buffalo and White Oak bayous inundated downtown Houston.
June 30, 1936	July 4, 1936	South Texas		Heavy rains set off a series of floods in South Texas river basins. The most significant flooding occurred near the peak rainfall areas in Gonzales County, which received twenty-one inches. In the Guadalupe Basin, Plum and Sandies creeks experienced the worst flooding.
September 13, 1936	September 18, 1936	San Angelo		Multiple storms produced rises on the main tributaries to the Concho River at San Angelo. Peak rainfall totals reached thirty inches.
January 19, 1938	January 25, 1938	East Texas		As much as 10.73 inches fell over the period. The Sulphur River rose to a higher stage than ever before known. Peak discharge was 92,000 cfs.
June 15, 1938		Panhandle		Nearly fourteen inches fell in a four-hour period in the Lake Creek basin. Peak discharge near Hedley on Lake Creek was 64,700 cfs.
July 16, 1938	July 25, 1938	Upper Colorado River		Multiple large rainstorms dropped heavy totals over the Upper Colorado River basin. Large floods moved down Brady Creek, as well as the San Saba and Colorado rivers.

START DATE	END DATE	LOCATION 1	LOCATION 2	DESCRIPTION
June 19, 1939	June 20, 1939	Upper Colorado River		As much as nineteen inches fell within ten hours in the Upper Colorado River basin, causing flood waves to move down the Upper Colorado River. Deep Creek at Snyder saw a peak stage of 21.5 feet—higher than any stage since 1892.
June 29, 1940	June 30, 1940	South Central Texas		The area near the Lavaca River basin received nearly 22.7 inches of rain over a two-day period. The resulting flood produced a stage that was eight feet higher than any previous stage on the Lavaca River at Hallettsville. The floodwaters inundated downtown Hallettsville and reached into the Lavaca County courthouse. Smithville recorded 20.4 inches for the two days. Recording flooding occurred on the small streams between Smithville and La Grange.
November 21, 1940	November 26, 1940	East Texas		Peak rainfall for November 24 and 25 fell near Hempstead, which received 16 inches in fewer than twenty-four hours and 20.46 inches in the two-day period. From November 20 to November 26, more than 15 inches fell over an area of 3,380 square miles, and more than 10 inches came down over another area of 17,570 square miles. The San Jacinto River near Huffman was approximately one foot higher than earlier known stages dating back to 1876. The peak discharge there was 253,000 cfs. Palestine received 12.06 inches.
September 26, 1946	September 27, 1946	San Antonio		Rainfall up to sixteen inches fell in south and southeast San Antonio. At Falls City the San Antonio River peaked at 33.8 feet, a flood stage not broken until the deluges of 2002 in the San Antonio area.
May 1, 1949		Fort Worth		Thunderstorms dropped heavy rain upstream of Fort Worth. The resulting rise on multiple forks of the Trinity River inundated the city.
October 3, 1949		Lufkin		Remnants of a hurricane dropped heavy rain and caused localized flooding near Lufkin.
September 13, 1951	September 15, 1951	South Texas		Up to twenty-one inches of precipitation fell near Hebbronville. Thousands of acres were flooded by the runoff.
September 9, 1952	September 11, 1952	Hill Country		Rainfall totals of nearly twenty-six inches fell over the southern Hill Country. Violent flash floods erupted along the Pedernales, Guadalupe, and Blanco river basins.
June 24, 1954	June 29, 1954	West Texas		Remnants of Hurricane Alice dropped record totals over sections of the Pecos and Devils River basins. Ozona was hit by a flash flood.
April 1, 1957	May 1, 1957	entire state		The record-breaking drought of the 1950s was broken by a series of heavy rainstorms throughout the state. Some of the most extreme floods occurred at Lampasas, Fort Worth, Christoval, and Waco.
October 28, 1960		Austin		In the Central Texas region, 7–10 inches of rain fell. Flash flooding in Austin caused 2½ million dollars in damage.
September 7, 1962		Fort Worth		Nearly eleven inches fell within three hours in the Fort Worth area. Flash flooding moved down Big Fossil and Denton creeks, and floodwaters damaged Richland Hills and Haltom City.
September 21, 1964	September 23, 1964	Dallas County	Tarrant County	More than twelve inches fell on the morning of September 21. Flash flooding occurred on Dallas area creeks, and Fort Worth and McKinney were also affected.

START DATE	END DATE	LOCATION 1	LOCATION 2	DESCRIPTION
June 11, 1965		Sanderson		Localized, intense rainstorm dropped eight inches above Sanderson. A flood wave moved down normally dry Sanderson Creek, inundating Sanderson at daybreak.
April 22, 1966	April 22, 1966	East Texas		In East Texas 20–26 inches fell over the period. Rivers and creeks flooded much of Northeast Texas.
April 28, 1966		Dallas		Early morning rains on Joes Creek, Turtle Creek, Bachman Branch, and White Rock Creek basins produced rapid flash floods that cut through north central Dallas.
September 18, 1967	September 23, 1967	South Texas		Hurricane Beulah moved into South Texas and dropped more than twenty inches of rain over a large area there. Near Falfurrias, nearly thirty-six inches fell. Many South Texas streams produced major floods that damaged lowlands and washed out bridges.
May 20, 1970		San Marcos		Picturesque San Marcos and the headwaters of the San Marcos River received heavy rains, causing the multiple creeks that feed the river to flood the city.
May 11, 1972		New Braunfels		An intense, localized deluge fell on Blieders Creek and the Comal River, producing a rapid rise that tore through New Braunfels.
May 23, 1975		Travis County		Intense thunderstorms dropped hail and heavy rain. Flash floods hit Austin.
June 15, 1976		Harris County		Thirteen inches fell on Houston and produced flash floods in the downtown and central part of the city. Flooding damaged the Houston Medical Center area.
March 27, 1977		North Central Texas		Tarrant, Somervell, and Dallas counties were flooded by heavy thunderstorms.
May 26, 1978		Canyon		Heavy, violent thunderstorms dropped intense rainfall in the creeks that flow through the Canyon area. The resulting rises merged to form a flood wave that moved down Palo Duro Canyon.
August 1, 1978	August 4, 1978	Hill Country	Big Country	Tropical Storm Amelia moved over the Hill Country and produced a world-record-intensity event in nighttime rainfall. Remnants moved north to the Albany area, where another record rainfall occurred, dropping more than two feet of precipitation near Albany. Massive floods ripped through the Hill Country and then Albany.
September 20, 1978	September 27, 1978	West Texas		Remnants of Hurricane Paul moved into West Texas. Totals of more than twelve inches fell east of El Paso and west of the Guadalupe Mountains. The runoff flooded low-lying areas to the north of the Big Bend region of Texas.
July 24, 1979	July 25, 1979	Harris County		Tropical Storm Claudette stalled and dropped forty-three inches of rain over Alvin. Local creeks, streams, and bayous flooded.
September 5, 1980	September 8, 1980	Southeast Texas	West Texas	Remnants of Hurricane Danielle brought heavy rains to Port Arthur (17 inches) and to Junction in the west (25 inches). The Llano River experienced a significant rise in response to the rains over the Junction area.
May 27, 1981		Travis County		This event is known as the Memorial Day flood in Austin. On Sunday night of Memorial Day weekend, a thunderstorm stalled over Shoal Creek in northwest Austin. In the darkness, normally dry Shoal Creek ripped through Austin from north to south.

START DATE	END DATE	LOCATION 1	LOCATION 2	DESCRIPTION
June 1, 1981		South Central Texas		Heavy rains fell in the corridor between Austin and San Marcos. On June 14 San Marcos received 13.98 inches of rain.
August 31, 1981		Southeast Texas	South Texas	Heavy rains over South and Southeast Texas, including peak totals of more than sixteen inches, produced rises on area streams.
October 10, 1981	October 14, 1981	North Central Texas		Clyde and Callahan counties received nearly 23 inches of precipitation in a thirty-four-hour span. Gainesville, Breckenridge, and Bridgeport recorded more than 25 inches of rain from the remnants of Hurricane Norma.
October 30, 1981	October 31, 1981	Southeast Texas		Multiple storms produced flooding over Southeast Texas. The most noteworthy flooding occurred on the Lavaca River, which produced a repeat of the 1940 flood in Hallettsville. Floodwaters again inundated downtown, including the courthouse square.
September 16, 1984	September 19, 1984	Rio Grande River		Cameron and Willacy counties received nearly twenty inches of rain. The resulting flooding was the worst since Hurricane Beulah in 1967.
October 19, 1984		Odem		Odem received more than twenty-five inches of rain, which produced severe flash flooding in the coastal areas near the town.
July 16, 1987	July 17, 1987	Hill Country		In perhaps the most tragic example of a localized flash flood hitting at the worst possible time, a thunderstorm dropped intense rain upstream of Comfort. A church bus tried to leave a camp outside of town but was stalled by a wall of water. Children in the bus were then swept away by the currents.
April 20, 1990		Brownwood		A storm dropped heavy rainfall into tributaries feeding Pecan Bayou upstream from Brownwood. The resulting rise topped the dam and Lake Brownwood and flooded the traffic circle area of the city.
December 18, 1991	December 31, 1991	entire state		An extended El Nino–based flooding pattern set up over the state. The area from the Hill Country to North Central Texas received 12–16 inches of rain, and extreme rises occurred on numerous rivers. The Colorado and Pedernales rivers pushed Lake Travis to its all-time high of 710 feet and also to within 4 feet of topping Mansfield Dam on Lake Travis. Downstream of Austin on the Colorado, flooding was extreme.
October 15, 1994	October 19, 1994	Southeast Texas		A fall weather pattern set up a slow-moving storm system over Southeast Texas, where peak totals of 28.9 inches were recorded. The area north of Houston was inundated by overflowing creeks and rivers, including the San Jacinto River.
May 5, 1995		Fort Worth	Dallas	On the evening of May 5, a severe thunderstorm cluster moved through Fort Worth and Dallas, producing large, deadly hail in the Fort Worth area, as well as a rapid flash flood in Dallas.
May 29, 1995		Kingsland		Heavy rains over the Sandy Creek basin created the second-highest recorded stage on Sandy Creek at Kingsland. In the middle of the night a flood wave moved down Sandy Creek and trapped residents near the confluence of Sandy Creek and Lake LBJ.

START DATE	END DATE	LOCATION 1	LOCATION 2	DESCRIPTION
October 28, 1996	October 29, 1996	Llano River		Nearly thirteen inches fell in the Llano River basin upstream from Llano. The rise on the Llano River at Llano topped thirty-one feet, the highest stage since the 1980 flood. Downstream from the confluence with the Llano River, the Colorado River rose rapidly.
February 19, 1997	February 20, 1997	Hamilton County		Almost ten inches fell in portions of Hamilton County. On Cowhouse Creek and the Lampasas River, flash floods washed away bridges. Pecan Creek flooded throughout Hamilton, and the Leon River spilled over its banks.
February 20, 1997	February 21, 1997	Llano River		Eight inches of rainfall west of Llano County sent the Llano River on a rapid rise. The peak stage in Llano was recorded at 28.8 feet. Where the Llano River joins the Colorado to form Lake LBJ, the surge damaged many boats and other watercraft.
April 10, 1997	April 11, 1997	Lavaca County		Widespread 6-inch totals and isolated totals of up to 14 inches produced multiple flash floods in the Lavaca County area. Highway 95 between Shiner and Yoakum was closed due to high water.
June 21, 1997	June 22, 1997	Hill Country		In the Hill Country, several areas received more than ten inches of rain. Flooding was particularly significant at D'Hanis, Bandera, and Brownwood and along the Llano River.
June 21, 1997	June 22, 1997	Hill Country		Many locations in the Hill Country recorded nearly 15 inches of rain from a series of storms. Bandera received 20 inches, and Tarpley 21. At Spring Branch, the Guadalupe River reached a stage of 45 feet. At Boerne, Cibolo Creek topped 16 feet, its highest level since 1964. South of Bandera, a small dam gave way, and the resulting flood wave wiped out a bridge on Bear Creek. On State Highway 16 over Privilege Creek, floodwaters severely damaged a bridge. D'Hanis was inundated when floods came down Parkers and Seco creeks. Garner State Park reported that thirty-one cars were washed away by the rise on the Frio River. The Sabinal River reached its highest stage since 1958. A surge from the James River fed the Llano River, which topped the 38-foot stage in Llano. As the heavy rains moved eastward, Coleto and Sandies creeks both spilled over their banks.
August 22, 1998	August 25, 1998	Del Rio		From the coast of Texas, Tropical Storm Charley drifted to Del Rio, where it dropped more than seventeen inches of rain overnight. An unprecedented flash flood surged down the San Felipe Creek basin and destroyed many of the neighborhoods built along the scenic creek.
October 17, 1998	October 19, 1998	Hill Country		When moisture from multiple hurricanes and an upper air system united over the San Antonio–New Braunfels–San Marcos region, a disastrous situation unfolded. A large area encompassing the Hill Country rivers received rains of 10–20 inches.
October 17, 2000		Abilene		Downtown Abilene was damaged by flash flooding after seven inches of rain fell within three hours.
June 6, 2001	June 9, 2001	Houston		Topical Storm Allison moved onto the shore south of Houston, then looped around the city and dropped almost thirty-six inches of rain. Unprecedented flooding inundated the central and eastern sections of Houston.

START DATE	END DATE	LOCATION 1	LOCATION 2	DESCRIPTION
August 30, 2001		Stockdale		Up to eleven inches of rain fell east of San Antonio. Floods along State Highway 123 topped the five-hundred-year recurrence interval. In Stockdale, more than one hundred homes were deluged, and town residents stated that this event was the worst in recent memory.
November 15, 2001		Central Texas		Intense rains fell in Hay, Travis, and Williamson counties. Rapid rises moved through local creeks, first stranding and then sweeping away several motorists. A large area reported 5–8 inches of rain, while some locations received nearly 10 inches. Williamson, Onion, and Brushy creeks experienced extreme rises. Near downtown Austin, Shoal Creek flooded Lamar Boulevard.
April 25, 2002		Albany		Up to a foot of rain powered a flash flood on North Hubbard and Gourd creeks at Albany. Mobile homes were lifted from their foundations and hurled onto the Highway 180 bridge at the edge of town.
May 24, 2002		Odessa		Intense, localized rains on the evening of May 24 produced high water in Odessa. Along the roadways, vehicles were stranded and required multiple rescues.
June 30, 2002	July 7, 2002	Hill Country	Abilene	Extended rainfall in the Hill Country northwest of San Antonio pushed flood waves down local streams. The Guadalupe River fed a rise into Canyon Lake that topped the spillway and carved a new canyon downstream of the dam. Once again New Braunfels flooded. Other Hill Country rivers damaged their basins as well, including the Medina, Sabinal, and Frio rivers. Heavy rains fell in the Abilene area, especially south of the city, near Buffalo Gap and Tuscola. Flooding on Abilene area creeks resulted from remnants of tropical moisture moving up from the Hill Country. Almost fourteen inches fell in the Jim Ned and Pecan Bayou watersheds. Downstream on Pecan Bayou, floods developed from Lake Brownwood.
September 8, 2002	September 9, 2002	Frio County	Atascosa County	Widespread 8–12 inch rains produced a large area of flooding from south of Hondo eastward to Atascosa County. Pearsall was one of the worst-hit towns.
June 3, 2003	June 4, 2003	Howard County		Severe thunderstorms brought baseball-sized hail and triggered flash floods. When vehicles stalled in the high water, their drivers had to be rescued. Parts of Coahoma and Forsan were flooded.
April 4, 2004		Toyah	Reeves County	Near Toyah, 8–12 inches of rain produced runoff that washed out a protective levee, allowing the waters to inundate the town. Later, Salt Draw surged with floodwater and washed out an eighty-six-foot section of the roadway and bridge on Interstate 20, which was closed due to the surge on the normally dry draw.
May 8, 2004		San Benito	Brownsville	Within 3–4 hours, 5–8 inches of rain fell, creating floods on the area creeks and resecas. Particularly affected were parts of Brownsville and Los Fresnos.
May 13, 2004		Hearne		In Milam County, 11 inches of rain fell, while Robertson County received 11–17 inches. Extensive flooding followed, especially in Hearne, where homes filled with as much as four feet of water. Travel on Highways 79 and 6 was blocked.

START DATE	END DATE	LOCATION 1	LOCATION 2	DESCRIPTION
July 25, 2004		Terrell County		In the early morning hours, 7–9 inches of precipitation fell, setting off intense flash floods along tributaries of the Pecos River. Noteworthy among these was an eighteen-foot wall of water that traveled down Dry Creek. On Independence Creek, buildings at the Chandler Ranch were severely damaged. Floodwaters ripped the pavement from the base of the roadways. After the currents receded, piles of sand and rock up to four feet high were left on the roads.
July 28, 2004		Dallas County		Areas south of Dallas were especially hard hit by the flood resulting from a seven-inch rain within twelve hours. Hundreds of homes were damaged.
September 25, 2004	September 27, 2004	Midland	Odessa	Midland was damaged by a flash flood. Then, on the evening of the September 27, a flash flood created by a stationary, intense thunderstorm struck Odessa. Monahans Draw brought water into the west Odessa area. Before dawn on September 28, another storm cell brought more rain, which produced yet another wave of flooding in the city.
November 21, 2004		Goliad County		Fifteen inches of rain fell in an eighteen-hour period over Goliad County. Coleto, Perdido, and Spring creeks experienced flash floods.
August 14, 2005	August 17, 2005	Big Country	Midland	An extensive area of 5–10 inch rainfall produced flooding in Coke, Fisher, Haskell, Jones, Shackelford, Sterling, and Tom Green counties. Near Silver, the North Concho and Colorado rivers flooded. In Rule, numerous houses were inundated by the runoff. In the Midland area, flash flooding occurred as a result of the downpours that were spawned when a front stalled for twenty-four hours.
March 19, 2006		Tarrant County	Dallas County	Flash flooding created rises that flooded Six Flags of Texas. In Dallas, homes were deluged with five feet of floodwater from the runoff.
May 31, 2006	June 1, 2006	Corpus Christi	Coastal Texas	A deluge of 11.47 inches within twenty-four hours fell in Corpus Christi, erasing a rainfall deficit in the city. Major roadways, including Interstate 37, were flooded. Within one hour, the rainfall total for the year to date had doubled. Heavy rains also fell throughout the region. On May 28 Victoria recorded 5.39 inches, and in Kleberg County, Ricardo recorded 14 inches.
August 1, 2006		El Paso		Tropical moisture caused thunderstorms to drop heavy rain over El Paso for seven days, creating devastating floods in that region. The Rio Grande River reached its highest level since 1912. Flooding in normally dry arroyos damaged many buildings and demolished several houses and places of business. Due to high water, Interstate 10 was closed for several hours. Throughout August and early September 2006, additional heavy rains fell, setting off more flash flooding in the El Paso and southern New Mexico region.

NOTES

Introduction

1. William G. Hoyt and Walter B. Langbein, *Floods* (Princeton, N.J.: Princeton University Press, 1955).

2. Jim E. O'Connor and John E. Costa, "Spatial Distribution of the Largest Rainfall-runoff Floods from Basins between 2.6 and 26,000 km² in the United States and Puerto Rico" [USGS report], *Water Resources Research* 40(1) (Jan. 2004).

APRIL 1900: Austin Dam Break

1. James H. Banks and John E. Babcock, *Corralling the Colorado: The First Fifty Years of Lower Colorado River Authority* (Austin: Eakin Press, 1988), 22.

2. Ibid.

3. Daniel W. Mead, "Report on the Dam and Water Power Development at Austin Texas," Daniel W. Mead and Charles V. Seastone, consulting engineers, 1917.

4. T. U. Taylor, "Austin Dam," Bulletin of the University of Texas, no. 164, University of Texas–Austin, 1910.

5. "Letter from Mr. J. P. Frizell," *Engineering News* (Apr. 19, 1900).

6. "Raging Torrents," *Austin Daily Statesman,* June 8, 1899.

7. David Humphrey, *Austin, An Illustrated History* (Northridge, Calif.: Windsor, 1985).

8. *Monthly Weather Review* (Apr. 1900).

9. Ibid.

10. "Flood Notes," *San Angelo Standard-Times,* Apr. 14, 1900.

11. "Heaviest Rain in Years," *San Antonio Express,* Apr. 8, 1900.

12. "Lockhart Rains," *San Antonio Express,* Apr. 8, 1900.

13. "Death and Ruin at Austin," *San Antonio Express,* Apr. 8, 1900.

14. "Breaking of the Dam," *San Antonio Express,* Apr. 9, 1900.

15. "Austin's Great Loss of Life and Property," *Austin Semi-Weekly Statesman,* Apr. 11, 1900.

16. "Death and Ruin at Austin."

17. "Account of the Failure by H. M. Chance, M. Am. Inst. M. E., dated Austin, Apr. 8," *Engineering News* (Apr. 19, 1900).

18. "Accounts of Several Eye-Witnesses," *Engineering News* (Apr. 19, 1900).

19. "Carry the News," *San Antonio Daily Express,* Apr. 8, 1900.

20. "Wild Alarm," *Austin American,* Apr. 7, 1900.

21. "Death and Ruin at Austin."

22. "Breaking of the Dam," *San Antonio Express,* Apr. 9, 1900.

23. "Death and Ruin at Austin."

24. Ibid.

25. *Monthly Weather Review* (Apr. 1900).

26. Ibid.

27. "Power House Is a Total Wreck," *Austin Daily Statesman,* Apr. 9, 1900.

28. Ibid.

29. "Capital City Is Recovering from the Effects of the Calamity and Aiding the Victims' Families," *San Antonio Daily Express,* Apr. 10, 1900.

30. "Austin's Great Loss of Life and Property."

31. "Austin's Ruined Dam," *San Antonio Daily Express,* Apr. 12, 1900.

32. "Carnegie's Great Gift," *San Antonio Daily Express,* Apr. 10, 1900.

33. "Failure of the Great Masonry Dam across the Colorado River at Austin, Texas," *Engineering News* (Apr. 12, 1900).

34. "Letter from Mr. J. P. Frizell, M. Am. Soc. C. E., Dated Boston, April 14, 1900," *Engineering News* (Apr. 19, 1900).

35. "Letter from Mr. J. T. Fanning, M. Am. Soc. C. E., Dated Minneapolis, Minn., April 13, 1900," *Engineering News* (Apr. 19, 1900).

36. "Letter from Mr. Emile Geyelin, Hydraulic Engineer, Dated Philadelphia, April 14, 1900," *Engineering News* (Apr. 19, 1900).

37. Letters to the editor: "Failure of the Austin Dam," *Engineering News* (May 3, 1900).

38. Ibid.

39. *Scientific American* (Apr. 28, 1900).

40. Ibid.

41. Taylor, "Austin Dam."

42. Mead, "Report on the Dam and Water Power Development at Austin Texas," 65.

DECEMBER 1913: Nolan Creek and Brazos River Floods

1. B. Bunnemeyer, "The December Floods in Texas," *Engineering News* 71(21) (May 21, 1914).

2. "Unprecedented Flood in Belton," *Temple Daily Telegram*, Dec. 2, 1913.

3. Ibid.

4. "Who Gave Alarm?" *Temple Daily Telegram*, Dec. 7, 1913.

5. "Story of Heroic Rescue," *Temple Daily Telegram*, Dec. 2, 1913.

6. "Born in Doomed House," *Temple Daily Telegram*, Dec. 3, 1913.

7. "Brazos River Is on Boisterous Boom This Afternoon," *Waco Daily Times-Herald*, Dec. 2, 1913.

8. "How Mother's Body Was Found," *Temple Daily Telegram*, Dec. 5, 1913.

9. "Belton Dead Are Rescued over a Wire," *Temple Daily Telegram*, Dec. 5, 1913.

10. "Greatest Overflow in County's History," *Temple Daily Telegram*, Dec. 3, 1913.

11. See "14 Persons Rescued," *Temple Daily Telegram*, Dec. 5, 1913.

12. See "14 Are Rescued," *Temple Daily Telegram*, Dec. 6, 1913.

13. "Brazos River Is on Boisterous Boom This Afternoon."

14. "Mexican Taken from Jail to Rescue Drowning Man," *Waco Daily Times-Herald*, Dec. 4, 1913.

15. "Summary of the Situation," *Waco Daily Times-Herald*, Dec. 4, 1913.

16. "Marooned on Train All Night," *Waco Daily Times-Herald*, Dec. 4, 1913.

17. Ibid.

18. "Water Receding at Marlin," *Austin Daily Statesman*, Dec. 6, 1913.

19. Bunnemeyer, "The December Floods in Texas."

20. Ibid.

21. "Swollen Rivers Slowly Receding," *Austin Daily Statesman*, Dec. 7, 1913.

22. Bunnemeyer, "The December Floods in Texas."

23. "Floodwaters Reach Gulf," *San Antonio Express*, Dec. 7, 1913.

24. Bunnemeyer, "The December Floods in Texas."

25. "Colorado River Very High and Going Higher," *San Antonio Express*, Dec. 3, 1913.

26. "Biederwolf Is Rained Out," *Austin Daily Statesman*, Dec. 4, 1913.

27. "History Repeated!" *La Grange Journal*, Dec. 18, 1913.

28. Ibid.

29. "Columbus an Island," *Temple Daily Telegram*, Dec. 5, 1913.

30. "Night in Columbus Is One of Terror Mingled with the Spectacular," *San Antonio Express*, Dec. 7, 1913.

31. Bunnemeyer, "The December Floods in Texas."

32. "Flood Water Is Standing in All the Low Places in Caldwell County," *San Antonio Express*, Dec. 3, 1913.

33. "San Marcos River High," *San Antonio Express*, Dec. 5, 1913.

34. Ibid.

35. "Loss Small Measured by Last Flood," *San Antonio Express*, Dec. 5, 1913.

36. Ibid.

37. "Convent Bend," *San Antonio Express*, Dec. 5, 1913.

38. "Heavy Damage to Bridge in Bexar County," *San Antonio Express*, Dec. 5, 1913.

39. "Suggest Conduit Relief," *San Antonio Express*, Dec. 5, 1913.

40. Ibid.

41. Ibid.

42. "Twice the Warning Has Come—Let Us Act," *San Antonio Express*, Dec. 5, 1913.

43. Ibid.

44. Bunnemeyer, "The December Floods in Texas."

45. Ibid.

APRIL 1915: Floods on Shoal and Waller Creeks

1. B. Bunnemeyer, "Climatological Data, Texas Section, April 1915," U.S. Dept. of Agriculture, Weather Bureau.

2. Ibid.

3. "Rainfall Greatest in Austin History," *Austin American*, Apr. 23, 1915.

4. "Deluge at Austin; Six Known Dead," *Dallas Morning News*, Apr. 23, 1915.

5. "Flood Damage $2 Million at Austin," *Austin American*, Apr. 24, 1915.

6. See "35 Persons Are Believed Drowned," *Austin American*, Apr. 23, 1915.

7. "Destruction and Gloom in Wake of Shoal Flood," *Austin American*, Apr. 24, 1915.

8. "Flood Damage $2 Million at Austin."

9. "Will Sue City?" *Austin American*, Apr. 24, 1915.

10. "Acute Suffering Result of Flood," *Austin American,* Apr. 24, 1915.

11. Ibid.

12. "Flood Damage $2 Million at Austin."

13. See "16 Known Dead in Austin Storm," *San Antonio Express,* Apr. 24, 1915.

14. "Swedish Tabernacle Destroyed at Manor," *Austin American,* Apr. 24, 1915.

SEPTEMBER 1921: Downtown San Antonio Flood

1. Frederick Law Olmsted, *Journey to Texas; or, A Saddle-trip on the South-western Frontier: with a Statistical Appendix* (New York: Mason Brothers, 1859), 149.

2. Metcalfe Report, 1920.

3. "Timely Showers Revive Ranges in Southwest Texas," *San Antonio Express,* Sept. 9, 1921.

4. J. D. Smith and L. Guttridge, *Jack Teagarden: The Story of a Jazz Maverick* (London: Cassell, 1960).

5. "Flood Mark Is 45 Inches over Deluge of 1845," *Austin American,* Sept. 11, 1921.

6. "Caught Unaware, Sleeping, Scores Are Suddenly Swept Off," *San Antonio Express,* Sept. 11, 1921.

7. "Human Features of Flood Tragedy," *San Antonio Express,* Sept. 11, 1921.

8. "Floods in Central Texas," USGS Water Supply Paper 488, Sept. 1921.

9. "Men in San Antone and Flood," *Austin American,* Sept. 11, 1921.

10. "Known Flood Dead 39, Scores Missing," *San Antonio Express,* Sept. 11, 1921; *Monthly Weather Review* 49(9) (1921).

11. "Warning in San Antonio Less than in Europe during War," *San Antonio Express,* Sept. 11, 1921.

12. "State Control of Flood Waters Is Needed, Says Ashe," *San Antonio Express,* Sept. 16, 1921.

13. "Repair the Damage—and Protect the City," *San Antonio Express,* Sept. 11, 1921.

14. "Flood Yet to Come," *Dallas Morning News,* Sept. 13, 1921.

15. Ibid.

SEPTEMBER 1921: Thrall Record Rainfall and Little River Flood

1. "10-Inch Rain Floods City Late Friday," *Austin American,* Sept. 10, 1921.

2. Clara Stearns Scarbrough, *Land of Good Water, Takachue Pouetsu: A Williamson County, Texas, History* (Georgetown, Tex.: *Williamson County Sun,* 1973), 370–76.

3. Ida Jo Marshall, ed., *Rockdale Centennial: A History of Rockdale, Texas, 1874–1974* (Rockdale, Tex.: *Rockdale Reporter,* 1974).

4. "Floods Do Much Damage," *Marble Falls Messenger,* Sept. 15, 1921.

5. George Lott, "The Unparalleled Thrall, Texas, Rainstorm," *Monthly Weather Review* 81(7) (July 1953): 195–203.

6. *Texas Almanac, 1994–1995* (Dallas: *Dallas Morning News*).

7. John F. Griffiths and Greg Ainsworth, *One Hundred Years of Texas Weather, 1880–1979* (College Station: Office of the State Climatologist, Department of Atmospheric Sciences, Texas A&M University, 1981).

8. J. P. McAuliffe, "Excessive Rainfall and Flood at Taylor, Texas," *Monthly Weather Review* 49(9) (Sept. 1921): 497.

9. Ibid.

10. B. Bunnemeyer, "The Texas Floods of September 1921," *Monthly Weather Review* 49(9) (Sept. 1921).

11. Lott, "The Unparalleled Thrall, Texas, Rainstorm."

12. "Record Flood Hits Taylor," *Taylor Daily Press,* Sept. 10, 1921.

13. "Willing Helpers in Time of Trouble," *Taylor Daily Press,* Sept. 10, 1921.

14. "Record Flood Hits Taylor."

15. Bunnemeyer, "The Texas Floods of September 1921."

16. "Central Texas Remembers the Great Deluge of 1921," *Waco Times-Herald.*

17. Ibid.

18. Ibid.

19. See "45 Lives Lost in Vicinity of Thorndale," *San Antonio Express,* Sept. 14, 1921.

20. "Rescue Crews Push Way into River Bottom," *Cameron Herald,* Sept. 22, 1921.

21. "Picturesque San Gabriel Gives Up 85 Bodies When Flood Waters Pass Crest," *San Antonio Express,* Sept. 14, 1921.

22. Ibid.

23. "Did the Whale Swallow Jonah? No, Jonah Swallows Ocean," *Taylor Daily Press,* Sept. 15, 1921.

24. Ibid.

25. Scarbrough, *Land of Good Water,* 370–76.

26. "Toll of Life Grows," *Taylor Daily Press,* Sept. 12, 1921.

27. "Grave Yard Refuge for Storm Victims," *Taylor Daily Press,* Sept. 12, 1921.

28. "Odor of Death Fills Air in the Vicinity of Youngstown," *Taylor Daily Press,* Sept. 13, 1921.

29. McAuliffe, "Excessive Rainfall and Flood at Taylor, Texas," 497.

30. Ibid.

31. Lott, "The Unparalleled Thrall, Texas, Rainstorm."

32. "San Gabriel Sector Hit Hard by Flood," *Cameron Herald*, Sept. 22, 1921.

33. "San Gabriel Gossip," *Cameron Herald*, Sept. 22, 1921.

34. Ibid.

35. "Belton Parks to Be Restored," *Temple Daily Telegram*, Sept. 14, 1921.

36. "Appeals for Aid for Flood Victims in Salado Section," *Temple Daily Telegram*, Sept. 13, 1921.

37. Ibid.

38. E. A. Limmer Jr., ed., *Story of Bell County, Texas*, vol. 1 (Austin: Eakin Press for the Bell County Historical Commission, 1988).

39. "Little River at Highest Stage Ever Known in Bell County," *Temple Daily Telegram*, Sept. 11, 1921.

40. C. E. Ellsworth, "The Floods in Central Texas in September, 1921," Water Supply Paper 488 (Washington, D.C.: U.S. Geological Survey, 1923).

41. "Bodies of Railroad Men Drowned in Little River Recovered," *Cameron Herald*, Sept. 15, 1921.

42. Marshall, ed., *Rockdale Centennial*.

43. Ibid.

44. Ibid.

45. Ibid.

46. Ibid.

47. Ibid.

48. Ibid.

49. Ibid.

50. Ibid.

51. Ibid.

52. Ibid.

53. Bunnemeyer, "The Texas Floods of September 1921."

54. "Floods Do Much Damage," *Marble Falls Messenger*, Sept. 15, 1921.

55. "Notes from Travis Peak," *Marble Falls Messenger*, Sept. 22, 1921.

56. Ellsworth, "The Floods in Central Texas in September, 1921."

JULY 1932: Guadalupe River Basin Flood

1. "Heaviest Rainfall in History and Worst Floods in the History of This Entire Section," *Uvalde Leader*, July 8, 1932.

2. "Aerial Survey of Guadalupe Shows Trail of Wreckage," *San Antonio Express*, July 4, 1932.

3. "Five Towns Isolated by Cloudbursts," *San Antonio Express*, July 3, 1932.

4. "Marooned Families Rescued by Boats," *San Antonio Express*, July 4, 1932.

5. "Planes Hurry Aid to Kerrville; Scores of Flood Victims," *Austin American*, July 5, 1932.

6. "Kerrville Fish Hatchery Losses," *Austin American*, July 7, 1932.

7. "Boy Marooned in Tree," *San Antonio Express*, July 2, 1932.

8. "Kerrville Begins Comeback Fight after Raging Flood," *Austin American*, July 6, 1932.

9. "Dr. Jewett Tells of Disaster," *Austin American*, July 6, 1932.

10. C. E. Good, "Aerial Survey of Guadalupe Shows Trail of Wreckage More than 80 Miles Long," *San Antonio Express*, July 4, 1932.

11. "20- to 30-Inch Downpour Sends All Streams on Rampage; Damage Will Be Enormous; Two Drowned," *Uvalde Leader News*, July 8, 1932.

12. Ibid.

13. "Flood News," *Uvalde Leader News*, July 8, 1932.

14. "Live Oak at Con-Can Reported Uprooted," *San Antonio Express*, July 4, 1932.

15. "Marooned Families Rescued by Boats," *San Antonio Express*, July 4, 1932.

16. "Around the Supper Table," *Brownwood Bulletin*, July 5, 1932.

17. *Brownwood Bulletin*, July 6, 1932.

18. "Flood Prevention," *Brownwood Bulletin*, July 7, 1932.

19. "Think," *San Antonio Express*, July 6, 1932.

20. Bandera County History Book Committee, *History of Bandera County, Texas* (Dallas: Curtis, 1986).

SEPTEMBER 1932: Devil's River and Rio Grande River Floods

1. "Flood of September and October 1932, International Portion of the Rio Grande: Special Flood Report" (El Paso: International Boundary Commission).

2. *Sutton County, 1887–1977* (Sonora, Tex.: Sutton County Historical Society, 1979).

3. "Flood of September and October 1932," 33.

4. "Ripples from the Rio Grande," *Laredo Times*, Sept. 4, 1932.

5. "Four Drowned When Rio Crumbles Laredo Bridge," *San Antonio Light*, Sept. 4, 1932.

6. "Receding Water Brings Safety to Three Men on Debris," *Laredo Times*, Sept. 4, 1932.

7. "Rescued Men Describe Peril," *San Antonio Light*, Sept. 5, 1932.

8. Ibid.

9. Ibid.

10. Ibid.

11. *Sutton County, 1887–1977,* History of *Devil's River News.*

12. "Flood of September and October 1932," 25.

MAY 1935: D'Hanis Flash Flood

1. "Climatological Data, Texas Section," U.S. Department of Agriculture, Weather Bureau, Mar. 1935.

2. Tate Dalrymple, "Major Texas Floods of 1935," USGS Water Supply Paper 796-C (Washington, D.C., 1939).

3. "D'Hanis Flood Damage Estimated at Million," *San Antonio Express,* June 2, 1935.

4. "Death Rides the Flood Tides," *Hondo Anvil Herald,* June 7, 1935.

5. Ibid.

6. Ibid.

7. Josie Rothe, "Deluge at D'Hanis," *Hondo Anvil Herald,* June 5, 1935.

8. "D'Hanis Flood Damage Estimated at Million."

9. "Friday Hondo Flooded," *Hondo Anvil Herald,* May 31, 1935.

10. "Death Rides the Flood Tides."

11. "Friday Hondo Flooded."

12. "Three Men Washed down Draw in Car Escape with Lives," *San Antonio Express,* June 6, 1935.

13. "Hondo-Sabinal Area Fears New Floods," *San Antonio Express,* June 3, 1935.

14. "Dead at D'Hanis Increase to Six," *San Antonio Express,* June 3, 1935.

15. "Local and Personal—May Breaks Record," *Hondo Anvil Herald,* June 7, 1935.

16. "Pioneer Resident Forecast Flood 20 Years Ago," *Uvalde Leader News,* June 7, 1935.

17. Ibid.

JUNE 1935: Llano and Nueces Rivers Floods

1. "Weather Report," *Junction Eagle,* Mar. 28, 1935.

2. *Llano News,* May 16, 1935.

3. "Good Rains in Hill Country Revive Ranches," *Junction Eagle,* May 23, 1935.

4. "Heavy Rains Fall in All Parts of County," *Fredericksburg Standard,* May 23, 1935.

5. Tate Dalrymple, "Major Texas Floods of 1935," USGS Water Supply Paper 796-C (Washington, D.C., 1939).

6. "High Span below Mason Wrecked," *San Antonio Express,* June 15, 1935.

7. "No Flood Danger," *Austin Statesman,* June 14, 1935.

8. "Rain Continues in This Section," *Rocksprings Record,* June 14, 1935.

9. "Flood," *Rocksprings Record,* June 21, 1935.

10. "Major Texas Floods of 1935."

11. "Camp Wood, Leakey, and Reagan Wells Signal Plane All O.K.," *San Antonio Express,* June 16, 1935.

12. "Texas Floods Take 8 Lives, Possibly More," *Dallas Morning News,* June 15, 1935.

13. "Nueces Breaks Both Highway and Railway Bridges," *San Antonio Express,* June 15, 1935.

14. "Loss at Uvalde Worst in History," *Rocksprings Record,* June 28, 1935.

15. "Montopolis Span Expected to Go Out in Big Rise," *Austin American,* June 15, 1935.

16. "Rail Bridge Stands," *San Antonio Express,* June 16, 1935.

17. "Big Dam Takes Hard Pounding from Colorado," *San Antonio* Express, June 16, 1935.

18. "Family Half-marooned by Overflow at Barton," *Austin American-Statesman,* June 16, 1935.

19. "Angry Colorado Recedes," *San Antonio Light,* June 16, 1935.

20. Austin History Center files, "Weather-Flood-CR," 1930–1937.

21. "Damage to Llano Pecan and Timber Crop Great," *Austin American,* June 27, 1935.

22. "Think," *San Antonio Express,* June 17, 1935.

23. "We Have Had Enough Rain," *Dallas Morning News,* June 17, 1935.

DECEMBER 1935: Downtown Houston Flood

1. "Sidelights," *Houston Post, Dec. 8, 1935.*

2. "Stockmen Faced with Prospect of Big Losses," *Houston Post, Dec. 8, 1935.*

3. See "1.25-Million Damage Suffered Here with One Reported Dead," *Houston Post, Dec. 9, 1935.*

4. Ibid.

5. Ibid.

6. "Houston Man Saves 21 from Flood Waters," *Houston Post, Dec. 9, 1935.*

7. "Sidelights," *Houston Post, Dec. 8, 1935.*

8. Ibid.

9. "One Building Collapses in Bayou Torrent," *Houston Post, Dec. 10, 1935.*

10. "Army of Workmen," *Houston Post, Dec. 11, 1935.*

11. "Sears Roebuck Damage Placed at $350,000," *Houston Post, Dec. 11, 1935.*

314

12. Ibid.

13. Ibid.

14. "Houstonians from All Walks of Life Call for Immediate Work on Flood Control Plan," *Houston Post*, Dec. 10, 1935.

15. Ibid.

16. Ibid.

17. "Sheppard Plans to Seek U.S. Flood Funds," *Houston Post*, Dec. 11, 1935.

18. Ibid.

19. "Bayou Crest Tops 1929 by 8 Feet," *Houston Post*, Dec. 10, 1935.

20. Ibid.

21. "Editorial: Action of Flood Control," *Houston Post*, Dec. 13, 1935.

22. "Norquest Urges Upper River Gauge," *Houston Post*, Dec. 11, 1935.

23. "Stockmen Faced with Prospect of Big Losses," *Houston Post*, Dec. 8, 1935.

24. "One Man Is Drowned and 30 Missing," *Houston Post*, Dec. 9, 1935.

25. "Sidelights," *Houston Post*, Dec. 8, 1935.

SEPTEMBER 1936: Concho River Flood

1. "Storm Goes in South of Corpus, Strikes in Thinly Settled Area," *San Antonio Express*, Sept. 14, 1936.

2. "No More Flood," *San Angelo Evening Standard*, Sept. 25, 1936.

3. "Killed Too Many Lizards," *San Angelo Standard-Times*, Sept. 20, 1936.

4. "Exaggeration," *San Angelo Evening Standard*, Sept. 17, 1936.

5. "San Angelo's $100,000 Worth of Fish Hatcheries Escape Water," *San Angelo Evening Standard*, Sept. 22, 1936.

6. "Did You Lose Boat?" *San Angelo Evening Standard*, Sept. 21, 1936.

7. "Off down Raging Concho," *Austin American*, Sept. 18, 1936.

8. "But How Could an Aviator Tell?" *San Angelo Standard-Times*, Sept. 20, 1936.

9. "City Seaport under Water," *San Angelo Evening Standard*, Sept. 17, 1936.

10. "High Spots and Low," *San Angelo Evening Standard*, Sept. 18, 1936.

11. "Flood Aftermath," *San Angelo Evening-Times*, Sept. 20, 1936.

12. Ibid.

13. Ibid.

14. "River Damage May Soar to Two Million," *San Angelo Evening Standard*, Sept. 18, 1936.

15. "Concho Flood Encores," *San Angelo Standard-Times*, Sept. 27, 1936.

16. Ibid.

17. Sam Ashburn, "Red Parking Ticket Adds Effect of Christmas Trees Day after Yuletide at Angelo's City Park," *San Angelo Standard-Times*, Sept. 20, 1936.

18. "New Game," *San Angelo Standard*, Sept. 27, 1936.

19. "Floods End Unemployment," *San Antonio Evening Express*, Sept. 22, 1936.

20. "Eldorado Lake," *San Angelo Standard-Times*, Sept. 27, 1936.

21. Tate Dalrymple, "Major Texas Floods of 1935," USGS Water Supply Paper 796-C (Washington, D.C., 1939).

22. "Recalls Father's Prediction, Angelo to Be Inundated," *San Angelo Standard-Times*, Sept. 27, 1936.

23. "Disaster on Colorado River at Bend," *Lampasas Leader*, Sept. 23, 1936.

24. "Crest Expected to Reach Austin during the Night," *Austin American*, Sept. 22, 1936.

25. See "30-Foot Flood Tests New Span," *Austin American*, Sept. 27, 1936.

26. *San Antonio Express*, Sept. 24, 1936.

27. "Colorado Stage," *San Antonio Express*, Sept. 22, 1936.

28. See "30–35 Foot Stage Expected," *San Antonio Express*, Sept. 22, 1936.

29. "Colorado Crest Goes A.W.O.L. above Austin, River Flattens Out Somewhere but Observers Not Sure Where," *San Antonio Express*, Sept. 23, 1936.

30. Ibid.

31. "Loss of Crest," *San Antonio Express*, Sept. 23, 1936.

32. "Flattening of Crest," *San Antonio Express*, Sept. 24, 1936.

33. "Rise May Clean Up Barton Creek," *Austin American*, Sept. 27, 1936.

34. Editorial, *Lampasas Record*, Oct. 1, 1936.

35. *San Antonio Express*, Sept. 24, 1936.

36. Dalrymple, "Major Texas Floods of 1936."

JULY 1938: Brady Creek and San Saba River Floods

1. "Brady Floodlights," *Brady Standard*, July 23, 1938.

2. "Oh, Boy, Million-Dollar Rain in McCulloch," *Brady Standard*, July 18, 1938.

3. "Moisture Falls over Area," *San Angelo Standard-Times*, July 20, 1938.

4. "Texas Floods of 1938 and 1939," USGS Water Supply Paper 914, 1944.

5. "Tremendous Wall of Water Nears Top of Big Levee," *Brady Standard*, July 22, 1938.

6. "Sauce," *Brady Standard*, July 22, 1938.

7. "Flood Waters Recede from Three West Texas Towns," *San Angelo Standard-Times*, July 25, 1938.

8. "Damages at Brady May Reach $600,000," *San Angelo Standard-Times*, July 25, 1938.

9. "Flood Damage Is Estimated at $500,000," *Brady Standard*, July 26, 1938.

10. "Brady Floodlights," *Brady Standard*, July 26, 1938.

11. "Menard, Brady Are Flooded; River Here Goes Out of Banks," *Austin American*, July 24, 1938.

12. Ibid.

13. "Brady, Menard, San Saba Hit Again by Floods," *San Angelo Standard-Times*, July 24, 1938.

14. "Rain Extends into Dry Areas of West Texas," *San Angelo Standard-Times*, July 22, 1938.

15. "At Least 2 Dead as Flood Rages in San Saba," *Austin American*, July 23, 1938.

16. "Brady, Menard, San Saba Hit Again by Floods."

17. "Flood Waters Recede from Three West Texas Towns."

18. Blondy Cross, "Real Heroes of the San Saba Flood Were the Small-town Boys Who Got There First and Stayed until Job Was Completed," *San Angelo Morning Times*, July 28, 1938.

19. Ibid.

20. Ibid.

21. "At Least 2 Dead as Flood Rages in San Saba."

22. "Man-made Flood Is Due to Reach Austin Saturday," *Austin American*, July 23, 1938.

23. "Refugees Flee Raging Colorado," *San Antonio Express*, July 29, 1938.

24. Ibid.

25. "Big Floods Are Blamed on Incompleted Central Texas Dams," *Austin American*, July 26, 1938.

26. "Colorado Dams Fail to Prevent Flood at Austin," *San Antonio Express*, July 27, 1938.

27. "Negligence Charges Are Hurled at CRA," *Austin American*, July 29, 1938.

28. "Colorado Dams Fail to Prevent Flood at Austin."

29. "Big Floods Are Blamed on Incompleted Central Texas Dams."

30. "Colorado Dams Fail to Prevent Flood at Austin."

31. Ibid.

32. "Lower Colorado Counties Stirred," *San Antonio Express*, July 28, 1938.

33. "LaGrange Bridge Collapses," *Austin American*, July 28, 1938.

34. Ibid.

35. "Columbus Meet Voices Protest," *San Antonio Express*, July 29, 1938.

36. "Refugees Flee Raging Colorado."

37. "Directors Absent at Meeting on Colorado Flood," *San Antonio Express*, July 31, 1938.

38. Ibid.

39. Ibid.

40. Ibid.

41. "Lower Valleyites Reveal Warning Given Authority," *San Antonio Express*, July 29, 1938.

42. Ibid.

43. "Austin Rotarian Charges Politics in Colorado Flood," *San Antonio Express*, Aug. 4, 1938.

44. "Starts Inquiry into Flood on Colorado," *San Antonio Express*, Aug. 9, 1938.

45. "Buchanan Dam Saved Austin," *Austin American*, Aug. 10, 1938.

46. "PWA Denies Dam Cause of Flood," *San Antonio Express*, Aug. 12, 1938.

47. "Officials Gratified," *San Antonio Express*, Aug. 12, 1938.

48. "Buchanan Dam Reduced Swell, Ickes Informed," *Austin American*, Aug. 12, 1938.

49. "A Few Facts Set Forth," *Dallas Morning News*, Aug. 12, 1938.

50. "Twisting Facts: *Dallas News* Misrepresents Report of U.S. Engineer in Effort to Discredit Public Power Policy," *Austin American-Statesman*, Aug. 14, 1938.

51. "For the People's Benefit, Dam System Is for Welfare and Protection of Citizens: An Editorial," *Austin American-Statesman*, Aug. 17, 1938.

52. "Dam Must Work to Repay Loan, Probers Told," *San Antonio Express*, Aug. 18, 1938.

MAY 1949: Downtown Fort Worth Flood

1. See "1922 Flood Drove City to Water Control Plan," *Forth Worth Star-Telegram*, Apr. 25, 1947.

2. "Dallas Is Facing Flood Threat," *Forth Worth Star-Telegram*, May 17, 1949.

3. "Same Old Outlaw," *Forth Worth Star-Telegram*, May 17, 1949.

4. "Autos and Furniture," *Forth Worth Star-Telegram*, May 17, 1949.

5. "Zoo Animals Have Own 'Splash Day,' Hittson Says," *Forth Worth Star-Telegram*, May 17, 1949.

6. "High-riding Trucker Gets Motor Here in 33 Hours," *Forth Worth Star-Telegram*, May 20, 1949.

7. Ibid.

8. Ibid.

9. Ibid.

10. "Man Jailed for Reckless Boat Driving," *Forth Worth Star-Telegram,* May 19, 1949.

11. "Food and Drug Stores Closed," *Forth Worth Star-Telegram,* May 18, 1949.

12. "Army Engineer Promises Quick Action on Levees," *Forth Worth Star-Telegram,* May 19, 1949.

13. "Clear Fork Rains Blamed for Flooded Condition," *Forth Worth Star-Telegram,* May 20, 1949.

14. Ibid.

SEPTEMBER 1952: Pedernales River Flood

1. "Continued Cool, Dry Weather Forecast," *San Angelo Standard-Times,* Sept. 7, 1952.

2. "Water-using Coolers Banned in San Angelo" and "Sonora Offers Water to Assist San Angelo," *San Angelo Standard-Times,* Sept. 9, 1952.

3. "Answer to Water Problem Rolled Downstream in '51," *San Angelo Standard-Times,* Sept. 9, 1952.

4. "Reuben's Half Acre," *Austin Statesman,* Sept. 9, 1952.

5. "Dunham Sees Showers Continuing This Week," *Austin Statesman,* Sept. 9, 1952; "Rain's Blessing Varied over Centex Counties," *Austin American,* Sept. 10, 1952.

6. "Broad Rain Dampens City," *San Angelo Standard-Times,* Sept. 10, 1952.

7. "Likely Flood Threatens Brady; Rain Dents, May Break Drought," *Austin Statesman,* Sept. 10, 1952.

8. "Rain Floods Isolate 5 Centex Towns," *Austin American,* Sept. 11, 1952.

9. "Floods in South Texas Cause 7 Deaths; San Marcos, Seguin, Comal Areas Hit," *San Antonio Express,* Sept. 12, 1952.

10. Ibid.

11. "Woodpile," *Brady Standard,* Sept. 12, 1952.

12. "Woodpile," *Brady Standard,* Sept. 16, 1952.

13. "Lesser of Two Evils . . . Thwarted Flood over Prolonged Drouth," *Brady Standard,* Sept. 12, 1952.

14. "Uninsured Merchants Put Faith in Hastily Erected Fort Sandbag," *Brady Standard,* Sept. 12, 1952.

15. "Brady Wins Two-crest Battle," *Brady Standard,* Sept. 12, 1952.

16. "Lesser of Two Evils."

17. "Woodpile," *Brady Standard,* Sept. 12, 1952.

18. "More about Brady," *Fort Worth Star-Telegram,* Sept. 11, 1952.

19. "Brady Offer Skyrockets," *San Angelo Standard-Times,* Sept. 11, 1952.

20. "Likely Flood Threatens Brady."

21. "Agricultural, Highway, and Fence Losses Make Flood Gillespie's Worst Disaster," *Fredericksburg Standard,* Sept. 17, 1952.

22. "Pleasant Hill News," *Fredericksburg Radio Post,* Sept. 18, 1952.

23. "Stonewall Area Devastated by Rampaging Floodwaters of Pedernales Last Week," *Fredericksburg Standard,* Sept. 17, 1952.

24. "Great Damage," *Fredericksburg Radio Post,* Sept. 18, 1952.

25. "Lyndon Has Near Miss," *Austin Statesman,* Sept. 12, 1952.

26. "Floods of September 1952 in the Colorado and Guadelupe [*sic*] River Basins, Central Texas," USGS Water Supply Paper 1260-A, 1954.

27. "From the Air: Guadalupe River Looked like Octopus Gone Mad," *San Antonio Express,* Sept. 12, 1952.

28. "Rains Changed Blanco River into Muddy, Monstrous Flood," *Austin American,* Sept. 13, 1952.

29. "Heavy Rains Are Gold to Farmers," *San Angelo Standard-Times,* Sept. 12, 1952.

30. Ibid.

31. Ibid.

32. "Record Rains Stored Away," *San Antonio Express,* Sept. 13, 1952.

JUNE 1954: Pecos River's Eighty-Six-Foot Wall of Water

1. "Storm Threats Fade along Texas Coast," *San Angelo Standard-Times,* June 26, 1954.

2. "Long Drought Breaking Up? Pecos Ranchmen Optimistic," *San Angelo Standard-Times,* June 27, 1954.

3. "Eagle Pass Isolated by Record Floods," *San Antonio Express,* June 29, 1954.

4. "Ten Feared Dead at Ozona—12 Missing," *San Angelo Standard-Times,* June 29, 1954.

5. "Flow of the Rio Grande and Related Data, Flood of 1954," Water Bulletin 24, International Boundary and Water Commission, 1954.

6. "Eagle Pass Isolated by Record Floods."

7. "Flood Rages in Valley," *Fort Worth Star-Telegram,* June 29, 1954.

8. "Ten Found Dead at Ozona—12 Missing."

9. Allan R. Bosworth, *Ozona Country* (New York: Harper and Row, 1964), 125.

10. Clipping from Fort Stockton Library files from *Fort Stockton Pioneer,* "Baker's Dozen."

11. "Eagle Pass Isolated by Record Floods," *San Antonio Express,* June 29, 1954.

12. "Flood Rages in Valley," *Fort Worth Star-Telegram,* June 29, 1954.

13. "Falcon Saving Valley Millions in Flood Damage," *San Antonio Express,* June 30, 1954.

MAY 1957: Lampasas Mother's Day Flood

1. "Rains Cause Flash Floods in Central Texas," *Temple Daily Telegram,* May 12, 1957.

2. "For First Time in Years, First Three Months above Average," *Lampasas Dispatch,* Mar. 28, 1957.

3. "Around Town," *Lampasas Dispatch,* May 2, 1957.

4. "Heavy Rains Friday Give Lampasans Scare," *Lampasas Dispatch,* May 2, 1957.

5. See "150 Families Evacuated," *Temple Daily Telegram,* May 13, 1957.

6. "The Flood Which Hit Lampasas Was Very Powerful, Deep, and Destructive," *Lampasas Record,* June 6, 1957.

7. "Strange Sights Seen after Lampasas Flood," *Waco Times-Herald,* May 13, 1957.

8. "Squad Car Helps Family in Escape," *Waco Times-Herald,* May 14, 1957.

9. "Lampasans Saved, Helped Each Other," *Temple Daily Telegram,* May 14, 1957.

10. Ibid.

11. "Injured Rodeo Champ Rescues His Family," *Temple Daily Telegram,* May 14, 1957.

12. "Lampasas Businessmen," *Temple Daily Telegram,* May 14, 1957.

13. "Thank You, Dean," *Lampasas Dispatch,* May 23, 1957.

14. See "28-Year-Old Mother Pulls 16 Others from Swirling Flood Waters Sunday," *Lampasas Dispatch,* May 23, 1957.

15. "Flood Leaves Lampasas Merchants, Residents Battered, Dazed, Dead," *Lampasas Dispatch,* May 23, 1957.

16. "Producers' Produce Takes Terrific Beating in Fourth Major Lampasas Flood," *Lampasas Dispatch,* May 30, 1957.

17. "Lampasas Business District Slowly Coming Back to Life," *Temple Daily Telegram,* May 19, 1957.

18. "'Mrs. Jodie' Left Switchboard for First Time in 29 Years," *Temple Daily Telegram,* May 14, 1957.

19. Ibid.

20. Ibid.

21. Ibid.

22. See "4' Rise Rolls down River; Lowlands Warned," *Temple Daily Telegram,* May 14, 1957.

23. Ibid.

24. "Three Years," *Lampasas Dispatch,* May 30, 1957.

25. "The Flood Which Hit Lampasas Was Very Powerful, Deep, and Destructive," *Lampasas Record,* June 6, 1957.

26. "Senator Johnson Pushes Dam Construction," *Lampasas Dispatch,* May 23, 1957.

27. "Watershed Flood Control Would Keep Damage Low," *Lampasas Dispatch,* May 30, 1957.

28. "Around Town," *Lampasas Dispatch,* June 13, 1957.

29. "Reservoirs Near Peak and Still Climbing," *Temple Daily Telegram,* May 15, 1957.

30. "Milam County Watches River but Worst Fears Unrealized," *Temple Daily Telegram,* May 15, 1957.

31. "Reservoirs Gain over West Texas," *San Angelo Standard-Times,* Apr. 20, 1957.

JUNE 1965: Sanderson Flash Flood

1. "Heavy Downpour Strands Train, Raging Waters Slow Rescue," *Odessa American,* June 11, 1965.

2. Ibid.

3. Richard A. Crawley, "Flood Effects on Sanderson Creek, Trans-Pecos, Texas, June 11, 1965," M.A. thesis, University of Texas–Austin, 1969.

4. Ibid.

5. Ibid.

6. Bob Mayo, "How Sanderson's Flood Came," *Fort Stockton Pioneer,* June 17, 1965.

7. Ibid.

8. Ibid.

9. Russell Ashton Scogin and Earl H. Elam, *The Sanderson Flood of 1965: Crisis in a Rural Texas Community* (Alpine, Tex.: Center for Big Bend Studies, Sul Ross State University, 1995).

10. "Flood Curb Studies Begun in Sanderson," *San Angelo Standard-Times,* June 20, 1965.

11. Ibid.

12. U.S. Weather Bureau storm data, June 1965.

13. "Death Toll Climbs to 15 in Sanderson Flood," *Odessa American,* June 11, 1965.

14. "Help Comes Quickly When Sanderson Hit by Disastrous Flood," *Odessa American,* June 13, 1965.

15. Scogin and Elam, *The Sanderson Flood of 1965.*

16. Ibid.

318

17. "Death Toll Climbs to 15 in Sanderson Flood."

18. "Flood Rescue Terror Recalled by Father of 2," *Fort Worth Star-Telegram,* June 12, 1965.

19. "Sanderson Flash Flood Kills 13; 300 Homeless," *San Angelo Standard-Times,* June 12, 1965.

20. "Terrell Residents Ready to Rebuild," *San Angelo Standard-Times,* June 12, 1965.

21. "Flash Flood at Sanderson," *Texas Highways* (Aug.–Sept., 1965) 12(8).

22. "Sanderson Flood Toll Reaches 16," *San Angelo Standard-Times,* June 14, 1965.

23. "Raging Torrent Caught Most of Victims Asleep," *Odessa American,* June 13, 1965.

24. "Terrell Residents Ready to Rebuild."

25. "Sanderson Flash Flood Kills 13; 300 Homeless."

26. "Terrell Residents Ready to Rebuild."

MAY 1966: Dallas Flash Flood

1. "Big D Column," *Dallas Morning News,* May 1, 1966.

2. "Two Snatched to Safety as Companion Drowns," *Dallas Morning News,* Apr. 29, 1966.

3. Ibid.

4. Ibid.

5. "Two Firemen Win Struggle," *Dallas Morning News,* Apr. 29, 1966.

6. Ibid.

7. "Randt Blasts City Officials," *Dallas Morning News,* Apr. 30, 1966.

8. "North Dallas Delegation to Petition Council for Flood Control Plan," *Dallas Morning News*, May 1, 1966.

MAY 1970: San Marcos River Flood

1. "Folks and Facts," *San Marcos Record,* May 21, 1970.

2. "Costly Flood Hits Hard; San Marcos Coming Back," *San Marcos Record,* May 21, 1970.

3. Ibid.

4. "San Marcos Flood Eases," *San Antonio Express,* May 16, 1970.

5. "Costly Flood Hits Hard."

6. Ibid.

7. "San Marcos Flood Eases."

8. "Costly Flood Hits Hard."

9. "We Dam Our Streams—Too Late," *San Marcos Record,* May 21, 1970.

10. "Costly Flood Hits Hard."

11. "KCNY Provides Essential Link in Time of Disaster," *San Marcos Record,* May 21, 1970.

MAY 1972: New Braunfels Flood

1. Victor Baker, "Flood Hazards along the Balcones Escarpment in Central Texas: Alternative Approaches to Their Recognition, Mapping. and Management" [circular] 75-5 (Austin: University of Texas, Bureau of Economic Geology, 1975.

2. A. B. Colwick, H. H. McGill, and F. P. Erichsen, "Severe Floods at New Braunfels, Texas, May 1972," American Society of Agricultural Engineers, Paper 73-206, June 1973.

3. "Blieders Dam Would Have Greatly Minimized Flood," *New Braunfels Herald and Zeitung,* May 18, 1972.

4. "Floodwaters Take 11 Lives," *Dallas Morning News,* May 13, 1972.

5. Herman Kelly, "Havoc along the Guadalupe," *Texas Highways* (July 1972) 19(7).

6. Baker, "Flood Hazards."

7. "Floodwaters Take 11 Lives."

8. "'Leben Schoen' No More," *San Antonio Express,* May 13, 1972.

9. "Flood Takes 15 Lives, Does $15 Million in Damage," *New Braunfels Herald and Zeitung,* May 18, 1972.

10. Ibid.

11. Colwick, McGill, and Erichsen, "Severe Floods in New Braunfels, Texas."

12. "Mayor Launches Petition for Flood Control Action," *New Braunfels Herald and Zeitung,* May 18, 1972.

13. "Blieders Dam Would Have Greatly Minimized Flood."

14. Ibid.

15. "Cleanup a Job for Young and Old in Posh Subdivision," *San Antonio Express,* May 13, 1972.

MAY 1978: Canyon, Texas, and Palo Duro Canyon Flood

1. "Flood Plain Information: Palo Duro Creek; Tierra Blanca Creek; Canyon, Texas," U.S. Army Corps of Engineers, 1971.

2. "Severe Weather Whips Panhandle," *Amarillo Daily News,* May 27, 1978.

3. *May 26, 1978: The Story of the Randall County Flood,* Carroll Wilson and the staff of *Canyon News,* (Canyon, Tex.: Staked Plains Press, 1978).

4. Ibid.

5. "Youth Stands on Knobs to Survive," *Amarillo Daily News,* May 28, 1978.

6. Ibid.

7. "Flood Victim Loses Library, Almost Lost Wife," *Amarillo Daily News,* May 30, 1978.

8. "Search Intensifies for Woman," *Amarillo Daily News,* May 29, 1978.

9. "Families Flee Waters," *Amarillo Daily News,* May 28, 1978.

10. "Palo Duro Canyon Nightmare Not Over," *Amarillo Daily News,* May 31, 1978.

11. "Campers: Why No Warning?" *Amarillo Daily News,* May 29, 1978.

12. Ibid.

13. "Boys' Ranch Crew Saves Man, Wife," *Amarillo Daily News,* May 31, 1978.

14. "High Water Traps Holiday Campers," *Amarillo Daily News,* May 28, 1978.

15. "Palo Duro Canyon Nightmare Not Over."

16. Ibid.

17. "Storms Kill 3; Floods Leave 300 Homeless," *Amarillo Daily News,* May 28, 1978; "Housing Addition Termed 'Serious,' " *Amarillo Daily News,* May 28, 1978.

18. "Last Week's Flood Worst in History," *Amarillo Daily News,* May 31, 1978.

19. "Army Flood Survey to Be Discussed June 5," *Amarillo Daily News,* May 31, 1978.

20. "Canyon Scouts Cut Trip Short," *Amarillo Daily News,* May 30, 1978.

21. Wilson and the staff of *Canyon News,* The Story of the Randall County Flood.

AUGUST 1978: Hill Country Flood

1. "Storm Amelia Fades over Sparse Texas Ranchland," *San Antonio Express,* Aug. 1, 1978.

2. Ralph Winingham, "Floodwaters Could Benefit Agriculture," *San Antonio Express-News,* Aug. 4, 1978.

3. David McLemore, "Vacation Becomes Nightmare," *San Antonio Express,* Aug. 3, 1978.

4. "Beauty Treed by High Water," *San Antonio Express,* Aug. 3, 1978.

5. Bill Cryer, "He Proves Report of Death Is Wrong," *Austin American-Statesman,* Aug. 5, 1978.

6. Grace Kitzman, "The Story of Peaceful Valley," *Bandera County History,* Bandera County Historical Association, 1986.

7. Greg Thompson, "Peaceful Rivers Become Killers; Hill Country Town Nearly Destroyed," *San Antonio Express,* Aug. 13, 1978.

8. Ibid.

9. David McLemore, "The Swollen Medina—Nature Gone Mad," *San Antonio Express,* Aug. 3, 1978.

10. David McLemore, "Bandera Digging Out," *San Antonio Express,* Aug. 4, 1978.

11. Donnis Baggett and Dan Watson, "Inundated Towns Dig Out of Mud," *Dallas Morning News,* Aug. 6, 1978.

12. "Disaster Areas Declared as Flood Deaths Reach 15," *Austin American-Statesman,* Aug. 4, 1978.

13. Ibid.

14. "Report 23 Deaths, Damage in Millions." *Kerrville Mountain Sun,* Aug. 10, 1978.

15. Donnis Baggett, "Neighbors Fight to Rescue People from Rising Water," *Dallas Morning News,* Aug. 4, 1978.

16. Glenn Garvin, "Five Drowned as They Slept," *Austin American-Statesman,* Aug. 4, 1978.

17. "Storm Data and Unusual Weather Phenomena," vol. 20, National Climatic Data Center, U.S. Dept. of Commerce, Aug. 1978.

18. Vickie Davidson, "Everything Gone," *San Antonio Express,* Aug. 3, 1978.

19. Mike Cox, " 'It Knocked Out Our Windows and Then Our Door,' " *Austin American-Statesman,* Aug. 3, 1978.

20. Ibid.

21. Davidson, "Everything Gone."

22. Mike Cox, "Member Laments Flooding of Comfort Tavern," *Austin American-Statesman,* Aug. 4, 1978.

23. Jerry Deal, "Motorist Swims to Safety from Riverlike Road," *San Antonio Express,* Aug. 3, 1978.

24. Bill Cryer, "Moving Out," *Austin American-Statesman,* Aug. 4, 1978.

25. Ibid.

26. Ibid.

27. "Around the Square," *Fredericksburg Standard,* Aug. 9, 1978.

28. "Flood Experiences," *Fredericksburg Standard,* Aug. 9, 1978.

29. Kay Powers, "Rise of 40 Feet Predicted on Lake Travis," *Austin American-Statesman,* Aug. 3, 1978.

30. Kay Powers, "43' Rise on Lake Travis Feared," *Austin American-Statesman,* Aug. 4, 1978.

31. Wade Roberts, "Flood Victims Come Back to Ravaged Homes," *San Antonio Express,* Aug. 4, 1978.

32. "Disaster Areas Declared as Flood Deaths Reach 15," *Austin American-Statesman,* Aug. 4, 1978.

33. Wade Roberts, "Flood Death Toll Climbs to 23," *San Antonio Express,* Aug. 9, 1978.

34. Wade Roberts, "Hill Country Toll Said Preventable," *San Antonio Express,* Aug. 11, 1978.

AUGUST 1978: Albany, Texas, Flood

1. *Abilene Reporter-News,* Aug. 3, 1978.

2. "Needed Rain Brightens Farmers' Gloomy Faces," *Abilene Reporter-News,* Aug. 4, 1978.

3. *Abilene Reporter-News,* Aug. 4, 1978.

4. See "6 Albany Deaths Reported," *Abilene Reporter-News,* Aug. 4, 1978.

5. "Businesses to Start All Over," *Abilene Reporter-News,* Aug. 9, 1978.

6. "Killer Rains Drench West Texas Town," *San Antonio Express,* Aug. 5, 1978.

7. "Rising Creek Trapped Surprised Abilenians in Albany," *Abilene Reporter-News,* Aug. 5, 1978.

8. "Floodwater Isolates Town," *Dallas Morning News,* Aug. 5, 1978.

9. "Albany Folks Recall the Terrifying Hours," *Abilene Reporter-News,* Aug. 20, 1978.

10. Ibid.

11. Ibid.

12. Ibid.

13. Ibid.

14. "Resident Thankful Life Was Spared," *Abilene Reporter-News,* Aug. 5, 1978.

15. "Survivors Face Shortage of Housing after Storm," *Dallas Morning News,* Aug. 6, 1978.

16. "Highway Dept. Takes Bids to Repair Flood-damaged Roads," *Albany News,* Aug. 11, 1978.

17. "Flooding Washes Away Future for Ranchers," *Dallas Morning News,* Aug. 6, 1978.

18. "Stricken," *San Antonio Express,* Aug. 6, 1978.

19. "Sixth Flood Victim Uncovered by Dozers," *Albany News,* Aug. 24, 1978.

20. "Restaurants Help Stranded, Feed Volunteer Rescue Workers," *Albany News,* Aug. 11, 1978.

21. "Flooding Washes Away Future for Ranchers."

22. "Flood Won't Run Many Off," *Abilene Reporter-News,* Aug. 8, 1978.

23. " Albany Airlifts More than 5 Tons," *Abilene Reporter-News,* Aug. 10, 1978.

24. "Briscoe Sees Good Job Done in Tour of Flood-ravaged West Central Texas," *Dallas Morning News,* Aug. 10, 1978.

25. "Water Brings Overflowing Joy and Sadness to Area," *Abilene Reporter-News,* Aug. 5, 1978.

26. "Flood Wipes Out McCarty Dam," *San Angelo Standard-Times,* Aug. 6, 1978.

27. "Floods Rush into Graham," *Dallas Morning News,* Aug. 7, 1978.

28. Ibid.

29. "Dry White Elephant Finally Became Full," *Abilene Reporter-News,* Aug. 7, 1978.

30. "Seeding of Clouds Continued during 24-Inch Albany Rains," *San Antonio Express,* Aug. 9, 1978.

31. Ibid.

32. Ibid.

33. E. E. Schroeder, B.C. Massey, and E. H. Chin, "Floods in Central Texas, Aug. 1–4, 1978: Report Prepared Jointly by the U.S. Geological Survey and the National Oceanic and Atmospheric Administration," USGS Professional Paper 1332, 1987.

MAY 1981: Memorial Day Flood in Austin

1. "Storms Douse City, Central Texas," *Austin American-Statesman,* May 24, 1981.

2. "Homeowners Flee Storm's Flooding," *Austin American-Statesman,* May 25, 1981.

3. Bill Douthat, "Austin Has No Systems for Early Flood Warning," *Austin American-Statesman,* May 27, 1981.

4. "Homeowners Flee Storm's Flooding."

5. Richard Abrams, "Neighborhood Is Devastated," *Austin American-Statesman,* May 26, 1981.

6. Cheryl Coggins, "I Guess It's Not Too Brilliant, but I Couldn't Leave My Dogs Behind," *Austin American-Statesman,* May 26, 1981.

7. Patrick Taggart, "I Thank God, Providence, and a Man in a Yellow Raincoat," *Austin American-Statesman,* May 26, 1981.

8. Mike Cox, "Rescue Efforts Frustrated," *Austin American-Statesman,* May 26, 1981.

9. Pete Szilagyi and Peggy Vlerebome, "City's Growth Could Make Future Shoal Creek Flood Worse," *Austin American-Statesman,* May 28, 1981.

10. Richard Abrams, "Jefferson Street Survivors Regroup amid Creek's Havoc," *Austin American-Statesman,* May 27, 1981.

11. Carolyn Bobo, "Businesses Insured, but Most Homes Aren't," *Austin American-Statesman,* May 26, 1981.

12. Abrams, "Jefferson Street Survivors."

13. Richard Abrams, "Gritty Spirit Abounds amid Flood Devastation," *Austin American-Statesman,* May 31, 1981.

14. Kerry Gunnels, "Flood Victims Brave Threat of New Rain," *Austin American-Statesman,* May 30, 1981.

15. John Kelso, "Jefferson Street Wrings Itself

Out after a Night of Terror," *Austin American-Statesman,* May 26, 1981.

16. "Drainage Neglect Disaster Factor," *Austin American-Statesman,* May 28, 1981.

17. "Flood Raises Questions," *Austin American-Statesman,* May 28, 1981.

18. Cheryl Coggins and Pete Szilagyi, "Daring Rescue," *Austin American-Statesman,* May 26, 1981.

19. Ibid.

20. Kirk Ladendorf, "City Businesses Take a Beating," *Austin American-Statesman,* May 26, 1981.

21. Ibid.

22. Abrams, "Gritty Spirit Abounds."

23. Ed Ward, "Austin's Music Survived Flood," *Austin American-Statesman,* May 27, 1981.

24. Jim Phillips and Mike Cox, "Survivor Saw Flood Sweep 2 Away," *Austin American-Statesman,* May 27, 1981.

25. Peggy Vlerebomee, "Three Saved by Lifeline from Plaza Torrent," *Austin American-Statesman,* May 26, 1981.

26. Julie Fernández, "Cities Picking Up Pieces from Flood," *Austin American-Statesman,* June 4, 1981.

27. "The Austin, Texas, Flood of May 24–25, 1981," U.S. National Research Council, 1982.

28. "Deadly Waters," *Austin American-Statesman,* May 26, 1981.

29. Jim Phillips, "Clements Optimistic about Aid," *Austin American-Statesman,* May 29, 1981.

30. "Flood-prone Area Not for Housing," *Austin American-Statesman,* June 3, 1981.

31. "The Austin, Texas, Flood of May 24–25, 1981."

32. "More Control for Watersheds," *Austin American-Statesman,* May 31, 1981.

33. Szilagyi and Vlerebome, "City's Growth Could Make Future Shoal Creek Flood Worse."

34. "The Austin, Texas, Flood of May 24–25, 1981."

35. Ibid.

36. Ibid.

37. Kay Powers, "More Rain Later in the Week," *Austin American-Statesman,* May 26, 1981.

38. Bill Douthat, "Austin Has No Systems for Early Flood Warning," *Austin American-Statesman,* May 27, 1981.

39. Ibid.

40. "Calls Inundate Weather Office," *Austin American-Statesman,* June 2, 1981.

41. "Storm Data and Unusual Weather Phenomena, June 1981 (Late Report)," National Climatic Data Center, U.S. Dept. of Commerce, storm data release (Oct. 1981) 23(10).

42. Pete Szilagyi, "Flooding Forces Evacuation of Rain-weary Central Texas," *Austin American-Statesman,* June 12, 1981.

43. Clayton Stromberger, "Scattered Showers? Weather Service Prediction All Wet," *Austin American-Statesman,* June 12, 1981.

44. Larry DeSaw, "New Round of Storms May Move into Area," *Austin American-Statesman,* June 16, 1981.

45. Terry Box, Terry Goodrich, and Kim Tyson, "Raging Torrents Leave San Marcos under Water," *Austin American-Statesman,* June 14, 1981.

46. Richard Abrams, "Soaked Evacuees Flee Homes Again," *Austin American-Statesman,* June 17, 1981.

47. Pete Szilagyi, "Storms Pummel Area; Man Killed in Flooding," *Austin American-Statesman,* June 5, 1981.

AUGUST 1998: Del Rio Flood

1. "Charley Rains on Central Texas," *Austin American-Statesman,* Aug. 22, 1998.

2. "Drought Gets Doused," *Austin American-Statesman,* Aug. 23, 1998.

3. "Deadly Flooding Came as Storm Stalled Inland," *Austin American-Statesman,* Aug. 25, 1998.

4. "Floodwaters Sweep down Rio Grande," *Houston Chronicle,* Aug. 25, 1998.

5. "Jim Bob Hill Recalls: 'It Was a Night from Hell,'" *Del Rio News-Herald,* Aug. 27, 1998.

6. "Del Rioan Recalls the Night of the Flood," *Del Rio News-Herald,* Aug. 27, 1998.

7. "Flood Kills 7 in South Texas Town," *Dallas Morning News,* Aug. 25, 1998.

8. "In Del Rio, Residents Find Little to Reclaim," *Austin American-Statesman,* Aug. 26, 1998.

9. "Val Verde to Receive Federal Aid," *San Antonio Express,* Aug. 27, 1998.

10. "Disaster Relief," *Del Rio News-Herald,* Sept. 8, 1998.

11. "Starting Over: Del Rio's San Felipe Neighborhood Picks Up Pieces after Deadly Flood," *Austin American-Statesman,* Sept. 27, 1998.

12. "Flood Kills 7 in South Texas Town."

13. "Floodwaters Sweep down Rio Grande."

14. "Town Ravaged by 1965 Flood Remains Secure Today behind Dams," *Del Rio News-Herald,* Aug. 28, 1998.

15. "State Rescue Team Prepares for Better Re-

322 sponse to Floods," *Austin American-Statesman,* Sept. 8, 1998.

16. "Border City Paralyzed by Rising Rio Grande," *San Antonio Express-News,* Aug. 27, 1998.

17. Ibid.

18. "Swollen Rio Grande Shows Pits to Laredo-area Residents," *Austin American-Statesman,* Aug. 28, 1998.

19. "Floods amid Droughts Just Typical Texas," *San Antonio Express-News,* Aug. 27, 1998.

OCTOBER 1998: Hill Country Flash Floods

1. "More Rain May Be on Way," *San Antonio Express,* Oct. 18, 1998.

2. "High Water Brings Stories of Rescues," *San Antonio Express,* Oct. 18, 1998.

3. "More Rain May Be on Way."

4. "Wisdom Pays Off for Hill Country," *San Antonio Express,* Oct. 18, 1998.

5. Ibid.

6. "Lamar Stores Take a Chance," *Austin American Statesman,* Oct. 20, 1998.

7. "New Braunfels Wary of Looters," *San Antonio Express,* Oct. 19, 1998.

8. "Bewitched by 'the Calm Comal,'" *Austin American Statesman,* Oct. 24, 1998.

9. "Dream Home Destroyed by 'beloved' Guadalupe," *New Braunfels Herald-Zeitung,* Oct. 19, 1998.

10. "Paper Will Print, Come Hell or High Water," *New Braunfels Herald-Zeitung,* Oct. 19, 1998.

11. "New Braunfels Wary of Looters."

12. "Tears of Sadness Fall as We All Rebuild for Future," *New Braunfels Herald-Zeitung,* Nov. 1, 1998.

13. "Out of the Woodwork" column, "Sudden Priority Shift," *Gonzales Inquirer,* Oct. 20, 1998.

14. "Record Flood Hits County," *Gonzales Inquirer,* Oct. 20, 1998.

15. "The Bright and Dark Sides of Nature," *Cuero Record,* Nov. 4, 1998.

JUNE 2001: Tropical Storm Allison Flood in Houston

1. Southeast Texas Forecast Discussion, 9:55 A.M., June 5, 2001, National Weather Service Houston/Galveston, Texas.

2. Ibid., 2:45 P.M.

3. Ibid., 8:45 P.M.

4. Ibid., 9:45 P.M., June 6, 2001.

5. Ibid., 2:55 P.M.

6. Ibid., 1:44 P.M., June 7, 2001.

7. Ibid., 3:37 A.M., June 8, 2001.

8. Ibid., 9:45 A.M.

9. Ibid., 2:45 a.m., June 9, 2001.

10. "Allison May Not Be Done," *Houston Chronicle,* June 10, 2001.

11. "Inside Allison's Bag of Tricks," *Houston Chronicle,* June 7, 2001.

12. "Allison's Deadly Punch Leaves Scars a Year Later," *Houston Chronicle,* June 3, 2002.

13. "Tropical Storm Allison Event Analysis," vol. 1, Final Technical Report, prepared by LJA Engineering and Surveying, Inc., Dec. 2002, 131.

14. "Displaced Residents Take Emergency Shelter," *Houston Chronicle,* June 10, 2001.

15. Southeast Texas Forecast Discussion, 10:22 A.M., June 9, 2001, National Weather Service Houston/Galveston, Texas.

16. "Allison's Deadly Punch Leaves Scars a Year Later."

17. Ibid.

18. "Out of the Dark: New Regard for Hospital's Caregivers," *Houston Chronicle,* June 3, 2002.

19. "Allison's Deadly Punch Leaves Scars a Year Later."

20. Ibid.

21. Ibid.

22. Ibid.

23. Ibid.

24. "Area Hospitals in State of Emergency," *Houston Chronicle,* June 9, 2001.

25. "Medical Center Warned on Flooding in '99," *Houston Chronicle,* June 14, 2001.

26. "Allison's Deadly Punch Leaves Scars a Year Later."

27. "For Theatre District, an Artistic Nightmare," *Houston Chronicle,* June 12, 2001.

28. "Allison's Deadly Punch Leaves Scars a Year Later."

29. "Why So Much in Basements?" *Houston Chronicle,* June 13, 2001.

30. "Roadways Paralyzed across City," *Houston Chronicle,* June 9, 2001.

31. "Can City Weather Bigger Storms?" *Houston Chronicle,* June 4, 2002.

32. Ibid.

JULY 2002: Guadalupe River Flooding

1. Forecast Discussion, 2:49 A.M., July 5, 2002, National Weather Service, San Angelo, Texas.

2. Ibid.

3. Ibid., 1:50 P.M., July 8, 2002.

4. Ibid., 9:00 P.M., July 1, 2002.

5. "Earlier Deluge Still the Record," *San Antonio Express*, July 3, 2002.

6. "Raging Waters Disrupt Peace in Jefferson Area," *San Antonio Express*, July 3, 2002.

7. Ibid.

8. "Dams in the Area Are Doing What They Were Designed to Do," *San Antonio Express*, July 7, 2002.

9. "Luckenbach Knocked Down but Not Out by Recent Flooding," *Fredericksburg Standard*, July 10, 2002.

10. "I Opened the Door, the Water Was Coming In," *Fredericksburg Standard*, July 3, 2002.

11. "Water Dumped on Area Creates Havoc for Emergency Crews," *Uvalde Leader-News*, July 4, 2002.

12. "Vacationers Finally Can Relax," *Uvalde Leader-News*, July 4, 2002.

13. "Strange Country Creates 100-Year Flood," *Uvalde Leader-News*, July 7, 2002.

14. "Resorts Suffer Damage from Flood of Century," *Uvalde Leader-News*, July 4, 2002.

15. "Utopia Gets More Damage, Rain Friday," *Uvalde Leader-News*, July 7, 2002.

16. Ibid.

17. "Sabinal River Floods Utopia," *Hondo Anvil-Herald*, July 11, 2002.

18. "Flood Blamed in Two Deaths," *San Antonio Express*, July 3, 2002.

19. "Historic Floods Challenge Area," *Hondo Anvil-Herald*, July 11, 2002.

20. "Canyon Lake Reaches Spillway," *San Antonio Express*, July 4, 2002.

21. "Not Like '98 Flood," *New Braunfels Zeitung-Herald*, July 5, 2002.

22. "Floods Swamp Hill Country," *Austin American-Statesman*, July 6, 2002.

23. "From Canoe, Resident Surveys Area Damage," *New Braunfels Zeitung-Herald*, July 7, 2002.

24. "Oh, My God, That's My House!" *New Braunfels Zeitung-Herald*, July 9, 2002.

25. "Flood Threat in Brownwood Not Over," *Abilene Reporter-News*, July 8, 2002.

26. "Chance of More Rain Has Officials Calling for Caution," *Abilene Reporter-News*, July 7, 2002.

27. "Flood Prompts Evacuations," *Abilene Reporter-News*, July 7, 2002.

28. Flood Statement, July 9, 2002, National Weather Service, Corpus Christi, Tex.

INDEX

~~~~~~~~~~

Abilene, 162, 232, 297

Academy, 45

Adams, Fred, 125

Adams Bayou (a.k.a. Adams Branch), 172, 297

Alazan Creek, 30, 31

Albany, 232–45, 297

Aledo, 129

Alley Theatre, 289

Alligator Creek, 43

Alpine, 157, 292

Amador, Lazaro, 14, 15

Amarillo, 129, 205

Angleton, 162

Arlington, 246

Armand Bayou, 286, 288

Armin, E. A., 124

Ashe, W. W., 35

Atascosa River, 298

Austin, 1–9, 10, 16, 17, 22–27, 29, 37, 79–82, 106–109, 136, 150, 162, 246–60, 277

Austin Dam, 1–9, 16, 17, 81

Bachman Branch (a.k.a. Bachman Creek), 186–88

Baker, Dr. Victor, 200

Bakersfield, 151

Balcones Escarpment, 28, 37, 39, 137, 192, 273, 291

Ballinger, 104, 105, 149

Bandera, 58, 66, 216–25, 227, 294

Bankersmith, 138, 147, 148, 291

Barksdale, 59, 77

Barnhart, 103

Barons Creek, 143

Barton Creek, 6, 37, 81, 108, 244, 260

Bashore, H. W., 125

Bastrop, 7, 17, 82, 122

Batesville, 54

Bay City, 18

Bear Creek (Junction), 230

Bear Creek (Parker County), 129

Beaver Creek, 230

Bedient, Dr. Philip, 290

Bee Creek (Westlake), 247, 255

Belton, 10–16, 37, 38, 43, 44, 46

Benbrook, 129

Benbrook Dam, 134, 135

Bend, 106

Ben Ficklin, 52, 94, 98

Ben Hur, 5, 7

Ben Meckel Draw, 110

Bentsen, Lloyd, Jr., 145, 256

Bernard Bunneymeyer, 39

Berry Creek, 38

Big Cypress Creek, 186

Bigham, John, 45

Big Spring, 151, 163

Big Walnut Creek, 27

Blackland Prairie, 37

Black Sunday, 72

Blackwell, 151

Blanco, 49, 66, 53, 136, 138, 148, 150

Blanco River (Blanco, Wimberley), 136, 148, 149, 195, 198

Blanco River (near Sabinal), 54

Blieders Creek, 200, 201, 203, 204, 278

Boerne, 66, 136, 138, 149, 150, 216, 292

Bomar, George, 272

Bosque River, 15, 172

Bosworth, Allan, 159

Brackenridge Park, 19, 20, 28, 30

Brackettville, 72, 136, 150, 246

Brady, 57, 111–18, 136, 138–42, 151, 216

Brady Creek, 57, 111–17, 138–42

Brady, E. C., 50

Brays Bayou, 286, 288

Brazos River, 10, 13, 14, 16, 48, 162, 241, 241

Bridgeport, 246

Briscoe, Governor Dolph, 230

Bronte, 151

Brookesmith, 105

Broome, 95

Brownwood, 57, 105, 111, 172, 296, 297

Bruceville-Eddy, 164

Brushy Creek, 27, 39, 41, 44

Bryan, 16

Buchanan Dam, 85, 106, 108, 111, 121, 123–25

Buchanan, J. P., 85

Buda, 193

Buffalo Bayou, 86–91, 288

Buffalo Gap, 297

Buffalo Lake, 206

Bull Branch, 39, 40

Bull Creek, 254

Bullhide Creek, 171

Bulverde, 200, 276

Bunton Branch, 187

Burgess, 13, 45

Burleson Creek, 164–68
Burnet, 3, 95

Cactus Hotel, 100
Caddo Lake, 186
Cal Farley's Boys Ranch, 213
Calliham, 55
Cameron, 13, 38, 45, 46
Camp Giesecke, 53
Camp Mystic, 51
Camp Rio Vista, 51
Camp Stewart, 51
Camp Verde, 225, 292
Camp Waldemar, 51
Camp Warnecke, 53
Camp Wood, 75, 77, 78, 152
Canyon, 205–15
Canyon Dam, 199, 216, 291, 295, 296
Canyon Lake, 226–28, 291
Carlsbad, 95
Carr, John, 244, 245
Carrizo Springs, 54
Castell, 73–75
Castroville, 68, 295
Cat Claw Creek, 297
Center Point, 53, 225
Chance, H. M., 5
Chenoweth, Dean, 99
Cherokee, 138, 142
Cherokee Creek, 142
Chocolate Bayou, 90
Choke Canyon Reservoir, 298
Christoval, 3, 97, 113
Cibolo Creek, 149, 200, 276
Circleville, 42
Clear Creek, 92, 286
Clear Fork of the Trinity River, 129, 130, 131, 135
Clements, Governor Bill, 256
Clifton, 162
Cobb, W. K., 141, 142
Coleman, 57, 150, 296
Colorado City, 174
Colorado River, 1–9, 10, 16, 27, 49, 79–82, 104, 105, 120–28, 142
Columbus, 7, 18, 82, 123, 124, 246
Comal River, 53, 147, 199–204, 277, 278
Comal Springs, 199
Comfort, 49, 53, 147, 226, 227, 292
Comstock, 157, 160
Concan, 54, 55, 293, 294
Concho River, 94, 97, 98, 113, 120
Cook's Slough, 54
Copperas Creek, 104
Corps of Engineers, 113, 134, 167, 169, 170, 204, 205, 228, 295, 297
Cotton Palace, 15
Cottonwood Creek, 186

Cotulla, 79
Cow Bayou, 164, 171
Cow Creek, 49
Cowhouse Creek, 171
Crawley, Richard A., 175, 177
Creedmoor, 37
Cresson, 129
Crofoot, E. J., 125
Cross Plains, 297
Crystal City, 54, 70
Cuero, 282, 283
Cumpton, Ken, 196
Cypress Creek (Comfort), 226
Cypress Creek (Houston area), 92, 286
Cypress Creek (Wimberley), 195, 276

Dalhart, 205
Dallas, 36, 129, 130, 186–91, 259
Dalrymple, Tate, 110
Dawn, 206
de la Cruz, Manuel, 62
Del Rio, 59, 61, 150, 153, 160, 217, 261–72
Deleon, 296
Denton, 186
Derby, 55, 65, 70
Devil's River, 59–61, 159
D'Hanis, 56, 66–72, 86, 295
Dilley, 55, 192, 292
Doss, 218
Dove Creek, 94
Dripping Springs, 247, 291
Dry (Westlake) Creek, 27, 255, 260
Dry Comal Creek, 200, 203, 204, 278
Dry Devils River Draw, 110
Dry Frio River, 294
Dryden, 153
Duck Creek, 191

Eagle Mountain Lake, 129
Eagle Pass, 39, 59, 61, 66, 152, 160
East Bernard, 93
Eckels, Judge Robert, 290
Eden, 57, 111, 112, 116, 137, 149
Edwards Plateau, 39, 59, 111, 137, 151
Eldorado, 95, 103, 112, 116
Ellsworth, C. E., 45
Elm Creek (Abilene), 297
Elm Creek (Ballinger), 104, 105
Elm Fork of the Trinity River, 130, 131
Elroy, 37
Engelhard, Fritz, 123, 124
Estelle, Earl, 231

Fairland, 49, 95
Falcom Dam and Reservoir, 160, 161
Fanning, J. T., 8
Farmers Branch, 135

Flatonia, 22

flood control, 36, 90–92, 94, 110, 111, 123–28, 129, 134, 135, 139, 146, 162, 170, 171, 186, 191, 198, 199, 204, 273, 275, 278, 286–88

Flores, Vincente Gonzales, 62–63

Floresville, 138

Floydada, 135

Floyd Branch, 186

Fort Clark, 59

Fort Stockton, 151

Fort Worth, 129–35, 246

Fort Worth Zoo, 132

Fredericksburg, 3, 136, 138, 142, 143, 150, 192, 218, 228

Freeport, 16

Frio River, 50, 54, 72, 77, 110, 262, 293, 298

Frizell, Joseph, 1, 8

Fugate, G. L., 86, 91

Galveston, 46, 69, 89, 284

Garden City, 50

Garner State Park, 55, 262

George Lott, 39

Georgetown, 37, 38, 41, 42, 163

Geyelin, E. C., 8

Gold, 138

Goldthwaite, 150

Goliad, 246

Golman, Joe H., 191

Gonzales, 18, 49, 274, 281, 282

Graham, 244

Grape Creek, 138, 143

Green, Ed, 47

Greens Bayou, 92, 286, 287

Groves, E. W., 8

Gruene, 274, 277, 279, 282

Guadalupe River, 3, 10, 18, 49–53, 136, 146–48, 199–204, 216–18, 224–28, 274, 277, 278, 281, 291, 295, 296

Guera, Belisario, 62

Gunter Hotel, 19, 32, 33, 35

Hallettsville, 22

Halls Bayou, 92, 287

Hamilton, 172

Hancock, Mayor Louis, 8

Happy, 208

Harper, 218, 246

Harris Creek, 15, 171

Hedwig's Hill, 74, 75, 83

Hempstead, 16, 48

Hereford, 206

Hernandez, Guadalupe, 62

Hico, 134

Hidalgo, 63

Hill, Robert T., 8

Hillendahl, 86

Hillsboro, 95

Holcombe, Oscar, 91

Holtzclaw Bridge, 45

Hondo, 50, 56, 66–70, 136, 138, 150, 192, 216

Hondo Creek, 56, 67

Hords Creek, 57

Houston, 86–93, 284–90

Howard Draw, 151, 154, 172

Hubbard Creek, 233, 235, 236, 237, 297, 298

Hueco Springs, 49

Hunt, 50, 51, 52, 136, 150, 216

Hunting Bayou, 286, 287

Huricane Beulah, 298

hurricane, 10, 39, 89, 240

Hurricane Alice, 151–54

Hye, 138, 144, 145, 291

Ickes, Harold, 124

Independence Creek, 151, 153, 154

Indian Creek, 105

Ingram, 52, 218

International Boundary and Water Commission, 60, 157

Jackson, H. H., 116

James River, 73

Jim Ned Creek, 57

Joe's Creek, 186, 187

John Hobbs, 196

Johnson, Lady Bird, 145, 146

Johnson, Lyndon B, 123, 144, 145, 170

Johnson City, 137, 138, 145, 146

Johnson Creek, 50

Johnson Draw, 151, 154, 158, 159

Johnson Fork Creek, 73

Jonah, 42

Junction, 72–74, 95, 104, 136, 138, 150

Kaufman, 95

Kelton, Elmer, 149

Kennedale, 129

Kerrville, 50, 52, 66, 95, 111, 136, 138, 150, 217, 218, 258, 292

Killeen, 171

Kingsland, 75, 106

Kingsville, 151

Kitzman, Grace, 220

Knippa, 55, 192

Koch, Joe and Matt, 68, 69

Kreuger, Senator Bill, 230

La Grange, 7, 17, 18, 82, 123, 246

La Pryor, 50

La Vernia, 276

Lake Austin, 5, 49

Lake Belton, 162, 172

Lake Bridgeport, 129

Lake Brownwood, 57, 105, 125, 297

Lake Buchanan, 106–108, 111, 121–28, 142
Lake Coleman, 297
Lake Colorado City, 172
Lake Dunlap, 53, 202
Lake Hubbard, 241
Lake McCarty, 241, 242
Lake McDonald, 1, 5
Lake Nasworthy, 94, 98, 172
Lake Placid, 148
Lake Texoma, 172
Lake Travis, 136, 146, 216, 230, 246
Lake Waco, 172
Lake Walk, 59
Lake Whitney, 162
Lakewood Church, 287
Lampasas, 10, 11, 95, 107–11, 162–72, 195
Lampasas River, 11, 44, 168, 169
Landa Park, 3, 199, 203, 277, 278
Laneport, 43
Langtry, 152, 153, 157, 160
Laredo, 29, 39, 60–63, 160, 199, 272
Las Moras Creek, 61
Lawn, 232, 297
LCRA, 85, 107, 108, 120–28, 136, 138
Leakey, 54, 65, 77, 78, 292, 293
Leander, 163, 246
Legion, 53
Leon Creek, 20
Leon River, 13, 44, 172
Leona River, 54
Lester Hurricane, 273
Liberty, 162
Liberty Hill, 247
Little River, 13, 44, 45, 46, 47, 48, 172
Little Walnut Creek, 27
Live Oak Creek, 54
Llano, 3, 72–75, 85, 111, 136, 138, 142, 150, 216, 247
Llano River, 64–65, 72–75, 104, 123, 136, 142, 230
Lockhart, 3, 274
Lometa, 106
Lorena, 11, 171
Lowrey Draw, 64
Lubbock, 95, 174, 192, 205
Luckenbach, 291, 293
Luckey, John, 106
Luling, 18, 22, 274, 282
Lyndon B. Johnson Park, 229, 230
Lytle Creek, 297

Mackey, John, 253
Madeline Hurricane, 273
Majestic Theatre (San Antonio), 35
Mansfield, J. J., 125
Marathon, 174, 292
Marble Falls, 16, 38, 49, 75, 95, 106, 138, 247
Marlin, 15, 172
Marshall Ford Dam, 123, 124
Mart, 11

Martin, Delbert, 165, 166
Martin, Robert H., 16
Martinez Creek, 30, 31
Mason, 73, 136, 150, 247
Maxdale, 168
Mayo, Bob, 177
McAllen, 63
McAullife, J.P., 38
McCamey, 172
McDonald, John, 1
McDonough, Clarence, 125, 127, 128
McGregor, 164, 171
Medina, 217, 219, 220, 286
Medina Lake, 56, 223, 295
Medina River, 56, 216–24, 294
Melvin, 57, 112, 116, 138
Menard, 95, 104, 112, 117, 136, 138, 150, 151, 172, 247
Mendoza, Higinio, 62
Mercury, 138
Meridian, 162
Meyer, M. C., 46, 47
Middle Concho River, 94, 97, 98, 101
Midland, 174
Milburn, 105
Miller, Tom, 5
Millers Creek Reservoir, 244
Mireles, Fortunato, 62
Mission, 63
Molyneaux, H. B., 60, 153
Monahans, 174
Montell, 50, 151
Montgomery Ward, 133
Moody, 164
Moody, Dan, 125
Moran, 236
Mrs. Jodie, 168, 169
Muleshoe, 174
Mustang Creek, 39, 40

Nalle, John, 1
National Weather Service (NWS), 200, 206, 212, 215, 217, 231, 247, 248, 258, 259, 274, 284, 285, 292
Neal's Lodge, 294
New Braunfels, 3, 10, 37, 49, 53, 66, 136, 138, 147, 199–204, 227, 258, 273–82
Nolan Creek, 10, 11, 12, 44, 45
Nolte, F. A., 40
Norquest, C. E., 92
North Bosque River, 162, 172
North Concho River, 94, 97–100, 102, 113, 137
North Llano River, 65, 73, 74, 104
North Prong Medina River, 222
North Prong of Hubbard Creek, 233, 235, 236
North San Gabriel River, 163
Noxville, 73
Nueces River, 50, 54, 64–65, 70, 72, 75, 77–79, 110, 298
Nueces River, 298
Nuhn, A. D., 204

Odessa, 174
Oilton, 152
Olmos Creek, 19, 20, 21, 28, 29, 30, 36, 274, 275
Olmos Dam, 275
Olmsted, Frekerick Law, 28
Onion Creek, 260, 277
Ozona, 103, 151–53, 158, 159, 172

Paint Rock, 94, 111, 138
Palo Duro Canyon, 205, 206, 212
Palo Duro Creek, 205, 206, 208
Palo Duro State Park, 174, 209, 212, 213
Palo Pinto Creek, 172
Pandale, 151, 153, 154
Parkers Creek, 56, 66–71
Pasadena, 92, 286
Patoski, Joe Nick, 253
Pecan Bayou, 57, 105, 172, 297
Pecan Creek (Near Leakey), 294
Pecos River, 60, 151, 154, 157, 172
Pedernales Falls State Park, 260
Pedernales River, 16, 49, 123, 136,
    142–46, 228, 260
Pedernales River Basin Map, 142
Piedras Negras, 59, 61, 160
Pinto Creek, 61
Pipe Creek, 218, 223
Plainview, 174
Plum Creek, 18, 193, 282
Polk Family, 11, 12
Prairie Dog Town Fork or the Red River, 205,
    206, 208
Purgatory Creek, 193, 195, 196, 198, 259

Quinlan Creek, 53

Randt, Frank, 191
Rankin, 174
Reagan, President Ronald, 256
Reagan Wells, 77, 78
Richards, Ann, 230
Richarz, C. J., 71
Richmond, 86
Rio Grande City, 61, 63, 65
Rio Grande River, 29, 59–61, 65, 160,
    161, 199, 271
Robert Lee, 59, 109
Rochelle, 138
Rockdale, 38, 46, 47
Rocksprings, 59, 66, 72, 73, 75, 110, 136,
    150, 159, 246
Rockwood, 105
Rocky Creek, 143
Rodriguez, Andy, 281
Roma, 63
Roosevelt, 95
Rose, Bob, 261
Rose, W. S., Jr., 44

Rothe, Josie, 68
Round Rock, 37, 247
Rudder, Earl, 141

Sabinal, 50, 56, 66, 67, 150, 192, 231
Sabinal River, 70, 200, 292, 294
Sabinal River Basin, 292
Salado, 11, 37, 44
Salado Creek (Salado), 13, 44, 45
Salado Creek (San Antonio), 19, 274, 275
San Angelo, 3, 50, 94–104, 111, 136, 137, 141, 142, 150,
    151, 172, 246, 291, 297
San Antonio, 3, 10, 16, 19, 20, 21, 28–36, 66, 70, 89,
    90, 150, 199, 274, 291, 292
San Antonio River, 10, 19, 29, 30–34, 199, 274, 288
San Antonio River Tunnel, 275
San Antonio Zoo, 30
San Felipe Creek, 261, 263–71
San Gabriel, 43
San Gabriel River, 41–45, 259
San Jacinto River, 92
San Marcos, 10, 18, 29, 37, 49, 137, 149, 192–98, 259,
    260, 274, 276
San Marcos River, 18, 149, 192–98, 260, 274, 276, 282
San Saba, 106, 112, 118–20, 136, 138, 150
San Saba River, 2, 57, 104–106, 111, 117–20,
    136, 142, 172
Sanderford, Roy, 46
Sanderson, 151, 157, 173–85, 195, 271
Sanderson Canyon, 174, 175, 178, 179
Sandy Creek (Kingsland), 104
Sandy Creek (Lake Travis), 260
Satsuma, 86
Scarbrough, Clara Stearns, 38, 42
Schlitterbahn, 277, 278
Scranton, 232
Sealy, 22
Sears Roebuck, 90
Seco Creek, 56, 66–71
Sedwick, 197
Segovia, 73
Seguin, 147, 148, 204, 227, 281
Selma, 138, 149, 276
Seymour, 94
Sheffield, 153, 154, 157
Shoal Creek, 3, 22, 23, 25, 246–54, 256, 257, 259
Sims Bayou, 286, 287
Sink Springs Creek, 192, 193, 195, 196
Sisterdale, 292
Sloan, 112
Smithville, 7, 82, 122
Snyder, 174
Soil Conservation Service, 162, 164, 167,
    170, 191, 195, 204
Somerville, 39
Sonora, 59, 64, 70, 95, 104, 110, 136, 150, 151
South Bear Creek, 129
South Bosque, 15

330

South Concho River, 94, 97–101, 113, 172
South Llano River, 64–65, 72–74
South San Gabriel, 163
Specht, Jack, 81, 82
Spicewood, 49
Spring Creek, 218, 228
Spring Creek (Irion County), 94, 97, 172
Stein, Joe, 47, 48
Sterling City, 95
Steves, Albert, 28
Stiles, 95
Stone, Albert, 128
Stonewall, 138, 143–45, 229, 230
Storms, Gracie, 167
Sugarland, 86
Sullivan, H.C., 46, 47
Sulphur Creek, 110, 162, 164–68, 171
Summers Mill, 45
Sunset Limited, 157
Surkey, George, 20
Sycamore Creek, 61
Sycamore Creek (Forth Worth), 129, 135

Tahoka, 95
Talpa, 70
Tarpley, 56, 70, 136, 150
Taulbee, E. O., 128
Taylor, 37–41, 44, 46, 47, 162
Taylor, T. U., 1, 9, 125, 127
Teagarden, Jack, 30
Temple, 10, 11, 37, 38, 46, 136, 150
Terlingua, 151
Terrett Draw, 95, 104
Texas Lutheran College, 204
Texas Medical Center, 288, 289
Texas State University, 192
Texas Water Development Board, 172
Thorndale, 40, 41
Thrall, 37, 38, 39, 40, 41, 216, 286
Three Mile Draw, 174, 177–79
Three Rivers, 79, 297
Throckmorton, 232
Tierra Blanca Creek, 205, 206, 208
Tilden, 55, 292
Tow, 106, 108
Trigo, Jose Rodrigues, 63
Trinity River, 36, 129–31, 135
Tropical Storm Allison, 284–86, 290
Tropical Storm Amelia, 216, 217, 232, 241, 245
Tropical Storm Charley, 261, 262
Tropical Storm Claudette, 286
Trough Creek, 200, 201
Turkey Creek, 54, 70
Turner, Bailey, 46, 47
Turner, Dean, 166
Turtle Creek (Dallas), 186, 187
Turtle Creek (Kerr County), 218

Utopia, 66, 294
Uvalde, 50, 53, 54, 66, 77–79, 137, 150, 246, 262, 292

Valera, 70
Valley Junction, 16, 48
Vander Zee, Rein J., 224
Vanderpool, 218, 292
Veidt, 196
Verde Creek, 218, 225
Veribest, 94
Victoria, 18, 49, 259, 283
Vince Bayou, 286
Voca, 118

Waco, 10, 13–15, 39, 45, 162
Waco Creek, 15
Waller Creek, 22, 23, 25
Walnut Creek (Austin), 247
Waring, 138
Washington, 48
Water Valley, 94, 98
Welfare, 147
Welk, Lawrence, 191
Werenskiold, N., 9
West Bernard, 93
West Bernard River, 92
West End Lake, 31
West Fork of the Trinity River, 129–31, 135
West Nueces River, 72, 73, 75, 77, 78
West Prong Medina River, 222
Westlake, 247, 255, 260
Wharton, 7, 18, 109
White Oak Bayou, 86–91, 286, 288
White Rock Creek, 186, 189
Whole Foods Market, 253
Wichita Falls, 162
Wilbarger Creek, 27
Williamson Creek, 27, 260, 277
Willow City, 143
Willow Creek, 27
Willow Spring, 195, 196
Wilson, Carroll, 206
Wimberley, 149, 195, 274, 276
Winchell, 105
Wink, 174
Winters, 137
Wirtz, A. J., 124
Wood, Charles, 281

Yettie Polk, 10
York Creek, 193
Youngsport, 168, 169
Youngstown, 43
Yuba City, Arizona, 167

Zapata, 63
zoo: Fort Worth, 132; San Antonio, 30

ISBN-13: 978-1-58544-590-5
ISBN-10: 1-58544-590-8

53500